FLORENTINE CODEX

Florentine Codex

General History of the Things of New Spain

FRAY BERNARDINO DE SAHAGUN

Book 2- The Ceremonies

Translated from the Aztec into English, with notes and illustrations
(Second edition, revised)

By

Arthur J. O. Anderson
School of American Research

Charles E. Dibble
University of Utah

IN THIRTEEN PARTS

PART III

Chapter heading designs are from the Codex

Published by

The School of American Research and The University of Utah

Monographs of The School of American Research

Number 14, Part III   Santa Fe, New Mexico   1981

CONTENTS

SECOND BOOK, WHICH TREATETH OF THE FEASTS AND SACRIFICES BY WHICH THESE NATIVES HONORED THEIR GODS IN THEIR STATE OF INFIDELITY

LIST OF ILLUSTRATIONS

following page 124

BOOK TWO–THE CEREMONIES

Segundo libro, que trata, del
calendario, fiestas, y ceri
monjas, sacrificios, y so
lenjdades: que estos na
turales, desta nue
ua españa, hazi
an: a honrra
de sus dioses.

Ponese al cabo, deste libro, por via de
apendiz: los edificios, officios
y serujcios: y officia
les, que auja
en el templo
mexicano.

De las Cerimonjas

SECOND BOOK, WHICH TREATETH OF THE FEASTS AND SACRIFICES BY WHICH THESE NATIVES HONORED THEIR GODS IN THEIR STATE OF INFIDELITY.

LIBRO SEGUNDO QUE TRATA DE LAS FIESTAS, Y SACRIFICIOS: CON QUE ESTOS NATURALES, HONRRAUAN A SUS DIOSES, EN EL TIEMPO DE SU INFIDELIDAD.

First Chapter, concerning the calendar and the feasts of fixed date, the first of which is the one which followeth.[1]

The first month of the year was called, among the Mexicans, Atl caualo, and in other parts Quauitl eua. This month began upon the second day of February, when we celebrate the Purification of Our Lady. On the first day of this month, they celebrated a feast in honor—according to some—of the Tlaloc gods, whom they held to be gods of rain; [or]—according to others—of their sister, the goddess of water, Chalchiuhtli icue; [or]—according to [still] others—in honor of the great priest or god of the winds, Quetzalcoatl. And we may say that [they celebrated the feast] in honor of all of these. This month and all the rest, which are eighteen [in number], each have twenty days.

Capitulo primero, del canlendario, de las fiestas fixas, la primera de las quales es lo que se sigue.

El primero mes, del año se llamaua entre los mexicanos Atl caoalo: y en otras partes quavitl eoa. Este mes començaua en el segundo dia del mes de Hebrero quando nosotros celebramos, la purificacion, de nuestra señora. En el primero dia deste mes: celebrauan vna fiesta a honrra (segun algunos) de los dioses tlaloques, que los tenjan por dioses de la pluuja: y segun otros de su hermana, la diosa del agua, chalchiuhtli ycue: y segun otros a honrra del gran sacerdote, o dios de los vientos quetzalcoatl: y podemos dezir, que a hõrra de todos estos. Este mes, con todos los de mas, que son deziocho tienen a cada veynte dias.

Atl caualo or Quauitl eua

In this month they slew many children; they sacrificed them in many places upon the mountain tops, tearing from them their hearts, in honor of the gods of water, so that these might give them water or rain.

The children whom they slew they decked in rich finery to take them to be killed; and they carried them in litters upon their shoulders. And the litter went adorned with feathers and flowers. [The

5[2]	d KL	Atl caoalo, o quavitl eoa	d	1[3]
1	e	En este mes matauan muchos njños	e	2
2	f	sacrificavanlos, en muchos lugares en	f	3
3	g	las cumbres de los montes: sacandoles	g	4
4	A	los coraçones a hõrra de los dioses del	A	5
5	b	agua, para que les diessẽ agua o llujia.	b	6
6	c	A los njños, que matauan: com-	c	7
7	d	ponjanlos con ricos ataujos para lleuar-	d	8
8	e	los a matar, y lleuauanlos, en vnas	e	9
9	f	literas, sobre los hõbros: y las literas,	f	10

---

1. The first nineteen chapters, largely a digest of more expanded material in Chapters 20–38, are presented unannotated; most of the translators' notes will be found in this later section. For these nineteen chapters the original has no corresponding Nahuatl text.

2. Marginal notation: *Cuẽta deste calendario.*

3. Marginal notation: *Cuenta del calẽdario romano.*

priests] proceeded playing [musical instruments], singing, and dancing before them.

When they took the children to be slain, if they wept and shed many tears, those who carried them rejoiced, for they took [it] as an omen that they would have much rain that year.

Also in this month they slew many captives in honor of these same gods of the water. They slashed them first, [with their swords,] fighting them as they were tied upon a stone like a mill wheel; and when they threw them down, wounded, they carried them off to tear their hearts from them in the temple which was called Yopico.

When they slew these captives, their owners—they who had taken them—went gloriously arrayed in feathers, dancing before them and showing their valor. This continued through all the days of this month. In this feast were enacted many other ceremonies, which are set down at length in its telling (*fol.* 15).

10 *g* yuan adornadas con plumajes, y con *g* 11
11 *A* flores: yuan tañendo, cantando, y bay- *A* 12
12 *b* lando delante dellos *b* 13
13 *c* Quando lleuauan a los njños a *c* 14
14 *d* matar: si llorauan, y echauan muchas *d* 15
15 *e* lagrimas, alegrauanse los, que los *e* 16
16 *f* lleuauan: porque tomauan pronostico, *f* 17
17 *g* de que aujan de tener, muchas aguas *g* 18
18 *A* esse año. *A* 19
19 *b* Tambien en este mes: matauan *b* 20
20 *c* muchos catiuos, a honrra de los mjsmos *c* 21
dioses del agua: acuchillauanlos primero peleando cõ ellos, atados sobre vna piedra, como muela de molino, y desque los derrocauan acuchillados: lleuauanlos a sacar el coraçon al templo, que se llamaua, iopico.

Quando matauan a estos captiuos: los dueños dellos, que los aujan captiuado, yvan gloriosamente ataujados cõ plumajes, y baylando delante dellos, mostrando su valentia. Esto pasaua por todos los dias, deste mes. Otras muchas cerjmonjas, se hazian en esta fiesta: las quales estan escriptas a la larga, en su historja. fo. 15.

The second month they named Tlacaxipeualiztli. On the first day of this month they celebrated a feast in honor of the god called Totec—[or], as another name, called Xipe—when they slew and flayed many slaves and captives.

Chapter 2
Tlacaxipeualiztli

From the captives whom they were to slay the owners themselves tore off the hair of the crowns of their heads and kept it as a relic. This they did in the *calpulco* before the fire.

When the masters of the captives took their slaves to the temple where they were to slay them, they took them by the hair. And when they took them up the steps of the pyramid, some of the captives swooned, and their masters pulled them up and dragged them by the hair to the sacrificial stone where they were to die.

Having brought them to the sacrificial stone, which was a stone of three hands in height, or a little more, and two in width,[1] or almost, they threw them upon it, on their backs, and five [priests] seized them—two by the legs, two by the arms, and one by the head; and then came the priest who was to kill him. And he struck him with a flint [knife], held in both hands and made in the manner of a large lance head, between the breasts. And into the gash which he made, he thrust his hand and tore from [the victim] his heart; and then he offered it to the sun and cast it into a gourd vessel.

After having torn their hearts from them and poured the blood into a gourd vessel, which the master of the slain man himself received, they started the body rolling down the pyramid steps. It came to rest upon a small square below. There some old men, whom they called Quaquacuiltin, laid hold of it and carried it to their *calpulco*, where they dismembered it and divided it up in order to eat it.

Cap. 2.

1	*d*	**KL**	**Tlacaxipeoaliztli**	*d*	22[2]
2	*e*	A los captiuos que matauan: arran-		*e*	23
3	*f*	cauãlos, los cabellos de la coronjlla, y		*f*	24
4	*g*	guardauanlos, los mjsmos amos, como		*g*	25
5	*A*	por reliqujas: esto hazian en el calpul		*A*	26
6	*b*	delante del fuego.		*b*	27
7	*c*	Quando lleuauan los señores de los		*c*	28
8	*d*	catiuos a sus esclauos al templo: donde		*d*	1[3]
9	*e*	los aujan de matar, lleuanuanlos por		*e*	2
10	*f*	los cabellos: y quando los subian, por		*f*	3
11	*g*	las gradas del cu, algunos de los cap-		*g*	4
12	*A*	tiuos, desmayauan, y sus dueños los		*A*	5
13	*b*	subian arrastrando por los cabellos,		*b*	6
14	*c*	hasta el taxon donde aujan de morir.		*c*	7
15	*d*	Llegandolos al taxon: que era vna		*d*	8
16	*e*	piedra de tres palmos de alto, o poco		*e*	9
17	*f*	mas, y dos de ancho o casi: echauanlos		*f*	10
18	*g*	sobre ella de espaldas: y tomauanlos		*g*	11
19	*A*	cinco, dos por las piernas, y dos por		*A*	12
20	*b*	los braços, y vno por la cabeça: y venja		*b*	13[4]

luego el sacerdote, que le auja de matar, y dauale con ambas manos, con vna piedra de pedernal: hecha a manera de hierro de lançon por los pechos, y por el agujero que hazia: metia la mano, y arrancauale el coraçon, y luego le ofrecia al sol, echauale en vna xicara.

Despues de auerles sacado el coraçon, y despues de auer echado la sangre en vna xicara: la qual recebia el señor del mjsmo muerto: echauan el cuerpo a rrodar por las gradas abaxo del cu, yua a parar, en vna placeta abaxo: de alli le tomauan, vnos viejos, que llamavan quaquacujlti, y le lleuauã a su calpul: donde le despedaçauan, y le repartian pa comer.

---

1. Actually a *palmo*, according to the *Diccionario de la lengua española* of the Real Academia Española, is equal to one-quarter of a *vara*; divided into twelve equal parts (*dedos* or fingers), it is the equivalent of about 21 cm or about eight and one-quarter inches.

2. Marginal notation: *Cathedra sancti petri.*

3. Marginal notation: *Martius habet dies xxxj.*

4. Marginal notation: *leandri archieṗi et conf.*

Before they dismembered the captives, they flayed them; and others put on the skins, and, [wearing them,] fought mock fights with other youths, as if it were a war. And those [of one band] took captive [those of] the other [band].

After what hath been set forth above, they slew other captives, battling with them—these being tied, by the waist, with a rope which passed through the socket of a round stone, as of a mill; and [the rope] was long enough so that [the captive] might walk about the complete circumference of the stone. And they gave him arms with which he might do battle; and four warriors came against him with swords and shields, and one by one they exchanged sword blows with him until they vanquished him. Etc.

Antes que hiziessen pedaços a los catiuos: los desollauan, y otros vestian sus pellejos, y escaramuçauan con ellos, con otros mancebos, como cosa de guerra: y se prendian los vnos a los otros.

Despues de lo arriba dicho: matauan otros captiuos, peleando con ellos: y estando ellos atados por medio del cuerpo, con vna soga, que salia por el ojo de vna muela, como de molino, y era tan larga, que podia a andar por toda la circũferencia de la piedra, y dauanle sus armas, con que peleasse: y venjan contra el quatro, con espadas, y rodelas, y vno a vno se acuchillauan con el, hasta que le vencian. Etc.

The third month they called Toçoztontli. On the first day of this month they observed a feast to the god named Tlaloc, who is the god of rain. On this feast they slew many children upon the mountains. They offered them as sacrifices to this god and to his companions, so that they would give them water.

Chapter 3
Toçoztontli

On this feast they offered the first fruits of the flowers which had bloomed earliest that year, on the pyramid named Yopico. And before they had offered them, none dared smell a flower.

Those in charge of the flowers, who are called *xochimanque,* celebrated a feast to their goddess, named Coatl icue, or by another name Coatlan tonan.

Likewise in this month, those who had worn the skins of the dead [sacrificial victims] whom they had flayed the previous month, took [them] off. They went to cast them into a cave in the pyramid which they called Yopico; they went in procession to do this, and [performed] many ceremonies. They went stinking like dead dogs. And after they had left them [in the cave], they washed themselves, [performing] many ceremonies. A number of the sick made vows to attend this procession, in order to recover from their sickness, and they say that some [of them] recovered.

The masters of the [sacrificed and flayed] captives, with all those of their households, did penance for twenty days: neither did they bathe nor wash their heads until the skins of the dead captives were deposited in the cave mentioned above. They said that they did penance for their captives.

After they had ended the penance, they bathed and washed themselves, and summoned all their kin and friends, and gave them food. And they performed many ceremonies with the bones of the dead captives.

Al tercero mes, llamavan toçoztontli: en el primer dia deste mes, hazian fiesta al dios llamado Tlaloc: que es dios de las pluujas. En esta fiesta, matauã muchos njños, sobre los montes: ofrecianlos en sacrificio a este dios, y a sus compañeros, para que los diessen agua.

Cap. 3.

1	c	KL Toçoztontli.	c	14
2	d	En esta fiesta: ofrecian las prjmicias	d	15
3	e	de las flores, que aquel año primero	e	16
4	f	nacian en el cu, llamado iopico: y	f	17
5	g	antes que las ofreciessen, nadie osaua	g	18
6	A	oler flor.	A	19
7	b	Los officiales de las flores, que se	b	20
8	c	llaman sochimanque: hazian fiesta, a	c	21
9	d	su diosa llamada Coatl ycue, y por otro	d	22
10	e	nombre coatlã tona.	e	23
11	f	Tambien en este mes: se desnu-	f	24
12	g	dauan, los q̃ trayan vestidos, los	g	25
13	A	pellejos de los muertos, q̃ aujan des-	A	26
14	b	ollado el mes pasado: yuanlos a echar	b	27
15	c	en vna cueua, en el cu, que llamauan	c	28
16	d	iopico: yuan a hazer esto, con pro-	d	29
17	e	cesion: y cõ muchas cerimonjas, yuan	e	30
18	f	hediendo, como perros muertos: y	f	31
19	g	despues que los aujan dexado: se	g	1[1]
20	A	lauauan, con muchas cerjmonjas:	A	2[2]

Algunos emfermos hazian voto, de hallarse presentes, a esta procesion, por sanar de sus emfermedades: y dizen, que algunos sanauan.

Los dueños de los catiuos, con todos los de su casa, hazian penjtencia, veynte dias: que nj se bañauan, nj se lauauan las cabeças: hasta que se ponjan los pellejos, de los captiuos muertos, en la cueua arriba dicha: dezian que hazian penjtencia, por sus captiuos.

Despues que aujan acabado la penjtencia: bañauanse, y lauauanse, y combidauan a todos, sus parientes, y amigos, y dauanles comjda: y hazian muchas cerjmonjas, con los huesos, de los catiuos muertos.

---

1. Marginal notation: *Aprilis habet dies xxx.*
2. Marginal notation: *Mariae egiptiaca.*

During all of these twenty days, until the coming of the next month, they practised singing in the houses which they called *cuicacalli*. They did not dance; rather, remaining seated, they sang canticles in praise of their gods. Many other rites were performed in this feast which are set forth at length in the accounting of them, *fol. 27.*

Todos estos veynte dias, hasta llegar al mes que viene: se exercitauan en cantar en las casas, que llamauan cujcacali, no baylauã, sino estando sentados: cantauan cantares a loor de sus dioses. Otras muchas cerjmonjas, se hazian en esta fiesta: las quales, estan escriptas, a la larga en su historia. fol. 27.

The fourth month they called Uei toçoztli. On the first day of this month they celebrated a feast in honor of the god named Cinteotl, whom they regarded as god of maize. In his honor they fasted four days before the arrival of the feast.

Chapter 4
Uei toçoztli

In this feast they placed reeds at the doors of the houses. They sprinkled them with the blood from their ears or from the calves of their legs. Besides these, the nobles and the rich set up in their houses some branches which they called *acxoyatl*. Likewise, they set up branches for their gods, and set forth flowers for [the gods] which each one had in his house.

After this, they went about the maize fields and brought stalks of the maize (which was still small), and they garnished them with flowers and went to place them before their gods, in the house called *calpulli;* and also they set food before them.

Having done this in the various suburbs, they went to the pyramid of the goddess whom they called Chicome coatl, and there, before her, they enacted skirmishes in the manner of battles. And all the girls bore upon their backs ears of maize [grown] the year before. They went in procession, to present them to the goddess Chicome coatl, and they returned them once more to their house[s] as blessed thing[s]; and from them they took the seed to plant next year. And also they put it [away] as the heart of the grain bins, because it was blessed.

They made of dough (which they call *tzoalli*) the image of this goddess in the courtyard of her pyramid; and before her they offered all kinds of maize, and all kinds of beans, and all kinds of *chía*. For they said that she was the maker and giver of all those things which are the necessaries of life, that the people may live.

Al quarto mes llamauan, Vey toçoztli: en el primero dia deste mes: haziã fiesta a honrra del dios llamado Cinteutl, que le tenjan por dios de los mahizes: a honrra deste, ayunauan quatro dias, ante de llegar la fiesta.

Cap. 4.

1	b	KL Vey toçoztli	b	3
2	c	En esta fiesta, ponjan espadañas a	c	4
3	d	las puertas de las casas ensangrenta-	d	5
4	e	uanlas, con sangre de las orejas, o de	e	6
5	f	las espinjllas: los nobles y los ricos,	f	7
6	g	de mas de las espadañas, enrramauan	g	8
7	A	sus casas, con vnos ramos, que llaman	A	9
8	b	acxoatl. Tambien enrramauan a sus	b	10
9	c	dioses, y las ponjan flores a los que cada	c	11
10	d	vno tenja en su casa.	d	12
11	e	Despues desto, yuan por los ma-	e	13
12	f	hizales, y trayan cañas de mahiz (que	f	14
13	g	aun estaua pequeño) y componjanlas	g	15
14	A	con flores y yuanlas a poner delante de	A	16
15	b	sus dioses, a la casa que llamauan	b	17
16	c	calpulli: y tambien ponjan comjda	c	18
17	d	delante dellos.	d	19
18	e	Despues de echo esto, en los barrios:	e	20
19	f	yuan al cu, de la diosa, que llamauan	f	21
20	g	chicome coatl: y alli delante della	g	22[1]

hazian escaramuças a manera de pelea: y todas las muchachas lleuauan a cuestas, maçorcas de mahiz del año pasado: yuan en procesion, a presẽtarlas, a las diosa chicome coatl: y tornauanlas otra vez a su casa como cosa bendita, y de alli tomauan la semjlla, para sembrar el año venjdero: y tambien ponjanlo por coraçon, de las troxes, por estar bendito.

Hazian de masa (que llaman tzoalli) la ymagen desta diosa, en el patio de su cu, y delante della: ofrecian todo genero de mahiz, y todo genero de frisoles, y todo genero de chien: porque dezian, que ella era la autora, y dadora de aquellas cosas, que son mantenjmjentos, para biujr la gente.

---

1. Marginal notation: *Sanctorum soteris et baii pontif.*

According to the accounts of some, they assembled the children whom they slew in the first month, buying them from their mothers. And they went on killing them in all the feasts which followed, until the rains really began. And thus they slew some in the first month, named Quauitl eua; and some in the second, named Tlacaxipeualiztli; and some in the third, named Toçoztontli; and others in the fourth, named Uei toçoztli: so that until the rains began in abundance, in all the feasts they sacrificed children. Many other ceremonies were performed in this feast. Etc.

Segun relacion de algunos, los njños que matauan, juntauanlos en el primero mes, comprandolos, a sus madres: y yuanlos matando, en todas las fiestas, sigujentes, hasta que las aguas començavan de veras: y ansi matauan algunos, en el primero mes llamado quaujtl eoa: y otros en el segundo, llamado tlacaxipeoaliztli: y otros en el tercero llamado toçoztontli; y otros en el quarto llamado vey toçoztli: De manera que hasta que començauan las aguas abundosamente, en todas las fiestas sacrificauan njños. Otras muchas cerjmonjas, se hazian en esta fiesta. Etc.

The fifth month they called Toxcatl. On the first day of this month they celebrated a great feast in honor of the god named Titlacauan, and for another name, Tezcatlipoca. This one they held to be god of the gods. In his honor, they slew, in this feast, a chosen youth who might have no blemishes upon his body, [who was] reared in all luxuries for the space of a year, [and] trained in the playing [of musical instruments], and in singing, and in speaking.

Chapter 5
Toxcatl

This feast was the most important of all the feasts. It was like Easter, and fell near Easter Sunday—a few days after. This youth, reared as hath been said, was very comely, and chosen from many. He had long hair—down to the waist.

When, on this feast, they slew the young man who had been reared for [the rôle], they at once produced another, who was to die after one year. He walked everywhere in the town finely arrayed with flowers in his hand, and with people who accompanied him. He greeted with good grace those whom he met. All knew that this one was the likeness of Tezcatlipoca, and they bowed before him and worshiped him whenever they met him.

Twenty days before this feast came, they gave this young man four comely young women reared for [the part], with whom for all the twenty days, he had carnal relations. And they changed his array when they gave him these young women: [they] clipped his hair like a war captain and gave him more finery [even] braver [than what he had had].

Five days before he was to die, they celebrated feasts for him and banquets, in cool and pleasant places. Many of the leading men accompanied him. On the arrival of the day he was to die, they took him to a pyramid or sanctuary which they called

Al quinto mes llamauan Toxcatl: el primero dia deste mes: hazian gran fiesta a honrra del dios llamado Titlacaoa, y por otro nombre Tezcatlibuca: a este tenjan por dios de los dioses: a su honrra matauan en esta fiesta vn mancebo escogido, q̃ ninguna tacha tuujesse en su cuerpo: criado en todos deleytes, por espacio de vn año, instruto en tañer, y en cantar, y en hablar.

Cap. 5.

1	A	KL	Toxcatl	A 23
2	b	Esta fiesta, era la principal de todas		b 24
3	c	las fiestas, era como pascua, y caya		c 25
4	d	cerca de la pascua de resurrection		d 26
5	e	pocos dias despues: este mancebo		e 27
6	f	criado, como esta dicho era muy bien		f 28
7	g	dispuesto, y escogido entre muchos:		g 29
8	A	tenja los cabellos largos hasta la cinta.		A 30
9	b	Quando en esta fiesta matauã al		b 1[1]
10	c	mãcebo que estaua criado para esto:		c 2
11	d	luego sacauan otro: el qual auja de		d 3
12	e	morir dẽde a vn año, andaua por todo		e 4
13	f	el pueblo muy ataujado con flores en		f 5
14	g	la mano, y con personas que le acõpa-		g 6
15	A	ñauan saludaua a los que topaua graci-		A 7
16	b	osamẽte: todos sabian que era aquel		b 8
17	c	la ymagẽ de Tezcatlipuca: y se pros-		c 9
18	d	trauã delante del, y le adorauan donde		d 10
19	e	qujera que le topauan.		e 11

20 f Viente dias antes que llegasse esta f 12[2] fiesta: dauã a este mancebo quatro moças, biẽ dispuestas y criadas para esto: con las quales todos los veinte dias tenja cõuersaciõ carnal: y mudauanle el traje, quando le dauã estas moças, cortauale los cabellos como capitã y dauãle otros ataujos mas galanes.

Cinco dias antes que muriesse: hazianle fiestas y vanquetes en lugares frescos y amenos: acompañauanle muchos principales: llegado el dia donde auja de morir: lleuauanle a un cu, o oratorio que llamauã tlacuchcalco: y ante que llegasse alli en vn lugar que

---

1. Marginal notation: *Maius hz dies xxxj.*
2. Marginal notation: *Nerei, Achilei atqz Pan.*

Tlacochcalco; and, before he arrived there, at a place which they called Tlapitzauayan, the women withdrew and left him. Arrived at the place where they were to kill him, he ascended the steps himself; on each of them he shattered one of the flutes which he had played as he walked, all during the year. When he had reached the summit [of the pyramid], they threw him upon the sacrificial stone; they tore out his heart; they brought down the body, carrying it in their hands; below, they cut the head off and ran through it [the crosspiece of the skull rack] which is called *tzompantli*. Many other ceremonies were enacted in this feast, which are set forth at length in their account, *fol.* 53.

llamauã tlapitzaoaiã, apartauãse las mugeres y dexauãle: llegãdo al lugar, donde le aujã de matar: el mjsmo se subia por las gradas, en cada vna dellas, hazia pedaços vna flauta de las cõ que andaua tañendo todo el año: llegado arriba, echauãle sobre el taxõ sacauanle el corcaçõ, tornauã a decendir el cuerpo abaxo en palmas, abaxo le cortauã la cabeça y la espetauã en vn palmo que se llama Tzompãtli: Otras muchas cerimonjas, se haziã en esta fiesta: las quales estan escriptas a la large en su historia. fo. 53.

The sixth month they called Etzalqualiztli. On the first day of this month they observed a feast to the rain gods. In honor of these gods, the priests of these gods fasted before their feast came for four days, which are the four last days of the previous month.

Al sexto mes llamauan Etzalqualiztli: en el primero dia deste mes: hazian fiesta a los dioses de la pluuja: a honrra destos dioses, ayunauã los sacerdotes destos dioses: quatro dias antes de llegar a su fiesta, que son los quatro postreros dias del mes pasado.

Chapter 6
Etzalqualiztli

In order to celebrate this feast, the priests and servants of the idols went to Citlaltepec for reeds; for they grew very large and handsome in the waters called Temilco. From there they brought them to Mexico to adorn the pyramids. On the road which they took, no one appeared; all wayfarers hid themselves, for fear of them. And if they came upon one, they took from him whatever he had, even leaving him naked. And if he resisted, they belabored him such that they left him for dead. And even if he bore tribute for Moctezuma, they took it from him. And for this they visited upon them no punishment; because, since they were servants of the idols, they had license to do these things, and others [even] worse, with no punishment. Many other ceremonies the priests of the temple performed in these four days, which are put forth at length in the account of the feast.

On the arrival of the feast of Etzalqualiztli, everyone made a kind of gruel or porridge which is called *etzalli* (a delicious food, which they liked well). All ate in their houses, and gave [of it] to those who came, and did a thousand follies on this day.

On this same feast, they punished terribly servants of the idols guilty of committing some fault in their service; [they mishandled] them in the water of the lagoon to such a point that they left them for dead. And thus they left them there at the edge of the water. From there their parents or relatives took them and carried them to their houses, half dead.

On this same feast they slew many captives and

Cap. 6.

1	*g*	KL Etzalqualiztli.	*g*	*13*
2	*A*	Para la celebracion desta fiesta: los	*A*	*14*
3	*b*	satrapas de los ydolos y sus mjnjstros,	*b*	*15*
4	*c*	yvã por junças a Citlaltepec: que se	*c*	*16*
5	*d*	hazẽ muy grãdes y muy hermosas en	*d*	*17*
6	*e*	vn agua que se llama temjlco, de alli	*e*	*18*
7	*f*	las trayan a Mexico: para adornar los	*f*	*19*
8	*g*	cues, por el camjno donde venjã, nadie	*g*	*20*
9	*A*	parecia: todos los camjnãtes se ab-	*A*	*21*
10	*b*	scondian de mjedo dellos, y si con	*b*	*22*
11	*c*	alguno encõtrauã: tomauãle quãto	*c*	*23*
12	*d*	traya hasta dexalle en pelo, y si se	*d*	*24*
13	*e*	defendia: maltratauãle de tal manera	*e*	*25*
14	*f*	q̃ le dexauã por muerto: y aunque	*f*	*26*
15	*g*	lleuasse el tributo para Motecuçoma se	*g*	*27*
16	*A*	le tomauan: y por esto njnguna pena	*A*	*28*
17	*b*	las dauã: porque por ser mjnjstros de	*b*	*29*
18	*c*	los ydolos, tenjã libertad para hazer	*c*	*30*
19	*d*	estas cosas, y otras peores sin pena njn-	*d*	*31*
20	*e*	guna. Otras muchas cerimonjas hazian	*e*	*1*[1]

los satrapas del templo en estos quatro dias que estan a la larga puestas en la historia desta fiesta.

Allegada la fiesta de Etzalqualiztli: todos haziã vna manera de puchas o poleadas que se llama Etzalli (comjda delicada a su gusto) todos comjan en su casa, y dauan a los que venjan, y hazian mjll locuras en este dia.

En esta mesma fiesta, a los mjnjstros de los ydolos que avian hecho algun defecto en el serujcio dellos: castigauanlos terriblemẽte en el agua de la laguna tãto que los dexauã por muertos: y assi los dexauã alli a la orilla del agua: de alli los tomauã sus padres o parientes, y los lleuauã a sus casas medio muertos.

En este mjsmo mes matauã muchos catiuos y otros

---

1. Marginal notation: *Junjus hz dies xxx.*

other slaves, arrayed in the ornaments of these gods named Tlalocs, in whose honor they slew them on their own pyramid. The hearts of those whom they killed they went to cast into the whirlpool or drain of the Lake of Mexico, which at that time was clearly to be seen. Many other ceremonies were performed. Etc.

esclauos, compuestos con los ornamentos destos dioses llamados tlaloques: por cuya honrra, los matauan en su mjsmo cu, los coraçones destos que matauã yvanlos a echar en el remolino a sumjdero de la laguna de Mexico, que entonces se via claramente. Otras muchas cerimonjas se hazian. Etc.

The seventh month they named Tecuilhuitontli. On the first day of this month they celebrated a feast to the goddess of salt, whom they called Uixtociuatl. They said that she was elder sister of the Tlaloc gods. In honor of this goddess they slew a woman decked in the ornaments with which they represented the same goddess.

Al septimo mes llamauan Tecujlhujtontli: En el primero dia deste mes: hazian fiesta a la diosa de la sal que llamauan Vixtocioatl: deziã que era hermana mayor, de los dioses tlaloques: matauan a honrra desta diosa vna muger compuesta con los ornamẽtos que pintauã a la mjsma diosa.

Chapter 7
Tecuilhuitontli

On the eve of this feast, all the old women sang and danced, as well as the young women and girls. They went held by some short cords which they carried in their hands, one [taking] one end, another the other [end]. These cords they named *xochimecatl*. They all wore garlands of wormwood [flowers] of this land, which are called *iztauhiatl*. A number of old men led them and ordered the singing. Among them went the woman who was the likeness of this goddess and who was to die arrayed in rich ornaments.

On the night before the feast, the women, with the same one who was to die, kept vigil; and they sang and danced all night long. At break of day, all the priests arrayed themselves and performed a very solemn dance. And all who were present at the dance held in their hands those flowers which are called *cempoalxochitl*. Thus dancing, they took many captives to the Pyramid of Tlaloc, and, with them, the woman who was to die, who was the likeness of the goddess Uixtociuatl. There they slew first the captives and then her.

Many other ceremonies were performed during this feast; and also [there was] great drunkenness, all of which is set forth at length in the account of this feast, *fol. 76.*

Cap. 7

1	f	KL Tecujlhujtontli.	f	2[1]
2	g	La vigilia desta fiesta cantauan y	g	3
3	A	dançauan todas las mugeres, viejas, y	A	4
4	b	moças y muchachas yvan asidas de	b	5
5	c	vnas cuerdas cortas que lleuauan en las	c	6
6	d	manos, la vna por el vn cabo, y la otra	d	7
7	e	por el otro: a estas cuerdas llamauan	e	8
8	f	sochimecatl: lleuauan todas gujrnaldas	f	9
9	g	de axenxos desta tierra que se llama	g	10
10	A	iztauhiatl: gujaualas vnos viejos, y	A	11
11	b	regian al canto en medio dellas yva la	b	12
12	c	muger que era la ymagen desta diosa,	c	13
13	d	y que avia de morir aderaçada con	d	14
14	e	ricos ornamentos.	e	15
15	f	La noche antes de la fiesta: velauan	f	16
16	g	las mugeres con la mjsma que auja de	g	17
17	A	morir, y cantauan, y dançauan toda la	A	18
18	b	noche: venjda la mañana: adereça-	b	19
19	c	uanse todos los satrapas, y hazian vn	c	20
20	d	areyto muy solemne: y todos los que	d	21

estauan presẽtes al areyto, tenjan en la mano aquellas flores que se llaman cempoalsochitl: assi baylando lleuauan muchos catiuos al cu, de Tlaloc: y con ellos a la muger que auja de morir que era imagen de la diosa Vixtocioatl: alli matauan primero a los captiuos, y despues a ella.

Otras muchas cerimonjas se hazian en esta fiesta, y tambien gran borracheria: todo lo qual esta a la larga puesto en la historia desta fiesta. fo. 76.

---

1. Marginal notation: *Marcellinj, petri, atqz Eras.*

The **eighth month** they called Uei tecuilhuitl. On the first day of this month they observed a feast to the goddess named Xilonen (goddess of the tender maize). On this feast they gave food to all the poor men and women—old men, old women, boys, girls— in honor of the goddess. They slew a woman, on the tenth day of this month, arrayed in the ornaments with which they represented the same goddess.

Chapter 8
Uei tecuilhuitl

For eight uninterrupted days before the feast, they fed men and women, young and old. Then, very early in the morning they gave them to drink a kind of gruel which they call *chienpinolli*. Each one drank as much as he wished. And at noon they placed all in order, seated in their rows, and they gave them tamales. He who gave them [out], gave each one as many as he could hold in one hand. And if one of them exceeded the bounds of custom so much as to take [tamales] twice, they mishandled him and took from him those which he had, and he went with nothing. This [feasting] the lords brought about in order to give comfort to the poor; for at this time, ordinarily, there is a want of the necessities of life.

All these eight days they danced and moved in rhythm, men and women together performing the ceremonious movement, all heavily adorned with rich vestments and jewels. The women wore their hair unbound; they went with hair down, dancing and singing with the men. This dance began at sundown, and they continued in it until nine o'clock. They carried many lights (like great torches) of resinous wood, and there were many braziers or bonfires which burned in the same courtyard in which they danced. In this dance or solemn movement they went with hands joined [to those of other dancers], or embraced—the arm of one grasping the body of another as in an embrace, and the other likewise [holding still] another, men and women [alike].

---

1. Marginal notation: *Sancti paulinj Ep̄i et conf.*
2. Marginal notation: *Julius hz dies xxxj.*
3. Marginal notation: *Pij papae et Mart.*

1	e	KL	Vei tecujlhujtl	e	22[1]
2	f		Dauan de comer a hombres y mu-	f	23
3	g		geres chicos y grãdes ocho dias con-	g	24
4	A		tinos, antes de la fiesta luego muy de	A	25
5	b		mañana dauãles a beuer vna manera	b	26
6	c		de maçamorra que llamã chienpinolli:	c	27
7	d		cada vno bueja quãto queria: y al	d	28
8	e		medio dia ponjãlos todos por orden	e	29
9	f		en sus rencleras sentados, y dauanlos	f	30
10	g		tamales: el que los daua, daua a cada	g	1[2]
11	A		vno quãtos podia abarcar con vna	A	2
12	b		mano: y si alguno se desmãdaua a	b	3
13	c		tomar dos vezes maltratauanle, y to-	c	4
14	d		mauanle los que tenja, y yvase sin	d	5
15	e		nada. Esto hazian los señores por con-	e	6
16	f		solar a los pobres: porque en este	f	7
17	g		tiempo ordinariamente ay falta de	g	8
18	A		mãtenjmjentos.	A	9
19	b		Todos estos ocho dias baylauan, y	b	10
20	c		dançauã: haziendo areyto hombres y	c	11[3]

mugeres todos juntos todos muy ataujados con ricas vestiduras y joyas: las mugeres trayan los cabellos sueltos, andauan en cabello baylando y cantando cõ los hombres començaua este areyto en ponjendose el sol, y perseuerauan en el, hasta ora de las nueue: trayã muchas lumbreras (como grãdes hachas) de tea, y aujan muchos braseros o hogueras, que ardian en el mjsmo patio dõde baylauan. En este bayle o areyto andauã trauados de las manos, o abraçados, el braço del vno asido del cuerpo como abraçado, y el otro asimjsmo del otro hombres y mugeres.

One day before they slew the woman who was to die in honor of the goddess Xilonen, the women who served on the pyramid (who were called *ciuatlamacazque*) performed a dance in the courtyard of this same pyramid, and sang the [hymns of] praise and the canticles of this goddess. They all went surrounding her who was to die [and] who went bedight in the ornaments of this goddess. In this way, singing and dancing, they kept watch all night before the day when she was to die.

And at dawn all the nobles and warriors performed a dance in this same courtyard, and with them also danced the woman who was to die, with many other women arrayed like her. The men went dancing in front, by themselves, and the women went behind them.

As soon as all, thus dancing, arrived at the pyramid where that woman was to die, they made her go above, up the steps. When she reached the top, one [of the priests] took her upon his back, shoulder against shoulder; and in this position, they struck off her head and then tore out her heart and offered it to the sun. Many other ceremonies were enacted in this feast. Etc.

Vn dia antes que matassen a la muger que auja de morir: a honrra de la diosa xilonẽ: las mugeres que serujã en el cu (que se llamauã cioatlamacazque) haziã areyto en el patio del mjsmo cu, y cantauan los loores y cantares desta diosa, yvan todas rodeadas de la que avia de morir, que yva compuesta con los ornamẽtos desta diosa. Desta manera cantando y baylando: velauan toda la noche precediẽte el dia en que avia de morir.

Y en amaneciendo todos los nobles y hõbres de guerra: hazian areyto en el mjsmo patio, y con ellos baylaua tambiẽ la muger que auja de morir, con otras muchas mugeres adereçadas como ella: los hombres yvan por si baylãdo delante y las mugeres yvan tras ellos.

Desque todos assi baylando: llegauã al cu donde auja de morir aquella muger, subiãla por las gradas arriba: llegada arriba tomauãla vno a cuestas espaldas cõ espaldas: y estãdo assi, la cortauan la cabeça y luego la sacauã el coraçon y le ofreciã al sol: Otras muchas cerimonjas se haziã en esta fiesta. Etc.

The ninth month they called Tlaxochimaco. On the first day of this month they held a feast in honor of the god of war, named Uitzilopochtli. In this they offered him the first flowers [grown] in that year.

Chapter 9
Tlaxochimaco

On the night before this feast, all busied themselves in killing fowls and dogs, in order to eat them, and in making tamales and other things concerned with food. Then, very early in the morning of this feast, the priests of the idols decked Uitzilopochtli with many flowers; and after the statue of this god was adorned, they decorated the statues of the other gods with garlands and strings and wreaths of flowers. And then they decked all the other statues in the *calpulcos* and young men's houses. And in the houses of the majordomos and leading men and common folk, all decorated with flowers the statues which they had in their houses.

Having decorated the statues of all the gods, they then began to eat that fare which they had prepared the night before; and, a little after eating, they started a kind of dance in which the noblemen, with women, together danced grasping each other's hands, and the ones embracing the others, arms thrown about each other's necks. They did not dance solemnly in the manner of a ceremonial dance, nor did they go through the movements of a ceremonial dance; but they went step by step, to the rhythm of those who beat [the drums] and sang, all of whom were standing, a little to one side of those who danced, near a circular altar which they called *momoztli*.

This chanting lasted until nightfall. Not only in the pyramid courtyards but in all the houses of the leading men and the common folk they beat [the drums] and sang with a great din until night. And the old men and the old women drank wine; but no young man nor young woman drank it. And if [any] of them did drink it, they punished them sorely. Many other ceremonies were performed in this, which are [described] at length. Etc.

Al nono mes llamauan Tlasochimaco: El primero dia deste mes hazian fiesta a honrra del dios de la guerra llamado Vitzilobuchtli: offrecianle en ella las primeras flores de aquel año.

Cap. 9

1	d	**KL**	**Tlasochimaco**	d 12
2	e	La noche antes desta fiesta ocupa-		e 13
3	f	uanse todos en matar gallinas y perros		f 14
4	g	para comer, en hazer tamales y otras		g 15
5	A	cosas concernjentes a la comjda: luego		A 16
6	b	de mañanjta el dia desta fiesta: los		b 17
7	c	satrapas de los ydolos, componjã cõ		c 18
8	d	muchas flores a Vitzilobuchtli, y des-		d 19
9	e	pues de compuesta la estatua deste		e 20
10	f	dios: componjan las estatuas de los		f 21
11	g	otros dioses con gujrnaldas y sartales		g 22
12	A	y collares de flores: y luego cõponjan		A 23
13	b	todas las otras estatuas de los calpules,		b 24
14	c	y telpuchcales: y en las casas de los cal-		c 25
15	d	pisques y principales y maceguales,		d 26
16	e	todos componjan las estatuas que ten-		e 27
17	f	jan en sus casas con flores.		f 28
18	g	Compuestas las estatuas todos los		g 29
19	A	dioses: luego començauan a comer		A 30
20	b	aquellas viandas que tenjan aparejadas		b 31

de la noche pasada, y dende a vn poco despues de comer: començauan vna manera de bayle o dança: en la qual los hombres nobles con mugeres juntamente baylauan asidos de las manos y abraçados los vnos con los otros: echados los braços sobre el cuello el vno del otro: no dançauan a manera de areyte, nj hazian los meneos como en el areyte, sino yvan paso a paso: al son de los que tanjan y cantauan los quales estauan todos en pie, apartados vn poco de los que baylauan, cerca de vn altar redondo que llaman momuztli—

Duraua este cantar hasta la noche: no solo en los patios de los cues: pero en todas las casas de principales y maceguales, tañjã y cantauan con gran bozeria hasta la noche: y los viejos y viejas beujan el vctli: pero njngun mancebo nj moça lo beuja: y si alguno lo beuja castigauanlos reziamente. Otras muchas cerimonjas se hazian en esta: que esta a la larga. Etc.

The tenth month they named Xocotl uetzi. On the first day of this month, they observed a feast to the god of fire, named Xiuhtecutli or Ixcoçauhqui. On this feast they cast into the fire, alive, many slaves, bound hand and foot, and before they had quite died, they took them forth, dragging [them] out of the fire, in order to tear out their hearts before the image of this god.

Chapter 10
Xocotl uetzi

During the feast of Tlaxochimaco, they went forth into the forest [and] cut a tree of twenty-five fathoms' height and brought it, dragging it, to the courtyard of this god. There they pruned off all its branches and raised it upright, and it remained thus standing until the eve of the feast. Then they again laid it upon the earth with much caution and [using] many devices that it might not bump [the ground]. On the day before this feast, early in the morning, many carpenters came with their tools, and they trimmed it and made it very smooth. After having trimmed it and decorated it with many kinds of papers, they tied ropes and other cords to it and raised it up with much shouting and din, and they made it firm.

As soon as the beam or tree was raised and adorned with all of its finery, then those who had slaves to cast alive into the flames adorned themselves with their plumage and rich ornaments, and they stained their bodies yellow, which was the livery of fire; and, taking their captives with them, they performed a dance all that day, until nightfall.

After the captives had kept vigil all that night on the pyramid, and after having performed many ceremonies with them, they cast into their faces some powder which they call *yiauhtli,* that they might lose their sense of feeling and not suffer so greatly [the

Al decimo mes llamauan Xocotl vetzi: En el primero dia deste mes, haziã fiesta al dios del fuego llamado xiuhtecutli o Jzcoçauhquj: en esta fiesta echauã en el fuego viuos muchos esclauos, atados de pies y manos, y antes que acabasen de morir, los sacauã arrastrando del fuego para sacar el coraçon delante la ymagen deste dios.

Cap. 10.

			Xocotl vetzi		
1	*c*	**KL**		*c*	*1*[1]
2	*d*	Durante la fiesta de tlasochimaco:		*d*	*2*[2]
3	*e*	yvã al monte cortauan vn arbol de al-		*e*	*3*
4	*f*	tura de veinte y cinco braças y trayanle		*f*	*4*
5	*g*	arrastrando hasta el patio deste dios:		*g*	*5*
6	*A*	alli le escamondauan todo, y le leuan-		*A*	*6*
7	*b*	tauan enhiesto y estaua assi enhiesto		*b*	*7*
8	*c*	hasta la vigilia vigilie de la fiesta en-		*c*	*8*
9	*d*	tonce le tornauã a echar en tierra cõ		*d*	*9*
10	*e*	mucho tiẽto y cõ muchos pertrechos		*e*	*10*
11	*f*	para que no diesse golpe: la vigilia		*f*	*11*
12	*g*	desta fiesta, bien de mañana venjan		*g*	*12*
13	*A*	muchos carpinteros con sus herrami-		*A*	*13*
14	*b*	ẽtas y mondauãle y hazianle muy liso.		*b*	*14*
15	*c*	Despues de mondado y de auerle com-		*c*	*15*
16	*d*	puesto cõ muchas maneras de papeles:		*d*	*16*
17	*e*	atauanle sogas y otros mecates y leuan-		*e*	*17*
18	*f*	tauanle con muchas bozes y muchos		*f*	*18*
19	*g*	estruendos y afixauanle muy bien.		*g*	*19*
20	*A*	Desque la viga o arbol estaua leuã-		*A*	*20*[3]

tada y adornada cõ todos sus aparejos: luego los que tenjã esclauos para echar en el fuego viuos adere-çauãse con sus plumajes y ataujos ricos: y tiñjanse el cuerpo de amarillo que era la librea del fuego y lleuando sus captiuos consigo: hazian areyto todo aquel dia hasta la noche.

Despues de auer velado toda aquella noche los captiuos en el cu, y despues de auer hecho muchas cerimonjas con ellos, enpoluorizauanlos las caras con vnos poluos que llamã yiauhtli: para que perdiessen el sentido, y no sintiessẽ tanto la muerte, atauanlos

---

1. Marginal notation: *Augustus hz dies xxxj.*
2. Marginal notation: *Petri ad vincula.*
3. Marginal notation: *Bernardi abbatis.*

pains of] their death. They tied them hand and foot, and, thus bound, they slung them over their shoulders, and walked with them as if performing a dance about the edge of a great fire and tall mound of live coals. Thus proceeding, they went casting them upon the mound of coals—now one, and, after a little, another. And him whom they had cast they let burn for a good while; and, still alive and tossing, they took him forth, dragging him out with something like a hook, and cast him upon the sacrificial stone. And, having opened his breast, they tore out his heart. In this manner suffered all those unhappy captives.

The tree was made fast by many ropes from the top, as the rigging of a ship hangeth from the topsail. On the top of this stood upright the statue of that god, made of a dough which they call *tzoalli*. When the aforesaid sacrifice had been offered, all the young men assailed [the statue] with great vigor. Many other ceremonies were enacted, as hath been written at length below, in this feast.

los pies y las manos, y assi atados ponjãlos sobre los hombros, y andauã con ellos como haziẽdo areyto en rrededor de vn grã fuego y grã mõton de brasa, ansi andando yvãlos arrojando sobre el monton de brasas: agora vno y desde a vn poco otro: y el que avian arrojado, dexauanle quemar vn buen interualo, y avn quando biuo y barqueando sacauanle fuera arrastrando con qual que garauato, y echauãle sobre el taxõ: y abierto el pecho sacauanle el coraçon: desta manera padecian todos aquellos tristes catiuos.

Estaua el arbol atado con muchas sogas de lo alto, como la jarcia de la nao: esta pendiente de la gabia en lo alto del, estaua en pie la ymagen de aquel dios: hecha de masa que llaman tzoalli: acabado el sacrificio ya dicho, arremetian con gran impetu todos los mancebos. Otras muchas cerimonjas hazian segun a la larga esta escripto adelante en esta fiesta.

The eleventh month they named Ochpaniztli. On the first day of this month they celebrated a feast to the mother of the gods, named Teteo innan, or Toçi, which meaneth "Our Grandmother." They danced in silence for the honor of this goddess, and in great silence slew a woman dressed with the ornaments with which they represented this goddess.

Al vndecimo mes llamauan Ochpanjztli: El primero dia, deste mes, haziã fiesta a la madre de los dioses llamada Teteu inna o Toci, que qujere dezir nuestra abuela: baylauan a honrra desta diosa en silencio y matauan vna muger en gran silencio vestida con los ornamentos que pintauan a esta diosa.

Chapter 11
Ochpaniztli

Five days before this month began, all the feasts and merry making of the previous month ceased. Entering this month, they danced eight days without singing and without beating the two-toned drum. These past, there came forth the woman who was the likeness of the goddess whom they name Teteo innan, arrayed with the ornaments with which they pictured the same goddess; and a great number of women came forth with her, especially the medicine women and midwives. And they split into two bands and fought, pelting each other with balls made of tree parasites and from the leaves of the *tuna* cactus and with balls made from the leaves of reeds, and with flowers which they call *cempoalxochitl*. This merry making lasted four days.

These ceremonies and others of like kind ended, they brought it about that that woman should not know she was to die, so that she should neither weep nor be saddened; for they held that to be an omen of evil. The night when she was to die having fallen, they decked her very richly, and persuaded her that they were taking her so that some great lord might sleep with her; and they bore her in great silence to the pyramid where she was to die. Having taken her up, one [of the priests] took her upon his back, shoulder against shoulder, and swiftly they struck off her head, and then they flayed her. And a stout youth put on her skin.

This one who wore the skin of the woman whom they had slain they then bore off with great solem-

Cap. 11.

1	b	**KL** Ochpanjztli.	b	21
2	c	Cinco dias antes que començasse este	c	22
3	d	mes: cesauan todas las fiestas y regozi-	d	23
4	e	jos del mes pasado entrando este mes,	e	24
5	f	baylauã ocho dias sin cantar, y sin	f	25
6	g	teponaztli: los quales pasados, salia la	g	26
7	A	muger que era ymagen de la diosa q̃	A	27
8	b	llaman teteu inna, compuesta con los	b	28
9	c	ornamẽtos con que pintauan a la	c	29
10	d	mjsma diosa, y salian grã numero de	d	30
11	e	mugeres con ella: especialmente las	e	31
12	f	medicas y parteras: y partianse en dos	f	1[1]
13	g	vandos y peleauan apedreandose con	g	2
14	A	pellas de pachtli y con hojas de tunas	A	3
15	b	y cõ pellas hechas de hojas de espa-	b	4
16	c	dañas, y con flores que llamã cempoal-	c	5
17	d	sochitl. Este regozijo duraua quatro	d	6
18	e	dias.	e	7
19	f	Acabado estas cerimonjas y otras	f	8
20	g	desta calidad: procurauan que aquella	g	9

muger no entendiesse que auja de morir porque no llorasse nj se entristeciesse porque lo tenjan por mal aguero: venjda la noche en que auja de morir, ataujauanla muy ricamente, y haziãla entender que la lleuauan para que dormjesse con ella algun gran señor: y lleuauanla con grã silencio al cu, donde auja de morir: subida arriba, tomauala vno a cuestas espaldas con espaldas, y de presto la cortauan la cabeça, y luego la desollauan: y con mancebo robusto vestiase el pelejo.

Este que vestia el pelejo desta que matauan: lleuauanle luego con mucha solenjdad y acõpañan-

---

1. Marginal notation: *September hz dies xxx.*

nity, and, escorted by many captives to the pyramid of Uitzilopochtli, here this same one, before Uitzilopochtli, tore out the hearts of four captives. The rest he left, that the priest might slay them.

In this month the lord drew up a parade of all the warriors and of the young men who had never gone to war. These he gave arms and insignia, and they became soldiers; so that from then on they could go to war. Many other ceremonies were enacted in this feast, which are set forth at length in its account.

dole de muchos catiuos al cu de Vitzilobuchtli: alli este mesmo delante de Vitzilobuchtli, sacaua el coraçon a quatro catiuos: y los de mas dexaualos para que los matasse el satrapa.

En este mes hazia alarde el señor de toda la gente de guerra: y de los mancebos que nũca aujan ydo a la guerra: a estos daua armas y diujsas, y asentauan por soldados: para que de alli adelante fuessen a la guerra. Otras muchas cerimonjas se hazian en esta fiesta que estan a la larga puestas en su historia.

The twelfth month they named Teotl eco, which meaneth "The Arrival of the Gods." They celebrated this feast in honor of all the gods; for they said that they had gone to a number of places. They observed a great feast on the last day of this month because their gods had arrived.

Chapter 12
Teotl eco

On the fifteenth day of this month the young men and boys strewed boughs on all the altars and shrines of the gods, both those which were in the houses and those which were along the roads and crossroads. And for this activity which they performed they gave them maize; [to some they] gave a large basket full of maize, and to others two or three ears.

On the eighteenth day arrived the god (who is always a young man whom they called Tlamatzincatl; that is, Titlacauan). They said that, because he was young and strong, he traveled better and arrived first. They then set forth food on his pyramid, and that night they ate and drank, and all made merry, especially the old men and the old women, who drank wine because of the arrival of the god. And they said that with this rejoicing they washed his feet for him.

On the last day of this month was the great feast; for they said that all the gods then arrived. On the eve of this day, at night, they made, on a mat, a very closely packed small cake of cornmeal, in the shape of a cheese. Upon this small cake the gods impressed the print of a foot as a sign that they had come. All night long the principal priest watched, and came and went many times to see when he would descry the print.

Seeing the mark of a footprint, the priest then cried out, saying "Our lord hath come!" Then the priests of the pyramid began to sound horns, and conch shells, and trumpets, and other instruments of those

Al dozeno mes llamauan Teutl eco, que qujere dezir la llegada le los dioses celebrauan esta fiesta, a honrra de todos los dioses, porque dezian que aujan ydo a algunas partes, hazian gran fiesta el postrero dia deste mes, porque sus dioses aujan llegado.

Cap. 12

1	A	KL	Teutl eco	A 10
2	b	A los qujnze dias deste mes: los		b 11
3	c	moços y muchachos, enrramauan		c 12
4	d	todos los altares y oratorios de los		d 13
5	e	dioses: assi los que estauan dentro de		e 14
6	f	las casas como por los camjnos y en-		f 15
7	g	cruzijadas, y por esta diligencia que		g 16
8	A	hazian dauãlos mahiz, algunos dauan		A 17
9	b	vn chiqujvitl lleno de mahiz, y a otros		b 18
10	c	dos o tres maçorcas.		c 19
11	d	A los deziocho dias: llegaua el dios		d 20
12	e	(que siempre es mancebo que le		e 21
13	f	llamauã tlamatzincatl: este es titla-		f 22
14	g	cauã) deziã que por ser mancebo y		g 23
15	A	rezio, camjnaua mejor, y llegaua pri-		A 24
16	b	mero: luego ofreciã comjda en su cu,		b 25
17	c	y aquella noche comjan y beujan y		c 26
18	d	regozijauãse todos: especialmente los		d 27
19	e	viejos, y viejos que beujan vino, por la		e 28
20	f	llegada del dios: y dezian que lo		f 29[1]

lauauã los pies con este regozijo.

El postrero dia deste mes era la gran fiesta: porque dizen que todos los dioses llegauan entonce: la vigilia deste dia, a la noche hazian encima de vn petate de harina de mahiz vn mõtonzillo muy tupido de la forma de vn queso: en este montonzillo imprimjan los dioses la pisada de vn pie en señal que avian llegado: toda la noche el principal satrapa velaua y yva y venja muchas vezes a mjrar quando veria la pisada.

En vinjendo el satrapa la señal de la pisada luego daua bozes diziendo, llegado a nuestro señor: luego comenzauan los mjnjstros del cu, a tañer cornetas, y caracoles, y trompetas y otros instrumentos de los

---

1. Marginal notation: *Dedicatio sancti Michael.*

which they then used. As soon as the instruments were heard, all the people hastened to offer food at all the pyramids and shrines. Again there was merry making, washing the feet of their gods, as is told above.

On the next day they said that the old gods arrived, after all [the rest]—because they moved more slowly, being old. On this day they had many captives to burn alive; and, a great mound of coals having been piled up, certain young men went dancing about the edge of the fire, disguised as monsters. And, thus dancing, they proceeded casting into the fire these miserable captives in the manner which is told above. Many other ceremonies were performed, as will be related below in this feast.

que ellos entonce vsauã: luego que se oyan los instru-mẽtos, acudia toda la gente a ofrecer comjda en todos los cues, y oratorios: otra vez se regozijauã lauando los pies de sus dioses, como arriba esta dicho.

El dia sigujente: dezian que llegauã los dioses viejos a la postre de todos: porque andauan menos por ser viejos. Este dia tenjã muchos catiuos para quemar biuos: y hecho grã monton de brasa, andauan baylando al rededor del fuego ciertos mancebos, dis-fraçados como monstros, y ansi baylando, yvan arrojando en el fuego estos tristes captiuos, de la manera que arriba esta dicho. Otras muchas ceri-monjas se hazian segũ se dira adelante en esta fiesta.

The thirteenth month they named Tepeilhuitl. In this month they celebrated a feast in honor of the high mountains, which are in all these lands of this New Spain, where large clouds pile up. They made the images of each one of them in human form, from the dough which is called *tzoalli,* and they laid offerings before these images in veneration of these same mountains.

Chapter 13
Tepeilhuitl

In honor of the mountains they made a number of serpents, of wood or of the roots of trees, and they fashioned them heads like [those of] serpents. They made also some lengths of wood, as thick as the wrist, and long. They called them *ecatotonti.* These, as well as the serpents, they overlaid with that dough which they call *tzoalli.* These pieces they provided a covering in the manner of mountains. Above, they placed the head, like the head of a person. Likewise they made these images in memory of those who had drowned in the water, or had died such a death that they did not burn them, but rather buried them.

After, with many ceremonies, they had placed upon their altars the aforementioned images, they also offered them tamales and other food; and also they uttered canticles of their praises, and they drank wine in their honor.

Upon arrival of the feast in honor of the mountains, they slew four women and one man. The first of these [women] they called Tepexoch. The second they called Matlalcueie. The third they named Xochtecatl. The fourth they called Mayauel. And the man they named Milnauatl. They decked these women and the man in many papers covered with rubber. And they carried them in some litters upon the shoulders of women highly adorned, to the place where they were to slay them.

---

1. Marginal notation: *October hz dies xxxj.*

Al tercio decimo mes llamauan Tepeilhujtl: En este mes hazian fiesta a honrra de lo montes emjnētes, que estan por todas estas comarcas desta nueua españa: donde se armã ñublados: hazian las ymagenes en figura humana a cada vno dellos de la masa que se llama tzoal, y ofrecian delante destas ymagenes, en respecto destos mismos montes.

Cap. 13.

1	g	**KL**	**Tepeilhujtl.**	g	30
2	A		Hazian a honrra de los montes: vnas	A	1[1]
3	b		culebras de palo o de rayzes de arboles,	b	2
4	c		y labrauanles la cabeça como culebra:	c	3
5	d		haziã tãbien vnos troços de palo gru-	d	4
6	e		esos como la muñeca largos llamauan-	e	5
7	f		los Ecatotonti: assi a estos como a las	f	6
8	g		culebras los investian cõ aquella masa	g	7
9	A		que llamã tzoal: a estos troços los in-	A	8
10	b		vestian a manera de montes, arriba les	b	9
11	c		ponjan su cabeça como cabeça de per-	c	10
12	d		sona: hazian tambien estas ymagenes,	d	11
13	e		en memoria de aquellos que se aujan	e	12
14	f		ahogado en el agua o avian muerto de	f	13
15	g		tal muerte que no los quemauan, sino	g	14
16	A		que los enterrauan.	A	15
17	b		Despues que cõ muchas cerimonjas,	b	16
18	c		aujan puesto en sus altares a las yma-	c	17
19	d		genes dichas: ofrecianles tambien ta-	d	18
20	e		males y otras comjdas: y tambien los	e	19

dezian cantares de sus loores, y beujan vino por su honrra.

Llegada la fiesta a honrra de los montes, matauan quatro mugeres y vn hombre: la vna dellas llamauã tepexoch: la segũda llamauã Matlalcueie: la tercera llamauan Sochtecatl: la quarta llamauã Mayauel, y al hombre llamauã Milnaoatl: adereçauan a estas mugeres y al hombre cõ muchos papeles llenos de vlli: y lleuauanlas en vnas literas en hombros de mugeres muy ataujadas, hasta donde las aujã de matar.

After they had slain them and torn out their hearts, they took them away gently, rolling them down the steps. When they had reached the bottom, they cut off their heads and inserted a rod through them, and they carried the bodies to the houses which they called *calpulco*, where they divided them up in order to eat them. The papers with which they arrayed the images of the mountains, after they had broken them to pieces in order to eat them, they hung in the *calpulco*. Many other ceremonies were performed in this feast, which are set down at length in its account.

Despues que las oujeron muerto, y sacados los coraçones: lleuauanlas pasito rodando por las gradas abaxo: llegadas abaxo cortauanlas las cabeças, y espetauanlas en vn palo, y los cuerpos lleuauanlos a las casas que llamauan Calpul: donde los repartian para comer: los papeles con que adereçauan las ymagenes de los montes despues de averlas desbaratado para comer, colgauanlos en el Calpul. Otras muchas cerimonjas se hazian en esta fiesta, que estan a la larga puestas en su historia.

The fourteenth month they named Quecholli. They observed a feast to the god name Mixcoatl. And in this month they made arrows and darts for war. They slew many slaves in honor of this god.

Chapter 14
Quecholli

When they made the arrows, for a space of five days all took blood from the ears, and [with] the blood which they pressed out of them they anointed their own temples. They said that they did penances in order to go to hunt deer. From those who did not bleed themselves, they took their capes as punishment. No man lay with his wife on those days; neither did the old men nor the old women drink wine; because they did penance.

At the end of the four days during which they made the arrows and darts, they made a number of very small arrows, and bound them in four's with each [bundle of] four torches. And, a small bundle of the four torches and the four arrows being made, they offered them upon the graves of the dead. They placed also, along with the arrows and torches, two tamales. All this remained for a whole day upon the grave, and at night they burned it and performed many other ceremonies for the dead on this same feast.

On the tenth day of this month, all the Mexicans and Tlatelulcans went to those mountains which they call Çacatepec. And they say that this mountain is their mother. On the day that they arrived, they made huts or cabins of grass, and they lit fires, and nothing else did they do that day.

Next day, at dawn, all forthwith broke fast and set out for the country and formed a great wing, wherewith they surrounded many animals—deer, rabbit, and other animals—and little by little they kept coming together until they rounded up all of them. Then they attacked and hunted, each one what he could.

---

1. Marginal notation: *November hz dies xxx.*

Cap. 14

1	ƒ	**KL**	**Quecholli.**	ƒ	20
2	g	Quando hazian las saetas por espa-	g	21
3	A	cio de cinco dias: todos se sangrauan	A	22
4	b	de las orejas y la sangre que esprimjan	b	23
5	c	dellas: vntauanla por sus mesmas si-	c	24
6	d	enes. Dezian que hazian penjtencias	d	25
7	e	para yr a caçar venados: los que no se	e	26
8	ƒ	sangrauan, tomauanles las mantas en	ƒ	27
9	g	pena: njngun hombre se echaua con	g	28
10	A	su muger en estos dias, nj los viejos ni	A	29
11	b	viejas beujan pulcre: porque hazian	b	30
12	c	penjtencia.	c	31
13	d	Acabados los quatro dias en que ha-	d	1[1]
14	e	zian las saetas y dardos: haziã vnas	e	2
15	ƒ	saetas chiqujtas y atauanlas de quatro	ƒ	3
16	g	en quatro con cada quatro teas: y assi	g	4
17	A	hecho vn manogico de las quatro teas,	A	5
18	b	y de las quatro saetas, ofrecianlas so-	b	6
19	c	bre los sepulchros de los muertos: pon-	c	7
20	d	jan tambien juntamente con las saetas	d	8

y teas dos tamales: estaua todo esto vn dia entero sobre la sepultura, y a la noche lo quemauan: y hazian otras muchas cerimonjas por los defũtos en esta mesma fiesta.

A los diez dias deste mes yvan todos los Mexicanos y Tlatelulcanos a aquellos montes que llaman Çacatepec: y dizen que es su madre aquel monte, el dia que llegauan hazian xacales o cabañas de heno, y hazian fuegos y njnguna otra cosa hazian aquel dia.

Otro dia en amaneciendo luego almorçauan todos, y salian al campo y hazian vna ala grande: donde cercauan muchos anjmales, cieruos, conejos, y otros anjmales y poco a poco se yvan juntando hasta acorralarlos todos: entonce arremetian y caçauan cada a qual lo que podia.

The hunt ended, they slew captives and slaves on a pyramid which they call Tlamatzinco. They bound them hand and foot, and carried them up the steps of the pyramid (as one carrieth a deer by the hind and forelegs to slaughter). They slew with great ceremony the man and the woman who were the likeness[es] of the god Mixcoatl and of his consort. They slew them on another pyramid which was called Mixcoateopan. Many other ceremonies [were performed]. Etc.

Acabada la caça: matauan captiuos y esclauos en vn cu, que llaman tlamatzinco ataualos de pies y manos, y lleuauãlos por las gradas del cu arriba (como qujen lleua vn cieruo por los pies y por las manos a matar) matauanlos con gran cerimonja: al hombre y a la muger que erã ymagẽ del dios Miscoatl y de su muger matauãlos en otro cu, que se llamaua Miscoateupan. Otras muchas cerimonjas. Etc.

The fifteenth month they named Panquetzaliztli. In this month they celebrated a feast to the god of war, Uitzilopochtli. Before this feast, the priests of the idols fasted for forty days and performed other severe penances, like going naked at midnight to carry branches to the mountains. Etc.

Al quinzeno mes llamauan Panquetzaliztli: En este mes haziã fiesta al dios de la guerra Vitzilobuchtli: antes desta fiesta los satrapas de los ydolos ayunauan quarenta dias y hazian otras penjtencias asperas como era yr a la media noche desnudos a lleuar ramos a los montes. Etc.

Chapter 15
Panquetzaliztli

On the second day of this month all began to perform a dance and to sing the canticles of Uitzilopochtli in the the courtyard of his pyramid. Men and women danced, all together. They began these canticles in the afternoon, and they ended at nearly ten o'clock. These dances and songs lasted twenty days.

On the ninth day of this month, they adorned, with great ceremonies, those whom they were to slay. They painted them in various colors; they decked them in many papers. Finally they performed a dance with them, in which went a woman paired with a man, singing and dancing.

On the sixteenth day of this month, the owners of the slaves began a fast; and on the nineteenth day, they began to perform a number of dances in which all, men and women, went grasping hands, and they danced winding back and forth in the courtyard of the aforementioned pyramid. A number of old men sang, and played [instruments] while the others danced.

After those who were to die had performed many ceremonies, there came down from the pyramid of Uitzilopochtli one attired in the ornaments of the god Paynal, and he slew four of those slaves in the ball court which was found in the courtyard which they called Teotlachtli. From there he departed and circled all the city, running; and in certain places he slew, in each one, a slave. And from that point [onward], two factions began a mock battle. Some died in the skirmishing.

Cap. 15.

1	e	KL Panquetzaliztli.	e	9[1]
2	f	El segundo dia deste mes começauã	f	10
3	g	todos a hazer areyto, y a cantar los can-	g	11
4	A	tares de Vitzilobuchtli, en el patio de	A	12
5	b	su cu, baylauan hombres y mugeres to-	b	13
6	c	dos juntos: comẽçauan estos cantares	c	14
7	d	a la tarde, y acabauan cerca de las diez:	d	15
8	e	durauan estos bayles y cantos veinte	e	16
9	f	dias.	f	17
10	g	A los nueue dias deste mes: apare-	g	18
11	A	jauã cõ grandes cerimonjas a los que	A	19
12	b	aujan de matar pjntauanlos de diuersas	b	20
13	c	colores, componjãlos con muchos pa-	c	21
14	d	peles: al fin hazian vn areyte con ellos,	d	22
15	e	en el qual vyan vna muger y vn hom-	e	23
16	f	bre pareados cantando y baylãdo.	f	24
17	g	A los deziseys dias deste mes: co-	g	25
18	A	mençauã a ayunar los dueños de los	A	26
19	b	esclauos y a los dezinueue dias, comen-	b	27
20	c	çauan a hazer vnas danças en que yvan	c	28

todos asidos de las manos hombres y mugeres, y dançauan culebreãdo en el patio del dicho cu, cantauã y tañjan vnos viejos entre tanto que los otros dancauan.

Despues de auer hecho muchas cerimonjas los que avian de morir decendian del cu de Vitzilobuchtli, vno vestido con los ornamẽtos del dios Paynal, y mataua quatro de aquellos esclauos en el juego de pelota que estaua en el patio que llamauã teutlachtli: de alli yva y cercaua toda la ciudad corriendo, y en ciertas partes mataua en cada vno vn esclauo: y de alli començauan a escaramuçar dos partialidades, murian algunos en la escaramuça.

---

1. Marginal notation: *Dedicatio Basilice saluat.*

After many ceremonies, at last they slew captives on the Pyramid of Uitzilopochtli, and also many slaves. And, having slain one, they sounded musical instruments. And on finishing [with one], they seized another, to slay him. And, on killing him, they again sounded [musical instruments]. Thus they did to each one until finishing them [all]. On ceasing to slay these unhappy ones, they started to dance and to sing, to eat and to drink, and thus the feast ended.

Despues de muchas cerimonjas: finalmente matauan captiuos, en el cu, de Vitzilobuchtli, y tambien muchos esclauos y en matando a vno tocauan los instrumẽtos musicales, y en cessando tomauan otro para matarle, y en matandole tocauã otravez; ansi hazian a cada vno, hasta acabarlos: acabando de matar estos tristes, començauan a baylar, y a cantar, a comer y a beuer, y ansi se acabaua la fiesta.

The sixteenth month they named Atemoztli. In this month they celebrated a feast to the rain gods, because for the most part in this month it began to thunder and to threaten rain; and the priests of the Tlalocs began to do penances and to offer sacrifices, so that the rains would come.

Chapter 16
Atemoztli

When it began to thunder, the priests of the Tlalocs, with great industriousness, offered *copal* and other fragrances to their gods and to all the statues of these. They said that then they came to give rain. And the common folk made vows to fashion the images of the mountains, which are called *tepictli,* because they are dedicated [to] those gods of the rain. And on the sixteenth day of this month, all the common folk prepared offerings to offer before Tlaloc. And [during] these four days they performed penances, and the men abstained from women, and the women from men.

Having come to [the time of] the feast, which they celebrated on the last day of this month, they cut lengths of paper, and they bound them to a number of poles, from bottom to top. And they set them up in the courtyards of their houses and made the images of the mountains of *tzoalli.* They fashioned for them their teeth of squash seeds, and their eyes of some beans which are named *aiecotli.* And then they offered them their offerings of food, and they worshipped them.

After having kept a vigil for them, and beaten drums and sung for them, they opened their breasts with a *tzotzopaztli,* which is an instrument with which the women weave, almost like a *machete;* and they took out their hearts and struck off their heads. And later they divided up all the body among themselves and ate it; and the ornaments with which

---

1. Marginal notation: *Saturninj marty.*
2. Marginal notation: *December hz dies xxxj.*
3. Marginal notation: *Expectatio beate Marie V.*

Al mes decimo sesto llamauan Atemuztli: En este mes hazian fiesta a los Dioses de la pluuja: porque por la mayor parte en este mes, començaua a tronar y hazer demuestras de agua: y los satrapas de los Tlaloques començauan a hazer penjtencias y sacrificios porque venjesse el agua.

Cap. 16.

1	d	**KL** **Atemuztli.**	d	29[1]
2	e	Quando començaua a tronar: los	e	30
3	f	satrapas de los Tlaloques con gran	f	1[2]
4	g	diligencia offrecian copal y otros per-	g	2
5	A	fumes a sus dioses, y a todas las estatuas	A	3
6	b	dellos: dezian que entonce venjan para	b	4
7	c	dar agua: y los populares hazian votos	c	5
8	d	de hazer las ymagines de los montes	d	6
9	e	que se llaman Tepictli: porq̃ son dedi-	e	7
10	f	cadas aquellos dioses del agua. Y a los	f	8
11	g	deziseis dias deste mes, todos los popu-	g	9
12	A	lares aparejauan offrendas para offre-	A	10
13	b	cer a Tlaloc: y estos quatro dias hazian	b	11
14	c	penjtẽcia, y abstenjanse los hombres	c	12
15	d	de las mugeres, y las mugeres de los	d	13
16	e	hombres.	e	14
17	f	Llegados a la fiesta que la celebrauan	f	15
18	g	el vltimo dia deste mes: cortauan tiras	g	16
19	A	de papel, y atauanlas a vnos barales	A	17
20	b	desde abaxo hasta arriba: y hincauan-	b	18[3]

los en los patios de sus casas y hazian las ymagines de los montes de tzoal: hazianles los diẽtes de pepitas de calabaça, y los ojos de vnos frisoles que se llaman aiecotli: y luego los ofrecian sus offrendas de comjda y los adorauan.

Despues de auerlos velado y tañido y cãtado: abrianlos por los pechos, con vn tzotzopaztli: que es instrumento con que texen las mugeres, casi a manera de machete: y sacauanles el coraçon, y cortauãles las cabeças: y despues repartian todo el cuerpo entre si,

they had arrayed them, they burned in the courtyards of their houses.

This done, they carried all these ashes and the ornaments with which they had provided them to the shrines which they call *aiauhcalco*. And then they began to eat and drink, and to make merry. And thus ended the feast. Many other ceremonies remain to be related, which are [set down] at length in the account of this feast.

comjanselo, y otros ornamẽtos con que los tenjan aparejados quemauanlos en los patios de sus casas.

Hecho esto: lleuauan todas esta cenjzas, y los aparejos con que aujan serujdo a los oratorios que llamã Aiauhcalco: y luego començauan a comer y a beuer, y a regozijarse. Y ansi concluyan la fiesta. Otras muchas cerimonjas se quedan por dezir que estan a la larga en la historia desta fiesta.

The seventeenth month they called Tititl. In this month they celebrated a feast to a goddess whom they named Ilamatecutli, and by another name, Tonan, and by [still] another name, Cozcamiauh. In honor of this goddess they slew a woman, and as soon as they had torn out her heart they struck off her head and performed a dance with it. He who went before carried the head by the hair, in his right hand, making [with it] the gestures of the dance.

Chapter 17
Tititl

This woman whom they slew in this feast they arrayed in the adornments of that goddess whose likeness [she was], called Ilamatecutli, and by another name, Tonan, which meaneth "Our Mother." This woman, thus bedight with the adornments [which are] set forth in the description, danced alone. A number of old men made music for her; and, dancing, she sighed and wept, mindful that soon she was to die. After midday, the priests arrayed themselves in the ornaments of all the gods, and went before her, and took her up to the pyramid where she was to die. Having stretched her out upon the sacrificial stone, they tore out her heart, and they struck off her head. Then one of those who went adorned as a god took [it], and, [with him] foremost, carrying it by the hair, they performed a dance with it. He who bore it in his right hand guided [them], and he made the dance gestures with it.

On the same day that the servants of the idols slew this woman, they performed certain mock-battles, and made merry, running—some behind the others —up and down the pyramid, enacting certain ceremonies.

On the next day, all the common folk made a number of sacks, like pockets, with some cords attached, as much as a fathom long. They filled those

Al mes decimo septimo llamauan Tititl. En este mes haziã fiesta a vna diosa que llamauã Jlamatecutli, y por otro nombre Tona, y por otro nombre cozcamjauh, a honrra desta diosa: matauan vna muger, y desque le aviã sacado el coraçon cortauanle la cabeça y hazian areyto con ella, el que yva adelante lleuaua la cabeça por los cabellos en la mano derecha, haziendo sus ademanes de bayle.

Cap. 17.
Tititl.

1 c KL
2 d A esta muger que matauan en esta d 20
3 e fiesta: componjanla con los ataujos de e 21
4 f aquella diosa cuya ymagen tenja que f 22
5 g se llama Jlamatecutli y por otro nom- g 23
6 A bre Tona qujere dezir nuestra madre A 24
7 b esta muger ansi compuesta con los b 25
8 c ataujos estan puestos en la historia, c 26
9 d baylaua sola: hazianla el son vnos vie- d 27
10 e jos, y baylando suspiraua y lloraua, e 28
11 f acordandose que luego auja de morir: f 29
12 g pasando el medio dia, componjanse los g 30
13 A satrapas con los ornamentos de todos A 31
14 b los dioses, y yvan delante della, y su- b 1[1]
15 c bianla al cu, donde auja de morir: c 2
16 d echada sobre el taxon de piedra, sa- d 3
17 e cauanla el coraçon, y cortauanla la ca- e 4
18 f beça, tomaua luego vno de aquellos f 5[2]
19 g que yva adornado como dios, y delan- g 6
20 A tero de todos y lleuandola por los ca- A 7

bellos: hazian areyto cõ ella gujaua el que la lleuaua en la mano derecha y hazia sus ademanes de bayle con ella.

El mesmo dia que matauã esta muger los mjnjstros de los ydolos, haziã ciertas escaramuças y regozijos: corriendo vnos tras otros el cu, arriba y el cu abaxo haziendo ciertas cerimonjas.

El dia sigujente todos los populares hazian vnas talegas como bolsas, con vnos cordeles atadas tan largos como vn braço: hinchian aquellas talegas de

---

1. Marginal notation: *Januarius hz dies xxxj*.
2. Marginal notation: *Epiphanjs domjnj*.

sacks with soft things, like wool, and they carried them hidden under their capes, and they struck, with the bags, all the women whom they might meet in the streets. This game reached such lengths that the boys also made bags and with them mauled the girls so much that they made them weep. Many other ceremonies were performed in this celebration, which are set forth at length in the account of this feast.

cosas blandas como lana y llegauanlas ascondidas debaxo de las mantas, y a todas las mugeres que topauan por la calle, dauanlas de talegazos: llegaua a tanto este juego, que tambiẽ los muchachos hazian las talegas y aporreauan con ellas a las muchachas tãto que las hazian llorar. Otras muchas cerimonjas se hazian esta fiesta q̃ estan a la larga puestas en la historia desta fiesta.

The eighteenth month they named Izcalli. In this month they celebrated a feast to the god of fire, whom they called Xiuhtecutli, or Ixcoçauhqui. They made an image in his honor, with great artifice, which appeared to throw off flames of its own accord. And every four years, in this same feast, they slew slaves and captives in honor of this god. And they pierced the ears of all the children who had been born in those years, and they gave them godfathers and godmothers.

Al mes decimo octauo llamauan Izcalli: en este mes hazian fiesta al dios del fuego que llamauan Xiuhtecutli, o Jxcoçauhquj: hazian vna ymagen a su hõrra de grã artificio que parecia que echaua llamas de fuego de si: y de quatro en quatro años en esta mesma fiesta esclauos y captiuos matauan a honrra deste dios: y agujerauan las orejas a todos los njños que aujan nacido en aquellos años y dauanlos padrinos, y madrinas.

Chapter 18
Izcalli

On the tenth day of this month they made a new fire at midnight, before the image of Xiuhtecutli, [which was] very curiously adorned. And, the fire having been lit, then, in the morning, the young men and boys came, and they brought various animals which they had hunted in the ten preceding days— some water [animals] and some land [animals]. And they offered them to the old men who were charged with safeguarding this god. And these cast into the fire all of those animals, so that they would cook. And they gave each one of these young men and boys a tamal made with amaranth, which they called *uauhquiltamalli,* which everyone in the city offered upon that day. All ate of these in honor of the feast day. They ate them very hot, and they drank and made merry.

Cap. 18.
Izcalli

1	b	**KL** Izcalli	b	8
2	c	A los diez dias deste mes: sacauã	c	9
3	d	fuego nueuo a la media noche delante	d	10
4	e	la ymagẽ de Xiuhtecutli muy curiosa-	e	11
5	f	mente ataujada: y encendidos fuegos,	f	12
6	g	luego en amaneciendo venjan los man-	g	13
7	A	cebos y muchachos, y trayã diuersos	A	14
8	b	anjmales que aujan caçado en los diez	b	15
9	c	dias pasados vnos de agua, y otros de	c	16
10	d	tierra: y offrecianlos a los viejos que	d	17
11	e	tenjan cargo de guardar a este dios: y	e	18
12	f	ellos echauã en el fuego a todos aque-	f	19
13	g	llos anjmales para que se asassen: y	g	20
14	A	dauan a cada vno destos moços y mu-	A	21
15	b	chachos vn tamal hecho de bledos que	b	22
16	c	ellos llamauã Vauhqujltamalli: los	c	23
17	d	quales todo el pueblo ofrecia aquel dia,	d	24
18	e	y todos comjan dellos por honrra de	e	25
19	f	la fiesta, comjanlos muy calientes y	f	26
20	g	beujan y regozijauanse.		g	27

On this feast, in ordinary years, they slew no one. But in the bissextile year, which was every four years, they slew, during this feast, captives and slaves and the impersonator of Xiuhtecutli, decorated in the manner which hath been told above, with many precious and curious adornments; they performed many great ceremonies upon the death of these [victims]— many more than on the other feasts already described. This is set forth at length in the account of this feast.

After they had slain these slaves and captives and the impersonator of Ixcoçauhqui, who is the god of fire, all the leading men and lords, the illustrious, and

En esta fiesta los años comunes no matauã a nadie: pero el año del bisexto que era de quatro en quatro años: matauan en esta fiesta captiuos y esclauos, y la ymagen de Xiuhtecutli, compuesta de la manera que arriba se dixo cõ muchos y preciosos y curiosos ataujos: hazian grandes y muchas cerimonjas en la muerte destos, muchas mas que en las otras fiestas ya dichas. Esto esta puesto a la larga en la historia desta fiesta.

Despues que aujan muerto a estos esclauos y captiuos, y a la ymagen de Jscoçauhquj que es el dios del fuego: estauan aparejados y adereçados muy rica-

the emperor himself were decked and arrayed **very** richly in costly adornments, and they began a dance of great solemnity and gravity which they called *netecuitotiliztli,* which meaneth "Dance of the Lords." This was performed only every four years, during this feast. On this same day, very early in the morning, before dawn, they began to pierce the ears of the boys and girls, and they applied to their heads a wig of parrot feathers, pasted on with *ocotzotl,* which is pine resin. Etc.

mente con ricos adereços todos los principales y señores y personas yllustres, y el mesmo Emperador: y començauan vn areyto de gran solemnjdad y grauedad: al qual llamauan Netecujtotiliztli, qujere dezir: areyto de los señores: Este solamente se hazia de quatro en quatro años en esta fiesta. Este mesmo dia muy de mañana ante que amaneciesse començauã a agujerar las orejas a los njños y njñas: y echauãlos vn casquete en la cabeça de pluma de papagayos, pegado con ocutzotl que es resina de pino. Etc.

The five remaining days of the year, which are the four last of January and the first of February, they named Nemontemi, which meaneth barren days. And they regarded them as unlucky and of evil fortune. There is conjecture that when they pierced the boys' and girls' ears, which was every four years, they set aside six days of Nemontemi, and it is the same as the bissextile which we observe every four years.

A los cinco dias restantes del año que son los quatro vltimos de Enero y el primero de hebrero llamauan Nemontemi, que quiere dezir dias valdios: y tenjanlos por aziagos y de mala fortuna: ay conjectura que quando agujerauan las orejas a los njños y njñas que era de quatro en quatro años, echauan seys dias de Nenontemj y es lo mjsmo del bisexto que nostoros hazemos de quatro en quatro años.

Chapter 19

These five days they held as of evil fortune and unlucky. They said that those who were born in them had evil outcomes in all their affairs, and were poor and wretched. They named them Nemo. If they were men, they named them Nemoquich; if it was a woman, they named her Nenciuatl. They dared do nothing in these days, because they were unlucky. Especially did they abstain from quarreling, because they said that those who quarreled in these days always remained with that custom. They held as a bad omen stumbling in these days.

These aforementioned feasts were fixed, and were always observed within the month, or a day or two ahead. Other feasts they had [which were] movable, which were celebrated during the course of the twenty signs, which made a round in two hundred and sixty days. And hence these movable feasts, in a year, fell one in one month, and another in another, and always varied.

Capi. 19.

1	A	Estos cinco dias tenjan por malafor-	A	28
2	b	tunados y aziagos: dezian que los que	b	29
3	c	en ellos nacian tenjan malos successos	c	30
4	d	en todas sus cosas, y eran pobres y mj-	d	31

seros llamauanlos Nemo, si eran hombres llamauanlos Nenoqujch, y si era muger llamauala Nencioatl, no osauan hazer nada en estos dias por ser malafortunados: especialmente se abstenjan de reñjr: porque dezian que los que reñjan en estos dias se quedauã siempre con aquella costumbre tenjan por mal aguero tropeçar en estos dias.

Estas fiestas dichas eran fixas que siempre se haziã dentro del mes o vn dia o dos adelante: Otras fiestas tenjan moujbles que se hazian por el curso de los veinte signos: los quales hazian vn circulo en dozientos y sesenta dias: y por tanto estas fiestas moujbles vn año cayan en vn mes y otro en otro y siempre variauan.

Of the Movable Feasts

The first movable feast was celebrated in honor of the sun, in the sign which is named ce ocelotl, in the fourth house, which is named naui ollin. On this feast they offered, to the image of the sun, quail, and they offered incense. And at noon they slew captives before it in honor of the sun. On this same day, all drew blood from their ears—children and those who were grown—in honor of the sun, and they offered it that blood.

De las fiestas moujbles.

La primera fiesta moujble se celebraua a honrra del sol en el signo que se llama ce ocelutl, en la quarta casa que se llama naolin: en esta fiesta ofrecian a la ymagen del sol codornjzes y incensauan: y en el medio matauã capituos delante della a honrra del sol. En este mesmo dia se sangrauan todos de las orejas chicos y grãdes a hõrra del sol y le ofrecian aquella sangre.

The Second Movable Feast

In this same sign, in the seventh house, all the painters and the seamstresses celebrated a feast. They

La segunda fiesta moujble.

En este mjsmo signo en la septima casa haziã fiesta todos los pintores, y las labrãderas ayunauã quarẽta

fasted, [some] for forty days, others for twenty, in order to prevail over chance, in order to paint well and to weave textiles well. For this purpose they offered quail and incense, and performed other ceremonies—the men to the god Chicome xochitl, and the women to the goddess Xochiquetzal.

The Third Movable Feast

In the third sign, which is called ce maçatl, in the first house, they celebrated a feast to the goddesses who are named Ciuapipilti, because they said that then they came down to the earth. They adorned their images with papers and offered them offerings.

The Fourth Movable Feast

In the sign which is called ce maçatl, in the second house, which is called ome tochtli, they celebrated a great feast to the god named Izquitecatl, who is the second god of wine; and not alone to him but to all the gods of wine, who were many. On this day they adorned his image very well on his pyramid, and offered him things to eat, and they sang and played [musical instruments] before him. And in the courtyard of his pyramid they set a large open jar of wine, and those who were wine merchants filled it to overflowing, and all who wished went to drink. They had some canes through which they drank. The wine sellers kept feeding the large jar, so that it was always full. Mostly, those who had newly cut the maguey did this. The first syrup which they took out they took to the house of this god as first fruits.

The Fifth Movable Feast

In the sign called ce xochitl, in the first house, they celebrated a great feast. The leading men and the lords danced and sang in honor of this sign, and they otherwise made merry. And then they brought forth the richest feathers, with which they adorned themselves for the dance. In this feast the lord gave gifts to the warriors and to the singers and to the palace folk.

The Sixth Movable Feast

In the sign named ce acatl, in the first house, the lords and the leading men celebrated a great festival to Quetzalcoatl, god of the winds. This feast they observed in the house called *calmecac,* which was the house where dwelt the priests of the idols, and where were trained the boys. In this house, which was like

dias, otros veinte por alcançar ventura para pintar bien y para texer bien labores, offrecian a este proposito codornizes y encienso, y haziã otras cerimonjas los hombres al dios Chicome sochitl y las mugeres a la diosa Sochiquetzal.

La tercera fiesta mouible.

En el tercero signo que se llama ce maçatl: en la primera casa hazian fiesta a las diosas que se llaman cioapipilti porque dezian que entonce decendian a la tierra, ataujauã a sus ymagines con papeles, y ofrecianlas ofrendas.

La quarta fiesta mouible

En el signo que se llama ce maçatl: en la segunda casa que se llama vme tochtli: hazian gran fiesta al dios llamado Yzqujtecatl, que es el segundo dios del vino, y no solamente a el: pero a todos los dioses del vino que eran muchos: adereçavan este dia muy bien su ymagen en su cu, y ofrecianle cosas de comjda, y cantauan, y tañjan delante del: y en el patio de su cu, ponjan vn tinajon de pulcre, y hinchianle los que eran taberneros hasta reberter, y yuan a beuer todos los que querian: tenjan vnas cañas con que beujã: los taberneros yuan ceuando el tinajon: de manera que siempre estaua lleno: principalmente hazian esto los q̃ de nueuo aujan cortado el maguey, la primera agua mjel que sacauan la lleuauan a la casa deste dios como primjcias.

La quinta fiesta moujble

En el signo llamado ce xochitl: en la primera casa, hazian gran fiesta, los principales, y señores, baylauan, y cantauan a honrra deste signo, y hazian otros regozijos: y sacauan entonce los mas ricos plumajes, con que se adereçauan para el areyto: y en esta fiesta, el señor hazia mercedes a los hombres de guerra, y a los cantores y a los del palacio.

La sexta fiesta mouible

En el signo llamado ce acatl: en la primera casa, hazian gran fiesta a quetzalcoatl dios de los vientos: los señores y principales: esta fiesta hazian en la casa llamada calmecac, que era la casa donde morauan los satrapas de los ydolos: y donde se criauan los muchachos, en esta casa que era como vn mones-

a monastery, was the image of Quetzalcoatl. On this day they adorned it with rich ornaments and placed before it offerings of perfumes and food. They said this was the sign of Quetzalcoatl.

The Seventh Movable Feast

In the sign which was called ce miquiztli, in the first house, the lords and leading men celebrated a great feast to Tezcatlipoca, who was the great god. They said that this was his sign. Since all of them had their shrines in their houses, where they kept the images of this god and of many others, on this day they decorated this image and offered it perfumes, flowers, and food, and sacrificed quail before it, tearing off their heads. This not only the lords and leading men did, but all the people to whose attention this festival came; and the same was done in the *calpulcos* and on all the pyramids. All prayed, and besought of this god that he grant them favors, for [it was thought] that he was almighty.

The Eighth Movable Feast

In the sign which was called ce quiauitl, in the first house, they celebrated a feast to the goddesses whom they named Ciuapipilti. These, they said, were the women who died in first childbed. They said that they became goddesses and that they dwelt in the house of the sun; and that when this sign reigned, they came down to the earth and afflicted with various sicknesses those whom they met outside of their houses. And hence, in these days, they dared not go out of their houses. They had shrines built in honor of these goddesses in all the suburbs where two streets [crossed], which they called *ciuateocalli,* or by another name, *ciuateopan.* In these shrines they had the images of the goddesses, and on these days they adorned them with papers which they called *amateteuitl.* On this feast of these goddesses they slew in their honor those condemned to death for some crime, who were in the jails.

The Ninth Movable Feast

In the sign named ce quiauitl, in the fourth house (which was called naui ecatl), because this house was very unlucky they slew in it the malefactors who were imprisoned. And likewise the lord had a number of slaves slain as a superstition. And the merchants and traders made a show or demonstration of the jewels in which they dealt, bringing them forth so that all might see them. And afterwards, at night,

terio, estaua la ymagen de quetzalcoatl: Este dia la adereçauan con ricos ornamentos, y ofrecian delante della perfumes, y comjda: dezian que este era el signo de quetzalcoatl.

La septima fiesta moujble.

En el signo que se llamaua ce mjqujztli: en la primera casa: hazian gran fiesta, los señores y principales a Tezcatlibuca, que era el gran dios, dezian que este era su sino, como todos ellos, tenjan sus oratorios en sus casas: donde tenjan las ymagines deste dios, y de muchos otros: en este dia, componjan esta ymagen, y ofrecianla perfumes, y flores y comjda: y sacrificauan codornizes delante della arrancandolas la cabeça. Esto no solamente lo hazian los señores, y principales: pero toda la gẽte, a cuya noticia venja esta fiesta, y lo mjsmo se hazia, en los calpules, y en todos los cues: todos orauan, y demandauan a este dios que les hiziesse mercedes: pues que el era todopoderoso.

La octaua fiesta moujble

En el signo, que se llamaua, ce qujaujtl: en la primera casa, hazian fiesta, a las diosas que llamauan Cioapipilti: estas dezian que eran las mugeres que murian del primero parto, dezian que se hazian diosas, y que morauan en la casa del sol, y que quãdo reynaua este sino, decendian a la tierra, y herian con diuersas emfermedades, a los que topauã fuera de sus casas. Y por esto en estos dias, no osauan salir de sus casas. Tenjan edificados oratorios, a honrra destas diosas: en todos los barrios donde auja dos calles: los quales llamauan cioateucalli, o por otro nombre cioateupan: en estos oratorios, tenjan las ymagines destas diosas: y en estos dias las adornauan con papeles, que llamauan amateteujtl. En esta fiesta, destas diosas matauan a su honrra los condenados a muerte por algun delicto, que estauan en las carceles.

La nona fiesta mouible.

En el signo llamado ce qujaujtl: en la quarta casa que se llamaua nauhecatl, por ser esta casa muy malafortunado, matauan en ella los malhechores, que estauan presos. Y tambien el señor hazia matar algunos esclauos, por via de supersticion: y los mercaderes, y tratantes hazian alarde o demostracion de las joyas, en que tratauan, sacandolas, para que las viessen todos: y despues a la noche, comjan, y beujan, to-

they ate and drank, and held flowers and those canes of perfume. And they sat in their seats. And each one began to boast of what he had gained, and of the distant parts which he had reached. And he belittled the others for their counting for little; [for] neither did they have as much as he, nor had they gone to distant places, as he had. In this the ones made a great mock of the others for a long space of the night.

The Tenth Movable Feast

In the sign which they named ce malinalli, in the second house, named ome acatl, they celebrated a great festival; for they said that this was Tezcatlipoca's sign. In this feast they fashioned the image of Omacatl, and one who felt devotion took it to his house that it might bless him and cause his goods to increase. And when this took place, he kept it and preferred not to let it go. He who would let this image go, waited until the next time when the same sign reigned. Then he returned it whence he had taken it.

The Eleventh Movable Feast

In the sign called ce tecpatl, in the first house, they brought forth all the ornaments of Uitzilopochtli; they cleaned them and shook them out; and they put [them] in the sun. They said that this was his sign and that of Camaxtli. This they did at Tlacatecco. Here they set out, on this day, many kinds of food, very well cooked, like that which the lords eat. They presented all of them before his image. After they had remained there a while, the officials of Uitzilopochtli took them up and divided them among themselves, and ate them. And they also incensed the image and offered it quail. They struck off their heads before it, so the blood should be shed before the image. And the lord offered all the precious flowers which the lords used, before the image.

The Twelfth Movable Feast

In the sign named ce oçomatli they said that the goddesses called Ciuapipilti came down to the earth and [that] they harmed the boys and girls, afflicting them with palsy. And if anyone, at this time, sickened, they said that [the Ciuapipilti] had caused it; that he had come upon them. And the fathers and mothers on these days did not let their children go outside the houses, so that they might not come upon these goddesses, whom they held in great dread.

mauan flores: y aquellas cañas de perfumes, y assentauanse en sus assientos: y començaua cada vno a jactarse, de lo que auja ganado, y de las partes remotas, donde auja llegado: y valdonaua a los otros de que eran para poco, nj tenjan tanto, como el, nj aujan ydo a partes remotas como el: en esto tenjan gran chacota, los vnos con los otros, por gran rato de la noche.

La decima fiesta mouible

En el signo que llamauan ce malinalli: en las segunda casa llamada vme acatl, hazian gran fiesta: porque dezian que esto sino era de Tezcatlibuca: en esta fiesta hazian la ymagen de Omacatl, y alguno que tenja deuocion, lleuauala a su casa: para que le bendixesse, y le hiziesse multiplicar su hazienda, y quando esto acontecja tenjala, y no la queria dexar: el que queria dexar esta ymagen esperaua, hasta que otra vez, reynasse el mjsmo signo: entonce la lleuaua adonde la auja tomado.

La onzena fiesta mouible.

En el signo llamado ce tecpatl. En la primera casa sacauan todos los ornamentos de Vitzilobuchtli, los linpiauan, y sacudian, y ponjan al sol: dezian que este era su signo, y el de camaxtle: esto hazian tlacatecco: aquj ponjan, en este dia, muchas maneras de comjdas, muy bien gujsadas, como las comen los señores: todas las presentauan, delante de su ymagen, despues de auer estado vn rato alli, tomauanlas los officiales, de Vitzilobuchtli, y repartianlas entre si, y comjanlas, y incensauan tambien a la ymagen, y ofrecianla codornizes, descabeçandolas delante della: para que se derramasse la sangre delante la ymagen: y ofrecia el señor todas las preciosas flores, que vsan los señores, delante la ymagen.

La dozena fiesta mouible.

En el signo llamado ce Oçumatli: dezian que decendian las diosas llamadas cioapipilti, a la tierra: y dañauan a los njños, y njñas, hiriendolos con perlesia. Y si alguno en este tiempo enfermaua, dezian que ellas lo aujan hecho, que se auja encontrado con ellas: y los padres, y las madres, estos dias no dexauan salir a sus hijos, fuera de casa: porque no se encontrassen, con estas diosas, de las quales tenjan gran temor.

The Thirteenth Movable Feast

In the sign which they called ce itzcuintli, [which] they said was the sign of fire, they held a great festival in honor of Xiuhtecutli, god of fire. In it they offered him much *copal* [incense] and many quail. They arrayed his image in many kinds of papers and with many rich adornments. Among the rich and powerful, they celebrated a great feast in honor of the fire, in their own houses; they held dinners and banquets in honor of the fire. In this same sign they held elections of lords and consuls, and in the fourth house of this sign they enacted the formalities of their elections, feasts, dances, and gift [giving]. After these feasts, they forthwith proclaimed war against their foes.

The Fourteenth Movable Feast

In the sign named ce atl, in the first house of this sign, they celebrated a feast to the goddess of water, named Chalchiuhtli icue. All those who dealt in water celebrated the festival—those who sold water, as well as those who fished, and those who gained other livelihoods which there are in the water. These arrayed her image and laid offerings before her, and revered her in the house called *calpulli*.

The Fifteenth Common Movable Feast

The lords, leading men, nobles, and rich merchants, when a son or daughter was born to them, paid much heed to the sign, the day, and the hour in which he was born. And of this they forthwith set out to inform the judicial astrologers, and to ask as to the good fortune or ill of the child who was born. And if the sign in which he was born was propitious, they had him baptized at once; and if it was adverse they sought the most favorable house of that sign [in which] to baptize him. When they baptized him, they banqueted the kinsmen and friends, so that they would be present at the baptism, and then they gave food and drink to all the guests, and also to the children of the whole suburb. They baptized him at sunrise in the house of his father. The midwife baptized him, uttering many prayers and performing much ceremony over the child. This [same] feast they also observe today in the baptism of their children, as to feasting, eating, and drinking.

The Sixteenth Movable Feast

As soon as the parents saw that their son was of

La trezena fiesta mouible.

En el signo que llamauan ce jtzcujntli: dezian que era el signo del fuego: hazian gran fiesta a honrra de xiuhtecutli, dios del fuego: en ella le ofrecian mucho copal, y muchas codornizes: componjan su ymagen, con muchas maneras de papeles, y con muchos ornamentos ricos: entre las personas ricas y poderosas, hazian gran fiesta, a honrra del fuego, en sus mjsmas casas, hazian combites, y vanquetes, a honrra del fuego. En este mjsmo signo: hazian la election de los señores y consules, y en la quarta casa deste sino: hazian la solẽnjdad, de sus electiones, combites, y areytos, y dones. Despues destas fiestas apregonauan luego la guerra contra sus enemigos.

La catorzena fiesta mouible

En el signo llamado ce atl: en la primera casa deste signo, hazian fiesta, a la diosa del agua llamada chalchiuhtli ycue: hazian la fiesta, todos los que tratauan en el agua: ansi vendiendo el agua, como pescando, como haziendo otras gragerias, que ay en el agua. Estos componjan su ymagen, y la ofrecian, y reuerenciauan, en la casa llamada Calpulli.

La quinta decima fiesta mouible comũ.

Los señores, y principales, nobles, y mercaderes, ricos quando les nacia algun hijo o hija; tenjan gran cuẽta con el signo en que nacia; y el dia, y la hora en que nacia: y desto yuan luego a ynformar a los astrologos, judiciarios: y a preguntar por la fortuna buena o mala de la criatura que nacia. Y si el signo, en que nacia era prospero, luego le hazian baptizar, y si era aduerso buscauan la mas prospera casa de aquel signo para le batizar. Quando le batizauan, combidauan a los parientes, y amigos: para que se hallassen presentes al batismo: y entonce dauan comjda, y beujda, a todos los presentes, y tambien a los njños, de todo el barrio: baptizauanle, a la salida del sol, en casa de su padre, baptizauale la partera, diziendo muchas oraciones: y haziendo mucha cerimonja sobre la criatura. Esta fiesta, tambien la vsan agora, en los baptismos de sus hijos, en quanto al combidar, y comer, y beuer.

La sexta decima fiesta mouible.

Desque los padres vian que su hijo era de edad para

age to marry, they spoke to him of their wish to seek a wife for him. And he replied, thanking them for this solicitude which they showed in marrying him. Then they addressed the leading man who had charge of all the young men, whom they called *telpochtlato,* and they told him that they wished their son to marry, since [the son] held doing so to be good. For this they held a great feast for him and for all the young men whom he had in his care; and for this they held conversation with him, after having given food and drink to him and to all those whom he had in his charge. And at the beginning of the conversation they laid before him an axe for cutting lumber or firewood. This axe was a sign that that young man took his leave, now, of the company of the other young men; for they wished him to marry. And thus the *telpochtlato* departed content. After this the relatives decided, among themselves, upon the woman whom they were to give [to the son], and summoned the marriage-makers, who were some old, honored women, that they might go to speak with the parents of the young woman. [The marriage-makers] went two or three times, and spoke, and returned with the reply. During this time, the relatives of the young woman spoke among themselves, and, having decided to give her to him, they gave their consent to the marriage-makers. After this they sought a day of good fortune, of a sign of good disposition [among] which were acatl, oçomatli, cipactli, quauhtli. Having chosen one of these signs, the parents of the young man made known to the parents of the young woman the day on which the marriage should be performed, and then began to prepare the necessary articles for the wedding—[those] to eat and to drink, as well as such [things] as capes, smoke tubes, and flowers. This done, they summoned the leading men and all the other people whom they wanted for the wedding. After the feast and [after] many speeches and ceremonies, those acting for the young man came at about nightfall to take the young woman. They carried her, with great solemnity, upon the back of a matron, and with many pine torches burning in two rows before her. Many people surrounded her, behind and ahead, until they brought her to the house of the parents of the young man. Having brought her to the house of the young man, they set them both by the hearth, which they always had in the middle of a hall, full of fire. And the woman was at the left hand of the man. Then the mother of the young man

casarse, hablauanle en que le querian buscar su muger: y el respondia, haziendoles gracias, por aquel cuydado, que tomauan de casarle: luego hablauan al principal que tenja cargo de todos los mancebos, que ellos llamauan Telpuchtlato: y dezianle como querian casar su hijo, que lo tuujesse por bueno: y para esto hazianle vn combite a el, y a todos los mancebos, que tenja a su cargo, y para esto le hazian vna platica, despues de auerle dado de comer, y de beuer a el y a todos los que tenja a su cargo: y en principio de la platica, ponjanle delante vna hacha de cortar madera o leña. Esta hacha era señal que aquel mancebo se despedia ya de la companja de los otros mancebos: porque le querian casar, y ansi el telpuchtlato yua contento. Despues desto determjnauan entre si los parientes la muger, que le aujan de dar, y llamauan a las casamenteras, que eran vnas viejas honrradas, para que fuessen a hablar a los padres de la moça, yuan dos, o tres vezes, y hablauan, y bolujan con la respuesta. En este tiempo los parientes de la moça se hablauan, y concertandose de darsela, dauan el si, a las casamenteras. Despues desto buscauan vn dia bien afortunado, de algun signo, bien acondicionado, quales eran acatl, oçumatli, cipactli, quauhtli, aujendo escogido alguno destos signos: los padres del moço hazian saber a los padres de la moça el dia en que auja de hazerse el matrimonjo, y luego començauan a aperejar las cosas necessarias, para las bodas, assi de comer como de beuer, como de mantas, y cañas de humo, y flores. Esto hecho conbidauan a los principales, y toda la otra gente, que ellos querian para las bodas. Despues del combite, y de muchas platicas, y cerimonjas: venjan los de la parte del moço a lleuar a la moça de par de noche, lleuauanla con gran solennjdad, a cuestas de vna matrona, y con muchas hachas de teas encẽdidas, en dos rencles delante della, yua rodeada della mucha gente, detras y delante, hasta que la llegauan a la casa de los padres del moço: llegada a la casa del moço, ponjanlos ambos, junto al hogar, que siempre le tenjan, en medio de vna sala, lleno de fuego, y la muger estaua, a la mano izqujerda del varon: luego la madre del mancebo, vestia vn vipil muy galano a su nuera, y ponjale junto a sus pies vnas naoas muy labradas: y la madre de la moça, cubria cõ vna manta, muy galana a su yerno, y atauasela sobre el hombro, y ponjale vn maxtli, muy labrado, a los pies. Hecho esto, vnas viejas, que se llaman titici, atauan la esqujna de la manta del moço con la falda del vipil de la moça. Assi se concluya el

placed a very fine shift upon her daughter-in-law, and put for her, by her feet, a richly embroidered skirt. And the mother of the young woman covered her son-in-law with a very fine cape, and tied it over his shoulder, and laid a very richly embroidered breech clout at his feet. This done, a number of old women, who are called *titici*, tied the corner of the young man's cape to the lower part of the young woman's shift. In this way was concluded the marriage, with many other ceremonies, and dinings, and drinking, and dances, which were given thereafter, as is contained in the account of the marriages.

They observed two other feasts which in part were fixed and in part were movable. They were movable because they were celebrated in interpolated years. One was observed every four years, and the other every eight years. They were fixed because they had year, month, and day assigned. In the one which was celebrated every four years, they pierced the ears of the boys and the girls, and they performed for them ceremonies for good growth, and they purified them over the fire. In the one which they celebrated every eight years, they fasted before it for eight days on bread and water, and enacted a dance in which they assumed the forms or characters of various birds and animals. And they said that they sought good fortune, as is set forth in the appendix of the Second Book.

These movable feasts, in some years, displace the feasts of the calendar, as also happeneth in our calendar.

matrimonjo, con otras muchas cerimonjas, y comeres, y beueres, y bayles, que despues se hazian, como se contiene, en la historia del matrimonjo.

Otras dos fiestas tenjan, que en parte eran fixas, y en parte eran moujbles: eran moujbles, porque se hazian por años interpolados. La vna se hazia, de quatro en quatro años, y la otra de ocho en ocho años: eran fixas porque tenjan año, mes, y dia señalados. En la que se hazia, de quatro en quatro años, horadauan las orejas a los njños o njñas: y hazianlos, las cerimonjas, de crezca para bien, y lustrauanlos por el fuego. En la que hazian, de ocho en ocho años: ayunauan antes della, ocho dias a pan y agua, y hazian vn areyto, en que tomauan figuras, o personajes, de diuersas aues y anjmales: y dezian que buscauan ventura, como esta escrito, en el apendiz del segundo libro.

Estas fiestas mouibles en algunos años echan de su lugar a las fiestas del kalendario: como tambien acontece, en nuestro kalendario.

Twentieth Chapter, which telleth of the feast day and the debt-payment which they celebrated during all the days[1] of the month, which they named, which they said was Atl caualo or Quauitl eua.[2]

It was [the month of] Quauitl eua [when] this feast day came, and when it took place, then the feast day was celebrated for the Tlalocs.

There was the paying of the debt[3] [to the Tlalocs] everywhere on the mountain tops, and sacrificial banners were hung. There was the payment of the debt at Tepetzinco or there in the very middle of the lake at a place called Pantitlan.

There they would leave the rubber-spotted paper streamers[4] and there they would set up poles called *cuenmantli*, which were very long. Only on them [still] went their greenness, their sprouts, their shoots.

And there they left children known as "human paper streamers," [5] those who had two cowlicks of hair, whose day signs were favorable. They were sought everywhere; they were paid for. It was said: "They are indeed most precious debt-payments. [The Tlalocs] gladly receive them; they want them. Thus they are well content; thus there is indeed content-

Jnic 20. capitulo, ytechpa tlatoa yn ilhuitl, yoan in nextlaoaliztli: in quichioaia, yn ipan vel ic cemilhuitl metztli; in qujtocaiotiaia, in qujtoaia atl caoalo, anoço quauitl eoa.

Quauitl eoa, ynin ilhuitl quiçaia: auh yn iquac y, vncan ilhujqujxtililoia in tlaloque:

nextlaoaloia, in noujan tepeticpac, yoã neteteuhtiloia, onnextlaoaloia, in tepetzinco, anoço vmpa in vel aytic, ytocaiocan pantitla:

vmpa concaoaia in teteujtl, yoan vmpa conquetzaia quaujtl, moteneoa cuenmantli, viujtlatztic, çan itech ieetiuh yn icelica, yn itzmolinca, yzcallo.

Yoan vmpa qujmoncaoaia pipiltzitzinti, in moteneoaia tlacateteuhti: iehoãtin in vntecuezcomeque, in qualli intonal: noujan temoloia, patiiotiloia: mitoaia, ca iehoantin vellaçonextlaoalti, vel qujnpaccacelia qujnnequj, ic vellamati, ic vellamachtilo, ynjc inca qujiauhtlatlanjoa, quiiauhtlatlano.

---

1. *cemilhuitl*: the term is usually translated as "one day," "all day," or "all the days." Angel María Garibay K., in "Relación breve de las fiestas de los dioses, Fray Bernardino de Sahagún," *Tlalocan*, Vol. II, No. 4 (1948), p. 291, renders it "the first day." Rémi Siméon in *Dictionnaire de la langue nahuatl ou mexicaine* (Paris: Imprimerie Nationale, 1885), in an extended discussion admits a meaning of "the first day," or "all the days." In the corresponding Spanish text Sahagún consistently uses the phrase *"en las kalendas."*

2. Sahagún, in the corresponding Spanish text, observes that Quauitl eua is the term used by the Mexicans. Cf. Manuel Orozco y Berra, *Historia antigua y de la conquista de México*, 4 vols. (Mexico: Tipografía de Gonzalo A. Esteva, 1880), Vol. II, p. 36: "Xilomanaliztli, — Atlacahualco, — Cuahuitlehua, — Cihuailhuitl. *Xilomanaliztli, ofrenda de xilotl ó jilotes; nombre usado por los de Tlaxcalla. Cuahuitlehua, quemazon de los árboles; nombre perteneciente á lugares fuera de México. Atlcahualco ó Atlacahualco, nombre admitido por los mexicanos; segun el P. Leon, detencion de las aguas, y es la interpretación de todas que más nos satisface. Cihuailhuitl, fiesta de la mujer. El símbolo religioso es la imágen de Tlaloc y un árbol reverdeciendo, con el agua entre las raíces."* Cf. also Francisco J. Clavijero, *Historia antigua de México*, 4 vols. (Mexico: Editorial Porrúa, S.A., 1945) Vol. II, pp. 401–402: *". . . el primer mes, cuyo nombre Acahualco o Atlacahualco, significa la cesación del agua, pues en el mes de marzo cesan las lluvias del invierno en los países septentrionales, en donde tuvo origen el calendario mexicano o tolteca. Lo llamaban también Quahuetlehua, lo que significa la vegetación de los árboles, que se verifica en este tiempo en los países fríos. Los tlaxcaltecas llamaban a este mes Xilomanilitztli, esto es, oblación de las mazorcas de maíz, porque en él ofrecían a sus dioses las del año corrido, para ayudar la siembra que por este tiempo comenzaban a hacer en los lugares altos."*

Garibay, in "Relación breve," p. 291, translates *cuahuitl ehua* as *palo se alza*; Eduard Seler, in *Einige Kapitel aus dem Geschichtswerk des Fray Bernardino de Sahagún aus dem Aztekischen übersetzt*, ed. Caecilie Seler–Sachs, Walter Lehmann, Walter Krickeberg (Stuttgart: Strecker und Schroeder, 1927), p. 54, translates the name as *die Bäume erheben sich (machen sich auf den Weg)*.

3. *nextlaoaloia*. Cf. *ixtlaua* in Alonso de Molina, *Vocabulario de la lengua mexicana*, ed. Julio Platzmann (Leipzig: B. G. Teubner, 1880), and in Siméon, *Dictionnaire*. Eduard Seler, in *Gesammelte Abhandlungen zur Amerikanischen Sprach-und Altertumskunde*, 5 vols. (Berlin: A. Asher und Co., 1903–23), Vol. II, p. 983, says: *"Die Kinderopfer an die Regengötter wurden geradezu* nextlaualli *'die bezahlte Schuld'* genannt."

4. Garibay ("Relación breve," p. 292) translates *teteuitl* as *tiras sagradas*.

5. In *ibid.*, Garibay renders *tlacateteuhme* as *tiras humanas* and makes it clear (Nahuatl sentence No. 4) that the term refers to the children who died. Seler, *Einige Kapitel*, p. 54, refers to them as *Menschen–Opferstreifen (Opferpapiere in Menschengestalt)*. They may actually have been paper streamers surmounted by a representation of a human head, and have symbolized the children who died. See illustration from *Biblioteca del Palacio MS* in Wigberto Jiménez Moreno, *"Primeros memoriales" de Fray Bernardino de Sahagún* (Mexico: Instituto Nacional de Antropología e Historia, Consejo de Historia, Colección Científica, No. 16, 1974), Lámina I.

ment." Thus with them the rains were sought, rain was asked.

And everywhere in the houses, in each home, and in each young men's house, in each *calpulco*,[6] everywhere they set up long, thin poles, poles coming to a point, on each of which they placed paper streamers with liquid rubber, spattered with rubber, splashed with rubber.[7]

And they left [the children] in many [different] places.

[First was] at Quauhtepetl.[8] And its same name, Quauhtepetl, went with the one who died there. His paper vestments were dark green.[9]

The second place where one died was the top of Mount Yoaltecatl. Its same name, Yoaltecatl,[10] went with the "human paper streamer." His vestments were black striped with chili red.

The third place was at Tepetzinco.[11] There died a girl called Quetzalxoch, [a name] which they took from Tepetzintli, which they [also] named Quetzalxoch. Her array was light blue.

The fourth place was Poyauhtlan,[12] just at the foot, just in front, of the mountain, at Tepetzintli. Its name, Poyauhtecatl, went with the one who died [there]. Thus he went adorned: he was painted with liquid rubber; he was touched with liquid rubber.

The fifth place, there in the middle of the lake, was a place called Pantitlan. The one who died there went with his name, Epcoatl. His vestments, which he went wearing, were set with pearls.

The sixth place to which they carried [a victim] was to the top of [the hill of] Cocotl; he also went with its name, Cocotl.[13] His array was varicolored, part chili-red, part dark green.

The seventh place was the top of Yiauhqueme; likewise the "human paper streamer" went with its

Auh yn novian calpan, in techachan: yoan in tetelpuchcalco, in cacalpulco, noujian qujquetzaia, matlaquauhpitzaoac, tzonioquaujtl, itech qujtlatlaliaia amateteujtl, vltica tlaulchipinilli, tlavlchachapatztli.

Auh mjeccan in qujmoncaoaia,

quauhtepec: auh yn vmpa onmiquja, çan ie no ie ytoca etiujia, in quauhtepetl: yn jamatlatquj, yiapaltic.

Jnic vccã miquja, icpac in tepetl ioaltecatl: çan ie no itoca ietiuh, in tlacateteujtl, ioaltecatl: yn jamatlatquj, tliltic, chichiltic ic oaoanquj.

Injc excan, tepetzinco: yn vmpa onmjquja cioatl, itoca quetzalxoch, ytech canaia, in tepetzintli, qujtocaiotiaia quetzalxoch, yn itlatquj catca texotic.

Jnic nauhcan, poiauhtlã, çan itzintla, çan ixpan in tepetl, tepetzinco: itoca ietiujia in miquja poiauhtecatl, ynic muchichiuhtiuja, vlpiiaoac, tlaulujtectli.

Jnic macujlcan, vmpa in atl itic itocaiocan pantitlan, in vmpa, onmjquja, itoca ietiuh, epcoatl: yn itlatquj, in caqujtiuja, epnepanjuhquj.

Jnic chiquaceccan: vmpa qujujcaia cocotl icpac, no itoca ietiuja cocotl: yn inechichioal catca, chictlapanquj, cectlapal chichiltic, cectlapal yiappalli.

Jnic chicoccan, icpac yn jiauhqueme: çan no itoca

---

6. *calpulco*: in the Spanish text, Sahagún consistently uses the term *calpulco* when he refers to the principal temple of the *calpulli*. Cf. Bernardino de Sahagún, *Historia general de las cosas de Nueva España*, ed. Angel María Garibay K., 4 vols. (Mexico: Editorial Porrúa, S.A., 1956; hereafter referred to as Sahagún, Garibay ed.), Vol. I, p. 263: "calpulco o parroquia de su barrio"; p. 345: "calpulco, *que era la iglesia de aquel barrio.*" On the *calpulli*, the fundamental territorial-economic-social-political-religious-lineage unit, see William T. Sanders, "Settlement Patterns in Central Mexico," in Gordon F. Ekholm and Ignacio Bernal, eds., *Archaeology of Northern Mesoamerica*, Handbook of Middle American Indians, Vol. 10, Robert Wauchope, gen. ed. (Austin: University of Texas Press, 1971), pp. 13–15.

7. See n. 5. Sahagún, in the corresponding Spanish text, refers to "*vnos papeles, llenos de gotas de vlli: a los quales papeles llamauan amateteujtl.*" For *tlavlchachapatztli*, cf. chachapani in Molina, *Vocabulario*.

8. Maps of the Valley of Mexico in colonial times locate most of the places and features mentioned by Sahagún, but the frequent repetition of place names is at times confusing. Of Quauhtepec, Sahagún's Spanish text says: "*es vna sierra emjnente que esta cerca del tlatelulco.*"

9. *yiapaltic*: cf. Charles E. Dibble and Arthur J. O. Anderson, *Florentine Codex, Book XI, Earthly Things* (Santa Fe: School of American Research and University of Utah, 1963; hereafter referred to as Dibble and Anderson, *Book XI*), p. 244.

10. The Spanish text explains: "*es vna sierra emjnente, que esta cabe guadalope.*"

11. *Ibid.*: "*es aquel montezillo, que esta dentro desta laguna, frontero del tlatelulco.*"

12. *Ibid.*: "*es vn monte, que esta en los termjnos de tlaxcalla, y alli cabe tepetzinco.*"

13. *Ibid.*: "*es vn monte que esta cabe chalco atenco.*"

name, Yiauhqueme. As to the clothing which he had with him, he was all dressed in dark green.

These were all the places where the debt-payments, the "human paper streamers," died.

And all went with their head-bands.[14] They were crammed with precious feathers; they had sprays of precious feathers. Their green stone necklaces went with them; they went provided with bracelets — they went provided with green stone bracelets. They had their faces liquid rubber-painted; their faces were painted with liquid rubber; their faces were spotted with a paste of amaranth seeds. And there were their rubber sandals; their rubber sandals went with them. They all went honored; they were adorned, they were ornamented with all valuable things which went with them. They gave them paper wings,[15] they were of paper; they each had paper wings. In litters were they carried; they went housed in precious feathers, there where each of them customarily went. They went sounding flutes for them.

There was much compassion. They made one weep; they loosed one's weeping; they made one sad for them; there was sighing for them.

And when they were brought to the place of vigil, in the Mist House,[16] there all night was to be spent in vigil. The offering priests and the *quaquacuiltin*,[17] those who were old offering priests, made them keep the vigil. And if any of the offering priests avoided them, they would call them "the abandoned ones." No longer did one join others in singing; nowhere was he wanted; nowhere was he respected.[18]

And if the children went crying, if their tears kept flowing, if their tears kept falling, it was said, it was stated: "It will surely rain." Their tears signified rain. Therefore there was contentment; therefore one's heart was at rest. Thus they said: "Verily, already the rains will set in; verily, already we shall be rained on."

And if one who was dropsical was somewhere, they said: "There is no rain for us."

And when the rains were already to pass, when

ietiuh, yiauhqueme, in tlacateteujtl: yn jtlatquj ietiuh, tlacemaqujlli, yn jiappalli.

Jzqujcan yn, in miqujia nextlaoalti, tlacateteuhti:

auh muchinti, ynmaxtlatzon ietiuh, quetzalxixilquj, quetzalmjiaoaio: inchalchiuhcozquj ietiuh, yoan momacuextitiuj, qujmomacuextitiuj chalchiujtl: tlaixolujlti, qujmixolhujaia, mjxmichioaujque, yoan ymolcac, ymolcac ietiuh, muchintin maujzçotiuj, tlacencaoalti, tlachichioalti, muchi tlaçotlanquj, yn jntech ietiuh, tlaçotlantiuj, qujmamatlapaltia, amatl, amaamatlapaleque: tlapechtica in vicoia, quetzalcallotiuja, yn vncã momantiujia, qujntlapichilitiuja:

cenca tlatlaocultiaia, techoctiaia, techoquizvitomaia, teicnotlamachtiaia, ynca elciciooaia.

Auh yn oaxitiloque toçocan, aiauhcalco, vncan ceiooal toçaujlo, qujntoçaviia tlamacazque: yoan in quaquacujlti, iehoan in ie veuetque tlamacazque. Auh in tlamacazque, yn o ceme ontetlalcaujque, motocaiotiaia mocauhque: aocmo tecujcananamiquj, aoccan onmonequj, aoccan onpoalo.

Auh in pipiltzitzinti, intla chocatiuj, intla imixaio totocatiuh, intla imixaio pipilcatiuh, mitoaia, moteneoaia, ca qujiauiz: yn imixaio qujnezcaiotiaia, in qujiaujtl, ic papacoaia, ic teiollo motlaliaia: iuh qujtoa, ca ie moquetzaz in qujiaujtl, ca ie tiqujiaujlozque.

Auh intla cana ca, ytixiuhquj, q'toaia, amo techqujiaujlota.

Auh yn ie qujçaz qujiaujtl, yn ie tlamiz yn ie

---

14. Seler, *Einige Kapitel*, p. 57, reads *ymaxtlatzon*, which he translates as *ihre eigentümliche Frisur*.

15. Corresponding Spanish text: *"ponjanlos vnas alas de papel como angeles."*

16. *Ibid.*: aiauhcalco is described as *"un oratorio que estaua iunto a tepetzinco de la parte del occidente."*

17. *quaquacuilti* (sing., *quacuilli*): in Seler's *Gesammelte Abhandlungen*, Vol. II, p. 987, it is suggested that the meaning of the term is probably *"der zum Haupte gewählt ist."* In Sahagún's *Histoire générale des choses de la Nouvelle-Espagne*, trans. D. Jourdanet and Rémi Siméon (Paris: G. Masson, Editeur, 1880; hereafter referred to as Sahagún, Jourdanet–Siméon ed.), p. 110, n. 2, the translators render the term *preneur de têtes*.

18. In the corresponding Spanish text, Sahagún explains in greater detail: *"Si alguno de los mjnistros del templo, y otros q̃ llamauan quaquacujlti, y los viejos se boluian a sus casas, y no llegauan a donde aujan de matar, los njños: tenjanlos por infames, y indignos de njngun oficio publico: de ay adelante llamauanlos mocauhque, que quiere dezir dexados."*

they were already to end, when already they were at their close, thereupon the curve-billed thrasher[19] pisang; it was the sign that continuous rains would set in. Then came the Franklin gulls.[20] And also came the falcons;[21] they came crying out. They were the sign that ice was to come; already it would freeze.

And at the time called Quauitl eua, then on the round stone of gladiatorial sacrifice there appeared, there came into view those to be striped. And of those who were only to die, it was stated: "They raise poles for the striped ones."[22] They were brought there to Yopico, [Xipe] totec's temple.[23] There they intimated to them how they were to die; they tore out their hearts; yet they were only putting them to the test. It was with the use of tortillas of ground corn which had not been softened in lime,[24] or "Yopi"-tortillas, that they tore their hearts from them.

And four times they appeared before the people; they were brought out before them; they were made to be seen by the people; they were made known to them. They gave each of them things; they gave each of them their paper vestments.

The first time they were given [things] with which they were adorned, they were red. They went red. They were red. Their paper vestments were red.

The second time their paper adornment was white.

The third time they went with vestments which were red.

The fourth time they were white.

Finally they adorned them, finally they gave them, finally [the victims] wore that in which their task would end, in which [the sacrificer] would put them to death, in which [the victims] would breathe their last, in which they would be striped. For this last time they took their red garments.

No more did they change [garments]: no longer did they keep changing them. And with liquid rubber they ornamented [the victims] with stripes.

And the captors, those who had captured men, who had captives, who had taken men, also anointed themselves with ochre; they covered themselves with

itzonco: njman ie ic tlatoa in cujtlacochi, ynezca, ynic ujtz, inic moquetzaz tlapaqujiaujtl: njman oalhuj, pipixcãme: no yoã oalhuj necujlicti, tletlecton, tzatzitinemj, ynezca ie uitz in cetl, ie ceuetziz.

Auh ynic mjtoaia quaujtl eoa: vncan necia, vncan onjxnecia, yn izqujntin oaoanozque temalacac: yoan in quexqujch çan miquiz, moteneoaia qujnquavitleoaltiaia yn oaoanti: vmpa ovico yiopico, yn iteupan Totec: vmpa qujntlaieecalviaia, in quenjn miquizque, qujmeltequja: çan oc qujntlaiecultiaia: iotlaxcalli, anoço iopitlaxcalli, ynic qujmeleltequja.

Auh nappa teixpan neci, teixpan qujxtilo, teittitilo, teiximachtilo, qujntlamamaca, qujnmamaca yn jmamanechichioal:

ynjc ceppa maco, ynjc chichioalo, tlauhio, tlauhiotiuj, tlatlactic, tlauhio yn jmamatlatquj.

Jnic vppa iztac, yn jmamanechichioal.
Jnic expa, oc cepa iehoatl yn intlatquj, ietiuh, tlauhio.
Jnic nappa, iztac,
iccen qujnchichioaia, iccen qujnmacaia, iccen qujtquj, ynjc ipan intequiuh vetziz, ynic qujntlatlatizque, ynjc ihjiotl quiçaz ynic oaoanozque ça iccen qujcuj, yn intlatquj, tlauhio:

aocmo quipatla, aocmo qujpapatla: yoan vltica qujnoahoanchichioa.

Auh in tlamanj, in temanj, in male, in teacinj, no motlauhoça, mopotonja, motzomaia yn jma, yn icxi iztac totoliujtica.

19. cujtlacochi: Toxostoma curvirostre (Swanson) in Dibble and Anderson, Book XI, p. 51.

20. pipixcame (sing., pipixcan): Larus pipixcan Wagler in ibid., p. 43.

21. necuiljctli, tletlecton: Falco columbarius in ibid., p. 45.

22. oaoanozque, oaoanti: Jiménez Moreno, "Primeros memoriales," p. 23, notes: "Es el verbo uauana, que significa 'rayar.' Debe entenderse — según el Dr. Alfonso Caso — que sobre el embijado de tiza (yeso), les pintaban rayas rojas longitudinales. También podría ser que les sajasen la piel y de las sajaduras brotase sangre." For the act of striping and a discussion of agricultural connotations of the ceremony, see Seler, Gesammelte Abhandlungen, Vol. II, pp. 719, 1000, 1073. See also Appendix to this volume, pp. 203-4.

23. Yopico. For location of the temple and its reference to Xipe Totec, see Seler, Gesammelte Abhandlungen, Vol. II, pp. 772, 781.

24. yotlaxcalli: Sahagún, Garibay ed., Vol. I, p. 60, refers to them as "panes ácimos que ellos llamaban yotlaxcalli."

feather down; they covered their arms, their legs with white turkey feathers.

And also they were given costly devices; these were not given for always. It was only at the time that one warmed them in the sun; it was only at the time that one danced the captives' dance. One only appeared with them; one only was seen with them; one only vaunted himself with them; one was with them only at the time it was a feast day; with them one only made known to men that his captive was a striped one.

And his shield went with him; it went resting on his arm. With it he went bending his knees. And his rattle stick went with him; he went rattling his rattle stick. He went planting the rattle stick forcefully [on the ground]; it rattled; it jingled.

And all were thus ornamented, all who had captives, who were takers of captives, whose captives would be striped when the feast day of Tlacaxipeualiztli arrived.

Auh no macoia, tlaçotlanquj tlauiztli, amo iccen macoia, çan ipã tlatotonjaia, çan ipan momalitotiaia: çan ic neci, çan ic itto, çan ic tetlamauiçoltia, çan ic ipan ilhujtla, çan ic tetlattitia, ynjc oaoano ymal:

yoan ychimal ietiuh, ymac mantiuh, ic momamantiuh: yoan ichicaoaz ietiuh, chicaoaçotiuh, qujtilquetztiuh in chicaoaztli, chachalaca, cacalaca.

Auh muchinti, iuh muchichioaia, yn ixqujchtin, maleque, in tlamanjme: yn jnmalhoan oahoanozque, yn iquac oacic ilhujtl tlacaxipeoaliztli.

46

Twenty-first Chapter, which telleth of the honors and the debt-payment which they used to render at the time of the entire second month, which was called Tlacaxipeualiztli.[1]

Tlacaxipeualiztli. This feast day came and was thus celebrated: it was the time when all the captives died, all those taken, all who were made captive, the men, the women, all the children.[2]

Those who had captives, when, on the morrow, their captives were to die, then began to dance the captives' dance, when the sun had passed noon. And all night one held a vigil for his captive there in his *calpulco*. And there he took hair from the crown of [the captive's] head [and] placed it before the hearth[3] when the night divided in half, when it was time to fast.

And when it dawned, then they made [the captive] leave, that he might go to die, he who would die on this very feast day. And during the whole day they flayed all of them. They were flayed; hence [the feast day] was called The Flaying of Men.

And the captives were given the names *xipeme* and *tototecti*.[4] Those who slew them were the offering priests. Those who had captives did not slay them; they no more than left them, they no more than left them in the hands of [the priests],[5] who went seizing them, pulling them by their heads; they went taking them by [the hair of] their heads; they went taking them by [the hair of] the tops of their heads. Thus they made them climb to the top of the temple.

Jnic cempoali oce capitulo, ytechpa tlatoa in tlama- uiztililiztli, yoan in nextlaoaliztli, in qujchioaia, yn jpan vel ic vntetl metztli, in mjtoaia, tlacaxipeoaliztli.

Tlacaxipeoaliztli: ynin ilhuitl qujçaia: auh inic mu- chioaia, iquac miquja, yn ixqujch malli, yn ixqujch tlaaxitl, yn ixqujch haxioac: yn oqujchtli, in cioatl, yn ixqujch piltzintli.

Jn maleque, in ie iuh muztla miqujzque inmal- hoan, iquac peoa, in momalitotia, in ie onmotzcaloa tonatiuh: auh ceiooal qujtoçauja yn jmal, in vncan icalpulco: yoan vncan qujtzoncuj, iquaiolloco, tle- cuilixquac qujtlalia, iquac in ioalli xeliuj, neçaoaliz- pan.

Auh in ooallatujc, vncan coneoaltia, inic mjquj- tiuh: in miquja vel ipan in jlhujtl: auh vel iuh cemjl- hujtl muchinti qujnxipeoaia, xipeoaloia: ic mjtoaia tlacaxipeoaliztli.

Auh in mamalti motocaiotiaia xipeme, yoan toto- tecti: in temictiaia, iehoantin in tlamacazque: amo iehoanti qujnmictiaia in maleque, çan tequjtl qujm- oncaoaia, çan tequjtl temac qujmoncaoaia, qujnqua- temotzultzitzqujtiuj, inquatla qujmantiuj, ymjcpac qujmantiuj, ynjc qujntlecauja teucalticpac.

---

1. This most spectacular of ceremonies — the flaying of men — was said by Fray Diego de Durán to have been invented by Moctezuma I's general Tlacaelel. See *Historia de las Indias de Nueva-España y las islas de Tierra Firme*, ed. José F. Ramírez, 2 vols. (Mexico: Imprenta de J. M. Andrade y F. Escalante, 1867–80; hereafter referred to as Durán, *Historia*), Vol. I, p. 174. Miguel Acosta Saignes, in *Tlacaxipeua-liztli, un complejo mesoamericano entre los caribes* (Caracas: Universidad Central, 1950), *passim*, argues that it is an ancient complex and in various aspects very widespread.

In Mexico, its place as a spring festival, celebrated when the soil was prepared for planting, is well recognized. Those who wore the human skins represented the renewal of vegetation. See Alfonso Caso, *The Aztecs, People of the Sun* (Norman: University of Oklahoma Press, 1958), pp. 49–51, where, besides, origin of the ceremony in Guerrero or Oaxaca is suggested.

2. Clavijero, *Historia antigua*, Vol. II, p. 149, adds that "*algunas de estas victimas solían ser los ladrones de oro y plata que eran condenados por la ley del reino a semejante sacrificio.*"

3. Seler, *Einige Kapitel*, p. 62, translates thus: "*legen es*" — the hair — "*vor dem Feuerherde nieder*"; Sahagún, in the corresponding Spanish text, says: "*Junto al fuego hazian esta ceremonia.*"

4. Corresponding Spanish text: "*a ellos los llamauan xipeme, y por otro nombre tototecti, lo primero, quiere dezir, desollados, lo segundo, quiere dezir, los muertos a honrra del dios totec.*"

Besides being worn as described, the skins are said by Juan de Tovar to have been used to forecast a wet or a dry year, and the chiefs directed agricultural work accordingly — George Kubler and Charles Gibson, *The Tovar Calendar*, Memoirs of the Connecticut Academy of Arts and Sciences, Vol. XI (New Haven: Yale University Press, 1951), p. 22.

5. In the Spanish text, Sahagún definitely states that the captive was delivered to the priest by the captor.

And when some captive lost his strength, fainted, only went continually throwing himself on the ground, they just dragged him.

But when one made an effort, he did not act like a woman; he became strong like a man, he bore himself like a man, he went speaking like a man, he went exerting himself, he went strong of heart, he went shouting. He did not go downcast; he did not go spiritless; he went extolling, he went exalting[6] his city.

He went with firm heart; he went saying: "Already here I go: You will speak of me there in my home land!"

And things being so, they were made to arrive at the top [of the pyramid], before [the sanctuary of] Uitzilopochtli.

Thereupon one at a time they stretched them out on the sacrificial stone. Then they delivered them into the hands of six offering priests; they stretched them out upon their backs; they cut open their breasts with a wide-bladed flint knife.[7]

And they named the hearts of the captives "precious eagle-cactus fruit." They raised them in dedication to the sun, Xippilli, Quauhtleuanitl.[8] They offered it to him; they nourished him.

And when [the heart] had become an offering, they placed it in the eagle vessel.[9] And these captives who had died they called eagle men.[10]

Afterwards they rolled them over; they bounced them down. They came breaking to pieces; they came head over heels; they each came headfirst; they came turning over and over. Thus they reached the terrace at the base of the pyramid.[11]

And from here they removed them.

And they were in the hands of the old men, the *quaquacuilti*, the old men of the *calpulli*. They took

Auh yn aca malli, vel çotlaoa, iolmiquj, ça chachapantiuh, ça qujvilana:

auh yn aca vel muchicaoa, amo mocioatlamachtia, moq'chchicauhtic, oqujcheoatiuh, moqujchitotiuh, mellaquauhtiuh, moiolchicauhtiuh, oalmotzatzilitiuh, amo tlacuecuetlaxotiuh, amo tlapolotiuh, tlateniotitiuh, qujiauhcaiotitiuh yn jaltepeuh:

yiollo qujmattiuh, qujoalitotiuh, ie nõiauh, annechonjtozque, vmpa nochan yn.

Auh yn ie iuhquj yn oaxitiloque tlacpac, ixpan in vitzilobuchtli:

njman ie ic ceceniaca qujmonteca in techcac, ic inmac in tlamacazque, qujnchiquacencaujaia, qujmaquetztiteca, qujmeltetequj, yca ixquaoac, patlaoac tecpac.

Auh yn jniollo, mamalti qujtocaiotia, quauhnochtli tlaçotli: conjoalia in tonatiuh xippilli, quatleuanjtl qujtlamaca, quizcaltia.

Auh yn oventic quauhxicalco contlalia, quauhxicalco contlalitiuj: auh in iehoantin mjquja mamalti, qujntocaiotiaia Coauhteca:

çatepan qujnoalmjmjloa, qujnoaltetecujchoa, chachalcatiujtze, maiotzincueptiujtze, motzotzoniquetztiujtze, mocuecueptiujtze, ynjc oalaci apetlac:

auh vncan, qujmonana:

auh ie inmac in vevẽtzitzin quaquacujlti, calpul-

6. Read *quitauhcayotitiuh*.

7. Seler, *Einige Kapitel*, p. 63, specifies a *"dicken breiten Feuersteinmesser."* Siméon, *Dictionnaire*, defines *ixquauac* as *"Couteau pour les sacrifices humains, fait avec du silex ou de l'obsidienne...."* Fray Toribio de Benavente Motolinía's "Historia de los indios de Nueva España," in *Colección de documentos para la historia de México*, ed. Joaquín García Icazbalceta, 2 vols. (Mexico: Librería de J. M. Andrade, 1858–66), Vol. I, p. 40, definitely states that the knife was of flint, not obsidian. Motolinía describes it as *"un navajon como hierro de lanza, no mucho agudo porque ... no se puede hacer muy aguda...."*

8. *quatleuanjtl*: in Bernardino de Sahagún, *Historia de las cosas de Nueva España*, ed. Francisco del Paso y Troncoso (Madrid: Hauser y Menet, 1905–07; hereafter referred to as *Real Palacio MS* Vols. VII and VI), Vol. VII, the text reads *quauhtlevanitl*, but it is possible that the *uh* has been crossed out.

9. Seler consistently renders the term *quauhxicalli* as *Adlerschale* (cf. *Einige Kapitel*, p. 64). In *Gesammelte Abhandlungen*, Vol. II, pp. 704–11, he breaks the word down into *quauitl* and *xicalli* (wooden vessel), and argues that the syllable *quauh* was always understood to mean eagle. The vessels seem actually to have been made of stone, and were used not only for the hearts but for the blood as well. Sahagún, no less consistently than Seler, uses the term *xicara de madero*.

10. Corresponding Spanish text: *"Despues sacados los coraçones, los llamauan quauhteca."* Seler, *Gesammelte Abhandlungen*, Vol. II, p. 704, translates *quauhtecatl* as *"der aus dem Adlerlande."* He adds (p. 709): *"Und zur Sonne, in das Haus der Sonne, nach dem Osthimmel, als ihr Diener, als* quauhtecatl, *gieng auch die Seele des Geopferten."*

11. *Apetlatl* is a small terrace projecting at the foot of the pyramid stairway (cf. Sahagún, Garibay ed., Vol. III, p. 54).

them there to their *calpulco*, where the taker of the captive had made his undertaking, had said his say, had made his vow.

From there they removed him in order to take him to the house of [the captor], in order to eat him. There they portioned him out; they cut him to pieces; they distributed him. First of all, they made an offering of one of his thighs to Moctezuma. They set forth to take it to him.

And as for the captor, they there applied the down of birds to his head and gave him gifts. And he gathered together his blood relatives; the captor assembled them in order to go to eat at his home.

There they made each one an offering of a bowl of stew of dried maize, called *tlacatlaolli*. They gave it to each one. On each went a piece of the flesh of the captive.

They named [the captor] "sun," "chalk," "feather," because he was as one whitened with chalk, decked with feathers.

The captor's being pasted with feathers was done because he had not died there in war or else [because] he would yet go to die, would go to pay the debt [in war or by sacrifice]. Hence his blood relations greeted him with tears; they encouraged him.

And on the morrow there was the striping.[12] Until early morning, when it was to dawn, they held vigil for them all night until night ended. Thus the captives, the striped ones, spent all night until the time it dawned.

From those whom they were to stripe, once more they took hair [from the crowns of their heads] at midnight.

Hence it was said: "The eagle man is taken upwards," because indeed he who died in war went, went looking, sat resting in the presence of the sun. That is, he did not go to the place of the dead.

And therefore he who took hair [from the crown of a captive's head] kept his hair safely.

Because thus he merited honor, flowers, tobacco, capes.

Thus his valor would not in vain perish; it was as if thus he took renown from the captive.

And he who took the captive was adorned, there at [the Temple of] Tecanman, in Tenochtitlan, with white turkey down; he was pasted with feathers as is set forth in [the Feast of] Quauitl eua.

---

12. See Chap. 20, n. 22.

vevetque: vmpa qujnujca yn incalpulco, yn vmpa omotlatlalili, omjto, omonetolti male:

vmpa conana, ynic qujujca ichan, ynjc qujquazque: vmpa qujxexeloa, qujtetequj, qujueueloa: oc ie achto qujtonaltia in motecuçuma ce ymetz, mantiuh in qujujqujlia.

Auh in tlamani, vmpa qujquapotonja, yoan qujtlauhtia: auh yn joaniolque qujntlalhuja, qujcentlalia, ynic tlaquatiuj ichan tlamanj:

vmpa qujntotonaltia cecen molcaxitl in tlaolpaoaxtli, q'nmamanjliaia, itoca tlacatlaolli, ypan ieietiuh cecen tlatectli yn jnacaio malli:

quitocaiotia tonatiuh, tiçatl, hiujtl: ipampa iuhqujn ytiçaio, yujio.

ypotonjloca omochiuh in tlamanj, ynic amo vmpa omjc iaopan, yn anoçe oc miqujtiuh, qujxtlaoatiuh, ic qujchoquiztlapaloa, quellaquaoa yn joaiolque.

Auh yn imuztlaioc, tlaoaoano: yn jioatzinioc, in ie oallatuiz qujntoçauja, iuh ceioal, iuh tlami ioalli, iuh contlaça in ceiooal, iuh ipan tlatuj, in mamalti, in oaoanti:

in qujnoaoanazque, oc no cepa qujntzoncuj, ioalnepantla:

ic mitoaia onacoqujxtilo in quauhtecatl, iehica ca iaomjquj, ixco iauh, ixcopa itztiuh, ixco monoltitoc in tonatiuh, qujtoznequj, amo mictlan iauh:

yoan ipampa in qujtzoncuja, qujmopialtiaia yn itzon:

iehica ca ic oqujmomaceuj, in mavizçotl, in xuchitl yn ietl, in tilmatli:

ynjc amo çan nenpoliuiz itiiacauhio: iuhqujnma ic contleiocujliaia malli.

Auh in tlamanj vmpa muchichioa in tecanma, tenochtitla, iztac totolihujtl, ynjc mopotonja, in iuh omoteneuh ipan quaujtl eoa.

49

And in the place where the *tototecti* waited,[13] they were in order, they were in rows upon white earth or upon grass, for there was white earth in the place where they waited.[14]

And wherever in the city grass was shaken out, upon it they placed, set up, exhibited, before all, the *xipeme* who had put on the skins of men.

And any who had become drunk, unruly like warriors, daring, foolhardy, full of spirit, lively, proud of their valor, playing the part of men, kept provoking them, menaced them, kept starting a fight, provoked them to battle.

And to arouse their wrath completely, verily to move them, verily in order to bring out their rage, their anger, they would snatch at their navels. They snatched at their navels; they pinched their navels.

Then the *xipeme* went in pursuit. Behind them, at their backs, marched a Totec, named the Youallauan; he followed them; he went menacing them. All the *tototecti* then set upon [the warriors]; they took after them; they went fighting them; they went capturing them; they went taking them in their hands. It was as if they were on the heels of their interceptors.

And [the others] went turning back, went circling back; with pine staves they went threatening them.

And if some of the interceptors were taken, the *xipeme* beat them repeatedly with the rattle sticks. They trampled them; they made them angry.

And they took one to Yopico. Not for nothing did he come out; not for nothing was he let free. Something was exacted for it, something was taken for it, perhaps a turkey hen, mayhap a great cotton mantle he offered one, etc.

As was said in the description of Xipe, just so was it done. Afterwards they visited, they entertained, they amused the *tototecti*, the *xipeme*.

Then began the gladiatorial sacrifice.[15] The captives were placed in order; the captors remained accompanying each one, remained bringing each one. Then also the striped ones came forth. An ocelot warrior swiftly led; he swiftly led them; he swiftly

Auh in vncan momanaia tototecti, tecpantimanj vipantimanj tiçapan, anoço çacapan: ipampa ca tiçatl antoca in vncan momanaia.

Auh in cana altepetl ipan, çacatl motzetzeloa, yn ipan qujnoalmana, qujnoalquetza, qujnoalteittitia: tlaixco qujnoalmana in xipeme, yn onmaqujaia tlacaeoatl.

Auh yn aqujque, mihivintia iautlaueliloque, mixtlapaloanj, acan ixmauhque, iollotlapaltique, iollochicaoaque, quipopoanj yn jntiiacauhio moqujchnenequj, qujmonpepeoaltia, qujmontlaehecalhuja, oiaiaopeoa, qujnmoiaiaopeoaltia.

Auh inic vel qujntlauelcujtiaia, ynic vel qujmolinjaia, ynic vel intlauel, inqualan qujcuja, qujmonxiccuja, qujmõxiccuj, qujmonxiccotona:

ic njman in xipeme tlapaynaltiaia ymjcampa inteputzco icatiuh ce Totec, itoca iooallaoan, qujntoca qujntlaiehecalhujtiuh, in muchintin tototecti: ic njman intech ietiqujça, qujntlalochtoca, qujniaochiuhtiuj, qujmaacitiuj, qujnmamacujtiuj iuhq'n incotztitech ietiuj, in teçaloanj:

auh oalmocueptiuj, oalmomalacachotiuj, ocoquauhtica quinoallaheecalhujtiuj.

Auh intla ceme anoia, in teçaloanj, qujnujujtequj in xipeme, in chicaoaztica, qujxixilia, vel qujncocoltia.

Auh iopico conujcaia, amo çan nen oalqujçaia, amo çan nen caoaloia, itla ic moqujxtiaia, itla ic onanoia, aço totoli, aço quachtli qujtemacaia. Et.a

Yn o iuh mito ipan itlatollo xippe, çan ie no iuh mochioaia: çatepan, in ontetotocaque, yn onteaujeltique, yn ontlapactique tototecti, xipeme:

njman ic peoa in tlaoaoano, tecpantimanj in mamalti, qujnnanamjctimani, qujujujcatimanj in tlamanj: njman no oalqujça in tlaoaoanque, yiacatiujtz, qujiacatitiujtz, in teiacantiujtz ocelutl ipan quiztiujtz,

---

13. Although in the following paragraphs the Nahuatl text refers to the *tototecti* and the *xipeme*, both names refer to the same persons. See n. 4.

14. In the corresponding Spanish text, Sahagún states: *"ponjanse todos sentados, sobre vnos lechos de heno, o de tiçatl, o greda estando alli sentados."* See also Appendix in this volume, p. 204.

15. A less detailed description of this same ceremony appears in the *Real Academia MS* as the latter part of its Chap. 17 (the *Florentine Codex, Book VIII*, Chap. 20). The similarity of the two accounts may explain why the *Real Academia MS* version was deleted when *Book VIII* of the *Florentine Codex* was prepared. See Arthur J. O. Anderson and Charles E. Dibble, *Florentine Codex, Book VIII, Kings and Lords* (Santa Fe: School of American Research and University of Utah, 1954), pp. 83–86.

guided them. He swiftly encountered them. He displayed his shield, his obsidian-bladed club; he raised them in dedication to the sun.[16]

Then once again he turned back; he retreated, he turned to the rear; once again he went back.

When this was done, there then followed him, there came second after him an eagle warrior; he came second. Similarly he raised his shield, his obsidian-bladed club in dedication to the sun.

Once again there emerged another ocelot warrior; he came out as third. He came quickly after one as third. He did the same. He swiftly entered.

Yet again an eagle warrior came forth; he did everything in the same way. All four came forth fighting; they raised their shields, their obsidian-bladed clubs in dedication to the sun.

No longer did they delay. As they were turning to the rear, at once they were coming forth. They came dancing; they each went turning about. They each went as if stretched on the ground; they each went on the ground; they each went stretched flat; they went looking from side to side; they each went leaping upwards; they each went fighting.

And when this was done, then the Youallauan came forth; he came forth quickly as Totec; he only followed them; he came quite last; he hung on quite behind them; he came quite last of all after all four of the great ocelot [and] eagle warriors. They only extended their arms; they only stretched out their arms; they raised their shields, their obsidian-bladed clubs in dedication to the sun.

Thereupon came forth, arrived, were ranged in order all the impersonators, the proxies of all the gods.[17] They were called the lieutenants, the delegates, the impersonators.

In just the same way they went. They went in order; they went together. Thus they came down; they started from there at Yopico, from the very top of the Temple of Yopitli.

And when they had come to arrive down below, on the ground, on the earth, they encircled the round stone of gladiatorial sacrifice. When they had encircled it, they seated themselves. They were in order upon large backed seats called roseate spoonbill feather seats.

And as they were extended, as they were extended in order, so the Youallauan[18] was leading; again he

conjttitia, conjaujlia yn ichimal, yn imaquauh, in tonatiuh:

njman oc cepa tzinquiça, tzinnenemj, tziniloti: oc cepa ycujtlaujc iauh:

in ie iuhquj njman qujoaltoquilia, qujoaloncaiotia, oallaoncaiotia in quauhtli, çan no yuj in conjaujlia tonatiuh, yn ichimal, yn imacquauh:

oc cepa no oalquiça, oc ce ocelutl, oallaecaiotitiuh, teecaiotitiujtz, çan no iuh qujchioaia calactiuetzi.

Oc no cepa centetl oalqujça, in quauhtli, çan ie much iuj in qujchioaia, oallaehecooaia in naujxti: conjaujliaia yn jnchimal, yn jnmacquauh in tonatiuh:

aocmo oaluecaoaia, ynic oaltzinilotia, çan njman ic oalquiztimanca, mitotitiujtze, momamantiuj: iuhquin tlalli ixco motetecatiuj, iuhqujn tlaltitech õujujh, mocacanauhtiuj, nanacaztlachixtiuj, haacocholotiuj, tlatlaieecotiuj.

Auh in ie iuhquj njman oalqujça, yiooallaoan, totec ipan quiztiujtz, ça oallatoqujlia, ça oallatzacujtiuh, ça oallacujtlapilooa, ça quinoalcentzacujtiuh in naujntin, veueinti in quaquauhti, yn oocelo, ça oalmaçoa, oalmaana, conjaujlia yn inchimal yn jmaquauh in tonatiuh:

njman ie ic oalqujça oalmoiacatia, oalmotecpana, yn ixqujchtin teixiptlaoan, yn jnpatilooan in ixqujchtin teteu: motocaiotiaia tepatiuhti, tepatillooan, teixiptlati:

çan ie no yuj in ujh motecpantiuj, cemonotiuj, ynic oaltemo: vmpa oalpeoa in iopico, vel icpac in teucalli iopitli.

Auh yn oacico tlatzintla, in tlalchi, in tlaltitech: njman qujiaoaloa in temalacatl, yn oconiaoaloque, motlatlalia tecpantoque, ypan veuey icpalli, itoca quecholicpalli.

Auh ynjc onoque, ynjc tecpantoque, ene teiacantica, ie no cuele teiacantica, tlaiacatitica, in iooallaoa:

16. Sahagún's Spanish has: "*leuantaban la rodela, y la espada hazia el sol, como demandando esfuerço al sol.*" Cf. also Pl. 5.

17. Durán, in *Historia*, Vol. I, pp. 176 ff., names Uitzilopochtli, Quetzalcoatl, Toci, Yopi, Totec, and Itzpapalotl.

18. Corresponding Spanish text specifies "*el principal sacerdote, de aquella fiesta, que se llamaua ioallaoa.*"

was first; he was in the lead; because it was his office, his personal privilege that he sacrifice to the gods, that he slay one; at his hands would perish, at his hands would be hacked open all the eagle men.

When this was done, then musical instruments were blown; conch shells, large seashells were blown; there was whistling with fingers placed in the mouth, and there was singing. With singing, with blowing of trumpets, [the Cozcateca] arrived. The Cozcateca placed themselves in order; their shoulders each went decked with heron feather flags. They encircled the round stone of gladiatorial sacrifice.

One [of the captors] quickly seized a captive. The captor, he who owned the captive, went holding him by the head in order to bring him to the round stone of gladiatorial sacrifice.

When they had brought him, they gave him pulque; and the captive raised the pulque four times in dedication,[19] and afterwards drank it with a long hollow cane.

Then still another man, [a priest], came; he beheaded a quail for the captive, the striped one. When he had beheaded the quail, he raised the captive's shield [to the sun], and he cast the quail away behind him.

When this was done, then they made [the captive] climb upon the round stone of gladiatorial sacrifice; and when they had set him up on the round stone of gladiatorial sacrifice, a man, the bear [priest], confronted him. He represented the one called "Old Bear."[20] It was as if he were the uncle of the striped one.

Then he took the "sustenance" rope, which reached to the center [of the stone and] which was fastened [to it]. Then he tied it about the waist of the captive.[21] And he gave him a war club decked with feathers, not set with obsidian blades.

And he placed before him four pine cudgels, his missiles to throw at one,[22] to defend himself with. And the captor, when he had gone to leave his captive on the round stone of gladiatorial sacrifice, thereupon went away; he stopped where he had been standing before; he stood dancing; from where he

iehica ca itequjuh, yneixcaujl catca, in tlamictiz, in tetlatlatiz, ymac polioaz, ymac xamanizq̃ yn ixqujch quauhtecatl:

in ie iuhquj njman tlapitzalo, tecciztli mopitza, qujqujztli, mapipitzoa, yoan cujco: cujcapan tlapitzalpan, in oalmoiacatia: motecpana in cozcateca, qujquequechpanotiuj aztapanjtl, qujiaoaloa in temalacatl.

Ce cantiqujça in malli, icpac cantiuh in tlamanj, in male, ynic qujujca temalacac:

yn ocaxitique, qujmaca vctli: auh yn vctli nappa coniavilia in malli: auh çatepan conj piaztica:

njman oc no ce tlacatl oallauh, çolin qujcotonjlia, in malli, in oaoantli, yn oconquechcoton çolin, conjaujlia yn ichimal malli: Auh in çolli, icampa conmaiauj.

In ie iuhquj, njman contlecauja in temalacaticpac: auh yn oconquetzque temalacac, çe tlacatl cujtlachtli ipan qujça, ipan mixeoa, itoca cuitlachueue, iuhqujn intla catca in oaoanti:

njman conana, in tonacamecatl, yn iiolloco antica, yn iiolloco ilpitica, njman ic concujtlalpia in malli, yoan conmaca; maquaujtl, tlapotonilli, amo itztzo.

Yoan ixpan contema nauhtetl ocotzontetl itlamotlaia, ic temotlaz ic momapatlaz. Auh in tlamanj, yn oconcaoato ymal temalacac: njman ie ic vitz, vncan oalmoquetza yn icaia, mihtotiticac, ixqujchcapa ontlachixticac, yn jmal conitzicac:

19. Seler, in *Einige Kapitel*, p. 69, says that the captor raised the pulque; Sahagún says the prisoner.

20. *"venja vno de los sacerdotes, o mjnistros del templo, vestido con vn cuero de osso"* — corresponding Spanish text. Cf. Dibble and Anderson, *Book XI*, p. 5. Seler translates *cuetlachtli* as kinkajou, in *Einige Kapitel*, pp. 69, 73.

21. Tied to the captive's ankle, according to Durán, *Historia*, Vol. I, p. 177.

22. In *ibid.*, and later (p. 284), descriptions respectively specify *"quatro pelotas, hechas de palo de tea,"* and *"quatro troços de palo de tea."*

was he stood watching; he stood looking at his captive.

Then they fought each other; they kept menacing each other; they threatened each other. They looked at each other well [to see] where they would smite each other, would cut each other in a dangerous place, perchance in the calf of the leg, or in the thigh, or on the head, or in the middle.

And if some captive was valiant, courageous, with great difficulty he surpassed [his adversary]. He met all four of the ocelot [and] eagle warriors; he fought them. And if they could not weaken him, then there went one who was left-handed. Then this one wounded his arms; he felled him; he felled him flat. This one appeared as [the god] Opochtli. And although the striped one already faltered, already weakened, also he quite acquitted himself as a man; he still acquitted himself as a man.

And when one only went faltering, only went on all fours, went fainting, only went undone, only vainly, only impotently, they snatched his war club. Thus the one who striped him, the striper, confronted him.

And on the other hand there was the one who no longer did anything, no longer used his arms, no longer defended himself with them, no longer attended to it, no longer took the trouble, no longer spoke. At once he faltered, he fainted, he fell on the surface, he threw himself down as if dead, he wished that breath might end, that he might endure it, that he might perish, that he might cast off the burden of death.

And then they quickly grabbed him, quickly seized him, held him thrown down, held him stretched out on the edge of the round stone of gladiatorial sacrifice.

And then at that time the Youallauan went [forth]; he came in the guise of Totec. He gashed [the captive's] breast, seized his heart, raised it in dedication to the sun. The offering priests placed it in the eagle vessel. And another man, an offering priest, carried the [hollow] eagle cane,[23] set it standing in the captive's breast [cavity] there where the heart had been, stained it with blood, indeed submerged it in the blood. Then he also raised [the blood] in dedication to the sun. It was said: "Thus he giveth [the sun] to drink."

And the captor thereupon took the blood of his

njman ic mopeoaltia, motlatlaiehecalhuja, motlaehecalhuja, vel qujnmottilia in canjn ymoujcan moujtequizque, qujmotequjlizque: yn aço in cotzco, anoço in metzpan, anoço in quappa, anoço in tlacotiian.

Auh yn aca malli, iolchicaoac, iollotlapaliuj, vel yujujh in qujcaoa: in naujxtin qujnnamjquj, qujnmaiztlacoa, yn oocelo in quaquauhti. Auh intlaca uel qujhiiocaoaltia, njman oiauh, opuchmaie, qujn iehoatl qujmamimictia, qujmaiauj, qujtentimaiauj: injn ipan mixeoaia in opuchtli. Auh intlanel ie çotlaoa, intlanel ie ihiiocaoa, no çan oaloqujcheoa: noma oqujcheoa, in oaoantli.

Auh in aca ça çotlaoatiuh, ça xonauhtiuh, iolmictiuh, ça tlapolotiuh: ça nenpanca, ça nenpictli in qujcujtiuetzi, yn imaquauh: ic qujoalnamjquj, in qujoaoana, in tlaoaoanquj.

Auh in neh aca, aoctle conchioa, aoctle onmaitia, aoctle ic oalmomapatla, aoctle conmochichioaltia, aocmo oalmocuetzoa, aocmo oalnaoati, çan njman iolmjquj, çotlaoa, chapantiuetzi, momiccatlaça: qujnequj, macuelieh yhiiotl onqujça, macuelieh conjhiiouj, macuelieh ompoliuj, macuelieh conmotlaxili, yn jmjquiztequjuh.

Auh niman ic qujcuitiuetzi, câ antiquiça, ca quetztimaiauj, câ quetztiteca, itenco in temalacatl:

auh njman iquac oiauh yn Iooallaoan, totec ipan quiztiuitz coneltetequj, conanjlia yn iiollo, conjaujlia in tonatiuh, quauhxicalco contlalia in tlamacazque: yoan oc no ce tlacatl tlamacazquj, conitqui, quappiaztli, ielpan contilquetza yn malli, yn vncan ocatca yiollo, conezçotia, vel eztitlan conpolactia: njman no ic conjaujlia in tonatiuh, mitoa, ic catlitia.

Auh yn tlamanj njman ic conquj[24] yn iezço ymal,

23. "vn cañuto, de caña hueca" (corresponding Spanish text).
24. Read cōcuj as in the Real Palacio MS.

captive in a green bowl with a feathered rim. The
sacrificing priests poured it in for him there. In it
went standing the hollow cane, also feathered. And
then the captor departed to nourish the demons. He
went everywhere; he went every place; he omitted
no place; nowhere did he forget in the *calmecacs*,
in the *calpulcos*. On the lips of the stone images, on
each one, he placed the blood of his captive. He
made them taste it with the hollow cane. He went
with his warrior's insignia.[25]

And when he had gone everywhere, when he had
gone to reach everywhere, then he left the insignia
at the palace, and he caused [the body of] his captive to be taken to the *calpulco* where they had
passed the night in vigil for him. There they flayed
him. Then [the captor] had [the flayed body] taken
to his home, where they cut it up, so that it would be
eaten, so that it would be [other] people's lot. And
it was said that they would be considered gods.[26] As
it is told elsewhere, so likewise was it done.

But the captor could not eat the flesh of his captive. He said. "Shall I perchance eat my very self?"
For when he took [the captive], he had said: "He
is as my beloved son." And the captive had said:
"He is my beloved father." But yet on someone
else's account he might eat of one's captive.

And the captor kept [the captive's] skin for himself; he went lending it to others. For twenty days
there was begging in it; it was passed from one to
another; it was worn all day. He who wore it customarily gave the captor all that was given [him],
all that he gathered. Afterwards [the captor] divided
up, distributed [the gifts] among [all of] them.
Thus he made use of his skin.

And when this was done, when they had finished
with the striped ones, then they danced, they went
in procession about the round stone of gladiatorial
sacrifice. All the impersonators [of the gods and]
those who had done the striping went in their array.
Thus did they who did the slaying go ending [the
ceremony]. All severally took with them the head
of a captive, of a striped one; with them they danced.
It was said: "They dance with the severed heads."

And the old bear man pulled up the "sustenance"
rope; he raised it in dedication to the four directions.
He went weeping, he went howling like one be-

xoxoujc xicalli, tlatenpotonilli, vncan qujoaltequjlia,
in tlamictique, ipan icatiuh piaztli no tlapotonilli.
Auh njman ic vncã eoa in qujntlatlaqualia diablome,
noujian nemj, izqujcan qujça acan qujmocauja, acan
qujxcaoa in calmecac, calpulco: in teme teixiptlaoan,
intenco qujmontlatlalilia yn jezço malli, piaztica quj-
monpaloltitiuh, tlaujcetinemj.

Auh yn onoviiampaneh, yn onoujampa aacito,
njman concaoa in tlauiztli tecpa: auh yn jmal vncan
qujoalujqujlia in calpulco, yn vncan oqujtoçaujque
ceiooal: vncan qujxipeoa, çatepan concaujliaia yn
ichan vmpa qujtetequj, ynjc qualoz, ynjc tetonaltiloz:
yoan mjtoaia teteuhtiloz, yn oiuh mito cecnj, çan ie
no iuh muchioaia.

Auh in male, amo uel qujquaia, yn jnacaio imal,
qujtoaia, cujx çan no ne njnoquaz: ca yn iquac caci,
qujtoa, ca iuhquj nopiltzin: Auh in malli, qujtoa ca
notatzin: auh tel tepal qujquaia intemal.

Auh yn ieoaio qujmopialtiaia in tlamanj, qujtetla-
neuhtitinemj, cempoalilhujtl ipan tlatlaeoalo, nepa-
patlalo, yn onneaqujlo cemjlhujtl: yn aqujn onma-
quja in quexqujch maco, in quexqujch qujnechicoa
conmacatimanj in tlamanj, çatepan qujtexexelhuja,
tetlatlamachia: ic qujtlaiecultia yn ieoauh.

Auh in ie iuhquj, yn ontlanque oaoanti, njman ic
mjtotia, qujiaoaloa in temalacatl, yn ixqujchtin teixiptlati, yn otlaoaoanque, mocencauhtiuj, çan iuh tlan-
tiuj yn oiuh tetlatlatique: muchintin cecentetl intlan
ca ana, yn jntzontecon mamalti, in oaoanti, ic mjto-
tiuj: mjtoa, motzontecomaitotia.

Auh in cujtlachueue, contilinja in tonacamecatl,
nauhcampa conjiaoa, chocatinemj, tehcoiouhtinemj,

25. *"yua conpuesto con sus plumages, y cõ todas sus ioyas"* (*ibid.*).

26. *teteuhtiloz*: Seler, in *Einige Kapitel*, p. 72, n. 1, holds, of *teteuhtiloz*, that it is derived from *teotia*, equivalent to *tonaltia*; *teotl* is
equivalent to *tonatiuh* or *tonalli*. Hence the meaning, to apportion as a favor.

reaved; he wept for those who had suffered, who had died.

And also from cities which were his enemies, from beyond [the mountains] those with which there was war, Moctezuma secretly summoned, secretly admitted as his guests the Nonoalca, the Cozcateca, the Cempoallans, the Mecateca. There was witnessing, there was wonder; then consequently there was breaking up, there was dispersal.[27]

And when there was the striping, at that same time were eaten tortillas of uncooked maize.[28] The onlookers took tortillas of uncooked maize there; they went as their refreshments; they sat eating them there.

And on the next day, the third day, then each began the bringing out of persons. It was very late at night that it was begun there at the great palace. The Tlatelolca began it; they ended it at the time of eating. Then the offering priests replaced them. They adorned themselves, they danced in quite mixed things, quite various arrays: butterfly nets, fish banners, clusters of ears of maize, coyote heads made of a paste of amaranth seeds, S-shaped tortillas, thick rolls[29] covered with a dough of amaranth seeds which they covered on top with toasted maize, and red amaranth (only it was red feathers), and maize stalks with ears of green or tender maize.

After midday the offering priests rested. Thereupon the Tenochca [and] the Tlatelolca joined, paired. The Tenochca formed two rows; also the Tlatelolca formed two rows. They went facing each other. Very slow was the dancing; very much in harmony went the dancing. Then there was emerging through the palace entrance; there was stopping. Moctezuma brought them forth; he went dancing. Two great rulers, Neçaualpilli of Texcoco [and] Totoquiuaztli, ruler of Tepaneca land, came each following him, went facing him. Great solemnity reigned while there was dancing.

And when night fell, when it was going dark, there was dispersal; then began the singing and

iuhqujn mjccaoati, qujnchoqujlia yn otlacotique, yn onmicque.

Auh no iehoanti, yn iiaooan altepetl, tlateputzca, ynjn ca manca teuatl, tlachinolli, qujmonnotzaia ichtaca, oalichtacacalaquja, yn jcooaoan motecuçuma: yn nonooalca, cozcateca, cempoalteca, mecateca, tlattitiloia, tlamaujçoltiloia: njman ic xitinooa, necacaoalo.

Auh yn jquac tlaoaoano, çan no iquac qualo, vilocpalli: in tlatlattaque vmpa conjtquj yn jnvilocpal, ymjttac ietiuh, vmpa qujquaquatoque.

Auh yn imuztlaioc, in ie ic eilhujtl: njman pepeoa in teq'qujxtilo, cenca oc hueca iooan in peoalo, in peoa, in vmpa vey tecpa: qujpeoaltiaia in tlatelulca, tlaqualizpan qujoalcaoaia: njman qujmonpatla tlamacazque, ynic muchichioaia, ynic mjhtotiaia, çan tlanenel, çan nepapã tlatqujtl, papalomatlatl, michpanjtl, ocholli, tzôcoiotl, tzoalli, tlachichioalli, xonecujllaxcalli, teumjmjlli, çan no tzoalli ic qujpepechooaia, qujmomochiotiaia panj: yoan oauhchichilli, çan tlapaliujtl catca, yoan cintopilli, eloio, anoço xiloio.

Yn omotzcalo tonatiuh, moceuja in tlamacazque, njman ie ic monepanuja, montlamanuja, in tenuchca in tlatilulca, vmpanti in tenuchca, no vmpanti in tlatilulca, mixnamjctiuj, cenca çan yujian, yn netotilo, cenca vel cooamantiuh in netotiliztli: njman oalqujxoa in tecpaqujiaoac, oalnemanalo, oalteujca in motecuçoma, oalmjtotitiuh, qujtzatzacutiuitze, qujoalitzcatitiuj, vmentin veueintin tlatoque Neçaoalpilli tetzcuco, totoqujoaztli, tepanecapan tlatoanj: vel mauiztli oonoc in nehtotiloia.

Auh ie tlapoiaoa, ie tlaixcuecuetziuj in necacaoalo, njman ic peoa, in cujcoanolo, mjtotiaia in telpuchte-

27. Durán (Historia, Vol. I, pp. 175–80) says that Moctezuma I invited "los señores de toda la redonda" — Texcoco, Tlacopan, Chalco, Xochimilco, Couixco, Matlatzinco, the Maçahuaques, and as many more as possible. "Los señores de las prouincias y ciudades," he continues, "admirados y asombrados de semejante sacrificio, partiéronse para sus prouincias y pueblos llenos de temor y espanto . . . dexó espantados á los forasteros. . . . Desde entonces todos los de las prouincias y ciudades comarcanas dexaron de tratar reueliones ni contiendas con los mexicanos, viendo quán adelante estauan y cómo tratauan á sus enemigos."

28. uilocpalli: "tortillas, como empanadillas, que hazian de mahiz, sin cozer," according to Sahagún's Spanish text. In Seler (Einige Kapitel, p. 74, n. 1) this is defined as the equivalent of macuextlaxcalli — "das 'Brot in Gestalt eines Armbandes.' . . . Es war ein Gebäck in Ringform, das aus eingekochten, in trockenem Zustande zermahlenen Maiskörnern, also aus Maismehl, nicht aus Maismasse, hergestellt wurde."

29. teumjmjlli: a description in Sahagún, Garibay ed., Vol. I, p. 61, reads, "Hacian de masa una figura de un hueso grueso, redondo y largo como un codo." Possibly these resembled the wrapped femur in Pl. 12.

dancing [with interlocked hands]. There danced the rulers of the youths, the leaders of the youths, who had gone to take four or more captives, as well as those who had gone to take one [or] two. And also these were called leading youths. And also the rulers danced. And also women danced with them (they were called mothers), only of their own accord;[30] they were not made to. And likewise pleasure girls, who amused themselves.

And the time that there was cessation was when already midnight came hurrying, at the time of the blowing of the trumpets. For twenty days such was the custom; such used to be customary. Then arrived the time when it was the Feast of Toçoztontli.

qujoaque, teachcaoa, in nauj cacitinemj, yn anoce oc quezqujnti ymalhoan: yoã in ce, vme, cacitinemj. Auh no motocaiotiaia hy, telpuchiiaque: no yoan in tlatoque mitotia. Auh no tehoan in cioa mjtotia: mjtoa tenaoan, çan illotlama, amo tequjuhtiloia: auh çan no iehoãtin yn aujianjme, in maaujltia.

Auh iquac necaoaloia, in ie hiciuhtiuh, ioalnepantla tlatlapitzalizpa: cempoalilhujtl, yn iuh tlamanca, yn juh tlamanja: vmpa onaci yn ipan toçoztontli.

---

30. Read *yyollotlama* as in the *Real Palacio MS*.

Twenty-second Chapter, in which are described the feast day and the debt-paying which they celebrated in the second month, called, known as Tlacaxipeualiztli.[1]

And when it was this [time], the rattle boards were sown[2] there at Yopico. And only they, the old men of the *calpulli* at Yopico,[3] sat singing, sat rattling their rattle boards until the day was done. Thus they sat passing all day, thus they sat celebrating the day, thus they sat displaying the day; they sat making the day wear away; they sat wearing the day away. Thus they continued to pass the day.

And flowers were offered. Hence was it said: "Flowers are offered." For all the various flowers which for the first time blossomed, the flowers which came [out] first, the flowers which came [out] ahead, were then given as offerings. No one first smelled them unless he would first make an offering, would give them as gifts, would lay them out as offerings. They were whatever small flowers they saw which spread out blossoming, spread out bursting, spread out popping into bloom — the flowers of spring. Small, little, tiny, minute ones, no matter how many, no matter how little, no matter how small, no matter how tiny, they bound them each together at the ends; they bound them up.

And in order to look for the flowers, they all went together to the fields to bring them in, although some of the field people sold them here.

And when this was done, they ate tamales of wild amaranth seeds.[4]

Especially the Coateca, they who belonged to the *calpulli* of Coatlan, venerated [this feast day]. They made offerings to their deity called Coatl icue or Coatlan tonan.

They placed their trust in her; she was their hope; they depended upon her; she was their support. To her they lifted their voices.

Jnic cempoali omume capitulo, vnca moteneoa yn ilhuitl, yoan in nextlaoaliztli in quichioaia in ipan ic vme metztli: in mitoaia, in moteneoaia, Tlacaxipeoaliztli.

Auh in iquac y, aiacachpixolo vmpa iopico: auh ça iehoanti, in calpulueuetque, vmpa pouhque iopico, cujcatoque, aiacachotoque, yc ouetzi cemilhujtl, ic tlacemilhuitiltitoque, ic tlalhujqujxtitoque, ic tlalhujnextitoque, tlalhuiçultitoque, ihujçulotoque, ic ueuetzi cemilhujtl:

yoã xochimanalo ynic mjtoa xochimanalo, ca in ixqujch nepapan xochitl, in iancujcan cueponj, yiacatiuitz: yn iiacac vitz xochitl ic tlamanalo, aiac achto qujnecuj, intlacamo achto ic tlamanaz, qujuenchioaz, qujuẽmanaz, in çaço tlein xochitotõti qujttaia, cuecuepontoc, cuecuepocatoc, tlatlatzcatoc, in tonalxuchitl, hacquj, aqujtoton, hacqujpipil, hacqujtetoton, çan quecizquj, çan quezqujtoton, çan quecizquipipil, çan quezqujquauhtoton qujcujcujtlalpia, qujilpia.

Auh ynjc xuchitetemoaia, qujcenpanocujtivj in milli, tel cequj qujoalnamacaia, in millaca:

auh yn iquac y, qujquaia tzatzapaltamalli:

oc cenca iehoanti qujmauiztiliaia in coateca, in coatlan calpulli itech pouja: qujtlamanjlia yn inteouh, itoca coatl ycue, coatlan tona:

yn jtech tlaquauhtlamati, yn jnnetemachil, yn jtech moquauhiotia, yn inquauhio, yn jtech motzatzilia.

---

1. The corresponding Spanish text specifies: ". . . *que hazian en el postrero dia, del segundo mes, que se dezia tlacaxipeoaliztli.*" In Chapter 3, this month is correctly named Toçoztontli.

2. *ioan moteneva ayacachpixollo* — "*Y se dice 'se siembran sonajas'*" (Garibay, "Relación breve," p. 294). Seler, in *Einige Kapitel*, p. 77, has, for *aiacachpixolo*, "*findet statt das Ausstreuen mit der Rassel.*"

3. "*los vezinos de aquel barrio,*" according to Sahagún's Spanish text.

4. Cf. Sahagún, Jourdanet–Siméon ed., p. 92, n. 3: *tzatzapaltamalli* — "*Peut-être pour* tzatzapatamalli, *de* tzatzapatli, *épine ou herbe piquante, et* atamalli, *sorte de tamal.*"

And at that same time were hidden away the skins;[5] the human skins were placed aside, left there at Yopico.

Any of the youths who had wished to, to whom it had been pleasing, who had wanted to, who had been drunk, had gone wearing [the skins].

And some had made vows to hide away the skins because perchance they were covered with sores, perchance had a scabby skin, or had maladies of the eyes. Though for some this was successful [and] thus they recovered, some did not recover.

Each one of the captors came forth from this home; they left; they went wearing the [captive's] skin. Paper streamers went upon their shoulders and upon the calves of their legs.

And as they went, they went jumping, they went stinking; they went in a group. So did they stink [that the stench] verily wounded the head. It could not be endured. There was holding of the nose when they were met, when they went among people.

And the skins were in pieces; they crackled; they were hard. And some just carried them in their arms in baskets, those which were completely dried hard, those which were decayed, those which were as stiff as a board.

And the captors came in lead of the *tototecti*. They went with their incense ladles, each with his incense ladle. They went with their gifts tied up in bundles: capes perchance painted with designs, or else brown ones[6] or crimson ones, or in two colors diagonally divided, or with the border striped with feathers. They had feathers striping the edge; they had feathers surrounding the edge.

And when there had been arriving at the place where the skins were hidden away, on the top of the Temple of Yopitli, Yopitli's temple, one dedicated [incense] to the four directions; the captors offered incense; they raised their incense ladles [to the sky]; they shook them.

And those who stood wearing the skins then took them off, stood divested [of them]. And when they had drawn off the skins, they cast them down, they threw them into a cave. And the captor went down to the bottom [of the temple pyramid]; he quickly left, he quickly deposited the coals in the fire basin.

And those who had gone to dispose of the skins which they had gone about wearing washed their

Auh çan no iquac eoatlatilo, onmotlatia, onmocacaoa, yn jmeoaio tlaca, vmpa iopico

onaactiuj: in çaço aqujn connequja, conmonectiaia, ontlaeleujaia in mihivintia telpopochti.

Auh cequjntin ic monetoltia, yn eoatlatizque: ipampa aço papalanja, aço çaçaoati, anoço ixcocoia: tel in aca, ipanti, ie pati, in aca amo pati:

ceceiaca inchan in tlamanjme oalpeoa, oaleoa conmaqujtiuj in eoatl, amateteujtl, ymacolpan mamãtiuh, yoan in tlanitzco.

Auh ynic vih, chocholotiuj, hiaxtiuj, centlalli mantiuh, ynjc yiaque, vel tetzonujtec, aisnamjquiztli: çan neiacapacholo ynjc namjco, ynic tetla qujça.

Auh yn eoatl, ocototzauh, ocacalachoac, oquaoac: auh in cequj ça chiqujuhtica qujnapaloa, yn oueltepioac, yn oquelochauh, oquappitzoac.

Auh in tlamanjme, qujniacantiuj in tototecti, intletlema, intletlema ietiuh: qujmoolpilitiuj yn innetlauhtil, tilmatli, aço tlacujlolli, anoço camopalli, anoço nochpalli, anoço nacazminquj, anoço teniujoaoanquj, yhujtenoaoanquj, yhujtentlaiaoalo.

Auh yn oaxioac, yn eoatlatiloian, yn icpac teucalli iopitli, iopiteucalli: nauhcampa ceceiaca ontlaiiaoaia, in tlamanjme ontlenamacaia, conjiaoa yn jntlema, conujujxoa.

Auh yn onacticac eoatl, njman mototoma, mototonticac: yn oqujoalcopin eoatl, contlaça ica onmaiauj yn oztoc. Auh in tlamanj, oaltemo tlatzãtla, qujoalcauhtiqujça, qujoaltentiqujça, tlehquazco in tecolli.

Auh yn oqujcaoato eoatl, yn onmaqujtiuja, amo

---

5. *eoatlatilo*: Seler, in *Einige Kapitel*, p. 78, uses the term *das Vergraben*; Garibay ("Relación breve," p. 295) has, for *yoan mitoaya hevatlatillo*, "y se llamaba, 'se ocultan las pieles'"; the corresponding Spanish text of Sahagún reads, "*escondian en alguna cueua*."

6. *camopalli*: cf. Dibble and Anderson, *Book XI*, p. 244.

faces not with water but rubbed their faces with flour, with cornmeal. They each scrubbed their faces; they used flour on their faces.

They left to be bathed there at the temple in their bathing place. They did not scrub each of them; they just struck them, they slapped them. [The sound] was like the breaking of ocean waves. Thus did the grease diminish; thus it could come to an end. And also it was when there was washing of the hair. The captor washed out the dirt; he used *amolli* [soap].[7]

For while they had fasted for their captives, they had never bathed themselves. They had soiled themselves as the twenty days had passed, together with those of their household who had never bathed themselves. They washed the heads of all; they soaped themselves. Hence it was said: "There is the washing of the hair," or, "There is the washing away of the filth," so had they soiled themselves.

And thereafter the owner of the captive set up, put in place in the courtyard [of his house] a woven twig ball[8] on three feet; it had little feet. On it he placed each of the paper adornments with which had been adorned the Totec [when he died].[9]

And from here he took out a man pleasing to look upon, acceptable, strong. Once again he was adorned [with the paper vestments of Xipe]. In them he took after people; he dispersed them; the man kept vexing them. He ran; he went sheltering himself under his shield; he went rattling his rattle board. They cried out at him; they chased him, stoning him; they pelted him with stones; they attacked him with stones.

He frightened everyone. When they dispersed, they said: "Now cometh he who hath washed his hair."[10]

And if he captured someone, if he quickly seized someone, he despoiled him, he ran off with his cape. However many capes he took from people, he carried them to the captor's house. In the courtyard on the ground he kept beating the capes.

Thereupon the captor set up his "pole of the flaying of men" in the courtyard; it betokened that this man [the captor] had flayed a captive.

And also, when he had done this, he suspended

mixamja atica, çan iotextli, tlaoltextli, inic onmixxaxaqualooa, ynic onmjxmamatiloa, mixiotexuja:

vncã oneoa, in teupan, ynic maltitiuh, yn innealtiaia, amo qujnmamatilooaia, çan qujntzotzona, qujntlatlatzinja, iuhqujn tlatlatzcatimanj, ic poujia, ic vel qujça in chiaoaliztli. Auh no yquac, netzonpaco in tlamanj, motzopaca, mamouja:

ipampa inic oquinneçaujlique, yn inmaloa, aic omaltique, omotzoiotique, inic oquiz cempoalilhujtl: cenvetzi yn inchantlaca, yn aic omaltique, qujnmuchiquacmaltia, mamoujia: ic mjtoa netzõpaco, anoço netzopaco, ynjc omotzoiotique:

auh çatepan itoalco, qujquetza in male, qujtlalia quauhtzontapaiolli, ey icxi, tzicujlicxe, ytech qujtlatlalia: yn jamatlatquj, ynjc omochichioaia totec.

Auh vncan conana ce tlacatl tlaqualittalli, tlauelittalli chicaoac: ie no ceppa ie ic muchichioaia, ipan tetotoca, tececenmana, tlacatl qujcocomonja, motlaloa mochimalcaltitiuh, qujcacalatztiuh ychicaoaz qujcaoatztiuj, qujtetoca, q'tepachotiuj, qujtecicali:

muchi tlacatl qujmauhtia, ipan macauj: qujtoa, Ie uitz tetzompacquj:

auh intla aca cana, intla aca qujcujtiuetzi, qujpepetlaoa, qujtlatlalochtia yn jtilma: in quezquj qujtecujlia tilmatli, ychan concaoa in tlamanj, itoalnepantla tlalli ic qujujujtequj in tilmatli.

Çatepan itoalco qujquetza, itlacaxipeoalizquauh, in tlamanj: ic qujnextia, yno ce tlacatl quixipeuh malli.

Auh yoan yn iquac y, tlaacopiloaia: auh ynaca oc

7. *amolli: ibid.*, p. 133.

8. Corresponding Spanish text: "*vn globo redondo, hecho de petate.*"

9. *Ibid.*: "*ponia todos los papeles, con que se auia adereçado, el captiuo quando murio.*"

10. Cf. Sahagún, Jourdanet–Siméon ed., p. 93, n. 1: *tetzompacqui* — "*C'est-à-dire que réjouit* (paqui) *le seigneur, le maître* (tzontli, *en composition* tetzon, *que s'emploie métaphoriquement pour dire: noble d'une haute famille*)." This would imply a double entendre.

[from it his trophy]; but its [remaining] flesh he first removed from the captive's thigh bone,[11] and from it he hung the sleeveless knotted cord jacket [and] a small spray of heron feathers.

And he wrapped the thigh bone thoroughly in paper; he provided it a mask; and this was called the god-captive.[12]

And when he had hung it up, he summoned [his friends and his kin] to a feast. There was eating; there was drinking. The old men [and] the old women became intoxicated.

And also a man decked himself in the captor's insignia. There was much contentment; he leapt about. Reeds were laid out. The old men of the *calpulli* gathered to sing for him.

And he offered white pulque in various gourds. He kept menacing it.

Afterwards it was as if he shot it. Then he drank it.

And when he had drunk it, then he also had it taken elsewhere. He did similarly in a third place; similarly in a fourth place.

Here they finished when he had done similarly in all places. It was done in no more than one day.

But song did not end in the song house until they went ending when it was [the feast of] Uey toçoztli.

conchololtiaia, yn iqueztepol malli: yoan mecaxi-colli, aztapatlactontli itech pilcac.

Auh in queztepolli, amatica qujqujqujmiloaia, qujxaiacatiaia: auh ynjn motocaiotiaia, malteutl.

Auh yn jquac tlaacopiloa, tecoanotzaia, tlatla-qualo, atlioa, in ueuetque, ylamatzitzin, tlaoana.

Auh no ce tlacatl ic muchichioa, yn jtlauiz tlamanj haauja, chocholoa. motelimana, qujcujcatitoque cal-puluëuetque.

Auh izqujatecontica qujmana tiçavctli, contlatla-iehecalhuja:
çatepan iuhqujnma conmjna, njman ic conj:

auh yn oconjc, ie no cecnj coniquanjlia, çan no iuh conchioa, çan ie no iuh qujchioa, ynjc excan, çan no yuj, ynic nauhcan:
vncan ontlamj iça ieh no iuh qujchioaia yn izquj-tlamantli: ça uel cemilhujtl, in muchioaia.

Auh in cujcatl, amo mocaoaia in cujcacali, ix-qujchica tlamjtiuh, yn ipan vey Toçoztli.

---

11. Sahagún's Spanish text suggests that the thigh bone was thus suspended. Seler, in *Einige Kapitel*, p. 81, has "trophy."
12. *Gefangenenfetisch*, in *ibid*.

Twenty-third Chapter, which telleth of the feast day and of the honors which they performed during all the days of the fourth month, which was known as Uey toçoztli.[1]

This [feast of] Uey toçoztli was thus celebrated: to begin with, for four days there was fasting in each person's home. [There] the young men set up the sedges, covered with blood, bloodied, sprinkled with blood, everywhere [in the houses].

They arranged them all in rows in each one's house. They offered the sedges,[2] erected them, set them up carefully before their gods. They injured the [white] bases, they bruised them, they cut the bases; there they rubbed in the blood.[3]

And any young man, quite of his own will, drew blood from his shanks or from his ears.

And where there were riches, where there was prosperity, in the houses of the lords, the leaders, the constables, the merchants, [the youths] laid out a bed of fir branches[4] for the sedge. There were balls of grass with designs, with the edges interlaced. In the middle of these they placed maguey thorns;[5] these they set [on the balls of grass]. They also were bloodied, sprinkled with blood. It was at eventide, when still a little sun [shone], when the sun had not yet entered his house, that they made their offerings.

And at night the women made *atole*, perchance a thick, white *atole*,[6] or an *atole* made of a dough of maize softened with lime, or a fruit *atole*. This *atole* was known as *aquetzalli*.

Thereupon they each swept their *calpulcos*. And when they had swept, then they poured the *atole* into various gourd vessels.

Indeed it spread shining,[7] it spread scintillating; it

Jnic cēpoualli omei capitulo, ytechpa tlatoa in ilhujtl: yoan in tlamauiztililiztli, in qujchioaia, yn jpan ic cemilhujtl, yc nauj metztli: in mitoaia vey toçoztli.

Inin vey toçoztli, ynic muchioaia, oc achtopa naujlhujtl neçaoalo, in techachan: qujquequetza telpopochti tolpactli, tlaehezujlli, heezço, tlaezçotilli noujã:

qujcentzacutimanca, in techacha, ymixpan qujmamanaia, qujquequetzaia, qujtitilquetzaia, yn jnteuoan in tolpactli, qujtzinichpeloa qujtacaloa, qujtzinixcoloa, vncan conalaoa in eztli.

Auh in eztli, çan teiollotlama, yn aqujn telpuchtli, itech qujqujxtiaia, ytlanitzco, anoço ynacaztitech.

Auh in necujltonoloia, in netlacamachoia: yn aço tetecuti, teiacanque, achcacauhti, puchteca, yn inchachan cacxoiatema, in tolpatlactli, çacatapaiolli, tlatenvimololli, tlatenxinepanolli: tlanepantla qujtlalia: vitztli, itech qujmamana no tlaezujlli, tlaezçotilli teutlacpa, oc achiton tonatiuh, iquac yn aiamo vncalaquj tonatiuh, in qujmamanaia.

Auh in ioaltica, yn oqujchiuhque cioa atolli: aço quauhnexatolli, anoço nextamalatolli, anoço xocoatolli: injn atolli moteneoa, aquetzalli:

njman ie ic tlatlachpana yn jncalpulco. Auh yn otlachpanque njmã ie ic qujteteca in atolli, izqujatecomac,

vel pepeiontimanj, pepetlantimanj, totontlapetztic,

---

1. Great Vigil (*Gran Velada*), according to Garibay ("Relación breve," p. 296). Durán (*Historia*, Vol. II, pp. 273, 276) refers to Uey toçoztli as *gran punzada* and to Toçoztontli as *"punzadurilla pequeña . . . cosilla pasada con alguna cosa de una parte á otra."*

2. In the *Real Palacio MS* the text reads *tolpatlactli*. For a description see Dibble and Anderson, *Book XI*, p. 195, where it is identified as *Cyperus* sp.

3. Corresponding Spanish text: *"ensangrentada, la parte de abaxo, donde tiene la blācura, con sangre de las orejas, o de las piernas."*

4. *cacxoiatema* (der. *acxoyatl* and *tema*): Garibay equates *acxoyatl* with *oyametl* in Sahagún, Garibay ed., Vol. IV, p. 320. See the description of *oyametl* in Dibble and Anderson, *Book XI*, p. 107, where it is identified as *Abies religiosa* (H. B. K.) Schlecht and Cham. In the corresponding Spanish text, Sahagún gives: *"vnos ramos que se llaman acxoiatl."*

5. Sahagún consistently translates *vitztli* as *"punta de maguey."* *Metl* (maguey) is the "generic term for agaves and other plants of similar appearance"; *Agave atrovirens* Karw. is the most important species (Robert L. Dressler, "The Pre–Columbian Cultivated Plants of Mexico," *Botanical Museum Leaflets*, Harvard University, Vol. 16, No. 6, 1953, p. 120).

6. *quauhnexatolli*: Sahagún, Garibay ed., Vol. II, p. 307: "*quauhnexatolli, que es hecho con harina muy espesa y muy blanca, hecho con* tequixquitl." Seler, *Einige Kapitel*, p. 84, specifies that the grains of maize were *"mit Pottasche gekochten."*

7. The *Real Palacio MS* adds *pepexōtymani* — it spread filled to the brim.

was gleaming with heat; its vapor diffused. And when it had cooled, when it was cold, when it had thickened, when it lay in place, it spread contracting, it spread quivering.

And when day broke, the young men [and] the priests walked everywhere; they walked to all places; they went from one dwelling to another; they went taking all the roads to the houses. Also the priests recognized only their own offering-places. One might not join in, when the gifts were made, when they asked alms.

But if they met one another, if they joined in, there was ill-feeling over it, there was dislike because of it, there was continued wrangling over it.

The youths took [their gifts] to the young men's house; there they sampled them.

And the priests carried [theirs] to the *calmecacs*.

Then they departed to their fields,[8] to get Cinteotl. In as many places as lay their fields, from each field, from each they went to take a stalk of green maize.[9]

And from the cleared fields they took only large maguey roots.[10] They carried them hence to their homes.

They decked their maize gods with flowers; they set them up in each *calpulco*. Then they arrayed them; they laid offerings for them.

And before them they laid out five fast foods; they laid them in a basket. And upon it went standing a hard-baked frog — hard, stiff,[11] its face painted blue, a woman's skirt about its hind quarters. And they laid down a basket of pinole with beans [and] toasted maize.

And they cut a section of reed; there they filled it, they crammed it with everything [which] lay before Cinteotl. They took a very little, a small amount, a tiny bit from everywhere. They let the frog carry it on its back.[12]

And when this was done, it was called *calonoac*, "there hath been resting in the houses," because it was only in the houses, only in each person's house, that honors were paid the maize gods.

And after sundown they left each of [the foods] there at Cinteopan, the Temple of Chicome coatl.

hypotoc quiztimanj: auh yn oceuh, yn oitztix, yn otetzaoac, yn omotlali, hi tzotzoliuhtimanj, ioiolcatimanj.

Auh yn otlathujc, in telpopochti in tlamacazque, noujian nemj, cencol nemj, tecalpanoa, qujcenocujtiuj in calli, no iehoantin yn tlamacazque: çan intlatlamanaia tlamattiuj, amo aca vel monepanoaia, ynic motlaueuenjaia, ynic motlaeujaia.

Auh intla monamjquja, intla monepanoa, ic motlauelia, ic motlauelitta, ic mihixnamiquj:

in telpopochti, telpochcali qujtquj, vmpa qujpaloa.

Auh in tlamacazque, calmecac qujtquj:

njman ic vmpeoa, yn jnmjlpan, cinteuanazque, yn izqujcan manj inmil, yn itech, yn ipan cecentetl milli, cecen cantiuj in toctli.

Auh in tlaxinmjlpan, çã mecoatl in conana, qujoalitquj, yn inchachan:

qujnxoxochiotia yn jncinteuoan, in cacalpulco qujquetza: vncan qujntlaquentia, qujntlamanjlia:

tlacatlaqualli ymixpan qujmanaia macujltetl, acaquauhcaxtica conmana: auh ipan icatiuh cujiatlaoatzalli, tepioacquj, quappitztic, tlaixtexoujlli. qujtzincuetia: yoan cen chiqujujtl pinolli, yoan eeio izqujtl conmana.

Auh cem ixtli qujtequj acatl vncan qujtemjtia, qujtentiquetza, yn izqujtlamantli, ixpan onoc cinteutl: tepitoton, tepizcantoton, achipipil, noujiampa qujcuj, qujmamaltia in cujatl.

Auh yn iquac y, moteneoa calonooac, cali onooac: iehica ca çan cali çan techachan in mauiztililoia cicinteu.

Auh in ie teutlac, vmpa qujmoncacaoa, cinteupan yn jteupan chicome coatl: vmpa qujnamoc, ic neaujl-

---

8. *ompepeva* in *Real Palacio MS.*

9. "*cañas de mahiz*" in corresponding Spanish text. Garibay ("Relación breve," p. 296) translates the term as *mata de maiz*; Molina, *Vocabulario*, as "*porreta o mata de mayz antes de q̃ espigue.*"

10. "*otras yeruas, que llamauan mecoatl*" in corresponding Spanish text. Orozco y Berra, *Historia antigua*, Vol. I, p. 330, referring to the maguey, says: "*Las raíces gruesas mecoatl, seruían de jabon.*"

11. Corresponding Spanish text: "*ponjan comjda delante del, desta ymagen, cinco chiqujujtes, con sus tortillas: y encima de cada chiqujujtl, vna rana asada, de cierta manera guisada.*"

12. Corresponding Spanish text: "*ponjan aquel cañuto sobre las espaldas de la rana, como que le lleuaua a cuestas.*"

There they pilfered them. There was merry-making over it; there was the taking of a belligerent attitude by each one; there was striking, there was whacking.[13] It was said: "There is the scattering of people like seeds."

And furthermore, they bore to Cinteopan, the Temple of Chicome coatl, the maize which was to be seed. They had young girls carry it on their backs.

Some [of the girls] had a long lock of hair on one side,[14] some had long hair, some already had hair wound about the head.[15] They bound the cobs of maize in groups of seven; these were the clusters [of cobs of maize]. They wrapped them in paper which was reddened; they painted them with liquid rubber; and they sprinkled on them drops of liquid rubber.

And they pasted the young girls' arms and legs with red feathers, and they painted their faces; on each they stuck two [circles] of tar, which were flecked with iron pyrites.[16] On both sides, on their cheeks, they had iron pyrites.

Thereupon they accompanied the young girls as they carried on their backs the dried maize, also called Cinteotl. They went going before them; they went scattering them; they went surrounding them. All faces were toward them. [But] no one might look at them, look at any one of them; no one joked with them.

And if someone joked with one of them, they chid him. One said to him:

"He with the occipital tuft of hair can speak! Canst thou talk? Be thou already concerned over how thy tuft of hair will fall off, thou with the little tuft of hair.[17] It is an evil-smelling tuft of hair, it is a stinking tuft of hair. Art thou not just a woman like me? Nowhere hath thy excrement been burned!" [18]

Some turned on her; they said:

"It is well. I am just going. I know. It is not true; it is not like that. Thou hast conferred a favor. So also wilt thou be. Anoint thy stomach with mud;

tilo, ic neiaiaotlalo, ic neujujteco, ic netlatlatzujteco, mjtoa tepixolo.

Auh no yoan, in cintli, xinachtli iez: vmpa conitquja, cinteupan, yn iteupan chicome coatl, qujnmamaltia ichpupuchti:

yn aca atzotzocoltone, yn aca tzonqueme, yn aca ie omaxtlauh: chichicoomolotl in qujilpia, iehoatl yn ocholli catca, camaquentia, tlauhio, colxaoa: yoan conolchichipitza.

Auh in ichpopuchti, tlapaliujtica qujnpotonja, in inmac, ymicxic, yoã qujnxaoaia, ovme qujnpilhuja chapopotli apetztzo, tlaapetzujlli, tlaapetziotilli: necoccampa incamatepa.

Niman ie ic qujnujca yn ichpopuchti, qujmamatiuj in cintli, no cinteutl motocaiotiaia: ymixpã hicatiuj, qujntepeuitiuj, qujmololhujtiuj, cemixtli invic: aiac in maca qujmjtta, qujncecemjtta, aiac qujncamanalhuja.

Auh intla aca tecamanalhuja, qujoalaoa qujoalilhuja:

no uellatoa in cuexpalle, vel teh titlatoa? ma ie ic xitlaocuia, quen uetziz in mocuexpal, cuexpaltone? cuexpaliiac, cuexpalpoto, amo çan tinocioapo? acan motlachinauja mocujtl.

Cequjntin quioalcuepaia, qujtoaia
ca ie qualli, ça onjia, ie nehoatl, nicmati, haçanelli, haçayuj, otitlacneli ca no te tiez: xonmitiçoqujuj, xonmjtichichiquj, ximocximalina, tlalli ic ximoujte-

---

13. Corresponding Spanish text: "alli andauan a la rebatina con ello, y lo comjan todo."

14. "Atzotzocolli, vel ahamoxtli. cabello largo que dexan a vn lado de la cabeça a las moças quando las tresquilan." Molina, Vocabulario.

15. omaxtlauh (der. axtlaualli): in ibid. (Spanish–Nahuatl section), "Cabellos compuestos y rodeados a la cabeça de la muger."

16. Corresponding Spanish text: "ponjanlas en la cara pez derretida que ellos llaman chapopotli, salpicada con marcaxita."

17. Corresponding Spanish text: "piensa en como hagas, alguna azaña, para que te quiten la bedija de los cabellos, que traes en el cocote, en señal de cobarde, y de hombre para poco, cobarde bisoño." For a detailed explanation of the meaning of cuexpalle see Sahagún, Garibay ed., Vol. I, p. 188, and Vol. II, pp. 330, 331.

18. Corresponding Spanish text: "tan muger eres como yo, nunca has salido detras del huego." Seler, Einige Kapitel, p. 87, n. 2, suggests that this may refer to a puberty ceremony.

scratch thy stomach; twist one leg about the other; [fall] striking thyself on the ground; fall stinking on the ground. There is a stone, a hard stone; strike thy face with the stone, strike thy face with it; make the blood spurt forth. Scratch thy nose with the stone, or bore a hole with a fire drill into thy windpipe; thou wilt spit [through] there. Just go away; just be an old maid."

But although the words of us men were like this, they were verily only vain, they were verily only weak words. For verily thus the women could torment [young men] into war; thus they moved them; thus the women could prod them into battle.

Indeed we men said:

"Bloody, painful are the words of the women; bloody, penetrating are women's words. Indeed we have gone; we have said that we shall not live. Perhaps we shall merit something, O our friend."

And when [the young girls] went carrying upon their backs the maize gods, as they took them to the Temple of Chicome coatl, [the ears of maize] were made hearts. They became their granary hearts. They laid them in the granary.[19]

And when the seed was sown, when it was the time for planting, this they sowed. They made seed of it; they scattered it as seed.

And they established, they celebrated this feast for Chicome coatl.

They formed her image as a woman. They said: "Yea, verily, this one is our sustenance"; that is to say, indeed truly she is our flesh, our livelihood; through her we live; she is our strength. If she were not, we should indeed die of hunger.

For he who eateth no tortillas indeed then fainteth; he falleth down: he droppeth quickly; there is a twittering as of birds in his ears; darkness descendeth upon him.

And, it was said, it was indeed this Chicome coatl who made all our food — white maize, yellow maize, green maize shoots,[20] black maize, black and brown mixed, variously hued; large and wide; round and ball-like; slender maize, thin; long maize; speckled red and white maize as if striped with blood, painted with blood — then the coarse, brown maize (its appearance is as if tawny); popcorn; the after-fruit; double ears; rough ears; and maturing green maize; the small ears of maize beside the main ear; the ripened green maize.

quj, tlalli xiqujpototztiuetzi: vmpa ca tetlhon, techachalli, ic xonmixtetzotzona, ic xonmjxtzotzona, eztli tiqualaacuchoz: ximoiacatechichiquj, noce xonmococotlecoionj, vmpa tioalchichichaz, çan xinemj, ça tiuhquj xinemj.

Auh maciuj yn iuhquj hin intlatol muchioaia toqujchti, ca ça nenpanca, ca ça in toneuhcatlatol: ca uel ic qujmontzintopeoaia in cioa iaoc, ic teioltoneoa, ic teioleoa, ic teiollo tzicujnia in cioa, in iaoc.

Ca qujttoa, in toqujchti

eço tecoco, yn jntlatol cioa, eço teitic acic in cioatlatolli, ca otiiaque, ça otiqujtoque, yn ahtinemizque: aço itla tomaceoal tocnjuhtze.

Auh in qujmamatiuj in cicinteteuh, yn oqujtquja iteupan chicome coatl, tlaiollotl muchioa: incuezcomaiollo muchioa, cuezcomac contema.

Auh yn iquac totoco, in ie toquizpã iehoatl qujtocaia qujxinachioaia, qujxinachioa.

Auh injn qujlhujtlaltia, qujlhujchiujlia in chicome coatl:

iuhqujn cioatl qujtlaliaia ixiptla. Qujtoaia, ca uel iehoatl in tonacaiutl: iuhq'nma qujtoznequj, ca nel tonacaio, tonenca, ic tiioltinemj, tooapaoaca: intlacamo iehoatl, ca tapizmiquizque.

Ca yn aqujn, atle qujqua tlaxcalli, ca njman çotlaoa, vetzi, meciuhtiuetzi, ynacaz, yicaoaca, tlaioalli ipã momana:

yoan mjtoa, ca in iehoatl chicome coatl, ca qujchioa yn ixqujch tonacaiutl: in iztac tlaolli, in coztic tlaolli, in xiuhtoctli, yiaujtl, yiauhnenel, iauhcacalquj, tlaolpatlachtli, in totolontic, in tlaolpicilli, tlaolpitzaoac: in xochicintli, ynjn iuhqujn ezoaoanquj, ezcujcujltic: njman iee in quappachcintli: iuhqujn quappachtli, itlachieliz, momochicintli, in molqujtl, cinmaitl, cintzatzapalli: yoan in xilotl, in cacamatl, in elotl:

---

19. Corresponding Spanish text: "*echauanlos, en el hondon, de la troxe dezian: que era el coraçon de la troxe.*"

20. For a description of the varieties of maize, beans, amaranth, and chía listed, see Dibble and Anderson, *Book XI*, pp. 279–87.

Then the beans — white beans, yellow beans, red beans, quail-colored beans, black beans, flesh-colored beans, fat red beans, wild beans; amaranth, the variety of amaranth called *cocotl*, fine red amaranth seed, [common] red amaranth, black amaranth, bright red or chili-red amaranth, fish amaranth [*michiuauhtli* or *chicalotl*], brilliant black amaranth seed; the bird-seed called *petzicatl*.

And also chía — white chía, black chía, wrinkled chía.

All these things, so they say, all of them they offered to [the goddess]. When it was her feast day they gave her human form; they laid all before her. The old men, those in charge of the *calpulli*, sang for her; they beheaded quail for her.

And her adornment [was thus]: she was anointed all in red — completely red on her arms, her legs, her face. All her paper crown was covered completely with red ochre; her embroidered shift also was red; her skirt was a bed covering. The ruler's shield was painted with designs, embellished in red. She was carrying her double ear of maize in either hand.

Thus ended [the festival of] Uey toçoztli, and thus ended, thus passed the vigil songs. And this was the time that there began the winding dance, the dance with song. It ended there at the time of [the feast of] Toxcatl.

njman iehoatl in etl, yn iztac etl, ecoztli, echichilli, çoletl, tliletl, aqujletl, aiecotli, quavecoc, oauhtli, cocotl, tlapalhoauhtli, xochioauhtli, tliloauhtli, teuoauhtli, anoço chichiloauhtli, mjchioauhtli, chicalotl, tezcaoauhtli, petzicatl:

no yoan in chien, iztac chien, tliltic chien, chiantzotzol.

Jn ixqujch y, iuh qujtoa, ca moch iehoatl, qujtemaca: in iquac ilhujuh, qujtlacatilia, muchi ixpan qujmanaia, qujcujcatia in veuetque, calpuleque: qujtlacotonjlia.

Auh yn jnechichioal motlaoçaia, muchi tlauhio, centlauhio, yn jmac, yn icxic, yn jxco: muchi tlacemaqujlli, tlaujtl yn jamacal yn ivipil tlamachio, no tlauhio, yn icue cacamoliuhquj, tlatolchimali cujlolli, tlauhpoiaoac, ycinma nenecoccampa qujtqujtica.

ic ontlamj, in vey toçoztli: yoan ic vntlamj ic qujça, in toçozcujcatl. Auh iquac vmpeoa in necocololo, cujcoanolo: vmpa vntlami, yn ipan toxcatl.

65

Sixth [Twenty-fourth] Chapter, which relateth the feast and the debt-paying which was celebrated during all the days of the fifth month, which was called Toxcatl.[1]

In the time of Toxcatl there was Tezcatlipoca's great festival. At that time he was given human form; at that time he was set up. Wherefore died his impersonator, who for one year had lived [as Tezcatlipoca].

And at that time was appointed his [new] impersonator, who would again live [as Tezcatlipoca] for a year.

For many impersonators were living, whom stewards in various places guarded; whom they maintained. About ten [so] lived. These were indeed selected captives; they were selected when captives were taken. There one was chosen if he was seen to be suitable, if he was fair of body. Then he was taken. They entrusted these to stewards. But one destined to be a slave, him the captor slew.

Indeed he who was thus chosen was of fair countenance, of good understanding, quick, of clean body, slender, reed-like, long and thin, like a stout cane, like a stone column all over, not of overfed body, not corpulent, nor very small, nor exceedingly tall.

Indeed it became his defect if someone were exceedingly tall. The women said to him "Tall fellow; tree-shaker; star-gatherer." He who was chosen as impersonator was without defects.

He was like something smoothed, like a tomato, like a pebble, as if sculptured in wood; he was not curly-haired, curly-headed; his hair was indeed straight, his hair was long. He was not rough of

Jnic chiquacen capitulo, ytechpa tlatoa, yn ilhujtl, yoã in nextlaoalli, in muchioaia, yn ipan ic cemjlhujtl ic macujlli metztli, in mitoaia, Toxcatl.

In ipan in toxcatl, vel yueiilhujuh catca in tezcatlipuca: vncan tlacatia, vncan moquetzaia: ipampa ca vncan miquja, yn jxiptla in cexiuhtica onen.

Yoan iquac njman noce vncan mixquetzaia yxiptla, yn oc no cexiuhtica nemiz:

ca miequjntin in nemja, teixiptlaoan in quinpia, in qujnnemjtiaia cacalpixque: aço quẽ matlactli in nemj: y iehoantin y, ca mamalti tlaqujxtilti qujxtiloia, yn iquac oalaxitiloia mamalti, vncan pepenaloia, intla aca ce oqualittoc, in qualli ynacaio: njman onano, qujmonpialtiaia in calpixque: auh iece ipan qujoalixquetzaia tlacotli, iehoatl qujmictia in tlamanj:

ca iehoatl ic pepenalo, in qualli itlachieliz, in mjmatquj, in mjmatinj, in chipaoac ynacaio, cujllotic, acatic, piaztic, iuhqujn otlatl, ipanoca temjmjltic, amo tlacaçolnacaio, amo tomaoac, amo no tetepiton amo no cenca quauhtic:

ca yiaioca muchioa, yn aqujn cenca quauhtic, qujlhuja in cioa: quauhtitin, quauhchachalan, citlalmaololo: yn aqujn pepenaloia, in teixiptla, atle yiaioca:

iuhqujn tlachictli, iuhqujn tomatl, iuhqujn telolotli, iuhqujn, quaujtl tlaxixintli, amo quacocototztic, quacolochtic, vel tzõmelaoac, tzompiaztic, amo ixquachachaquachtic, amo ixquatotomonquj, amo ix-

1. Of this name, Orozco y Berra, *Historia antigua*, Vol. II, p. 37, writes: "Toxcatl, Tepopochuiliztli. *De todas las interpretaciones dadas á la palabra* toxcatl, *la más genuina, á nuestro entender, es la dada por Gama, tomada del P. Acosta: 'una soga gruesa torcida de sartales de maíz tostado.'* "

Clavijero, *Historia antigua*, Vol. III, p. 402, explains that "*La figura del mes quinto es la de una cabeza humana con una cadena debajo, para representar aquellas sartas de maíz tostado que se ponían al cuello, y con las cuales adornaban también al ídolo de Tezcatlipoca, por lo que el mes tomó el nombre Toxcatl*"; and (p. 152) "*unos sacerdotes teñidos de negro y vestidos del traje del ídolo, lo bajaban en unas andas bien aderezadas al pie de la escalera. Los mancebos y vírgenes del templo rodeaban las andas de una cuerda gruesa compuesta de sartas de maíz tostado y ponían al ídolo una sarta al cuello y una guirnalda en la cabeza. A esta cuerda por ser de granos secos y símbolo de la sequedad que pretendían evitar con sus plegarias, llamaron* toxcatl, *el cual nombre se dió por esta ceremonia al mes quinto de que hablamos.*"

Garibay ("Relación breve," p. 298) also suggests as a translation for the name "our dryness, our drought" — "*nuestra secura.*"

Jiménez Moreno, "Primeros memoriales," p. 31, notes: "*Precisamente se llevaban collares de maíz tostado (de allí quizá la idea de 'cosa seca') en esta fiesta* Tózcatl, *pues podría aquí significar lo mismo que* cózcatl (collar). *Pero, siendo ésta fiesta de* Tezcatlipoca *no es improbable que se tenga* Tózcatl *como posible forma arcáica de* Tézcatl ('espejo' *y en ocasiones 'laguna'). En el castellano de México, un espejo se llama también 'luna' y no debe olvidarse que* Tezcatlipoca *era un dios lunar.*"

forehead; he had no pimples on his forehead; he did not have a forehead like a tomato; he did not have a baglike forehead. He was not long-headed; the back of his head was not pointed; his head was not like a carrying net; his head was not bumpy; he was not broad-headed; he was not rectangular-headed; he was not bald; he was not of rounded forehead; he was not of swollen eyelids; he was not of enlarged eyelids; he was not swollen-cheeked; he was not of injured eyes; he was not of injured cheeks; he was not bulging of eye; he was not cloven-chinned; he was not gross-faced; he was not of downcast face; he was not flat-nosed; he did not have a nose with wide nostrils; he was not Roman-nosed; he was not concave-nosed; he was not twisted-nosed, not bent-nosed, not crooked-nosed; but his nose was averagely placed; he was straight-nosed. He was not thick-lipped, he was not gross-lipped, he was not big-lipped,[2] he was not bowl-lipped, he was not large-lipped; he was not a stutterer, he was not ring-tongued, he was not rough-tongued;[3] he did not speak a barbarous language; he did not lisp, he did not speak with a lisp, he was not dumb. He was not buck-toothed, he was not large-toothed, he was not fang-toothed, he was not yellow-toothed, he was not ugly-toothed, he was not rotten-toothed; his teeth were [like] seashells; they lay well; they lay in order; he was not bowl-toothed. Nor was he scarred of eye; he was not poor of vision; he was not small-eyed; he was not scarified of eye; he was not blinded; he was not little-eyed; he was not tiny-eyed; he was not yellow-eyed; he was not hollow-eyed, not sunken-eyed; he was not cup-eyed; he was not round-eyed; he was not tomato-eyed; he was not of pierced eye; he was not of perforated eye; he was not of bruised eyes. He was not scarred of neck; he was not [as if] of choked neck; he was not of lacerated neck, of double chin, of swollen neck. Nor was he large-eared, nor was he long-eared. He was not stiff-necked; he was not twisted-necked; he was not rigid-necked; he was not long-necked; he was not very long-necked; he was not wry-necked; he was not crook-necked. He was not long-handed; he was not one-handed; he was not handless; he was not fat-fingered. He was not emaciated; he was not fat; he was not big-bellied; he was not of protruding navel; he was not of hatchet-shaped navel; he was not of

quaxitontic, amo ixquaxiqujpiltic, amo quametlapiltic, amo cuexcochujtztic, amo quachitatic, amo quapatztic, amo quapatlachtic, amo quaoacaltic, amo quaxoxomalacquj, amo ixquamamalacachtic, amo ixquatolpopoçactic, amo ixquatolmemetlapiltic, amo campoponaztic, amo ixujujlaxtic, amo canujujlaxtic, amo ixpopotztic, amo no camachaloacaltic, amo ixmetlapiltic, amo ixpechtic, amo iacapatztic, amo iacacocoiactic, amo iacaxaxacaltic, amo iacacaxtic, amo iacachittoltic, amo iacaujttoltic, amo iacanecujltic, çan vel icac yn ijac, iacapiaztic, amo tenxipaltotomaoac, amo texipaltotomac, texipaltotomactic, amo tencaxtic, amono tenmetlapiltic: amono eltzatzacquj, amo nenepilchanpuchtic, amo nenepilchacaiultic, amo popoloc, amo tentzitzipi, amo tentzitzipitlatoa, amo tenmjmjcquj, amo tlanpantic, amo tlancujcujtztic, amo coatlane, amo tlancocoztic, amo tlanxoiauhquj, amo tlanpalanquj: iuhqujn tecciztli itlan, vel onoc vipantoc, amo tlancaxtic, amo no ixtitiqujltic, amo ixnacatic, amo ixujtzaltic, amo itztztziqujltic, amo ixpopoiontic, amo ixpipiltic, ixpipiciltic, ixcocoçaltic, amo ixcocomoltic, amo ixatlacomoltic, amo ixcacaxtic, amo ixtotolontic, amo ixtotomatic, amo itztzatzapitztic, amo itztzatzamoltic, amo ixtacaltic, amo quechtitiqujltic, quechmotzoltic, quetztzitziqujltic, quechnacatic quechxixiqujpiltic, amo no nacazpatlactic, amo no nacazvilaxtic, amo quechtiltic, amo quechtepotzotic, amo quechacquj, amo quechujiac, amo quechujtlatztic, amo quechnecujltic, amo quechnenetic: amo maviujtlatztic, amo matzicoltic, amo macuecuetzin, amo mapiltotomactic, amo itiujlaxtic, amo cujtlatoltic, amo cujtlapetztic, amo xicquizquj, amo xictopoltic, amo xiccueio, amo ittitzotzoltic, amo cujtlapechtic, amo tzintopoltic, amo tzincuecuexactic, tzintamalcuecuexac.

2. Read *tēxipaltotomac, tēxipaltotomactic* as in the *Real Palacio MS*.

3. The *Real Palacio MS* adds *popolactic*.

wrinkled stomach; he was not of shrunken stomach. He was not cringing; he was not of hatchet-shaped buttocks; he was not of flabby buttocks; he was not of flabby thighs.

For him who was thus, who had no flaw, who had no [bodily] defects, who had no blemish, who had no mark, who had on him no wart, [no such] small tumor, there was taken the greatest care that he be taught to blow the flute, that he be able to play his whistle; and that at the same time he hold all his flowers and his smoking tube.[4] At the same time he would go playing the flute, he would go sucking [the smoking tube], he would go smelling [the flowers].

So [his flute], his flowers, his smoking tube went together when he followed the road.

And while yet he lived, while yet he was being trained in the home of the steward, before he appeared [in the presence of the people], very great care was taken that he should be very circumspect in his discourse, that he talk graciously, that he greet people agreeably on the road if he met anyone.

For he was indeed much honored when he appeared, when already he was an impersonator. Since he impersonated Titlacauan, he was indeed regarded as our lord. There was the assigning of lordship; he was importuned; he was sighed for; there was bowing before him; the commoners performed the earth-eating ceremony before him.

And if they saw that already his body fattened a little, they made him take brine; with it they thinned him; they thinned him with salt. Thus he became thin; he became firm; his body became hard.

And for one year he [thus] lived; at the time of Toxcatl he appeared [before the people], and at that time died the man who had been impersonator for one year, who had been led along the road, who had waited for one year, who had [thus] passed one year. Just then he went being substituted; one was set in his place [from among] all whom the various stewards were guarding, were maintaining, at the time that [the first impersonator] appeared [before the people].

Thereupon he began his office. He went about playing the flute. By day and by night he followed whatever way he wished.

His eight servitors went following him. Four [of them] had fasted for a year. Their hair was shorn

Jn aqujn iuhquj y, atle itlacauhca, atle yiaioca, atle ytlaciuhca, atle ytlaciuizço, atle ytech ca etzotzocatl, xitomaciuiztli: njmā cenca necujtlaujlo, inic vel momachtiz, yn tlapitzaz: ynic vel qujpitzaz, yujlacapitz: yoan inic vel muchi ipan qujtzitzquiz yxochiuh, yoan yieuh, ipan tlapitztiaz, tlachichintiaz, tlanecutiaz:

iuhqujn centlalli mantiuh yn ixochiuh, yn jyieuh, yn iquac vtli qujtocaia.

Auh in çan oc nemj, in çan oc oapaoalo, yn ichan calpixquj, yn aiamo ixneci, cenca vel necujtlaujloia, ynic vel mjmatiz, ica itlatol, vellatoz, vel tenotza, vel tetlapaloz in vtlica, intla aca qujnamiquiz:

ipampa ca cenca mauiztililoia yn iquac oixnez, in ie teixiptla: ynic ixiptlati Titlacaoan, ca totecujo ipan machoia, netecuiotilo, tlatlauhtilo, yca elciciooa, ixpan nepechteco, ixpan ontlalqua in maceoaltzintli.

Auh intla ie qujtta, in ie achi tomaoa ynacaio, iztaiotl qujltequjtiaia, ic qujquaoatzaia, quiztaioquaoatza, ynic pipinja, tepitzauj, tlalichauj yn jnacaio.

Auh cexiujtl in nemja ipan toxcatl, yn ixnecia: auh iquac miquj ce tlacatl yn oteixiptlatic ce xiujtl, in ce xiujtl, ooallaotlatoctic, in ce xiuitl oqujtlaz, in ce xiujtl ooallaujcac: ça çan ic mopatlatiuja yn ixquetzaloia, yn ixqujchtin qujnpiaia, in qujnnemjtiaia cacalpisque, yn iquac oixnez:

njman ic compeoaltia, yn itequjuh, in tlapitztinemj: cemilhujtl, yoan ceniooal: çan connequja in campa ieh vtli qujtocaz:

qujtocatinemj yn iachoan chicueintin: navin mocexiuhçauhque, moquatexoloxima, moquateçonoa,

4. "*Caña o cañuto de çahumerio, acaietl*," in Molina, *Vocabulario*; "*cañas de humo*" in Sahagún's corresponding Spanish.

as if they were one's pages; their hair was cut; their hair was clipped; they were not clipped smooth like a gourd; they were not clipped bald like a gourd; their heads were not smooth like pots; they did not stick [hair] to the head.

And also there were four constables, masters of youths. They cut their hair similarly; their hair arrangement was similar. It was arranged upright for them on their foreheads.

At this time Moctezuma adorned [the impersonator]; he repeatedly adorned him; he gave him gifts; he arrayed him; he arrayed him with great pomp. He had all costly things placed on him, for verily he took him to be his beloved god. [The impersonator] fasted; hence it was said: "He fasteth in black," [for] he went with his face smoke-black. His head was pasted with feathers, with eagle down. They only covered his hair for him; it fell to his loins.

And when he was attired, he went about with popcorn flowers[5] laid upon his head; they were his crown of flowers. And he was dressed in these same on both sides; they drew them out to his armpits. This was called "the flowery stole."

And from his ears on both sides went hanging curved golden shell pendants.[6] And they fitted [his ears with] ear plugs made of turquoise, turquoise mosaic. And a shell necklace was his necklace. Moreover, his breast ornament was of white seashells.

And then his lip pendant, his slender lip pendant, was of snail shell. And down his back went hanging what was like a cord bag called *icpatoxin*.[7]

Then on both sides, on his upper arms, he placed golden bracelets, and on both sides, on his wrists, he went placing turquoise bracelets taking up almost all his forearms. And he went putting on only his net cape like a fish net of wide mesh with a fringe of brown cotton thread.[8] And his costly breechclout reached to the calves of his legs.

And then he went placing his bells on both sides, on his legs. All gold were the bells, called *oyoalli*.[9] These [he wore] because they went jingling, because they went ringing; so did they resound. And his

motlatetecilhuja, amo maiochiquj, amo maioichiquj, amo moquacoconaloa, amo moquatetzicoa

Auh no naujntin, teachcaoan, tetiachcaoan, çan ie yujn moxima yn iuhca innexin, motlaeoatimanjlia, yn jmjxquac.

Jquac vel qujcencaoa, qujcecencaoa in Motecuçuma, qujtlamamaca, qujchichioa, qujieiecquetza: muchi tlaçotlanquj, yn jtech qujtlalilia: ipampa canel ic ytlaçoteouh ipan qujmati, moçaoa, ic mjtoa motlilçaoa, mixtlilpopotztinenca, moquapotonjaia, quauhtlachcaiotica: çan q'ujaqujliaia yn itzon, ycujtlacaxiuhian vetzia.

Auh yn omocencauh izqujxochitl in icpac contecatinemj, icpacxochiuh: yoan çan ie no ieh in necoccampa ic mapanaia, yciiacacpa qujqujxtiaia: in moteneoa suchineapãtli.

Auh yn jnacaztitech nenecoc pipilcatiujia teucujtlaepcololli: yoan conaqujaia icoiolnacoch, teuxiujtl in tlachioalli, tlaxiuhçalolli: yoan chipolcuzcatl, yn jcuzquj, oc cepa yielpancuzquj iztac cilin.

Auh njman ie yteçacauh, iteçacapiaz tecciztli: auh ycujtlapan pilcatiuh itoca Jcpatoxi, iuhqujn icpaxiqujpilli:

njman ie nenecoc teucujtlamatemecatl contlatlalitiuh in jacolpã, yoan in nenecoc imaquechtlan, xinmaquiztli in contetecatiuh, achi vel qujtlatlamja yn jmatzotzopaz: auh çan ycuechin in qujquentiuh, iuhqujn xoujlmatlatl ic cocoiaoac, tochiacatl ynic tentlaiaoalo: yoan ytlaçomaxtli qujmetztopeoa:

auh njman ie ycoiol nenecoc, icxic in contlalitiuh, muchi teucujtlatl in coiolli, mjtoa oiooalli: iehoatl inic xaxamacatiuh, ynic tzitzilicatiuh, ynic caquizti:

---

5. *Beureria huanita* Hemsley, according to Seler, *Einige Kapitel*, p. 97, n. 1. Cf. also Dibble and Anderson, *Book XI*, p. 202.

6. Corresponding Spanish text: *"como çerçillos de oro."*

7. Corresponding Spanish text: *"lleuaua a las espaldas, un ornamento como bolsa, de vn palmo en quadro de lienço blanco, con sus borlas y flocadura."*

8. Cf. Sahagún, Garibay ed., Vol. II, p. 311. In the corresponding Spanish text, Sahagún refers to *tochomjtl* (rabbit fur), we think mistakenly. *Tochiacatl* (or *tochacatl*), it would appear, is string or thread, while *tochomitl* is a thong of rabbit skin.

9. *oyoalli* (*oyoualli*) can be translated as bell or shell rattle. It is also the name of a shell neck pendant worn by the gods of dance. We follow the corresponding Spanish in our translation.

obsidian sandals had ocelot skin ears. Thus was arrayed he who died after one year.

When Toxcatl went drawing near, when it approached him, when already it went reaching him, first he married; he looked upon a woman; he was married at the time of Uey toçoztli.

And he shed, he put in various places, he abandoned what had been his ornaments in which he had walked about fasting in black. His hair was shorn; he was provided a tuft of hair upon his forehead, like that of a seasoned warrior. They bound it; they wound it round and round. They bound it with [brown cotton thread] called *tochyacatl*; it was tied with a slipknot. And his forked heron feather ornament with a quetzal feather spray they bound to his warrior's hairdressing.[10]

It was for only twenty days that he lived lying with the women, that he lived married to them. The four women in whose company he lived had also lived for a year guarded in the steward's establishment.

The name of the first one was Xochiquetzal; the second was Xilonen; the third was Atlatonan; the fourth was Uixtociuatl.

And when it was already the eve of [the feast of] Toxcatl, still five [days] from it, on the fifth day [from it], five days before the feast of Toxcatl would pass, they began each to sing [and dance].

At this time, in all these days, one knew nothing more of Moctezuma. They who yet had been his companions provided people with food, provided people with favors.[11]

On the first day they sang [and danced] at a place called Tecanman. On the second day it was in the place where was guarded the image of Titlacauan, in the home of him who was the steward who guarded it. On the third day it was at Tepetzinco, in the middle of the lagoon. The fourth time it was at Tepepulco, which is also quite near Tepetzinco.

When they had sung [and danced], thereupon he embarked in a boat. The women went, going with him. They went consoling him; they went encouraging him. The boat proceeded to a place called Aca-

yoan itzcac ocelunacace: yujn in muchichioaia, in iehoatl miquja ce xiujtl:

yn iquac ie oalacitiuh toxcatl, in ie itech ompachiuhtiuh, yn ie itech onacitiuh, achtopa tlapaliuhcatia, cihoatl qujttaia, mocioaoatiaia ipan vey toçoztli.

Auh qujtepeoaia, qujtlatlaliaia, quicaoa, yn jnechichioal ocatca, yn ipan omotlilçauhtinenca, moxima, mjxquatzontia, iuhqujnma iautequjoa, ontlalpia, ontlacuja: ynic ontlalpia, itoca tochiacatl, xittomonjlpitica: yoan yaztaxel, quetzalmjiaoaio, itzotzocol itech qujlpia:

çan cempoalilhujtl in oncioacuchtinemi, yn oncioaoatinemj: naujntin in cioa q'nujcatinenca, no cexiuhtica in pialoia calpixcan:

y ce itoca xochiquetzal, ynjc vme xilone, ynjc ey Atlatona, ynjc nauj, vixtocioatl.

Auh in ie itentla Toxcatl, oc macujltica, tlamacujlti, oqujuh macujlilhujtl qujçaz yn ilhujtl Toxcatl, in peoa cujcujca:

yn iquac y, yn izquilhujtl y, aocmo onmachiztia yn motecuçoma, oc ie ycenujc catca, tetlaqualtia tetlauhtia,

ynic cemilhujtl cujcujca, itocaiocan tecanma: ynjc omjhujtl, vncan in pialoia, in teixiptla in titlacaoan, yn ichã aqujn calpixquj, yn oqujpiaia: ynic eilhujtl tepetzinco, vmpa in anepantla, ynic nappa tepepulco, çan no itlan in tepetzinco.

Yn oncujcujcac njman ie ic onmacalaquja, itlan ietihuj in cioa, qujiollalitiuj, quellaquauhtiuj: vmpa vnqujça, vmpa onatenqujça, vmpa qujmonacana in acalli, ytocaiocan acaqujlpan, anoçe caoaltepec:

---

10. *tzotzocolli:* this warrior's hairdress protrudes over the forehead.

Seler, in *Gesammelte Abhandlungen*, Vol. I, p. 208, states: "*Bei der andern Frisur wurde das Haar über der Stirn hoch in die Höhe gezaust und vom Scheitel ab lang herabfallen gelassen und dort am Nacken mit einem Riemen umwickelt, in den bei festlichen Gelegenheiten ein Federschmuck eingesteckt wurde.*" In Vol. II, p. 521, Seler adds that this hairstyle is adopted by the young warrior after his first military exploit.

11. Corresponding Spanish text: "*el señor se quedaua solo en su casa, y todos los de la corte, les seguian, y se hazian solemnes banquetes, y areytos, con muy ricos ataujos.*"

quilpan or Caualtepec; there it proceeded to the shore; there it landed them.

For here they were left, rather near Tlapitzauhcan. The women then returned. And only they who for the time had become [and] were his servitors went following him while yet he lived.

Thus was it said: when he arrived where [the impersonators of Titlacauan] used to die, [where] a small temple called Tlacochcalco stood, he ascended by himself, he went up of his own free will, to where he was to die. As he was taken up a step, as he passed one [step], there he broke, he shattered his flute, his whistle, etc.

And when he had mounted all the steps, when he had risen to the summit, then the offering priests seized him. They threw him upon his back on the sacrificial stone; then [one of them] cut open his breast; he took his heart from him; he also raised it in dedication to the sun.

For in this manner were all [these] captives slain. But his body they did not roll down; rather, they lowered it. Four men carried it.

And his severed head they strung on the skull rack. Thus he was brought to an end in the adornment in which he died. Thus his life there ended; there they terminated his life when he went to die there at Tlapitzauayan.

And this betokened our life on earth. For he who rejoiced, who possessed riches, who sought, who esteemed our lord's sweetness, his fragrance — richness, prosperity — thus ended in great misery. Indeed it was said: "No one on earth went exhausting happiness, riches, wealth." [12]

And here in Mexico, at the time of Toxcatl, there was made, there was made in human form, [a figure of] Uitzilopochtli here at the Temple of Uitznauac, in its *calpulco.* They set it on the serpent bench.

This serpent bench was hewn of wood as if of serpents. Four lay supported by their tails; their heads were on the four sides.[13]

They kept covering [Uitzilopochtli's] mesquite wood members with fish amaranth dough; his figure was indeed always hewn[14] of mesquite wood, which they covered.

ipampa ca vncan ontecaoaloia, achi ie ytlan in tlapitzauhcan: in cioa vncan oalmocuepa: auh ça iehoã inmatian muchioa, yn jachoan ocatca, yn oqujtocatinenca in iq̃c oc nemj.

Juh mjtoa yn oacic, in vncan mjqujia teucaltontli icaia, itoca tlacochcalco: çan inoma in tleco, çan monomatlecauja, in vmpa mjqujz: in ce tlamamatlatl contlecauja, in ce conpanauja, ce vncan qujxamanja, qujpuztequj yn itlapitzal, yn jvilacapitz, etc.

Auh yn oqujpantlaz, yn izquj tlamamatlatl, yn opanuetzito tlacpac: njman qujcujtiuetzi in tlamacazque, conaquetztiteca in techcac: njman ie ic queltetequj, conanilia yn iiollo, no conjaujlia in tonatiuh:

ca çan muchi tlacatl iuh mictiloia, in mamalti. Auh yn jtlac amo qujoalmjmjlooaia, çan qujoaltemoujaia, qujnauhcaujaia:

auh yn jtzontencõ, tzompatitech conquauhço, iuh tlantica, yn iuh ipã omjc ynechichioal: ic vmpa ontlamj yn jnemjliz, vmpa contzonqujstia yn jnemjliz, yn vmpa omjqujto Tlapitzaoaian.

Auh ynjn ca qujnezcaiotia, in tlalticpac tonemjliz: ca in aqujn paquj, motlamachtia, in qujtta in qujmaujçoa in itzopelica, yn jaujiaca in totecujo, in necujltonolli, in netlamachtilli: injc tzonqujça vey netolinjliztli: ca iuh mjtoa, aiac qujtlamitiuh in tlalticpac, paqujliztli, necujltonolli, netlamachtilli.

Auh yn nican mexico, yn iquac Toxcatl: motlalia motlacatlalia, in Vitzilopuchtli: vncan in vitznaoac, teucalco, ycalpulco: coatlapechco contlalia:

ynjn coatlapechtli, quaujtl in tlaxixintli, iuhqujn cocoa, naujntin in motzinnamjctoque: nauhcampa caca yn jntzontecon:

mjchioauhtzoalli, ynjc qujpepechoaia, yn jmizqujo, ca mizqujquaujtl, in tlaxintli, yn ixiptla muchipa catca, yn oqujpepechoque:

---

12. This is a reference to the characteristics of Tezcatlipoca. Cf. Charles E. Dibble and Arthur J. O. Anderson, *Florentine Codex, Book VI, Rhetoric and Moral Philosophy* (Santa Fe: School of American Research and University of Utah, 1969; hereafter referred to as Dibble and Anderson, *Book VI*), pp. 7–10.

13. Corresponding Spanish text: "*hazian para ponerla un tablado, los maderos del, eran labrados, como culebras, y tenjan las cabeças, a todas quatro partes, del tablado contrapuestas, las vnas a las otras de manera que a todas quatro partes auja colas y cabeças.*"

14. *tlaxintli: tlaxixintli* in the *Real Palacio MS.*

Thereupon they gave him his various articles of raiment; they put on him his sleeveless jacket painted with representations of human limbs.

And over that they covered it,[15] over that they clothed it in a cape of nettles. It was like a netted cape.

And they fitted on him his paper headdress, made with feathers, called *anecuyotl*. Above his feather headdress stood a flint knife, also made of feathers, half of it blood-colored.

Then they dressed him in a godly cape. It was costly; it was all made, embellished, designed with precious feathers; it was provided with the red-eye border; its edge was quite all of roseate spoonbill [feathers]. And in its center lay a large golden disc.

And his bones were made of fish amaranth dough, shaped like cylinders. They were called *teomimilli*. They laid each one before him; they lay reaching high; they were hip-high.

And the cape with which they lay covered, which lay spread before him, was designed with severed heads, the palms of hands, hip bones, ribs, tibias, lower arm bones, footprints. With them it was painted.

And this cape was called *tlaquaqualo*.

And yet one more thing they spread out for him; they spread out what was named the sacred roll. In this form it was said to be his breechclout.

And this was a paper, white paper, not yellow paper,[16] a finger thick, a fathom wide, and twenty fathoms long.[17]

With godly arrows, cut at the tip — darts — they supported it. They were made only that they might support it; that his breechclout might be supported.

In three places were they plumed with white turkey feathers; first on their points, second on their shafts, third there on their stems.

When they had ornamented [the figure of Uitzilopochtli], the young seasoned warriors, the masters of the youths, the youths took it up. His breechclout went laid out before him, went spread out before him. They went in procession; they went dancing [and singing].

njman ie ic qujmamaca yn jtlatq': conaquja yn jxicol, tlacoaquallo, ynic tlacujlolli:

yoan panj cononoloa, panj conquentia, ytzitzicaztilma: iuhqujn cuechintli:

yoan conaquja yamacal, yujtica tlachioalli, motocaiotia anecuiotl: hivitzoncal, icpac icac tecpatl, çan no hiujtl ic tlachioalli eztlapanquj:

njman conquetia teuquemjtl tlaçotlanquj: muchi tlaçoiujtl ynic tlachiuhtli, ynic tlaiecchioalli, ynjc tlacujlolli, ynic tlatenchilnaoaiotilli, yn jten, çan moch tlauhquechol: auh yn jnepantla manj, cuztic teucujtlacomalli.

Auh yn jomjio muchioaia, mjchioauhtzoalli, mjmiltic, motocaiotiaia teumjmjlli: qujtetema ixpan veca acitoc, injc vecapan cenquappantli.

Auh yn tilmatli ic tlapachiuhtoc, yn jixco çouhtoca, tlacujlolli, tzontecomatl, macpalli, queztepolli, omjcicujlli, tlanitztli, matzotzopaztli, xocpalli, ynic tlacujlolli catca.

Auh ynjn tilmatli, motocaiotiaia tlacoaqualo:

yoan oc no centlamantli, ixpan contequjlia, ipan conteca in teumjmjlli itoca, iuh mjtoa ymaxtli:

Auh ynjn amatl catca quaoamatl, amo texamatl: ynic tilaoac cenmapilli: auh ynjc patlaoac cenmatl: auh ynjc vijac cempoalmatl:

teumjtl, tlatzontectli, tlacochtli ynjc qujnpapaloa: çan ic muchioaia injc qujnpapalozque, ynjc monapaloz ymaxtli:

excan in tlapotonjlli catca, iztac totoliujtica, injc cecnj, vel yiacac, ynjc vccan ytlaxichchocan, ynjc excan, vncan yn jmamazçocan:

yn oqujcencauhque, cacoqujxtia in telpuchtequjoaque, yoan in teachcaoan, in telpopuchti, ixpan onotiuh, ixpan çouhtiuh yn jmaxtli, tlaiaoalotiuj, qujttotitiuj:

---

15. *cononoloa*: read *conololoa* as in *ibid*.

16. Cf. V. W. von Hagen, *The Aztec and Maya Paper Makers* (New York: J. J. Augustin, 1944), pp. 60, 72 esp. In *Gesammelte Abhandlungen*, Vol. II, p. 656, a note by Seler states: "Quauhamatl *ou* texamatl *est la matière fournie par la couche libérienne de quelques arbres du genre Ficus. Il servait de papier pour les peintures ou les livres, et d'étoffe pour faire les parures, les vêtements et autres objets que le culte des dieux nécessitait*."

17. Corresponding Spanish text: "*vn papelon, que tenja veynte braças de largo, y vna de ancho, y vn dedo de grueso*." Estimates of the units of measurement vary. Cf. a detailed discussion in Victor M. Castillo F., "Unidades nahuas de medida," *Estudios de Cultura Náhuatl*, Vol. 10, Mexico, 1972, pp. 195–223.

When they brought it to the foot of the temple, when already they carried it up, at the four [corners] cords had been tied by which they might take it up, by which they might carry it up. They went stretching [the cords] so that it would not twist.

Thereupon they began to climb. They went rolling the breechclout up; they went reeling it; they reeled it; they went reeling it up.

They went throwing aside the godly arrows. Those whose task it was went taking them, went gathering them, went collecting them.

And when they had risen to the top, when they had raised [the figure of Uitzilopochtli] to the summit, thereupon they placed [the paper roll] upon the serpent bench. They placed it before him. They bound it to [the serpent bench]; they bound it tightly, they bound it firmly.

When they had gone to place it [there], then they descended. There those who had tasks, the offering priests, the stewards who guarded it were left.

Then all the people came down.

And this came to pass, that they went up in the evening when there was still a little sun. And also in the evening an offering was made.

And the tamales which they ate were fruit tamales, [which] were chili-red, or tamales made of maize softened with lime, or bean and cornmeal cakes,[18] colored tamales, tamales of coarse white flour, and [tamales] rolled up in amaranth seed dough.

These cylindrical tamales wrapped up in amaranth seed dough were the tamales they distributed at the temple.

And when it dawned, thereupon offerings were made in each one's home; only some made offerings before the devil [Uitzilopochtli].

And quail were beheaded. Everyone — women, men — [did so].

Moctezuma began [the offering]. He himself, with his own hands, beheaded four quail.

And the fire priest beheaded still other quail; he only laid his hands on them.[19]

Thereupon the commoners broke out; they threw themselves [into it] together. Everyone, men [and] women, beheaded quail.

And when the quail were beheaded, they cast them toward [the figure of] Uitzilopochtli; they threw them toward it.

yn ocaxitique ytzintlan teucalli, in ie qujtlecauizque, ca nauhcampa ixticaca mecatl, injc cacoqujxtizque, ynjc qujnapalozque, qujtitilinjtiuj, ynjc amo monecujloz:

njman ie ic qujpeoaltia in tlecoz, qujlacatzotiuj, qujcujxtiuj, qujtecuja, qujtecujxtiuj: yn jamamaxtli

qujoallaztiuj, in teumjtl concujtiuj, qujnechicotiuj, qujcententiuj in tequjppaneque.

Auh yn opanuetzito tlacpac, yn oqujpantlazque: njman ie ic conteca coatlapechco, ixpan qujtequjlia, itech qujlpia, qujcacatzilpia, qujteteuhilpia,

yn ocontlalito: njmã oaltemoa, vmpa onmocaoa in tequjpaneque, tlamacazque, in tlapixque, in qujpiaia:

njman ie ic oaltemo in ixqujch tlacatl.

Auh ynin mochioaia, in acoqujçaia: teutlacpa oc achi tonatiuh, yoan no teutlacpa muchioa ventli:

yoã in qujquazque tamalli, xocotamalli chichiltic, anoço tenextamalli, anoço quatecujcujlli, tlapactamalli, quauhnextamalli, yoan tzooalilacatzolli:

ynjn mjmjltic in tamalli, tzoalli ynjc tlailacatzolli, qujcẽmana ỹ in tamalli in teupan.

Auh yn otlathujc, njman ie ic tlatlamanalo intechachan, çan aca in ontlamanaia vel ixpan tlacateculotl:

yoan tlacotonalo ixqujch tlacatl, yn cioatl in toqujchti:

conpeoaltia yn Motecoçuma, nauhtetl in çolin yn inoma, yn iioma qujcotona.

Auh yn oc cequj, çoçolti, tlenamacac, in qujncotona, çan inpã conmantiuh yn jma:

njman ie ic tlatzomonj, cenuetzi in maceoaltzĩtli, yn ixqujch tlacatl in tlacotona, yn oqujchtli in cioatl.

Auh yn iquac tlacotonalo, yujc contlaça yujc conmaiauj, in Vitzilopuchtli.

18. Alvaro Tezozomoc, *Histoire du Mexique*, trans. H. Ternaux–Compans, 2 vols. (Paris: P. Jannet, 1853), Vol. I, p. 269, has, for *quatequicuiltamalli*, bean and cornmeal cakes with bird or other meat.

19. Seler, *Einige Kapitel*, p. 104, suggests that the priest merely touched them to behead them symbolically.

And the quail, when their necks were wrung, went fluttering away; they went thrashing; they went striking the earth; they kept throwing themselves to the earth.

And the masters of the youths took them up, gathered them up, plucked them,[20] roasted them, salted them; they cured them in brine.

Some they destined for Moctezuma, and the rest they destined for his officials — only the noblemen — and also for the masters of the youths, those who were leaders; also those who were offering priests.

And all took their large braziers — not their polished braziers. In them were coals and wood shavings. They heaped them up; they set them on fire; they made them take fire; they fired them with pine splinters. There they burned exceedingly.

And they took white incense and coarse incense.[21] And when already it was the proper time that already incense be offered, they laid coals in the incense ladle; on it they cast the white incense. With this they raised it in dedication to Uitzilopochtli.

Thus they warmed him, thus they incensed him not only there at the great temple but also furthermore in each one's home, in each one's *calpulco*. Incense was offered to all of their gods in whom they believed.

And after they had dedicated the fire [and incense to the gods], thereupon they cast [the coals] into the hearth [in the courtyard].

And the women, the maidens painted their faces; they pasted themselves with red feathers.

And they fastened their sacrificial paper streamers firmly to canes. [The streamers] were painted in black in what was called a scroll design.

And the rich [women and girls] thus fastened thin cotton blankets [to canes] likewise painted with a scroll design.

And two masters of youths who had spread black paint on their faces stood above, before the hearth. They stood in the leading position. They carried on their backs pine wood cages with small paper banners, only they carried them [with tumplines which crossed] the chest.

They began the dancing for the women. In this manner was the dance: they danced leaping; they danced just in the fashion of women. And the

Auh in çoçolti in oquechcotonaloque, tlapapatlatztinemj papatlacatinemj, tlalli ic moujujtequj, tlalli ic momomotla:

auh in teachcaoan qujnpepena, qujnnechicoa, qujnvihtlatla, qujntleoatza, qujmiztaioujia, qujmiztaioquauhoatza:

cequj qujtonaltia yn Motecuçoma, auh yn oc cequj qujntonaltiaia yn jtechiuhcaoan, çaniioque in pipilti. Auh no iehoantin in teachcaoan, tlaiacatique: no iehoan in tlamacazque,

yoan muchi tlacatl qujtquja yapãtlecax, amo iehoatl in petztlecaxitl, vncan ietiuh tlexochtli, yoan tlaxipeoalli, contepeuhtitlalia, contlecauja, contlecujtia, ocotica contlemjna, vncan tlâtlâtla.

Yoan qujtquja iztac copalli: yoã quauhiocopalli: auh yn iquac yn ie inman, in ie tlenamaco, in tlexochtli qujoaltema, tlemâco, ipan contepeoa yn iztac copalli, ic conjiaujlia yn Vitzilopuchtli:

ic qujtotonjlia, ic qujpopochuja, amo çanyio vncan in vey teupã, çan no yoan intechachan, intecacalpulco, popochujlo in ixqujchtin inteteuoan inpan qujnmatia.

Auh yn oconiauhque tletl njmã ie ic contema tlexicco:

auh in cioa ichpopuchti, moxaoaia, mopotonjaia tlapaliujtica:

yoan intêteuh acatica qujquappachoa, tliltica tlacujlolli, motocaiotia acaxilquj:

auh in motlacamati, canaoac ynjc qujquappachoa: çan no acaxilquj ynjc tlacujlolli:

Auh vmentin in tiachcaoã mixtlilpopotzque, haco manj, tlexictli ixpan, qujiacatitimanj ococalli in qujmama, amapapaiocatotonti, çan quelpanmama.

qujnpeoaltilia yn cioa in netotiliztli, ynic mjtotia chocholoa, çan mocioaittotia: auh in cioa çan tlattic in manj, yn jnteteuh coomemauja, qujtotitimanj,

20. *qujnvihtlatla*: read *quinvihvitla* as in the *Real Palacio MS*.
21. Thus identified in Seler, *Einige Kapitel*, p. 105.

women were in the middle; they held their sacrificial paper streamers in both hands. They were dancing; they were leaping about. And the offering priests also danced. It was said: "They make the Toxcatl-leap."[22]

There were conical paper rosettes fastened upon [the priests'] foreheads; they had conical paper rosettes fastened to their foreheads. They decked their heads with white turkey feathers. And they smeared honey on their lips; their lips went gleaming. They had paper breechclouts. And their various grackle-staves had grackle feathers;[23] they were like their cups, and their round balls at the base were likewise of grackle feathers. The grackle-staves were also called their thrasher[-staves].[24]

And where they went grasping [the staves] were papers painted with scroll designs. And these [priests], as they danced, went in procession. They went striking their grackle-staves [on the ground].

And only in the *calpulcos* were those who beat the drum for them. They were only seated. They beat only the upright drums; they sat rattling gourd rattles; they sat erecting gourd rattles; they beat turtle shells; they struck turtle shells; they sat using turtle shells.

And all the masters of the youths, the young seasoned warriors, and the youths were spread out elsewhere as they danced what is called the serpent dance.

And hence it went being called the serpent dance. It was because they went back and forth, they went from side to side, they met one another face to face, they went holding one another's hands as they danced.

And also a number of women, maidens, danced. It was their vow. They danced the popcorn dance. As thick as tassels of maize were their popcorn garlands. And these they went placing on [the girls'] heads. They were painted. And to the thickness of their thighs reached where they were pasted with feathers; and it reached up to their shoulders. And they went with those who danced; they went mingling with them.

Of these it was said that they embraced; they embraced one; they embraced Uitzilopochtli.

chocholotimanj: auh in tlamacazque no mjhtotia, mitoa toxcachocholoa:

amaixquatechimaletimanj, amaixquatechimaleque, moquaquapotonja iztac totolivitica: yoan motetenne-cuvia tetentzotlantiuj, ymamamaxtli, yoan intzatza-natopil, tzanaivitl, in iuhquj ytecomaio, auh yn itzin-teloloio, çan no tzanaivitl: no motocaiotia ycujtla-cuchcho, in tzanatopilli.

Auh ynjc quitzitzqujtiuj, amatl acaxilquj, ynjc tla-cujlolli: auh in iehoantin, hin, ynjc mjtotia, tlaiaoa-loa, ic tlaxixiltiuj yn jntzanatopil:

auh çan calpulco, in qujntlatzotzonjliaia, çan cacate eheoaticate: çan tlalpan veuetl in qujtzotzona, aiacachotoque, aiacachquetztoque, aiotl qujtzotzona, aioujtectoque, aiochiuhtoque.

Auh yn ixqujch teachcaoan, in telpuchtequjoaque, yoan in telpopuchti, cecnj manj in mjtotia, moteneoa mococoloa.

Auh ynjc mjhtotia mococoloa, iehica aujc viujh, ixtlapal viuj, mjxnanamiquj, in matitech maantiujh ynjc mjtotia.

Auh no cequjntin cioa ichpopuchti, mjtotia inne-tol, momomochiitotia: centzontecomatl ynjc toma-oac catca, ynmomochicozquj, yoan ymicpac conteca-tiuj, moxaoa, yoan inmetztomaoaian aci, ynjc mopo-tonja, yõ ymacolpan onacia: intlan mamantiuj, intzatzalan mantiuj, in mjtotia.

Jn iehoantin hin moteneoa tlanaoa, tenaoa, quj-naoa in vitzilopuchtli:

22. Corresponding Spanish text: "*Tambien los satrapas del templo, dançauan tambien con las mugeres, ellos y ellas baylãdo, saltauan: y llamauan a este bayle toxcachocholoa, quiere dezir, saltar, o baylar de la fiesta de toxcatl.*" Garibay ("Relación breve," p. 298) translates *toxcachochololoya* as "*se salta el salto de Toxcatl.*"

23. *tzanatl: Cassidix palustris* (Swainson) in Dibble and Anderson, *Book XI*, p. 50.

24. *cuitlacochin: Toxostoma curvirostre* (Swainson) in *ibid.*, p. 51.

And these maidens were very well guarded, that one might not covet them, that one might not joke with them.

And all who danced the serpent dance were well guarded, that none might fall into covetousness.

And if any were seen joking with one [of the maidens], then the masters of the youths struck him to the ground. They dragged them; they kicked them; they stepped on them.

Because they punished them indeed in the temple; they indeed had done wrong. They said to them: "Indeed there penance is done; there a feast day is celebrated."

So night fell as there was dancing. Thus the feast day ended when the day came to an end.

And next morning, when [the feast day] was over, there also was dancing; there was also dancing of the serpent dance.

And at this time died Ixteucale, he who had lived together with Titlacauan. And him also they named Tlacauepan and Teicauhtzin.

And his paper raiment was painted with black discs. His paper headdress had eagle feathers. His headdress was in disorder. Over the middle of his forehead a flint knife made of feathers was standing.

And also he had his cape of netting; over it there went hanging a small net bag, and his maniple went hanging from his arm. It was of the skin of a wild beast.[25] He went fastening [golden] bells [to his legs]. He danced with the others; he danced the serpent dance. He went erect at the head of the others.

And it was purely of his own will when he was to die. When he was to wish it, when he wished it. thereupon he delivered himself into the hands of those where he was to die.

Offering priests called *tlatlacanaualti* seized him, stretched him out [on the sacrificial stone], held him, cut open his breast. His heart they held up in dedication to the sun.

And his severed head also they strung up on the skull rack. In the same way he came to his end, even as Titlacauan, [whose head] was strung up [on the skull rack].

And just at this time the offering priests cut the skin on people; [with a stone knife] they cut the skin of youths, of young boys, and even verily small

auh in iehoantin ichpopuchti, cenca vel pialoia, ynjc aiac qujmjxeleuiz, ynjc aiac qujncamanalhuiz.

Auh yn ixqujchtin yn mococoloa, vel mopiaia ynjc aiac vncan moleuiz:

auh intla aca itto, tecamanalhuja: njmã tlalli ic qujujtequj, in teachcaoan, qujnujujlana, qujntitilicça, qujmiicça:

iehica in qujnmjctiaia ca teupan, ca tlaaujlqujxtia, qujmjlhuja: ca vncan tlamaceoalo, vncan ilhujtlalo.

çan iuh oniooa in netotilo, ic ontlamj in cemilhujtl, in ontzonquiz ilhujtl.

Auh yn jmuztlaioc, in apeoalco no netotilo, no necocololo:

auh iquac mjquj, yn Jxteucale, ynin neoan onenca Titlacaoan: auh ynjn no motocaiotia, tlacavepã, yoan Tehicauhtzin.

Auh ynjc tlacujlolli, yn jamatlatquj, tezcapocio yn jamacal, quahujujio, momoiaoa yn jvitzoncal: tecpatl iquanepantla icatiuh, tlapalihujtl ynic tlachioalli:

yoan no ycuechin, icampa vetztiuh, icpatoxi, yoan imatacax imac pilcatiuh, tequaneoatl, oiooalli contlalitiuh, tehoan mjhtotia, mococoloa, teiacantinemj, teiacac ycatinemj.

Auh çan iillotlama, in quenman miquiz, in quẽman connequiz, yn oqujnec, njman ie ic onmotemaca, yn vncan mjquiz:

qujoalana in tlamacazque, motocaiotia, tlatlacanaoalti, qujtitilinja, caana, queltetequj: yn iiollo conjaujlia in tonatiuh:

auh yn itzontecon, çan no tzompatitech conquauhço, çan no iuh tlantica yn iuh quauhçotica titlacaoan.

Auh çan no iquac y, tepaxotla in tlamacazque, qujnpaxotla in telpopuchti, in telpuchpipil: yoan yn oc vel pipiltotõti, yn coçolco onoque: ynic quin-

25. Corresponding Spanish text: *"tambien en vno de los braços, otro ornamento, de pellejo de bestia fiera, a manera del manjpulo que se vsa en la missa: a este llamauan ymatacax."*

children who lay in the cradles. Thus they cut the skin on their stomachs, on their breasts, and on both sides of each on their upper arms and on their forearms.

This was done only at the time of Toxcatl, when it ended, each year; thus ended [the feast].

paxotla ymelpan, ymelchiqujppan, yoan nenecoc ymacolpan, yoan inmatzotzopazpan:

çan yio iquac y, in muchioaia, yn ipan toxcatl: ape-oalco, cexiuhtica ic ontlatzonqujça.

Twenty-fifth Chapter, which telleth of the feast and of their offerings which they made during all the days of the sixth month, which was called Etzalqualiztli.[1]

Etzalqualiztli. Before the arrival of this feast, at the time when it was celebrated, first the offering priests fasted for Tlaloc. For four days,[2] before their fasting began, first they gathered reeds there at Citlaltepec. For indeed at that place were formed very long reeds called *aztapilin* or *tolmimilli*[3] — very long, very high, and very white at the base; and rounded, like a stone column.

And there where they gathered them, at a place in the water called Temilco [or] Tepexic oztoc, they plucked them by their white ends.

And when they had gathered them, thereupon they arranged them, they tied them together at the base in groups; they wrapped them up; they wrapped the groups of reeds up.

Thereupon they used the tumplines; they each used a tumpline. Then there was their carrying on their backs; there was carrying of the burdens upon their backs; there was the carrying of the burdens upon their backs [with the tumpline across] their foreheads. Thereupon they left; there was departing; there was coming to go. None carried [the reeds] crosswise upon his back; they only all departed carrying them on their backs.

And when the offering priests went to gather the reeds, and as they returned, the road [which they followed] remained deserted. No others took it; travelers followed it no more.

And if they came upon any men, they there then despoiled them of their possessions, they robbed them, they took all from them, they made them drop their possessions. And if they defended themselves, then [the priests] abused them; they threw them flat on the ground, they stepped on each of them,

Jnic cenpoalli ommacuilli capitulo, itechpa tlatoa yn ilhujtl, yoan yn jntlamanaliz in quichioaia, yn ipan ic cemilhujtl, ynic chiquacen metztli, in moteneoaia Etzalqualiztli.

Etzalqualiztli: ynin ilhujtl, yn aiamo onaxioa, in ipan muchioaia: achtopa motlalocaçaoaia in tlamacazque: nahuilvitl yn aiamo vmpeoa, inneçaoaliz achtopa ontolanaia, vmpa in citlaltepec: iehica ca cenca viiac yn vmpa muchioaia tullin, itoca aztapilin, anoço tolmjmjlli: cenca viac, cenca vitlatztic, yoan cenca tziniztac: yoan mjmjltic temjmjltic.

Auh yn vmpa conanaia, qujtezcopina, itocaiocan in atlan, temjlco, tepexic, oztoc:

auh yn oconanque, njmã ie ic qujchichioa, qujcujcujtlalpia, qujqujmiloa, qujtotolqujmjloa:

njman ie ic qujmecapallotia, qujmemecapallotia, njman netlamamaltilo, tlamamalo, tlaixquamamalo: njman ie ic oaleoa, oaleoalo, viloatz, aiac qujxtlapalmama yn aztapili, çan moch queoacamama.

Auh ynjc vih tolanazque, tlamacazque, yoan inic oalmocuepa, cactimoquetza in vtli, aocac qujtoca, aocmo qujtoca in nenenque:

auh yntla acame oqujnnamjcque, njman vncan qujntlacujcujlia, qujntlanamoielia, qujntlacencujlia, qujntlatlaçaltia: auh intla momapatla, njman qujnmjctia, qujntetentimaiauj, qujmihicça qujntitilicça, impan chocholoa, tlalli ic qujujujtequj, qujntlatlal-

---

1. Sahagún (Garibay ed., Vol. I, p. 116) says: "*hacian una manera de puchas, o poleadas que se llama* etzalli"; and in *ibid.*, p. 166: "*este* etzalli *era hecho de maíz cocido, a manera de arroz, y era muy amarillo.*" Durán, *Historia*, Vol. II, p. 210, defines *etzalli* as boiled corn and beans. In "Relación breve," p. 298, Garibay has "*Comida de manjar de frijoles.*"

2. The *Real Palacio MS* varies as follows: "*ynin ylhuitl ypã y̆ quiçaya. matlactli omome metztli mayo. auh yn ayamo onaxiva. yn ipã ylhuitl. achtopa motlalocaçavaya. yn tlamacazque navilhuitl.*" Seler, *Einige Kapitel*, pp. 112–13, translates: "*Dieses Fest fiel auf den 12. Mai. Und ehe man an das Fest kam, fasteten die Priester zu Ehren Tlalocs vier Tage.*"

3. In the Spanish text, Sahagún translates *aztapilpetlatl* as "*petates jaspeados, de juncias blancas, y verdes.*" In Dibble and Anderson, *Book XI*, p. 195, *tolmimilli* is identified as *Cyperus* sp., and the description says that the name of its white base is *aztapilli* or *oztopilli.*

they kicked each of them, they leapt upon each of them, they beat the ground with each of them, they scattered them like so many surveyor's cords,[4] they made them cry out, they beat them repeatedly, they beat their backs repeatedly, they beat the skin off of them, they straightened their backs.[5]

And when they had each been robbed, when they had each been stripped, they there only turned back, they only went back there to their homes.

And indeed if they took the very tribute, Moctezuma was not wrathful therefor. For they [who robbed] were penitents. He esteemed them; he gave them protection; he revered them because they were offering priests, because they did penance; they laid offerings before [the gods]. For they were offering priests.

And when they had come reaching [the temple], when they had gone bringing the white reeds, thereupon were pierced and strung together the white reeds. They fashioned green and white reed mats,[6] and they bound the reeds; they made reed seats, and they made reed seats with backs for one to rest on. In the same manner green and white reed seats with backs were fashioned of white reeds.

Thereupon they somewhat bound the reeds, the thin reeds, at their midpoints. And when they had bound them at their midpoints, thereupon they were arranged in order; on the ground they went bound, they went tightly bound with maguey roots, with maguey fibers.

And when this was done, when already the fasting in honor of Tlaloc was to begin, when night fell, then the offering priests crowded themselves into the houses [of the *calmecac*]; there was crowding into the houses — the warrior offering priests [who had taken three or four captives], and the offering priests [who had captured only one];[7] then the offering priests who were singers, who beat [the drums]; then all the lesser offering priests, and those who were still children, the novices, the little offering priests.

And when this had come to pass, then were spread out before the hearth the white and green reed mats, the white and green reed beds.

And when they had stretched out the white and

mecamauj, qujntzatzatzitia, qujnujujtequj, qujncujtlaujujtequj, qujxipetlavitequj, qujncujtlamelaoa.

Auh yn ontlacujcujliloque, yn onpepetlaoaloque, çan vncan mocuepa, çan vncan iloti yn jnchan:

intla nellacalaqujlli, vel qujcuja, amo ic qualanja in Motecuçoma iehica ca tlamaceuhque, compopoa contepopoaltiaia, qujpopooaia ynjc tlamacazque, ynic tlamaceoa, ymixco ymixpac qujmanaia, ynic tlamacazque.

Auh yn oacico, yn ocaxitico aztapili: njman ie ic moço, moçoço, in aztapili: qujchioa yn aztapilpetlatl, yoan qujilpia in toli, tolicpalli qujchioaia, yoan qujchioaia tepotzoicpalli netlaxonj: çãnoie ic muchioa in aztapili, aztapiltepotzoicpalli.

Niman ie ic acquj qujcujcujtlalpia, in tuli in tulpitzaoac: auh yn omocujcujtlalpi, njman ie ic mouipana, tlalpan molpitiuh, mocacatzilpitiuh menelhoatica metzonmecatica.

Auh in ie iuhquj in ie vmpeoaz, netlalocaçaoaliztli: yn oiooac njman mocacaltema, necacaltemalon tlamacazque: in tlamacazcatequjoaque tlamacazcayiaque: njman iehoan in tlamacazque cujcanjme, tlaujtequjnj: njman ie muchintin, in tlamacazcateicaoan, yoan in oc pipiltotonti tlamacazcatoton, tlamacatoto.

Auh in ie iuhquj, njman ie ic onmoteca, tlecujlixquac, in aztapilpetlatl, in aztapilpepechtli:

auh yn onmoçouh aztapilpetlatl: njman ic muchi-

---

4. *quītlatlalmecamayavi* in the *Real Palacio MS*.

5. *quīcuitlamemelahua* in *ibid*.

6. In the corresponding Spanish text Sahagún states that the reeds were alternated: *"luego las cosian, y componjan, contrapuestas, y entrepuesto, lo blanco a lo uerde: a manera de mantas pintadas."*

7. The number of captives is given in the corresponding Spanish text.

green reed mats, then the fire priest ornamented himself. He put on his sleeveless jacket, and on his left arm he placed [the maniple] called *matacaxtli*.[8]

And with it he took the incense bag, and [in his right hand] he took his incense ladle. Thereupon he offered incense. He stood forth at the entrance; he stood forth in the courtyard.

The fire priest raised[9] it to the four directions. And when this was done, he cast the coals into the brazier. He then went in; he sat before the hearth.

There in his turn he laid down four offering-balls of dough made of maize. Very cautiously, very gently, very warily he placed them. If he made one of them roll, they seized him because of it; he was seized because of it. The offering priests said unto him:

"We offering priests have detained thee, for thou hast rolled it."

And the fire priest then went within. Then he sat down; he undid, he removed [his adornment]. Then all the offering priests came forward; each one in turn was setting in place the offering-balls of dough.

And some left four large tomatoes, or else small ones,[10] and some spread out four green chilis.[11]

Very well were they watched; closely were they watched; closely were they continually watched in case perchance someone might roll something, in case he might move something, in case perchance someone might displace something with his hand, in case perchance someone might knock something with his hand. And if someone rolled something, they detained him, they discovered him, they marked him.

And if they noted on one a little dirt, or a cobweb, or a small piece of cotton perchance on his head, perchance on his cape, they detained him because of it; they marked him. Perchance he stumbled, he slipped, or he struck something. All [such] were detained.

For four days this was done, and four nights, that there was living with prudence.

chioa in tlenamacac, conmaquja yn ixicol, yoan conaquja yn iopuchcopa, itoca matacaxtli:

yoan itlan conana in copalxiqujpilli, yoan concuj in itlema: njman ie ic tlenamaca, qujiaoac oalmoquetza, itoalco oalmoquetza:

nauhcampa in conjaoa yn tlenamacac: auh in ie iuhquj, contema tlequazco tlexochtli, mec calaquj, onmotlalia tlecujlixquac:

vncan contema nauhtetl ynepapatlaia, ventelolotli, cencan tlamatzin, cencan juja, cencan matca in contlalia: intla centetl oqujmjmjlo, ic caci, yc axioa, conjlhuja in tlamacazque.

Otimjtzacique tlamacazque, ca otitlamjmjlo.

Auh in tlenamacac, mec calaquj: njman ic motlatlalia, moxixitinja, moueueloa; njman ic onmoiacatia yn ixqujchtin tlamacazque, ceceiaca cõtlalitimanj yn jnnepapatlaia, in ventelolotli.

Auh in cequjnti xitomatl, anoço izoatomatl in concaoaia nauhtetl: auh in cequjntin chilchotl in contemaia, nauj:

cenca vellachielo, vel neixpetzolo, vel neixpepetzalo, yn açaca tlamjmjloz, yn açaca tlaoliniz, yn açaca tlamapetoniz, yn açaca tlamaxopeoaz. Auh intla aca otlamjmjlo, caci, conjximati, conmachiotia:

yoan intla aca ytech qujttazque, tlaçoltontli, anoço tocatzaoalli, anoço ichcatontli: aço icpac, anoço itilmatitech, ic caci, conmachiotia: anoçe motepotlamja, moticujnja, anoço motlaujtequj, muchi ic neaxioa:

naujlhujtl ynjn muchioaia, yoã nauhioal, in nematcanemoaia.

---

8. *matacaxtli*: see Chapter 24, n. 25.

9. Sahagún (Garibay ed., Vol. I, p. 308) distinguishes three grades of priests — "tlamacazton *(que) es como acólito*; . . . tlamacazque, *que es como diácono*; . . . tlanamácac, *que es como sacerdote. De estos sacerdotes los mejores elegían por sumos pontífices.* . . ."

10. Francisco Hernández, *Historia de las Plantas de Nueva España*, 3 vols. (Mexico: Imprenta Universitaria, 1942–46), Vol. III, p. 699: ". . . *son mayores que avellanas aunque menores que las nueces, están encerrados en una membrana a modo de vejiga, . . . y pasan del verde al amarillo o al púrpura*. . . ." Physalis sp.?

11. *nanavi* in the *Real Palacio MS*.

And when this was done, then the old priests[12] took away [the offerings]. They took away for themselves what they required; they ate them. For four days they took for themselves the things which had been offerings.

And when midnight had not yet arrived, then shell trumpets were blown.[13] And when they were blown,[14] then there was the unclothing of each one and the cutting of maguey spines and the piercing of the ears. Thereupon were the spines stained with blood, and there was the smearing [of the priests] with blood. And when this was done, then there was the arising [of all].

There was going; there was bathing; there was going blowing musical instruments; they went blowing shell trumpets. Whistles were blown.[15]

And all the offering priests each carried their tobacco bags on their backs, and had their cord necklets, each one his cord necklet from which went hanging their little tobacco bags, each of which went filled with dyed, powdered tobacco.[16] And the fire priest went leading them. With him went his incense ladle; and his maguey thorns went with him. And, with them, he grasped his incense bag.

And leading them went a man, an old priest. He went bearing on his shoulders the mist rattle board, also called the sorcerer's staff. It was wide, very wide, excessively wide; and it was long, very long. And it rattled; he went along rattling it.

Not one remained in the *calmecac*. It went all cleaned out; it arose empty; the *calmecac* was empty.

And only four singers were left there. They sat singing, they sat beating the horizontal drum, they sat rattling the turtle shell rattle, they sat rattling the gourd rattle, they sat blowing the shell trumpet; they sat sounding the shell trumpet.

And when they went reaching the water's edge, the offering priests' bathing place, the mist houses were at the cardinal points. Thereupon there was stretching out of each one, there was their seating

Auh in ie iuhquj, njman ic quiquanja in quaquacujlti: qujmocujlia intech monequj, qujqua: naujlhujtl in qujmocujliaia, in motlaueuenjaia:

auh yn aiamo onaci ioalnepantla, mec tlapitzalo: auh yn ontlapitzaloc, njman ic nepepetlaoalo, yoan neuitzteco, yoan nenacazteco: njman ie ic mezuja in vitztli, yoan neçua: auh in ie iuhquj mec nequetzalo.

Viloa, onnevtemalo, tlapitzalotiuh, qujpitztiuj, in tecciztli, cohcouiloc chililitli.

Auh in muchintin tlamacazque, qujmamama yn imiyiequach, ynmecacozquj, inmemecacozquj, itech pipilcatiuh yn imiiequach, ontetentiuh yiaqualli: yoan qujniacantiuh in tlenamacac, ytlemauh ietiuh, yoan yuitz ietiuh: yoan itlan cana icopalxiqujpil.

Auh ce tlacatl quacujlli teiacantiuh, qujquechpanotiuh, aiochicaoaztli, no itoca naoalquaujtl, patlaoac, patlactic, patlacpol: yoan viiac, vitlatztic, yoan cacalaca, qujcacalatztiuh

aocac ce onmocaoã calmecac, cemjchictiuh, cactimoquetza, cactiuetzi in calmecac.

Auh çan naujntin in vmpa onmocaoa cujcanjme, cujcatoque, teponaçotoque, aiochiuhtoque, aiacachotoque; qujpitztoque in qujqujztli, qujqujçotoque.

Auh yn oacito atenco, yn jnnealtiaia tlamacazque: nauhcampa in manca yn aiauhcalli, njman ie ic neteteco, netlalilo, tlatzitzilca, tlaviujioca, tlacuecuechca, netlantzitzilitzalo:

---

12. In the corresponding Spanish text, Sahagún describes "*vnos viejos, que llamauan quaquacujltin: los quales trayan las caras teñjdas de negro, trasqujladas: saluo en la corona de la cabeça, que tenja los cabellos largos, al reues de los clerigos.*"

13. *tlapitza* means "to blow something" — a trumpet, flageolet, flute, or other wind instrument. We follow Sahagún's corresponding Spanish where designating specific instruments.

14. The *Real Palacio MS* text reads: "*tlatlapitzalo auh yn ontlatlapitzaloc.*"

15. The *Real Palacio MS* reads *cohcouilotl chililitli*. Seler, in *Einige Kapitel*, p. 117, translates this passage thus: "*man bläst Muschelhörner und Tonpfeifen, auch solche in Gestalt von zwei Tauben.*" However, in *Gesammelte Abhandlungen*, Vol. II, p. 702, he states: "*Neben ihnen wurden thönerne Pfeifen*, chilitli *oder* cohcouilotl *genannt, viel gebraucht.*"

16. Corresponding Spanish text: "*todos lleueuan a cuestas, vnas taleguillas, atadas con vnos cordelejos de ichtli, con vnas borlas al cabo: y de otras colgauan, vnas tiras de papel pintadas, cosidas, con las mismas talegas, que llamauan yiequachtli: y en aquellas talegas lleuauã vna manera de harina, hecha a la manera de estiercol de ratones, que ellos llamauan yiaqualli, que era cõficionada con tinta, y con poluos de vna yerua que ellos llaman yietl, que es como beleños de castilla.*"

themselves, there was trembling, there was shivering, there was quaking with cold, there was the chattering of teeth.

When this was done, then spoke the old man called the old precious stone priest; he said:

"[Behold] the place where the serpents are wrathful, the place where the water gnats buzz, the place where the ruddy ducks take off, the place where the white reeds rustle."

When he had said this, thereupon there was plunging into the water, there was going churning the water, there was going beating it with their hands, there was going beating it with their feet, there was going beating the water with their feet; they went shouting, they went twittering; they mimicked all the birds.

Some spoke like ducks; they hummed. Some mimicked gulls;[17] they spoke like gulls. Some mimicked jabirus;[18] they spoke like jabirus. Some spoke like white herons.[19] Some spoke like little blue herons.[20] Some spoke like brown cranes.[21]

Where they bathed, in the midst of things were poles.[22] For four days it was so done. And when this was done, then there was emerging from the water, there was ornamenting. Then there was returning; they went back. In just the same manner they went; they each went naked; they were naked.

And when they had reached [home], when they had each disposed themselves in the houses, thereupon were thrown down, were spread out the white and green mats everywhere in the *calmecac*.

Thereupon there was the wrapping up of each, there was the covering up of each. Then there was the stretching out of each upon the white and green mats. They were cold. There was lying as if dead. They lay cold. They lay sleepless. They sat hunched. They sat crouched. Some just lay sleepless, some slept continuously, some slept lightly, some dreamed, some talked in their sleep, some started up in their sleep. There was thundering, there was snoring, there was groaning, there was whimpering, there was [lying] twisted in sleep.

Later, at full noon, there was arising. And when

in ie iuhquj njman ic tlatoa, in veue itoca chalchiuhquaqujlli: qujtoa.

Coatl yçomocaiã, amoiotl ycaoacaian, atapalcatl ynechiccanaoan, aztapilcuecuetlacaian:

yn oconjto y, njman ie ic onnetepeoalon atla, tlachachaquatztinemj, yn atlan, tlamaujtectinemj, tlacxiujtectinemj, atlacxiuitectinemj, tzatzitinemj, ycaoacatinemj, qujntlaiehecalhuja yn ixqujchtin totome:

cequj canauhtlatoa, tlacacauja, ceq'ntin qujntlaiehecalhuja, in pihpitzti, pipitztlatoa: cequjntin qujntlaiehecalhuja, yn acacalome, acacalotlatoa: cequjntin aztatlatoa, cequjntin axoquentlatoa, cequjn tocujlcoiotlatoa:

yn vncan maltiaia yn, tlanepantla manca in cuenmantli: naujlhujtl yn juh mochioaia yn: auh yn ie iuhquj mec oalquixoa yn atlan, nechichioalo, njman ie oalnecuepalo, ycuitlaujc oalujloa, çan ie no iuj in Vitze, tlapitztiujtze, pepetlauhtiujtze, tlapetlauj.

Auh yn onacico, yn onmocacaltemaco, njman ie ic moteteca, moçoçoa yn aztapilpetlatl, yn noujan calmecac:

njman ie ic netlatlalpililo, nequequentilo, mec neteteco, yn aztapilpetlapan, cecec mjcoatoc, cececextoque, yitztitoque, mococototztlalia, motatapaiollalia: cequjntin çan iitztoque, cequjntin cocochi, cequjntin çan cochcanaoatoque, cequjntin temiquj, cequjntin cochtlatoa, cequjntin cochitleoa, tlaquaqualaca, tlacotaliuj, tlaqujqujnaca, tlatetena, tlanecujliuj in cochioa:

qujn cennepantla tonatiuh in neeheoalo. Auh in

---

17. *pipitztli*: tentatively identified as *Larus franklini* in Dibble and Anderson, *Book XI*, p. 39.

18. *acacalotl: Jabiru mycteria* (Lichtenstein) in *ibid.*, p. 43.

19. The *aztatl* is identified as *Leucophoyx thula* (Molina), "snowy egret," in *ibid.*, p. 28. However, we follow the prevailing usage and use the term "heron."

20. *axoquen: Florida caerulea* (Linnaeus) in *ibid.*, p. 28.

21. *tocuilcoiotl: Grus canadensis* (Linnaeus) in *ibid.*, p. 27.

22. "*varales hincados*" in Sahagún's Spanish text.

there had been arising, then the fire priest arrayed himself in order to offer incense, to burn it. He went everywhere, to all the temples; the old priests went ahead of him.

And when he had gone everywhere offering incense, thereupon food was eaten; there was eating. There was gathering around; there was grouping around. Severally they gave them their food, all kinds of sauce. For four days they only tasted it.

And if someone were to exchange his sauce with someone, they detained him because of it, they seized him because of it; he was seized because of it. And when food was eaten, no one let a drop of the sauce fall there on the ground where the sauce had been placed. If anyone spilt a little sauce, for all this he was detained; there was punishing.

And when this was done, when they had eaten, thereupon there was going to gather fir branches [or] reeds, green reeds.

And when there had been going forth, when there had been gathering, thereupon [the branches or reeds] were bound at their midpoints;[23] they were somewhat bound up. And when they had been bound at their midpoints, when already it was time that they be deposited, then there was breaking up, there was running, there was running by each one. They carried the reeds upon their shoulders.[24]

Quickly they deposited each of them everywhere in each of the temples of the demons.

And if anyone were to stumble and fall, and if anyone went not there, if he strayed, for this he was detained.

And if anyone did not keep up, if he did not keep up with one, if anyone straggled, if he did not deposit reeds along with the others, they detained him because of it; there was confinement because of it.

And this was done for four days.

And for these four days he who was detained could yet be freed, could yet free himself, could yet escape in return for perhaps a turkey hen, for perchance a breechclout, perchance a cape, perchance a maguey fiber cape, perchance for a small manta.

And the poor, these freed themselves with balls of dough,[25] a wooden vessel [full].

oneeheoaloc, mec muchichioa in tlenamacac, ynic tlenamacaz tlatotoniz, noujian qujça in jzqujcan teteupan, qujiacantinemj in quaquacujlti.

Auh yn ōtlenamacato noujian: njman ie ic tlaqualo tlatlaqualo, neiaiaoalolo, neoolololo: ceceiaca qujmonmaca yn intlaqual, yn quenamj molli qujmonmaca, navilhujxti in çan ice qujpalozque.

Auh intla aca qujpatilizque ymol, ic caci, ic conaci, ic onaxioa: yoan in jquac tlaqualo, aiac achi qujchipinja yn molli, yn vncan tlalpan; tlatlalteco in molli, intla aca achi qujchipinja molli, muchi ic neaxioa, ic netlanamjctilo.

Auh in ie iuhquj yn ontlaqualoc, njman ie ic viloa yn acxoiatl mocuiz, ie yn acatl, acaxoxouhquj.

Auh yn ooalujloac, yn onmocujto: njman ie ic tlacuitlalpilo, acquj molpia: auh yn ontlacujcujtlalpiloc, in ie inman motemaz, njman ic tlatzomonj, netlalolo, netlatlalolo, qujquechpanoa in acatl:

qujtetentiqujça yn izqujcan in teteupan tlatlacateculo.

Auh intla aca motlaujtequiz: yoan intla aca amo vmpa itztiaz, intla miscuepaz, ic axioa.

Auh intla aca, amo qujcxiaci, intlacamo teicxiaci: intla aca icxicaoalo, yn amo tehoan contemaz acatl, ic caci, ic nemaltilo.

Auh ynjn naujlhujtl in muchioaia: auh in naujlhujtl y, yn aqujque axioa, oc vel momaqujxtia, oc vel moqujxtia, oc vel maqujça: aço totolin yca, aço maxtlatl ica, aço tilmatli, aço ichtilmatli, aço tequachtli ica.

Auh yn jcnotlaactl iehoatl in uentelolotli, ic moqujxtiaia, cen quauhxicalli:

23. *tlacuicuitlalpilo* in the *Real Palacio MS.*

24. *quiquequechpanoa* in *ibid.*

25. "*bolillas de massa*" in Sahagún's Spanish text.

And [as for] all that by which one was freed, all this the captor, he who detained one, he who captured one, took.

But when it was already the fifth day, when it was already the feast day, no one could free himself; even if it were something very great in return for which he was to free himself, no longer did [the captor] accept it.

And when it was already the feast day, all the common folk made cooked maize and beans for themselves; they made *etzalli* for themselves. They fell to it as one. There was no one who did not prepare maize and beans for himself.

When they were cooked, then they were continually eaten; they continually presented it to one another; they continually invited one another to meals.

And some of the happy ones, the pleasure girls, and some of the brave warriors danced from time to time. Thus they just diverted themselves.

Thus were they adorned: they had circles about their eyes; they had their maize staves. They kept going to enter each one's home. They danced the *etzalli* dance. With them they went grasping a handled jar, the *etzalli* jar.

And as they kept on dancing they chanted: "When I do, when I do, [give me] a little of thy *etzalli*. If thou givest me none, I shall break a hole into thy house."

And the householders then gave them a pile of *etzalli*. They went placing it in the *etzalli* jar.

Those who kept on dancing gathered some in fives, some in sixes, some in sevens.

This *etzalli* dance began at midnight. Only when it was dawn was there dispersing, was it quiet.

And when the sun arose, then the fire priest adorned himself. He put on his sleeveless jacket;[26] over it he placed his [thin, transparent] netted cape, called the mist cape or the dew cape, adorned with [crossed] motmot feathers. Then he carried on his back the round paper rosette,[27] and he went placing a pleated paper neck ornament on the nape of his neck.[28]

auh yn jxqujch nequjxtilonj, moch qujmocujlia in tlamanj, in teaci, in teacinj.

Auh in ie ic macujlilhujtl, in ie yquac ilhujtl, aocac vel moqujxtiaia, inmanel itla cenca vey ic moqujxtiaia, aocmo qujceliaia.

Auh in ie iquac ilhujtl, yn ixqujch tlacatl maceoalli, qujmochiujliaia etzalli, metzalhujaia, vel cenvetzi, aiac yn macamo metzalhujaia:

auh yn iquac oicucic, njman quaqualo, netech qujmomamaca, nepanotl ic mococooachioa.

Auh in cequjntin papaqujnj, yn ahaujeni: yoan in cequjntin tiacaoan, mamaceoa çan ic mellelqujxtia:

injc muchichioa mixteiaiaoaltia, incintopil, cacalactinemj in techachan, etzalmaceoa: intlan caantinemj xocujcolli etzalcomjtl.

Auh ynjc mamaceoaia queoaia. Yn naie yn naie tla achi in metzal, intlacamo xinechmaca, njmjtzcalxaxapotlaz.

Auh in chaneque, njman qujoalmaca, cen tlaolololli etzalli, contlalitiuj yn etzalcomjc:
cequj macujlli, cequj chiquacen, cequj chicome, mantinemj in mamaceoa.

Jnjn etzalmaceoaliztli, ioalnepantla in peoaia, çan ic tlatlalchipaoa, in necacaoalo, cactiuetzi,

auh yn ooalquiz tonatiuh, njman ie ic muchichioa in tlenamacac, conmaquja yn ixicol, pani conmololoa aiatl, itoca aiauhquemjtl, anoço aoachquemjtl, tzitziuhio: njman conmomamaltia, in tlaquechpaniotl, yoan conmatiuh y cuexcochtlan amacuexpalli:

26. "*vna manta delgada trasparente, que se llama aiauhquemjtl*" in the corresponding Spanish text. Elsewhere Sahagún mentions "*mantas delgadas que llaman ayatl*" (Sahagún, Garibay ed., Vol. IV, p. 49).

27. "*vna flor de papel grande vncida redonda, a manera de rodela*" in the corresponding Spanish text. Later, in the same chapter, he describes the *tlaquechpaniotl* as "*ornamento, que va sobre el pescuezo.*" In *Gesammelte Abhandlungen*, Vol. II, pp. 850, 851, 885, Seler refers to it as "*die breite Nackenschleife*" and adds: "*am Nacken ist das* tlaquechpanyotl, *die Binde mit den breiten Schleifenenden aus gefälteltem Papier, angegeben die das Abzeichen der Berg-, Regen- und Wassergottheiten ist.*"

28. In *ibid.*, p. 487, "*eine aus Papier geschnittene Imitation des Schopfes, den man den Knaben, denen im Uebrigen das Haupthaar rasirt wurde, am Hinterkopf stehen liess. Wir werden dasselbe Merkmal unten noch bei den* Tepictoton, *den Berggöttern, angegeben*

And his forehead was painted blue; besides, he put iron pyrites on it; he sprinkled iron pyrites.

And with him he went grasping a paper incense bag, with shells attached, covered with seashells,[29] also known as a seashell incense bag. It went filled there with *yauhtli*, with ground up *yauhtli*.[30]

And an old priest bore upon his shoulders the mist rattle board.

And a number of offering priests carried in their arms rubber molded like men, called rubber gods.

Some bore in their arms [pieces of] incense, quite round, conical [in shape]. On their points went erect quetzal feathers, called quetzal feather tassels.

And when this was done, when the trumpets were played, thereupon there was their placing in order on the road. Then there was departing.[31]

And as many as had been detained [for transgressions] they arranged, each one, in order; they grasped each one firmly; they took them each by the napes of their necks, they seized each one firmly by the head; some they grasped, each one, by the ends of their breechclouts.

And for the novice offering priests who had been detained they made reed rests as for earthen jars for each one. There each one went. They went bearing [the novice priests] upon their shoulders.[32]

And as for those a little better [in size], they went grasping each one by their hands.

And when they had set forth, then was the time that they turned upon [the transgressors]; they set upon them, they abused them, they cast them each to the ground. If somewhere there was a puddle of water, there they threw them; they kept sliding them, they kept rolling them; they went sliding them in the mud, they went mingling them with the mud. Just so they forced them to the water's edge, to the place where they immersed one in the water, to a place called Totecco.

And when it had been reached, the fire priest and still other fire priests from various places thereupon [sacrificially] burned the papers and the incense gods and the rubber gods. And the *yauhtli* they

yoan mixquatexoujaia, oc cepa ipan conapetzujaia, conapetzotiaia:

yoan itlan cantiuh yiataztli cuechcho, tlacuechiotilli, no iuh mjtoa cuechiataztli, vncan tentiuh yiauhtli, yiauhtlatextli:

yoan ce quacujlli conquechpanoa, aiauhchicaoaztli:

auh in cequjntin tlamacazque, qujnanapaloa vlli, iuhqujn tlaca ic tlachichioalti, motocaiotia vlteteu:

cequjntin qujnanapaloa copalli, çan mjmjlmjltic quaquauitztic, icpac y icatiuh quetzalli, ytoca quetzalmjiaoaiotl.

Auh in ie iuhquj ỹ otlapitzaloc, njman ie ic onneotemalo, mec viloa.

Auh in q̃xqujchtin, yn oaxioaque, oqujntetecpanque, qujntzitzitzqujtimanj, incuexcochteuh qujmaanjlitimanj, qujnquaquatemotzoltzitzqujtimanj, cequjntin inmaxtlaujcoltitech qujmaantimanj.

Auh in tlamaztoton, yn oaxioaque, toliaoalli qujnchichiujliaia, vncan iehetiuj, qujnquechpanotiuj:

auh in ie achi qualtoton, inmatitech qujmaantiuj.

Auh yn iquac ie oneoa, njman iquac qujnpeoaltia in qujncujcujtiuetzi, qujnmictia qujnmamaiauj, intlacana manj qujiaoatl, vmpa qujmontlaça vmpa qujnpepetzcoa, qujnmjmjloa, qujnçoqujpetzcotinemj, qujçoqujnelotinemj, çan iuh qujmonaxitia yn atenco, in teatlan papacholoian, itocaiocan totecco.

Auh yn iquac yn onaxioac in tlenamacac, yoan oc cequjntin tletlenamacaque, njman ie ic qujtlatia yn amatl, yoan copalteteu, yoan vlteteu: yoan yn jiauhtli, qujtetepeoa, qujcecenmana in tolpepechpan.

---

finden.'' The corresponding Spanish text reads: *"al colodrillo, vnas flores de papel, tambien froncidas, que sobrauan a ambas partes de la cabeça, a manera de orejas de papel, como medios circulos,"* and later in the same chapter, *"era ornamento, que se ponjan tras el colodrillo, como vna flor hecha de papel."*

29. *tlacuechchotilli* in the *Real Palacio MS*.

30. Identified as *Tagetes lucida* in Dibble and Anderson, *Book XI*, p. 145.

31. Following *mec viloa*, the *Real Palacio MS* contains a few lines which are missing in the *Florentine Codex: auh tlanepãtla ycatiuh ytoca acacpalli, acatl, in tlachichiualli yuitl ycpac y ycatiuh ome, amatl ytech pilcatiuh, ytech çouhtiuh, ynic tlacuilolli acaxilqui, quinapalotivi, cenca quimauiztilitivi —* "and in the midst of them went what is called a reed seat, made of reeds, with two feathers [upright] upon it. Paper went hanging from it, spreading out from it, painted lengthwise with stripes. They went carrying it with much reverence."

32. *quĩquequechpanotiui* in the *Real Palacio MS*.

85

scattered in various directions; they spread it over each of the reed beds.

And when this was done, it was as if the water was wounded when there was the casting [of the transgressors] into the water. There was what was like a roar; the water rose straight up. And if anyone tried to come up, they submerged him. He went deep.

And if any were experienced in water, when [the escorts] had submerged them, they went for good. They came up at a distance; then they jumped out, they fled, they escaped.

And some [the escorts] indeed suffocated; they indeed fainted. They left them quite hurt; they left them as if lying dead at the water's edge; they stretched them each out.

And some, who had swallowed water continuously, bitter water, [their relatives] held head down so that what they had swallowed might come out through their noses, through their mouths.

And when this was done, then there was departing, there was going back. Once again they went blowing the shell trumpets.

And those who had been repeatedly submerged in the water went only to their homes. Their home folk accompanied them. They each went sick, they each went trembling, they each went shivering to recover their breath[33] at their homes.

And when there was going to reach the *calmecac*, once again there was a spreading out; the mats of green and white reeds, and also the reeds, were spread out. Once again fasting began; it was called "fasting during the day." For four days they also fasted during the day. No longer was there detaining [for transgressions]; no longer was anything eaten during the day.

Then began the adorning [of the priests]. The novice offering priests adorned the offering priests. They prepared all the divers paper vestments, the round paper rosettes, the pleated paper neck ornaments, and the paper bags for incense, only they bought them [at the market], and the necklaces of wood, only they were sold in the market place.

And when the four days had passed in which there was fasting during the day, then at dawn began the arraying [of the priests].

Then were bedight the various fire priests and all the offering priests. At dawn there was the putting

Auh yn iquac muchioa y, yn atl iuhqujn tzopontimanj, ynic teatlan papacholo: iuhqujn tlacaoacatimanj, vel macoquetza yn atl: auh yn aca oalpanuetziznequj conpolactia, centlanj iauh.

Auh yn aca amatinj, yn oconpolactique, çan iccen iauh, vecan onpauetzi, njman ic choloa, moieltia, momaqujxtia:

auh in cequjntin vel qujmjhiiocaoaltia vel çoçotlaoa, ça mjmjcque in qujncaoa, ça q'nmictoccaoa atenco qujnoaltetema:

auh in cequjntin oqujtotoloque atl, in chichic atl, qujntzonicpilooa ic oalqujça, yn iniacac yn jncamac, yn oqujtotoloca.

Auh in ie iuhquj njman ic oalujlooa, icujtlaujc oalujloa oc cepa oallapitztiuj:

auh yn oatlanpapacholoque, çan inchan vihuj, qujnujujca in inchantlaca, cocoxtiuj, viujujxcatiuj, tzitzitzilcatiuj, yn oconihiiocuizque inchan.

Auh yn oaxioato calmecac, oc cepa tlateteco, moteteca yn aztapilpetlatl, yoan no motetema yn atulin, oc cepa vncan peoa in neçaoaliztli, itoca netlacaçaoaliztli, no naujlhujtl in motlacaçaoaia, aocmo neaxioa, aocmo tlacatlaqualo:

njman ic vncã ompeoa in tlatlachichioalo, qujtlachichiujliaia in tlamacazque, tlamaztoton, qujcecencaoa yn ixqujch amatlatqujtl, in tlaquechpaniotl, yn amacuexpalli, yoã yn jiataztli, çan qujmococoujaia, yoan in tlacopacozcatl, çan monanamacaia tianquizco.

Auh yn oacic naujlhujtl, ynjc netlacaçaoalo, njman ioatzinco in peoa in techichioalo:

njman mochichioa in tletlenamacaque, yoan yn ixqujch tlamacazquj, ioatzĩco yn onneaqujlo, in tla-

---

33. In the *Real Palacio MS* the phrase reads: *yn oc ompa quihyyocuizque.*

on of the round paper rosettes. And they put on their heads the pleated paper neck ornaments. There was the application of the pleated paper neck ornaments; there was painting blue of the foreheads. Their foreheads were painted blue, and they were painted, they were painted after the manner of Uixtociuatl.[34] And with them they each grasped the incense bag; they were with them; they were grasped, each one. The various fire priests had their ocelot skin incense bags with small, white seashells. In four places shells hung from the incense bags.

And the incense bags of the offering priests were made only of paper painted like ocelot skin, painted to look like ocelot skin. Some [incense bags] represented the northern phalarope;[35] some represented the duck. Their incense bags each went filled with powdered *yauhtli*.

And when this was done, then there was coming together; the feast day was celebrated. The fire priest of the Temple of Tlaloc led the others. He went putting on his quetzal and heron feather crown, and his face was coated with liquid rubber. He put on his mist jacket, his rain mask or his Tlaloc mask. His long, tangled hair fell to his loins. Behind him came chanting all the offering priests. Thus they went to the Temple of Tlaloc.

When they reached there, thereupon the fire priest of the Temple of Tlaloc stopped. He spread out white reeds and *quequexquic*[36] and *nopal*, strewn with *yauhtli*, provided with *yauhtli*.

Then he placed [on the mats] four round green stones. And when he had placed them there,[37] then they gave him a small wooden hook, stained blue; with it he went striking each one of the round green stone balls. As he went striking each one, he went turning around.

And when this was done, then he scattered *yauhtli*. And when he had scattered it, then they gave him the mist rattle board. He rattled, he shook it; he raised it in dedication [to the god].

And when it was ended, then there was the departing of each one, there was the dispersing of each one, there was the disappearing of each one, there was the scattering of each one; they each went to the

quechpaniotl: yoan contlaliaia ymjcpac, amacuexpalli, neamacuexpaltilo, yoan neixquatexoujlo, mjxquatexoujaia, yoan michioaia, moujxtoichioaia: yoan intlan caana yn iataztli: tetlan tlaano in tletlenamacaque, ynooceloyiataz cuecuechcho, nauhcampa in pipilcac, cuechtli, yn itech yiataztli.

Auh in tlamacazque ymjataz, çan amatl in tlachichioalli, tlaoceloicujlolli, oceloicujliuhquj, in cequjntin atzitzicujlotl ipan mixeoaia: in cequintin canauhtli, ipan mjxeoaia, yn jmiataz, tetentiuh, yn jiauhtextli.

Auh in ie iuhquj, mec tenanamjco, ilhujtlalo: teiacana in tlalocan tlenamacac, quetzalaztatzontli, yn onactiuh: yoan mjsolhuj yaiauhxicol, iqujiauhxaiac, anoço itlalocaxaiac in conmaquja, ycuitlacaxiuhian vetzi yn ipapa ycampa icaoacatiuj yn jxqujchtin tlamacazque, ynic vih yn iteupan tlaloc:

yn onacique njman ie ic onmoquetza, in tlalocan tlenamac, conchaiaoa in aztapili, yoan in quequexqujc, yoan nopalli, yiauhtitlan tlaaqujlli, tlayiauhujlli:

njmã ic contlalia in chalchiuhtelolotli nauhtetl: auh yn ocontlali mec conmaca, quauhchicoltontli, tlatexoujlli, ic conujujtectiuh, cecentetl in chalchiuhtelolotli: yn jquac qujmonujujtectiuh, oalmocueptiuh.

Auh in ie iuhquj, njman contepeoa yn jiauhtli: auh yn ocontepeuh, njman conmaca yn aiochicaoaztli, concacalatza, conujujxoa, coniyiaoa.

Auh ỹ ontzonquiz, njman ic viujlooa, cecenmanoa, momoiaooa, xitinooa, viuj yn jncacalmecac: auh yn tlamaztoton, çan qujnujujca yn inchachan.

---

34. Seler, in *Einige Kapitel*, p. 125, has "*man . . . bemalt das Gesicht in der Art des bewegten Wassers.*"

35. *atzitzicujlotl*: identified as northern phalarope, *Lobipes lobatus*, or sanderling, *Crocethia alba* (Pallas), in Dibble and Anderson, *Book XI*, p. 28.

36. In a description of the Huaxteca and their region, Sahagún writes: "*se dan muy bien todos los bastimentos y muchas frutas que por acá no se hallan, como es la que dicen* quequexquic" (Sahagún, Garibay ed., Vol. III, p. 203). In Vol. IV, p. 351, it is identified as *Xanthosema violaceum*. Seler, in *Einige Kapitel*, p. 126, calls it *Pfeilkrautblätter*, and cites Hernández's definition as *Sagittae plinionae*.

37. The *Real Palacio MS* reads *contlatlalia* and *ocontlatlali*.

various *calmecacs*. But the novice offering priests they only took, each one, to their several homes.

And when there had been going to gather in the *calmecac*, then there was dispersing [of their ornaments]; there was the seating of each one.

And at night, thereupon there began the celebration of the feast day on the top of the Temple of Tlaloc.

The horizontal drum was beaten, trumpets were played, conch shells and reed pipes were blown. There was song. The horizontal drums lay croaking; they lay growling; it was as if they lay droning; and gourd rattles were rattled.

They caused those who were to die, the likenesses of the rain gods, to spend the night in vigil.

And when midnight came, when the night divided in half, then began the slaying. The captives went leading; they died. They began as the fundament of [those to follow]. And when they died, thereupon died [the impersonators of] the rain gods.

Then also was the time when all the paper offerings burned, and the quetzal feathers and the various [other] precious feathers, and some of the green stones — well formed, those which were in no way blemished, which had no defects, as well as some of the rubber-colored stones, those which were blackish, those which were brown, those which were dark.

And when they slashed open the breasts of [the victims], when they opened the breast of one of them, they seized his heart; they went to place it in a vessel painted blue, named the cloud vessel, which was painted with rubber on four sides. And its accouterments were papers dotted with drops of liquid rubber, much rubber; they were covered with rubber.

All this they likewise did to all the impersonators. All their hearts they continued casting there [in the cloud vessel].

And when this was done at midnight, when there had been the killing, all the bystanders, who had been watching continually, all went with their hands continually filled with their artemisia flowers.[38] They went thrusting them, they went lunging with them to and fro, they went fanning themselves, [and they went fanning their children with them.][39] It was said that thus they frightened away the worms;

Auh yn onnetecoto calmecac, mec nexixitinjlo, netlatlalilo:

auh yn oniooac njman ie ic peoa, in tlalhujmamanj, in teucalticpac tlalocan:

teponaçolo, tlapitzalo, iehoatl in mopitza tecciztli, yoan acatecciztli: cujco, yn teponaztli, mjmjlcatoc, nanalcatoc, iuhqujn qujqujnacatoc, yoan aiacacholo:

qujntoçauja in miquizque yn imixiptlaoan tlaloque.

Auh yn oacic ioalnepantla yn iquac xeliuj ioalli: mec peoa in micoa, iacattiuj in mamaltin miquj: iuhqujn inpepechoan muchioa: auh yn onmjcque, njman ie ic miq' in tlaloque:

njman no yquac tlatla, yn ixqujch nextlaoalli amatl, yoan in quetzalli, yoan in nepapan tlaçoihujtl: yoan cequj chalchiujtl yn jcucic, yn atle itlaciuiz, yn amo tlaciujce: yoan cequj olchalchiujtl, iaiauhquj, iaiactic, anoço yiauhtic.

Auh yn iquac qujmeltetequj, in ce onpeti yiechiqujuh, conanjlia yn iiollo, contlalitiuj comjc, tlatexoujlli motocaiotia, mixcomjtl, nauhcampa in tlavlxaoalli: auh yn itlaquen amatl tlavlchipinilli, cenca vllo moca vlli:

much iuh qujnchioa yn izqujntin teixiptlaoan, much vmpa contlaztimanj yn jniollo.

Auh yn iquac muchioa ioalnepantla, ynjc mjcoa: yn ixqujchtin tlatlattaque, in tlatlachia, muchi imiiztauhiaxochiuh, inmac tetentinemj, qujtlatlaujtzotinemj, aujc qujtlaztinemj, ic mêcapeujtinemj, yn inpilhoã, qujlmach ic qujnpeujaia in ocujlti, ynic amo yxocujlloazque: cequjntin in nacaztitlan caaquja, cequjn çan qujmamapictinemj.

---

38. Identified as *Artemisia mexicana* Willd. in Dibble and Anderson, *Book XI*, p. 165.

39. The *Real Palacio MS* adds *yuan yc quimecapeuitinemi.*

88

that their [children's] eyes might not become wormy. Some put the flowers in their ears. Some just went holding them in each hand.

And when this was done, when were slain [the captives and the likenesses of the rain gods], thereupon the offering priests came down. They brought down all the offerings — the rubber-spattered sacrificial banners, and the maguey fiber capes painted with designs, also called "mist-faced," and the green stones, and the quetzal feathers, and the incense pieces which looked like men. And they brought down the cloud vessel; it went filled there with hearts.

Then they took them directly to the water's edge, to a place called Tetamaçolco.

And when they had gone to arrive, thereupon they loaded a boat; they filled a boat with all the offerings. And all the offering priests embarked. Thereupon it was poled. It was filled. Those who poled it clung [to the poles]. They poled speedily. The poles were all in blue; they were painted blue; they were colored blue. And they had rubber ornamentation; they had rubber painting; they were rubber-ornamented.

And when they went to arrive in mid-water, at a place called Pantitlan,[40] there they brought the boat in. And when they had brought it in, thereupon trumpets were played. The fire priest arose in the prow of the boat. Then they gave him the cloud vessel, which went filled there with hearts. Thereupon he cast it in the midst of the water, before the stakes [which were in the water]. It immediately was swallowed; it immediately pierced [the water].

And then the water foamed, kept surging, roared, crackled continually, crackled as it surged. Bits of foam formed.

Thereupon were hung out, tied to the stakes, to the poles, the sacrificial banners. And they bound on green stones, but some of them they cast, scattered, strewed on the water.

And when this was done, thereupon there was going forth. And when there was coming to go forth, when there was going forth there at the opening in the [barrier of] stakes, then [the fire priest] took up the incense ladle, on which he arranged four sacrificial banners. Thereupon he dedicated [the incense ladle with papers]; when he had dedicated

Auh in ie iuhquj yn onmjcoac, njman ie ic oaltemoa in tlamacazque: qujoaltemouja yn ixqujch nextlaoalli, in teteujtl: yoan ichtilmatli tlacujlolli, yoan itoca aiavixo: yoan in chalchiujtl, yoan quetzalli, yoan copalli, tlatlacatlachia: yoan qujoaltemouja in mixcomjtl, vncã tetentiuh yn iollotli:

njman qujtlamelaoaltia atenco, itocaiocã tetamaçolco.

Auh yn oacito njman ie ic conacalaquja, conacaltema yn ixqujch nextlaoalli: yoan onmacaltema yn ixqujchti tlamacazque, njman ie ic tlanelolo, ontetemj onpipilcatoque in tlaneloa, tequjtlaneloa, in aujctli muchi texoio, tlatexoujlli, tlatexoaltilli, yoan tlaulxauhtli, tlaulxaoalli, vlxauhquj.

Auh yn oacito anepantla, itocaiocan pantitlan, njman ic concalaquja yn acalli: auh yn oqujcalaquj-que, njman ie ic tlapitzalo: in tlenamacac acaliacac onmoquetza, njman conmaca in mixcomjtl, yn vncan tentiuh iollotli: njman ie ic contlaça anepantla, ynixpã cuenmantli, iuhquin ontlachaquanitiuetzi, ontlatzoponitiuetzi:

auh njman poçoni yn atl, momoloca, quaqualaca, xixittomj, xixitemomoloca, apopoçoqujllotl motlatla-lia:

njman ie ic mopipiloa, moolpia in teteujtl, in quauhtitech yn itech cuenmantli: yoan in chalchiujtl qujilpia, yoan cequj atlan contepeoaia, conchaiaoa, concenmana.

Auh in ie iuhquj, njman ie ic oalqujxoa: auh yn oqujxoaloco, yn oalqujxooac, yn vncan qujiaoaten-pan, yn iqujiaoaioc cuenmantli: njman ic concuj in tlemaitl, vncan conmamana nauhtetl teteujtl: njman ie ic conjiaoa, yn oconjiauh, mec conmaiauj, ica on-majauj, contlaça, ica ontlamotla:

---

40. The *Real Palacio MS* adds *auh yn oacito pantitlan* — "and when they had gone to reach Pantitlan."

them, then he scattered them. He scattered them [on the water]; he cast them down; he threw them [on the water].

And when he had cast them away, then they turned the boat about. Then there was the return; there was poling. Some went in the prow; some went in the stern.

And when they had come to reach Tetamaçolco, where there had been embarking at the place of embarkation, thereupon there was bathing; then there was going on the part of each one.

And the boat they then went to beach at its resting place at the place for beaching boats.

And when dawn broke, thereupon there was washing of the blue color from foreheads. The offering priests were there at the offering priests' bathing place.

And whoever had only hidden himself, who had only concealed himself when there was fasting for Tlaloc, when there was detaining, later with the washing of the blue stain from their foreheads, they there plunged him into the water.

And when this was done, then there was a quick departure. Then were taken out each of the reed beds; they were each carried out of the *calmecac*. They were each taken out; they threw them, each one, behind the building.

Enough. Here ended the feast of Etzalqualiztli.

auh yn ocontlaz mec qujmalacachoa yn acalli: mec oalnecuepalo, tlanelolo cequj tlaiacatitiuj, cequj tlacuexcochtitiuj.

Auh yn oacico tetamaçolco, yn vncan neacalaqujlo, in neacalaqujloia, njman ie ic neaaltilo, mec viviloa.

Auh yn acalli, njman ic vi qujtecazque, yn jonoia, yn acaltecoian:
auh yn otlatujc, njman ie ic nequatexopaco: in tlamacazque vmpa yn jnnealtiaian, tlamacazque.

Auh yn aqujn çan motlati, in çan mjnax, in iquac netlalocaçaoaloia, yn axioac, qujniquac ica nequatexopaco: vmpa atlan qujpapachoa.

Auh yn ie iuhquj mec viloatz, mec tlaqujqujxtilo, tlaeeoalo in tolpepechtli in vncan calmecac: tlaqujqujxtilo, calteputzco contlatlaça.

Je ixqujch, vncan tlamj y, yn ilhujtl, in etzalqualiztli.

Twenty-sixth Chapter, in which are related the feast day and the honors done during all the days of the seventh month, which was named Tecuilhuitontli.[1]

Tecuilhuitontli. When this was in progress, the minor feast of the lords was celebrated also for twenty days. And at this time died, at this time her fate befell her, at this time died a sacrificial death [the likeness of] Uixtociuatl, god[dess] of the salt people, the salt makers.

This Uixtociuatl, so it was said, was thought to be the elder sister of the rain gods. And it was thought that the rain gods were her brothers. In one thing she angered them, she offended them: that she mocked at her brothers. And then they banished their elder sister to the salt beds. There she went to discover salt — how it existed, how it was formed, how were made the salt jars; and also grains of salt.[2]

And on this account, greatly did the salt flats people honor her.

And the array of [the likeness of] Uixtociuatl was [thus]: her face paint, her ornamentation, was yellow. This was of yellow ocher or [the yellow of] maize blossoms. And her paper cap had quetzal feathers in the form of a tassel of maize; it had many quetzal feathers; it was full of quetzal feathers. It was as if they turned it green; it was all turned green; they were outspread; they were divided; it was as if it were vivid green; it became green.

And there were her golden ear plugs. She had golden ear plugs. And the golden ear plugs glittered, flashed. They were very yellow; they were like squash blossoms. And her shift was designed like water; it was designed as if with water [waves].[3] And the border of her shift had a design of green stones; it was designed as if of green stones; the border was of billowing clouds; it had a cloud design. And her skirt was designed in the same fashion.

Jnic cēpoualli on chiquace capitulo, vncan motene- oa yn ilhuitl, yoan in tlamauiztililiztli, in muchioaia, yn ipan vel ic cemilhujtl, ic chicome metztli, in mjtoaia: Tecujlhujtontli.

Tecujlhujtontli: yn in qujçaia in muchioaia, in tecuilhujtontli, no cempoalilhujtica: auh vncā mj-quja, vncan itequjuh vetzia vncan teumjquja in vixtocioatl, yn jnteouh iztatlaca, iztachiuhque.

Jnjn vixtocioatl, iuh mjtoa qujlmach inveltiuh, catca in tlaloque: yoan qujlmach yioq'chtioan in tlaloque: centlamātli ic qujnqualanj, ic qujniolli-tlaco, inca mocaiauh, yn joqujchtioan: auh njman ic qujtotocaque yn jnveltiuh vmpa yn iztapan: vmpa qujnextito yn iztatl, yn juh ioli, yn juh tlacati, yn juh muchioa iztacomjtl, yoan iztaxalli.

Auh ipampa y, cenca qujmauiztiliaia yn iztapa-neca, yn iztapātlaca.

Auh in vixtocioatl, yn jnechichioal catca, yn jxaoal, yn jnechioal cuztic: iehoatl in tecoçaujtl anoço to-mjoli: yoan yamacal, quetzalmjiaoaio, quequetzalo, moca quetzalli, iuhqujn, xoxoqujuj, xoxoqujuhti-manj, momoiaoa, xexeliuj, iuhqujn xoxopaleoa, xoxoxouja:

yoan yteucujtlanacoch, teucujtlanacoche: auh in teucujtlanacochtli, pepetlaca, pepepetlaca, cenca coz-tic, iuhqujn aioxochqujlitl: yoan yujpil tlaaicujlolli, aycujliuhquj: auh yn iten yn ivipil, tlachalchiujcuj-lolli, chalchiujcujliuhquj, tēmixmolonquj, tlaten-mjxicujlolli: auh yn icue çan ie no iuhquj ynic tla-cujlolli,

---

1. "*Fiestecilla de los señores,*" according to Garibay ("*Relación breve,*" p. 300); "*das Kleine Herrenfest*" or "*Kleines Herrenfest*" in Seler (*Einige Kapitel,* pp. 130, 131).

2. "*Grano de sal, o sal de la mar*" in Molina, *Vocabulario.*

3. Corresponding Spanish text: "*Tenja el vipil labrado, con olas de agua.*" Cf. also Plate 24.

And on her ankles[4] she had placed bells, golden bells, or rattles. On the calf of her legs she had bound ocelot skins on which were the bells. And when she walked, much did she rustle, clatter, tinkle, continuously tinkle.

And her sandals, her foam sandals, [had] side pieces. The side pieces were of loose cotton yarn with flecks of raw cotton woven in, put in by hand. And the tassels of her sandals were similarly of loose [cotton]. And her sandal thongs were of the same loose [cotton].

And her shield had water lily leaves [and flowers];[5] it was painted with a waterlily leaf [and flower] design; it was as if painted with a water lily leaf [and flower] design. It was hung with yellow parrot feather pendants.[6]

And the yellow parrot feather pendants were made [into tassels] like the forepart of a locust.[7] They were [also] made of eagle feathers, of eagle down, and of cut [pieces of] quetzal feathers, and of troupial feathers,[8] and of the yellow belly and breast feathers and the ruddy tail feathers of parrots called *teoxollotl*.[9] The shield was rimmed with a circle of yellow parrot feathers.

When she danced, she kept swinging the shield around in a circle; with it she crouched around.

And her reed staff[10] was hung with papers; it had papers. And they were spattered with liquid rubber; they had rubber. In three places [the staff] had cup-like flowers; it had various cup-like flowers. And where there were the various cup-like flowers, there in each one there was *yauhtli*. On each of them were [crossed] motmot feathers; they were provided with [crossed] motmot feathers.

When she danced, she walked leaning on it, she walked thrusting it into the ground. She went marking the dance rhythm with it.[11]

And for ten days there sang [and danced] for her

yoan icxic contlalia coiolli, teucujtlacoiolli, anoço tzitzilli: itlanitzco in qujlpiaia, ocelueoatl yn ipan onoc coiolli: yn iquac nenemj cenca yxaoaca, yxamaca, xaxamaca, tzitzilica, tzitzitzilica,

yoan ycacac ipoçulcac, yn icacnacaz, in cacnacaztli, icpatl potonquj inic tlaqujttli, ynjc tlamaiqujttli: auh yn icacxochio, çan no ie in potonquj: auh yn jcacmecaio, çan ie no ic yn potonquj:

yoan ichimal atlacueçonaio, tlaatlacueçonanjcujlolli, atlacueçonanjcujliuhquj, toztlapilollo:

Auh in toztlapilolli, yn jiacachapullo muchioa, quauhyujtl, quanmoloctli, yoan quetzalpoztectli, yoan çaquan, yoan xollotl, matlatlauhquj, motocaiotia teuxollotl, toztenoloio in chimalli.

Jn iquac mjtotiaia, qujmamalacachoa yn jchimal, ic momamana:

yoan yoztopil tlaamaiotilli, haamaio, yoan tlaulhujlli, vllo: excan in tecomaio, tetecomaio: auh yn vncan tetecomaio, vncan mamanj yiauhtli, tziuhtli yn ipan mamantiuh, tzitziuhio:

in iquac mjtotia, ic motlaquechitinemj, qujtitilquetztinemj, ic ontlayiauhtiuh.

Auh matlaqujlhujtl, in qujcioapancujcatiaia, ix-

---

4. *"las cargantas de los pies"* in Sahagún's Spanish text.

5. Corresponding Spanish text: *"Tenja vna rodela pintada, con vnas ojas anchas, de la yerua que se llama atlacueçona."* For *atlacuetzonan*, Garibay, in Sahagún, Garibay ed., Vol. IV, p. 322, gives *" 'Madre de las olas' . . . Prob. Priaropus crassipes."* According to Dibble and Anderson, *Book XI*, p. 126, the broad round leaves of the *atzatzamolli*, probably *Castalia gracilis*, are called *atlacueçonan*.

6. *toztli* is identified as adult yellow-headed parrot, *Amazona ochrocephala* (Gmelin) in Dibble and Anderson, *Book XI*, p. 23.

7. *"con flores en los cabos, hechos de pluma de agujla"* in corresponding Spanish text. *Chapulin*, however, may be an element in *jiacachapullo*.

8. Identified as *Gymnostinops montezuma* (Lesson) in Dibble and Anderson, *Book XI*, p. 20.

9. Cf. *ibid.*, p. 22.

10. *yyoztopiltopil* in the *Real Palacio MS.*

11. Cf. *tlayaua* in Siméon, *Dictionnaire*: *"faire certains gestes en dansant."* The corresponding Spanish text reads: *"quando baylaua en el areyto, yuase arrimando al baston, y alcandole [sic] a compas del bayle."*

in the manner of women[12] all who came together, who gathered together of the salt people, the salt makers — the old women, and the mature women, and the maidens, and those who were maidens recently matured.

While yet there was sun, while it yet shone, then they began to dance. They went arranged, they went arranged each one in order; they were arranged, they were arranged each one in order. It was with cords called "flower cords" that they held one another, that they went stretched out. Their artemisia flowers went placed on their heads.

And they went singing; they cried out loudly; they sang in a very high treble. As the mockingbird takes it, [so] was their song. Like bells were their voices.

The old men led them. They loosed the song; they went directing them in their song — the chief men of the *calpulli*, the old men of the *calpulli*. And they were named keepers of the god[dess].

And [the likeness of] Uixtociuatl went erect in the midst of them. A brilliant feather ornament preceded her; an old man carried it in his arms. And this [ornament] was called Uixtociuatl's brilliant plumage.[13]

And for [the likeness of] Uixtociuatl they daily sang the women's song until the ten days had passed. And when they had gone to pass the ten days, in the evening they began holding vigil for her. At no time did they sleep; they made themselves go without sleep. Thus the night went.

And as [the impersonator of] Uixtociuatl danced, the old women held her; they went holding her as they made her dance.

Likewise the captives danced all the night, those who were to be the first to die, who would be as her fundament, whom they would make her fundament.

And when dawn broke, when it was verily the feast day, then were arrayed the offering priests, those who were to slay the victims. These were called Uixtoti.[14] They were adorned like Uixtotin; they were painted with the face paint of Uixtotin. They had their round paper rosettes, their pleated paper neck ornaments. And their [head] insignia

qujchtin cenqujça, qujcecencaoa yn iztatlaca, yn iztachiuhque: yn jlamatlaca, yoan yn jniolloco cioa, yoan ichpupuchti, yoan in ie ichpupuchchicacti:

oc vnca in tonatiuh, oc tona in peoa mjtotia, tecpantiuj, tetecpantiuj, motecpana, motetecpana mecatica, motocaiotia xochimecatl ynic maana, ynic motitilinjtiuj: ymjhiztauhiaxochiuh, ymicpac contecatiuj:

yoan cujcatiuj, cenca tzatzi, cenca tlapitzaoa: iuhqujn tzontli cana incujc: iuhquj in coiolli intozquj:

qujniacana in ueuetque, cuicatlaça qujncujcatlaxilitiuj in calpuleque, in calpulueuetque: yoan motocaiotia teuoaque.

Auh in Vixtocioatl, tlanepantla icatiuh, ce petlacotl qujiacana, ce tlacatl veue in qujnapaloa: auh ynjn mitoaia vixtopetlacotl.

Auh in iehoatl vixtocioatl, momuztlae in qujcioapancujcatiaia, yn ixqujchica matlaqujlhujtl onaci: auh yn oacito matlaqujlhujtl, teutlacpa im peoa qujtoçauja, qujcujcatia iuh ceiooal, aquenman cochi, acochiztli qujmochioaltia, iuh vetzi in ioalli.

Auh in Vixtocioatl, mitotia caana, caantinemj yn ylamatque in qujtotia:

no iuh ceiooal in mjtotia mamalti, in iacatiazque mjquizque, in iuhquj ypepechoan iezque, in qujnmopepechtizque.

Auh yn otlathujc, yn iquac ie vel ilhujtl, mec muchichioa in tlamacazque, in tlamictizque: in iehoan y, motocaiotiaia Vixtoti, movixtochichioa, moujxtoychioa, intlatlaquechpaiouh, yoan ymaamacuexpal: auh yn jntlauiz, quaviztitl muchioa, quetzaltzontecomaio quãmolocio.

---

12. Seler, in *Einige Kapitel*, p. 133, translates: "*Und zehn Tage lang sang (und tanzte) man für sie nach Weiberart.*" Garibay in "Relación breve," p. 300, translates *civapan cuicaya* as "*se cantaba como mujer.*" Jiménez Moreno (*"Primeros memoriales,"* p. 36) translates the same phrase as "*en el* Ciuapan *se cantaba.*"

13. Corresponding Spanish text: "*vn plumaje muy hermoso, hecho a manera de manga de cruz.*"

14. It would appear that both the offering priests and the captives were called *uixtotin*. The corresponding Spanish text reads: "*quando era la fiesta, aderecauanse los satrapas, que aujan de matar a esta muger que la llamauan, como a la diosa* Vixtocioatl, *y a los captivos: a los quales llamauan vixtoti.*"

were made [like] the claws of eagles, with quetzal head feathers, with eagle down.

And the legs of the eagles were made also of eagle down. These insignia [were supported] each upon carrying frames, each with holes [in the frames, in which the insignia were inserted]. Here were the insignia; [the frames] were then each tied, each bound around the stomach [with cotton bands], tied tightly, tied firmly. And their cords, the cords of each one, were wide bands, wide woven bands.[15]

And all the common folk who looked on, all carried, each one, their flowers; each one their tagetes flowers;[16] and some carried, each one, their artemisia flowers.

And when this was done, then they bore [the likeness of] Uixtociuatl to the summit of the Temple of Tlaloc. And they took up the captives who were as her fundament, whom she would use as a fundament, whom she would make her companions, her companions in death, who would be the first to die.

And when they had taken them up to the Temple of Tlaloc, then there was the slaying of the captives. And when the captives had died, only [then the impersonator of] Uixtociuatl came afterwards; she was last of all, she went last of all, she came quite last after them, she presided over the very end.

And when this was done, thereupon they laid her down on the offering stone. They stretched her out upon her back. They each laid hold of her; they each pulled tightly her hands, her feet. They bent her breast up greatly; they bent down her back. And her head they pulled tightly so that they took it nearly to the ground. And they bore down upon her neck with the beak of a swordfish,[17] barbed, serrated, spiny — spiny on either side.

And the slayer stood ready; he arose upright for it. Thereupon he cut open her breast. And when he had opened her breast, the blood gushed up high; it gushed far. It was as if it rose; it was as if it showered; it was as if it boiled up.

And when this was done, he took her heart from her; he placed it in the green jar, which was called the green stone jar.

And when this was done, loudly were the trumpets blown. And when it was over, then they brought

Auh in quauhtli imetz muchioa, no quãmolocio, ynjn tlaviztli câcacaxo, côcocoio, yn vncã onmana tlauiztli, ic maapana, ic moxixillancujtlalpia, ic motetevilpia, ic mocacatzilpia: auh yn jmecaio, yn jmemecaio, tlaxochtli, tlaxochpitzactli.

Auh in jxqujch tlacatl maceoalli, in tlatlatta, muchintin inxoxochiuh incecempoalxochiuh: yoan cequjntin ymiiztauhiaxochiuh.

Auh in ie iuhquj mec qujtlecauja in Vixtocioatl, yn icpac tlaloc: yoan qujntlecauja in mamalti, in iuhqujma ypepechoan, in q'nmopechitiaz, in qujnmoujcaltiz, yn imiquizteujcalhoan, yn iacatiazque miquizque.

Auh yn oq'ntlecaujque tlalocan, mec temictilo in mamalti: auh yn onmjcque mamalti, ça ontlatoqujlia in Vixtocioatl, ça ontlatzacuja, ça ontlatzacutiuh, ça ontetzacutiuh, ça tlatzinpachotiuh.

Auh yn ie iuhquj, njman ie ic conteca in techcac, conaquetztiteca, caanjlia, qujtitilinjlia, yn jma, yn jcxi, cenca uel quelcueloa, qujcujtlachicueloa: auh yn itzonteco, ynjc qujtilinjliaia, cẽca tlaltitech qujujcaia: auh ynic qujquechpachoa, acipaqujtli itlaujtequja, chichiqujltic, tzitziqujltic, viuitztic, necoc campa in ujujtztic.

Auh in tlamjcti, ça yc icac, omach ic moquetz, njman ie ic queltetequj: auh yn ompet yielchiqujuh, yn eztli oalmopipiazquetza, veca in onmopiaçoa, iuhquin momoloca, iuhqujn pipica, iuhqujn popoçoca.

Auh in ie iuhquj, mec conanjlia yn iiollo, contlalia xoxoujc xicalco: qujtocaiotiaia chalchiuhxicalli.

Auh yn iquac muchioa y, cenca tlapitzalo: auh in ie iuhquj mec qujoaltemouja yn jnacaio, yoan yn

---

15. Corresponding Spanish text: *"lleuauanle ceñjdo, con vnas vendas de manta coloradas del anchura de dos manos."*

16. *Tagetes erecta* L., in Dibble and Anderson, *Book XI*, p. 200.

17. Corresponding Spanish text: *"ponjanla sobre la carganta, vn palo rollizo, al qual tenjan dos, apretandole: para que no pudiesse dar vozes, al tiempo que la abriessen, los pechos. Otros dizen, que este era vn ocico de espadarte, que es vn pez marino, que tiene vn arma, como espada: en el ocico, que tiene colmjllos, de ambas partes: con este la apretauan la carganta."*

94

down the body, as well as the heart, of [the likeness of] Uixtociuatl. They came covered by a precious cape. And this came to pass in the early dawn.

And when it was over, when it was so, when there was ceasing of the part of each one,[18] then there was going, there was dispersing on the part of each one; there was going on the part of each one to their several homes. Those who had provided the feast carried out the feast, each one; celebrated the feast, each one. There was a feast; there was a feast in each place; the feast was observed in each place; the feast was held. There were invitations severally to banquet; there were acceptances severally.

And the old women, the old men, the salt people, the salt makers, the salt preparers, and the salt merchants, the salt traffickers, the people of the salt marshes each drank pulque. There was, on the part of each one, the drinking of pulque; there was the intoxication of each one. In their midst they poured out the pulque with a flower-decked jar.

One of the men made them intoxicated. He set it out; he distributed it. This was one who had not made his wife pregnant [nor] whose wife was pregnant. But if the one who made them intoxicated had impregnated his wife, he would not make them intoxicated; there would be no intoxicating. They would only imitate those who are drunk. The pulque would affect no one.

And when the day had ended, when they had celebrated the feast day, when it was night, then there was lying about. And some who were indeed intoxicated perhaps affronted others, perhaps belabored others, perhaps cried out at others. But afterwards they each fell exhausted,[19] they each slept, they slept as they fell. And anyone who had quitted the pulque, who had quitted it because he was sated — it was called sleep-producing pulque — afterwards, next day, he drank it, he finished it.

And any who had mishandled another, who had perhaps brawled with him, or had cried out at him, later, when day broke, when he had recovered his senses, supplicated [the injured one] with this same pulque in order to appease him. And the one to whom [injury] had been done, who had been shouted at, who had been shamed, then was appeased with the pulque; the offense was pardoned. Such did not remember against [the one who had been drunk] their disputes, their injuries, etc.

Here ended, here concluded Tecuilhuitontli.

iiollo Vixtocioatl, tlatlapachiuhtiujtz tlaçotilmatica. Auh ynin muchioaia, çan ioatzinco:

auh yn ontzonquiz, yie iuhquj yn onecacaoaloc, njman ic viujloa, cecēmanoa, viujloa in techachan, yn jlhujoaque, hiylhujchioa, hiilhujtlamati, ilhujtla, hiilhujtla, iilhujtlamacho, ilvichioalo, mococooanotza, motlatlacamati:

yoan yn jlamatque in veuetque, yn iztatlaca yn iztachiuhque, yn iztatlatique, yoan yn iztanamacaque, yn iztanecujloque, yn iztapan tlaca: tlâtlaoana tlâtlaoano, motlatlaoantia, tlanepantla xochapaztica qujoalmana yn vctli:

ce tlacatl tetlaoantia, qujteteca, qujtemamaca, amo iehoatl in tlavtztia, in vtztli ycioauh. Auh intla tlautztia tetlaoanti, amo teiujntiz, amo yujntioaz: çan teyujcopina, aiac itech quiçaz in vctli.

Auh yn ouetz cemjlhujtl, yn onjlhujtlaque yn oiooac, mec neteteco: auh in cequjntin yn oveliujntique, aço teixco, teicpac nemj, aço temjctia, aço tetzatzilia. Auh çatepan quaquauhtenuetzi, cocochi, cocochuetzi: auh yn aqujn, yn oc qujcaoa vctli, in qujxujcaoa, itoca cochvctli, qujn imuztlaioc in quj, in qujtlamja:

auh yn aqujn temicti, yn aço teaoac, yn anoço tetzatzili, qujniquac yn otlatvic, yn omuzcali: çan ie no ie in vctli ic tetlatlauhtia, ynic teiolceuja. Auh yn aioni, in tzatzililonj, in pinauhtilonj, njman moiolceuja yn ica vctli, motlapopolhuja, amo qujmolnamiqujlia, yn inneaoaliz, yn innemictiliz etc.

Nican tlamj, nican tzonquiça in Tecujlhujtontli.

18. Before *yn onecacaoaloc* the *Real Palacio MS* has *yn onecaualoc*.
19. *quaquauhtevetzi* in the *Real Palacio MS*.

Twenty-seventh Chapter, which telleth of the feast day and of the debt-paying which they celebrated during all the days of the eighth month, which was called Uey tecuilhuitl.[1]

Eighth feast day: this was Uey tecuilhuitl.

And before the arrival of the feast day, first there was eating on the part of each one. Everyone came together — the poor of Mexico and those who tilled the fields. When at dawn it was still quite dark, there was the drinking of *chiampinolli.* It was dissolved in a boat; they sweetened it with honey. And it was drunk from a vessel called *tiçapanqui.* Each one had a vessel for drinking from which he drank. Each one used the vessel, and some used the vessel twice. All fell to; two [vessels] were consumed. None held back; there were small children, old women, small boys, small girls; indeed there was everyone.

And anyone who could no longer finish it, who could no longer put his mouth to it, who could no longer put his lips to it, set it aside for himself. Some brought, each one, their vessels, some their gourds, in which they placed their leftovers. And anyone not provided with his vessel, who was without his vessel, without his bowl, just took it in his clothing; he made the atole go in his clothing. None made pretences; none cheated with the atole.

But if anyone did cheat with his atole, if he once more tried to enter among the others, there they repeatedly struck him with green canes; they whacked him.

And when this was done, when it had been drunk, for a while there was resting on the part of each one. Just there there was lying down; there was coming together on the part of each; there was gathering together on the part of each; there was conversing on the part of each. It was as if there was murmuring, as if they murmured, as if they twittered. And still others, who were setting aside[2] the atole, later could lie drinking it themselves; they lay giving it little by little to their small children to drink.

Jnic cempoalli on chicume capitulo, ytechpa tlatoa in ilhuitl yoan in nextlaoaliztli, in qujchioaia, yn ipan ic cemilhujtl ynic chicuey metztli: in mitoaia Vei tecujlhujtl.

Inic chicuetetl ilhujtl: iehoatl in vei tecujlhujtl.

Auh yn aiamo onaxioa ilhujtl, achtopa tlatlaqualoa: ixqujch tlacatl cenqujçaia, in motolinja in mexica, yoan in millacatzitzinti, in ioatzinco çan oc tlayoa, iehoatl in chianpinolli, mopatlaia acalco, qujnecpanja. Auh ynic tlayoa caxitl, motocaiotia tiçapanquj: cecen caxitl yn ioa, in quj: cecen caxoa auh in cequjntin, ooncaxoa, cenvetzi, ontetlamj, aiac mocaoa in pipiltzitzinti, in jlamatzitzin, in oqujchpipiltotonti, in cioapipiltotonti, in ie ixqujch tlacatl.

Auh in aqujn, aocmo vel qujiecoa, in aocmo qujcamaaci, in aocmo qujtenaci, motlacavia: cequjntin qujvivica in incocon cequjntin inxixical in vncan qujteca innetlacavil: auh in aca atle icõ monemachti, in atle icon, in atle icax; ça qujcuexanoa, concuexanaltia, in atolli, aiac motlapiquja, aiac matolixcuepa:

auh intlaca matolixcuepa, in oc ceppa tetlan calaqujznequj, vmpa qujvivitequj acaxoxouhquj ica, qujtlatlatzvitequj.

Auh in ie iuhquj in ontlaioac, oc achitonca nececevilo, çã vncan onoac, neoolololo, nececẽtlalilo, nenonotzalo, iuhqujn tlacaoacatimanj, iuhqujn tlatlacaoaca, iuhqujn tlachachalaca: auh in oc cequjntin, in oqujmocavica atolli, qujn ice vel qujtoque, yiolic qujmjititoque in impilhoantzitzin.

---

1. *"Fiesta grande de los Señores,"* according to Garibay ("Relación breve," p. 301); *"das 'grosse Herrenfest,' "* according to Seler (*Einige Kapitel,* p. 138).

2. *oquimocacauica* in the *Real Palacio MS.*

And when midday arrived, when it was time to eat, once again there was indeed the spreading out, the placing in order, the arranging of rows,[3] the forming of rows, the forming of lines. The small children were held by the hand; they were borne on the back.

And when there had been the spreading out, then the servers who were to take the food in their capes each girded their loins and each bound their hair with reed blades. [And those who were to take the food in their capes] would give it to the people, would distribute it to the people.[4] He who served one began with the first. Thus did he serve one: as many tamales as he could take hold of [with one hand], all those did he give him. They were perchance tamales of maize treated with lime, or tamales made with fruit; some were tamales of maize blossoms, some were tamales with twisted ends, some were honey tamales. And of the twisted-end tamales some had grains of maize, some had green beans and grains of maize.

And those who served looked to the small children. Very well did they serve them; great regard did they have [for them]. And there were some servers who offered tamales only to those whom they knew. They offered them to such familiars as perchance their kin or their friends. Perchance twice, thrice they offered them food.

And no one cheated with the tamales. But if they saw anyone try to cheat with the tamales, if it was seen, they struck him; they struck him repeatedly, leaving marks on him with a cord made of reeds.[5] As much as had been given him they took all away from him; they took from him all his tamales, his own which they had left with him, his own which had [wrongly] come to him.

And there were some to whom nothing came; it broke off with them — those who only came last after the others, who were only last, who only hung on at the tail [of the line]. Although indeed they crowded their way among the others, as they went forcing them apart in order to enter among them, nothing at all was given them. Therefore at first there was much forcing apart of the crowd, much jostling, because they feared lest[6] with them it be cut off.

Auh in oacic nepantla tonatiuh, in jquac tlaqualizpan, ie no ceppa vel neteteco, nevivipanolo, nececenpanalo, netetecpano, necuecuentililo: in pipiltzitzinti tematitech teaano, temamamalo.

Auh in onetetecoc mec mocujcujtlalpia, yoan moquaquailpia toltica: in tequjtque, in tlacuexanozque, in tetlamacazque, in tetlamamacazque, yiacac valpeoa in tetlamacac, injc tetlamaca, in quexqujch veliti qujtzitzquja tamalli, ixqujch qujtemaca, in aço tenextamalli, in anoço xocotamalli, cequj mjiaoatamalli, cequj iacacoltamalli, cequj necutamalli: auh in tamalli, cequj iacacollaoio, cequj iexococolotlaoio:

auh in tetlamacaia in qujmittaia pipiltzitzinti, cenca vel qujntlamacaia, cēca tlatlaocultiaia, auh in cequjnti tetlamacaque, çan qujteiximatcamaca in tamalli: qujmjximatcamaca in aço ivaniolque, in anoço injcnjoan, aço vppa, expa in qujntlamaca.

Auh aiac motamalaixcuepaia: auh in aqujn qujttaia motamalaixcuepaznequj, intla ittvz, qujvivitequj, qujtatacapitzvitequj tolmecatica: in quexqujch omacoca mochi qujcujlia, qujcencujlia in jtamal, inevian conmocavilia, inevian ōmonexotla.

Auh in cequjnti aoctle intech aci impan tlacotonj, iehoantin in ça tetzacuticate, in ça tlatzacuticate, in ça tlacujtlapiloa, in manel vel tetlamopitzmamali in temaxelotiuh, injc tetlan calaquj: çan njman aoctle maco: ipampa in acachto, cenca nemamaliva, cenca netotocholo, in mjmacaci, in maca ipan tlacoton.

---

3. *necempanalo* in *ibid.*

4. In the *Real Palacio MS* the passage is phrased: *yuan yn tlacuexanozque.* The bracketed words in our translation include the addition.

5. Corresponding Spanish text: *"nadie tomaua dos vezes y si alguno se atreuja a tomar dos vezes, dauanle de açotes cō vna espadaña, torcidas."*

6. *maaca* in the *Real Palacio MS.*

And among those with whom it was cut off there was weeping. They said:

"What can we do, we who are poor? In misfortune hath the feast day come! To what avail is our misery? Miserable are our small children!"

And if they saw that somewhere else perchance food was still eaten, they ran over there. There was running; they betook themselves there, they crowded there like the importunate. Although [those who ate] chased them away, beat them hence, beat them on the head, they only the more threw themselves at one, they only the more forced themselves violently on one.

And this was done for seven days while there was eating. And for this reason was this done,[7] that the ruler was pleased to show benevolence to one, that he showed benevolence to the common folk. For indeed there was much hunger; at this time dried grains of maize were costly; then there was much want; they were tired; it was very much a time of our death.

And until the time that the feast day of the lords came, upon every day there was song. When singing and dancing began,[8] there was very little sun; the sun had been shining bright. Thereupon fire was laid in the braziers; fire was placed in the braziers.

And the braziers lay in various rows; they lay in various lines; they lay in six rows. And each row was of ten [braziers]. And the braziers were so wide, each one, that two [men] took one in their embrace, and each was as tall as a man.[9]

And when this was done, then there was issuing from the house of song. They came singing, they came dancing. Between each pair [of men] came the women, the courtesans, the pleasure girls, the best ones, the chosen ones, those set apart.

And they went joining with,[10] went taking by the hands[11] those worthy of honor, the masters of the youths, and the young seasoned warriors, and the shorn ones, the Otomí, and the noblemen. [These last] were not arranged in order with them; they only placed themselves behind them, near them.

And the women were indeed adorned; they were indeed carefully bedight. All good were their skirts,

Auh in quexqujchtin impan tlacotonj, nechoqujlilo: qujtoaia,

quennel titotolinja, onenvetz in cemjlhujtl, tle nen totlaihiioviliz motolinja in topilhoantzitzin.

Auh intla ontlachia in oc cecnj, in açoc tlaqualo, ie ne vmpa motlaloa, netlalolo, vmpa motquj, vmpa onxoqujvi, iuhqujn amo pevilmatque, in manel qujnoaltoca, qujnvalhujtequj, in qujnvalquavitequj: ça cenca tevic mopetlativi, ça cenca tetlamopitzmamali.

Auh inin chicomjlhujtl in muchioaia, in tlatlaqualoia: auh injc mochioaia y, çan jc tetlaoculiaia in tlatoanj, in qujntlaoculiaia in maceoaltzintli: iehica ca cenca maianaloia, in jquac cenca tlaçotia in tlaolli, cenca oncã mjhiioviaia, mociavia: cenca vncã tomjqujan catca.

Auh in jxqujchica oalaci tecujlhujtl, izqujlhujtl cujcoia: im peoaia cujcoanaliztli, cenca ça achiton tonatiuh, cenca ça pepetzcatica in tonatiuh: njman ie ic tleteco tlaviltec, ipan in tlaviltetl motlatlalia tletl.

Auh in tlaviltetl viuipantoca, tetecpantoca, chiquacenpantitoca: auh in cempantli, matlatlatetl, actimanca: auh ynjc totomaoac catca tlaujltetl, hoontlacujtlanaoatectli: auh ynjc quaquauhtic catca, cecen quapantli:

auh in ie iuhquj, mec oalqujxoa, in cujcacali, cujcatiujtze, mjtotitiujtze, intzatzalan actiujtze in cioa: iehoantin in maaujltia, yn aujenjme: iehoantin in tlatzonanti, in tlapepenti, in tlacenqujxtilti:

auh yn qujnnanamictia, yn inmatitech qujmantiuj, çan iehoantin in mauiztililonj in teachcaoan, yoan in telpochtequjoaque, yoan in quaquachicti, yn otomj, yoan in pipilti: amo tehoan motecpana, çan jllotlama, incãpa onmoquetza tetlan.

Auh in cioa uel mocencaoa, vel moiecchichioa, much qualli in conmaquja, yn jncue, yn jvipil: yn

7. *ynin yuim mochiuaya* in *ibid.*

8. *cuicoaloya* and *cuicoyanaliztli* in *ibid.*

9. Corresponding Spanish text: "*gran copia de braseros altos, cerca de vn estado, y gruessos, que apenas los podian dos abraçar.*" Literally, *hoontlacujtlanaoatectli* may be rendered "two can take [it] in their embrace."

10. *quīnanamictiui* in the *Real Palacio MS.*

11. *quimaantiui* in *ibid.*

their shifts which they had put on. Some of their skirts had [designs of] hearts; some had a mat design like birds' gizzards; some were ornamented like coverlets; some had designs like spirals or like leaves; some were of plain, fine weave. All had borders,[12] all had fringes; all [the women] had fringed skirts.

And some of their shifts had tawny [streamers] hanging, some had smoke symbols,[13] some had dark green [streamers] hanging, some had house designs, some had fish patterns, some were only of plain, fine weave. And their neck [openings] were all large and their borders were also very deep; they were wide.

And when they danced, they unbound their hair; their hair just covered each one of them like a garment. But they brought braids of their hair across their foreheads.

And they were not decked with feathers; neither were their faces adorned with paint.

And thus were bedecked the masters of the youths: their array consisted of the cape of netting. And the brave warriors, they who had straw lip pendants,[14] had white net capes with seashells set in fish patterns. [These] were called their carmine-colored capes.

And as for all the men, whether brave warriors [or] youths, their net capes were only black, all with eyelets on the border,[15] and they had, each of them, their turquoise [ear plugs].

And those who led had only bell-shaped ear plugs.[16] And those who had bell-shaped ear plugs[17] also had their small lip pendants matching [their ear plugs]. Some were like lizards, some lip pendants were like dogs, some like a broad-leafed water plant or rectangular.

And the youths who had the hairdress of a warrior had, each one, their lip pendants made in the form of a circle containing four smaller circles.

And all the people who were just youths had the plain round lip plugs which they set in place.[18]

And the breast plates of the masters of the youths,

incue cequj iollo, cequj totolitipetlaio, cequj cacamo-liuhquj, cequj ilacatziuhquj, anoço tlatzcallotl, cequj çan petztic, muchi tene, muchi tlatenio, muchi cuetenio.

Auh yn invipil, cequj quappachpipilcac, cequj pocuipilli, cequj pocujpilli, cequj iapalpipilcac, cequj cacallo, cequj mjmjchcho, cequj çan petztic. Auh yn jtozquj much ueuei: yoan yn iten cenca no papatla-oac, papatlactic.

Auh yn iquac mjtotia, qujtoma yn jntzon, çan intzon qujquequentinemj: auh yn jntzon ipiloaz, ymixquac qujoalteca.

Auh amo mopotonja, amono moxaoa.

Auh ynic muchichioaia in teachcaoan, yn jnnechi-chioal catca, iehoatl in cuechintli: auh in tiacaoan, in teçacaoaque, ymiztaccuechin cilin ynic mjmjchcho, motocaiotia innochpalcuechin.

Auh in ixqujch tlacatl in çacan tiiacaoã, telpo-puchti: çan tliltic yn jncuechin, muchi tenjxo, yoan muchintin inxixiuh:

auh in tlaiacatia, çan incocoiolnacoch: auh in cocoiolnacoche: auh yn jntenpilol, qujnamictia, cequj aujtlatztli, cequj itzcujntenpilolli, cequj apa-tlactli, anoço tlaxantectli.

Auh yn telpopuchtin, in ie tzotzocoleque, ymaa-chichilacachtempilol:

auh yn ixqujch tlacatl in çan telpopuchti, çan ie-hoatl yn aiaoaltempilolli in contlalia.

Auh in teachcaoan, ymelpancuzquj, ymeelpancuz-

12. *tetene* in *ibid*.

13. *cequi pocujpilli* is repeated in the *Florentine Codex*.

14. *yn tēçacauaque* in the *Real Palacio MS*.

15. *tenixxo* in *ibid*.

16. In the corresponding Spanish text, Sahagún mentions copper, which may have been the material of which the bells were made.

17. *coyolnacocheque* in the *Real Palacio MS*.

18. Corresponding Spanish text: "*lleueuan vnos beçotes redondos, como vn circulo, con quatro circulillos en cruz, dentro en la circunferencia, que era algo ancha: todos los otros mancebos, lleuauan vnos beçotes, a manera de circulo, sin otro labor.*"

the breastplates of each one, were made of small, white seashells. All the neck bands with pendants[19] of the shorn ones, and Otomí, were of white gastropod shells.

And the shorn ones had attached lip plugs in the form of birds, and the Otomí had attached lip plugs formed like the broad leaf of a water plant.

And those of the brave warriors who were very proud each bought for himself genuine gastropod shell neck bands, very clear and limpid. And those who only came last, who only followed, each bought for their neck bands those which were only yellow; and they were not hard, neither were they very costly.

And those who had taken captives, the leaders of the youths, had their feather shoulder devices in the form of birds. They went carrying them upright over their heads.

And the seasoned warriors carried upon their shoulders feather devices formed like trees. In three places there were eagle feather clusters bound with ocelot skin. And at the base they were wound in three places with red cotton thread.

And some raised up quetzal feathers in the form of calliandra flowers, some a forked heron feather ornament; some set up the head plumage in bird form, some a device made of imitation quetzal feathers.

And on their legs, on their left ones, they placed hooves, real deer hooves. And their thongs were of this same deerskin cut thin, cut in narrow strips.

And thus were they variously painted. Some placed a black stain on their cheeks called "black cheek ash vase"; they applied iron pyrites to it. And some carried a black [stripe] upon their foreheads, from ear to ear; it was called "black sweat"; they also applied iron pyrites to it. And some extended diagonally a black [stripe], called *auitolli*, on their faces; they also applied iron pyrites to it.

And thus was their hair shorn. All had shorn their hair in the manner of masters of the youths; all together they had shorn their hair in the manner of masters of the youths. And those who had their temples shaven had each shaved their temples well; they had scraped them down well with a [sharp] piece of turtle shell. And they applied yellow ocher to them; they applied downy hairs to them.

And when this was done, when already they

quj, cilin in tlachioalli: auh in quaquachictin, yn otomj, incuzcachachapac: iehoatl in chipulin.

Auh yn quaquachicti qujnamjctia, iehoatl in tototenpilolli: auh yn otomj qujnamjctiaia, iehoatl yn apatlactli tenpilolli.

Auh yn aqujque in mocecenmati, in tiacaoan, qujmococouja teuchipuli in cuzcatl, cenca chipaoac: auh in ça tlatzacuja in ça tlatoqujlia, iehoatl yn achipulin qujmocoujaia, yn incuzquj, çan cuztic, amono tlaquaoac, amono cenca patio.

Auh in tlamanjme, in telpuchiaque, intototlamanal, in cõquequetztinemj yn imicpac.

Auh in tequjoaque, quauhtzontli in qujmamaia, excan yietiuh, quauhtlalpilonj, ocelueoatica in tlaqujmilolli: auh in itzintlã excan in chichilicpatica tlacujxtli.

Auh in cequjntin, xiloxochiquetzalli in conquetza in cequjntin aztaxelli, in cequjntin quatototl in conquetza, in cequjnti yntlatlachichioalquetzal.

Auh yn imicxic ymopuchcopa in cõtlaliaia chocholli, vel iehoatl in maçachocholli: auh yn jmecaio, çan no iehoatl yn maçaeoatl, tlapitzaoacatectli, tlapitzaoacaxotlalli.

Auh ynic mjchioaia, mjiec tlamantli, cequjtin tlilli incamapan contlaliaia, itoca tlilcamanexcomjtl, capetzujaia: auh in cequjntin ymixquac qujujca in tlilli, in nacaztitlan conaxitia, motocaiotia tliltzotl, no capetzujaia, auh in cequjntin imixtlan caana tlilli: itoca aujtolli no capetzuja.

Auh ynic moximaia, muchintin motiachcauhximaia, cenuetzia in motiachcauhximaia: yoan yn incanaoacan qujconaloaia, vel qujcoconaloaia, vel caiochiquja: yoã qujtecoçãnujaia, qujtomjiolhujaia.

Auh in ie iuhquj yn iquac ie mjtotia, tlepilli, oco-

19. Seler, *Einige Kapitel*, p. 144, has *deren Perlenhalsband* for *yncozcachachapac*.

danced, torches, pine fire brands, guided them. They went burning, they went sputtering, they went crackling. And as the young seasoned warriors carried them in their arms, they were much weighed down; it was as if they ran on their buttocks. And the resin, as it were, fell in large drops, and the live coals went scattering one by one on the ground, went spreading one by one on the ground. And the [charred] pine fell bit by bit to the ground.

And along the sides, only from fire ladles held in the hand was there light. They who gave light were youths who had fasted for twenty days. They were spread out in a circle; they ranged on the sides. On one side were those of Tenochtitlan; on the other side were those of Tlatilulco.

And they did not dance; they did only one thing, they only provided people light. And they kept watch, they kept a close watch on people. Their eyes were indeed on their charge, that no one take it upon himself, that none there make eyes at the women, in case anyone should go jesting there [with a woman]. If anyone was seen, [if] he yet only intended it, [if] he tried it — perhaps later, next day, or later, two days hence, they punished him. They beat him repeatedly with pine boughs[20] which went burning. Verily, they left him for dead.

And when there was dancing, sometimes Moctezuma emerged, came forth to dance, and sometimes he came not forth; it was only as his heart felt.

And that they might go in line when they danced, they held one another by the hand, they held one another about the waist.

And some they grasped by their hands. There was grasping of the hands. And thus they went going with their feet, thus they made the dance movements; they went together with their feet. And they whirled about repeatedly; they went passing by the braziers; they went passing among them; they went entering into all the rows of braziers. When they had gone to reach there where [the space] ended, once more they circled back; they returned [whence they had started].

And when there was a cessation, already it was late at night, already time for there to be sleeping, as when the eyes are blinked. Today it would be perchance already the hour of nine.

And when it was enough, when it had been stopped, when the ground drums faded out, then

pilli, qujniacana tlatlatiuh, cuecuetlacatiuh, cocomocatiuh: auh in qujnapaloa telpuchtequjoaque cenca eticiuj, iuhqujn tzitzintlacça: auh yn ocotzotl, iuhqujn chachapaca, yoan in tlexochtli tetepeuhtiuh, cecenmantiuh: yoan in ocotl oalichachaiaca.

Auh in tlatenco, çan matlematica in tlaujlo: iehoantin in tlaviaia telpopuchti, in mocempoalçauhque, tlaiaoalotimãca, ixtlapantimanj: cectlapal manj in tenochca, no cectlapal manj, in tlatilulca.

Auh amo mjtotia, çan qujxcaujaia, çan ixqujch tetlaujliaia: yoan tlapieia, vel teixpieia, vel ymix intequjuh catca, ynic aiac ytla vncan qujmotequjtiz, ynic aiac vncan teixtlaxiliz, yn açaca vncan vetzcatiuh: intla aca oittoc, çan oc conjxxotia, coniximati, aço qujn jmoztlaioc, anoço qujn iviptlaioc, in qujtlatzacuiltia, qujujujtequj ocoquauhtica, tlatlatlatiuh, ca micquj in qujcaoa.

Auh yn iquac netotilo, in Motecuçoma, in quenmanjan, oalqujçaia, oalmjtotiaia: auh iñ quenmanjan amo oalqujçaia, çan yiollo tlamatia:
auh ynic tecpantiuj, in mitotia, monaoa, mocujtlanaoa.

Auh in cequjntin, inmatitech maana, nematitech neaaano: auh ynic qujiauhtiuj, yn imicxi, ynic tlayiaoa, çan ceniauh yn imicxi: yoan ontzitzinqujça, itlan qujqujztiuj in tlaujltetl, itzalan quiquiztiuj, itic cacalactiuj, yn izqujpantli tlaujltetl: yn oacito yn vmpa tlantoc, oc cepa momalacachoa, in cujtlaujc, oalmocuepa.

Auh in necaoaloa, ie tlaquauhiooa, ie netetequjzpan: yn iuh mixtlaxilia axcan aço ie chicunauj ora.

Auh in ie ixqujch, yn onecacaoaloc, yn ompet veuetl, mec cecenmanoa, viujloa, yn ixqujchtin viuj

20. See Plate 28.

there was dispersing on the part of each one, there was going on the part of each one; all betook themselves to their homes. The great noblemen were left there by torch light; they went lighted by torches; they went giving them torchlight to their homes.

And the women who had danced with people holding them by the hand then were assembled when already there had been song and dance; they led them away, even as was done with the masters of the youths. They gathered [the women] together, grouped them, rounded them up, placed them together, grouped them together, indeed hunted them out, lest one might go somewhere, lest one be forced to accompany someone, lest some perverse youth might take one away.

None the less, the noblemen addressed the matrons that they might go releasing some [of the women], might go releasing one. Not only of their own accord did [the women] go somewhere; only at someone's word was it done.

And when they released them, [the girls] were given gifts. Gifts were given there, and food was given there. And also gifts were given each of the mistresses of the women,[21] the matrons. They put them aside for themselves; they each put them aside for themselves; they took their leftovers to their several homes.

And as for the masters of the youths: the master of youths of front rank, worthy of honors, asked for the women only in secret, not before others. Perhaps he went to await her in his home, or else he asked for her elsewhere. Just so, they ate in secret.

And the woman came forth only at night; she spent only the night [with him]; she departed when it was well into the night.

But if one was noted living in concubinage, there was anger because of it, there was concern over it. For all this there was assembling, for this there was consulting there in the song house.

There, before everyone, they punished him. For this they cut off his warrior's hair dress; they took from him all his possessions, his adornment, his lip pendant. Thereafter they beat him repeatedly with a pine stick; they verily caused him to swoon. They singed his head with fire; his body smoked; it blistered.

And when they had indeed caused him to swoon, with this they cast him forth.

---

21. *tlauhtiloya* in the *Real Palacio MS.*

yn inchachan: in veuei pipilti, oncacaoalo, tlavilpan, tlaujlilotiuj, qujntlatlaujlitiuj yn inchan.

Auh yn cioa yn otenaoaque, njman mocentlalia, in ie oncujcoianoloc, in qujiacana, yn iuhq' yn tiachcaoan muchioa, qujnnechicoa, qujntecpichoa, qujmololoa, qujncenqujxtia, qujcentecpichoa, vel qujmixpepena, yn ma aca canapa ia, yn ma aca moteujcalti, in ma aca telpuchtlaueliloc qujujca:

tel in pipilti, qujmonilhujaia in cioa tlaiacanque, ynic cequjntin qujncaoatiuj, tecaoatiuj: amo çan moiocoiaia yn canapa via, tetencopa muchioaia.

Auh yn ontecaoaia, vmpa motlauhtiaia, vmpa tlauhtiloia, yoã vmpa tlamacoia: auh no tlatlauhtiloia, in cioatachcaoan, in cioateiacanque, motlacauja, motlatlacauja, quitquj yn inchachan innetlacaujl.

Auh in teachcaoan, in teachcauh, tlaiacatia, in mauiztililonj, çan ichtaca in qujnnaoatia cioa, amo teixpan, aço ichan in qujchietiuh, anoço canapa in qujnaoatia: çan iuhquj, yn ichtacaquaia.

Auh in cioatl, çan oaliooalqujça, çan moiooalpoloa, oc ueca ioan in qujça:

auh intla aca ittoz, in momecatitinemj, ic tlaqualanjaia, ic tlaiolitlacoaia, ica necentlalilo, yca nenonotzalo, in vncan cujcacali:

vncan teixpan qujtlatzacujltia, ic qujtzotzocoltequj, muchi qujcujlia in ixqujch ytlatquj, yn inechichioal, yn itempilol: çatepan qujujujtequj, ocoquauhtica, vel qujhiiocaoaltia, qujquatlechichinoa, tlêtlecaleoa, haaquaqualaca, yn inacaio.

Auh yn ouelqujhijocaoaltique, yca oalmaiauj:

They said unto him:

"Go, rascal! Perchance thou art a man, perchance thou art a brave warrior! How can we care for thee? Wherever our foes come rising against us, let us die as brave men!"

And these were the words which they said unto him; indeed much else.

And when with this they had cast him forth, he just slowly crept away; he left going from one side to the other; he just went confused; he left full; he withdrew forever; nevermore was he to sing and dance with the others.[22]

And the mistress of the women just expelled the [erring] woman. Nevermore was she to sing and dance with the others; nevermore was she to hold others by the hand. Thus the girls' matrons established; thus they resolved.

And the woman who had erred withdrew forever. Never again was she to expect that once more she would sing and dance with others.

And the one whom they had punished because of the woman then married her; he quieted the affair.

And before the real feast day came which was called Uey tecuilhuitl, on the tenth day, then the woman [who was the likeness of] Xilonen died. Her face was painted in two colors; she was yellow about her lips, she was chili-red on her forehead. Her paper cap had ears at the four corners; it had quetzal feathers in the form of maize tassels; [she wore] a plaited neck band. Her neck piece consisted of many strings of green stone; a golden disc went over it. [She had] her shift with the water lily [flower and leaf design], and she had her skirt with the water lily [flower and leaf design. She had] her obsidian sandals, her carmine-colored sandals. Her shield and her rattle stick were chili-red. In four directions she entered, or she entered the sand.

For this reason it was called *xalaqui*: in this way she foretold her death — that on the morrow she would die.

She began the feast day when she entered Tetamaçolco. The second place where we had been arriving, we went to reach [to accomplish the ceremony], and it was a place named Necoquixecan. The third place in which she entered was Atenchicalcan. For this reason was it called Atenchicalcan, that here gushed forth the water, and also here faded away the wind. The fourth place she entered was there at Xolloco. There she concluded.

qujlhuja,

Xiiauh nocne aço toqujchtli, aço titiiacauh, quen timitztocujtlauja: çaçocan techquetzaqujuh in toiaouh, maça toqujchmiqujcã:

yoan in tlatolli qujlhujaia, vel oc mjec.

Auh yno ica oalmaiauhque, ça iaiatiuh, chichicoeoatiuh, ça xonauhtiuh, tẽtentiuh, iccen tlatlalcauja, aoqujc teoan cujcoanoz.

Auh in cioatl çan qujtotoca, in cioatetiachcaoan: aoqujc no teoã cujcoianoz, aoqujc no tenaoaz, ic qujcennaoatia, qujcenmacaoa, yn ichpuchtlaiacanquj.

Auh in cioatl yn otlatlaco, iccenmaian tlatlalcauja, aoq'c ceppa motemachiz, yn oc ceppa teoan cujcoanoz.

Auh in iehoatl yn otlatzacujltiloc, yn ipampa cioatl, njman ic qujmocioaoatia, qujiauceujlia.

Auh yn aiamo aci in iquac ie uel ilhujtl, yn moteneoa vei tecujlhujtl, yn iquac tlamatlacti, iquac miquja, in xilonen cioatl, michchictlapan, ynic michiuh yn itẽco coztic, auh yn ixquac chichiltic: yiamacal nauhcampa nacace, quetzalmjiaoaio, cozcapetlatl: yn icozquj chalchiujtl miiecpantli, teucujtlacomalli yn ipan mantiuh, yiaxochiavipil yoan yaxochiacue yhitzcac, ynochpalcac: yn ichimal yoã yn ichicaoaz chichiltic, nauhcampa yn aquja, anoço xalaquja:

ynic mjtoa xalaquj, ic qujmachiltia yn jmjquiz, in miquiz muztla:

in cemilhujtl conpeoaltia yn aquj, tetamaçolco, ynic vccan vncan in taciticatcan, tacito: yoan itocaiocan necoqujxecan: ynjc excan vncan yn aquja, yn atenchicalcan, ynic moteneoa atenchicalcan, ca vncan, oalcholoaia yn atl, yoan no vncan oalpopoliujaia yn ecatl: ynic nauhcan aquja, vmpa xolloco, vmpa ontzonqujçaia,

22. *quicoyanoz* in *ibid.*

[These] just sustained, just carried along the four year-bearers — Reed, Flint knife, House, Rabbit;[23] thus do the year-bearers go describing circles, go whirling around [as they measure time].

And when this was done, [the impersonator of] Xilonen was to die at dawn. All during the night songs were sung after the manner of women. Vigil was kept. Everybody kept vigil; they slept not; the women remained sleepless; they sang her songs; they sang for her.

And when day broke, then began the dancing. Verily everyone, the masters of the youths, the youths, the leaders, and the seasoned warriors had, each one, their maize stalk. These were named "bird banners."

Likewise the women danced, those who belonged to Xilonen. They were pasted with red feathers and they were painted with yellow ocher. Also, thus were their faces divided: they were yellow with ocher about the lips, and they were light red with arnotto[24] on their foreheads. They had their wreaths of flowers upon their heads; their garlands of tagetes flowers went leading.

These women were known as offering priestesses. They mingled not with the men; they just remained apart. They went encircling [the likeness of] Xilonen; they went enclosing her. They went singing for her after the manner of women. These women were called "the hanging gourd."

And the masters of the youths went dancing before [the impersonator of Xilonen]; they followed a serpentine course.

And for this reason were the women known as "the hanging gourd": the two-toned wooden drum, which they beat as they went, had going tied to it a water gourd, which went under, at the bottom of the drum; it looked as if it went hanging. They who beat the two-toned drum only went carrying under their arms the little drum which they went beating with the rubber-tipped drumsticks.[25]

çã qujtoctiaia, çan qujujcaltiaia, yn nauhtetl xiuhtonalli: yn acatl, in tecpatl, in calli, in tochtli, ynic tlaiaoalotiuh, ynic momalacachotiuh, in xiuhtonalli.

In ie iuh ioatzinco miquiz in Xilonen: ceiooal in cioapan cujcoia, toçooaia, muchi tlacatl ixtoçooaia, amo cochia, mocochiçoloaia in cioa, queoaia queviliaia yn icujc.

Auh yn ie otlatujc, njman ic peoa in netotilo, vel ixqujch tlacatl in tiachcaoan, in telpopuchti, yn iiaque, yoan in tequjoaque, incicintopil: ynjn motocaiotia totopanjtl.

No mjtotia in cioa, yn itech pouja in xilonen, mopopotonjaia tlapaliujtica: yoan moxaoaia tecoçauhtica: no ic qujcotona, yn inxaiac, yn jntenco, tecoçauhtica: auh yn imixquac tlapalachiotica, ymjicpacxochiuh, inxoxochicozquj cempoalxuchitl yiacatiuh.

Yn iehõã yn, cioa, moteneoa cioatlamacazque, amo qujmonnelooa yn oqujchti, çan nonqua mantiuj, cololujtiuj, qujtepeujtiuj in Xilonen: qujcioapãcujcatitiuj: in iehoantin y, cioa moteneoa tecomapilooa.

Auh in tiachcaoan ixpan mjtotitiuj, mococolotiuj:

auh ynic moteneoa tecomapilooa, ca in teponaztli in qujujtectiuj, itech çaliuhtiuh in atecomatl, yhicampa iteputzco ietiuh in teponaztli, iuhqujn pilcatiuh ic neci: in teponaçoa çan qujciacaujtiuh in teponaztontli in qujujtectiuh olmatica.

23. Entering the sand was evidently a ceremony literally enacted, and logical in view of the attributes of the deities whose festivities were honored by it. The explanation in both Sahagún's Spanish text and the Aztec column is not explicit. The four places in which Xilonen entered the sand may be identified in modern Mexico City and are associated with water and sand. *Aquia* is probably an assimilation of *aaquia*. Angel María Garibay K., personal communication.

Seler (*Einige Kapitel*, p. 150) translates *aquia anoço xalaquia* as "*ging sie (in die Erde) oder in den Sand hinein.*"

The corresponding Spanish text, quoted at length, is: "*Ataujada con estes ataujos, cercauanla muchas mugeres, lleuauanla en medio, a ofrecer encienso a quatro partes: esta ofrenda hazia a la tarde, antes que muriesse. A esta ofrenda llamauan xalaquia, porque el dia siguiente auja de morir: el vno destos lugares se llama tetamaçolco, el otro se llama necocyxecan, el otro se llama atenchicalcan, el quarto se llama xolloco. Estos quatro lugares, donde ofrecian era en reuerencia, de los quatro caracteres de la cuenta de los años.*"

24. *Bixa orellana* L. in Dibble and Anderson, *Book XI*, p. 241.

25. Corresponding Spanish text: "*a las mugeres, yvanlas tañedo* [sic], *con vn teponaztli, que no tenja mas que vna lengua encima, y otra debaxo: y en la debaxo, lleuaua colgado, vna xicara en que soelen beuer agua, y assi suena mucho mas, que los que tienen dos lenguas,*

And the offering priests attended them. They went blowing wind instruments; it was shell trumpets that they went blowing. And they went scattering powdered *yauhtli*; they went strewing it, they went casting it [as] they went to meet [the likeness of] Xilonen.

And the fire priest, who was to slay [the likeness of] Xilonen as an offering was well arrayed [and] adorned. He bore an eagle claw device upon his back; it went surrounded by quetzal feathers. His holder was of eagle down [with] quetzal feathers. His flint knife was of gold. He had his rosette on his back; it was of paper workmanship. Etc.

A man carried the mist rattle board upon his shoulders; it rattled in three places. And when they had gone to arrive at the place where [the impersonator of] Xilonen was to die, then the fire priest came to receive her. Before her he set up the rattle board; he rattled it, and with *yauhtli* went forth to receive her, and scattered it toward her.

And thereupon they took her up to the Temple of Cinteotl. Then they laid her upon the back [of a priest] — not upon the offering stone; rather, she died upon [a priest's] back. And when there was dying upon his back, it was called "it has a back."

Thereupon she performed her service. [The sacrificing priest] severed her head. When she had [thus] performed her service, when they had slain her, thereupon he took her heart from her; he placed it in the blue gourd. They who knew, who were well experienced, knew where they placed it, where they required it.

And at this time were eaten, for the first time, tortillas of green maize. For the first time was offered, for the first time was chewed the cane of green corn. And for the first time were cooked amaranth greens. And for the first time the sweetness of flowers — tagetes, tobacco flowers [— was smelled].

And when it was Uey tecuilhuitl, there was dancing which was the particular function of the women: old women, maidens, mature women, little girls. The maidens, who had looked upon no man, were plastered with feathers; their faces were painted.

Everyone made plain tamales, made fruit tamales for themselves. They offered them to each of their gods.

Auh in tlamacazque, tenanamjquj tlapitztiuj, tecciztli in qujpitztiuj: yoan yn iauhtextli in qujpipixotiuj, qujcecenmatiuj, qujtetepeuhtiuj, conjxnamjctiuj in Xilonen.

Auh in tlenamacac, in tlamjctiz, vel mocencaoa, muchichioa, quauhiztitl in qujmama, quetzalli ynic moiaoatiuh, quãmoloctli, yn itecomaio ietiuh quetzalli cuztic teucujtlatl yn itecpaio ietiuh, ytlaquechpaniouh ietiuh, amatl in tlachiuhtli, etc.

Ce tlacatl qujquechpanoa, in aiochicaoaztli, excan in cacalaca: auh yn oacito yn vncan miquiz xilonẽ, njman quioalnamjquj in tlenamacac, ixpan qujoaltilquetza in chicaoaztli, qujcacalatza: yoan yiauhtli ic qujoalnamiquj, yuicpa qujoalchaiaoa.

Auh ie ic contlecauja in cinteupan, çatepan conteca in tecujtlapan, amo techcac, çan tecujtlapan in miquja: auh yn icujtlapan mjcoaia, motocaiotia tepotzoa:

njman ie ic tlacoti, qujquechtequj, yn otlacotic, yn ocontlatlatique, njman ie ic conanjlia yn iiollo, xoxouhquj xicalco qujoallalia: iehoã qujmati in machiceque catca in campa qujtlalia, in campa qujnequja.

Yoan iquac iancujcan qualoia, in xilotlaxcalli: iancujcan tlamanalo, iancujcan moquaquaia in ooatl: yoan iancujcan mopaoaci in oauhqujlitl, yoan iancujcan ynecu in suchitl, in cempoalsuchitl, in jesuchitl.

Auh yn iquac in vei tecujlhujtl netotiloia, çan inneixcaujl in cioa, yn jlamatque, yn ichpopochti, yn iniolloco cioa cioapipiltotonti: in ichpopochti yn aiacan qujtta oqujchtli, mopotonjaia, moxaoaia.

Ixqujch tlacatl motamaluja moxocotamalujaia: qujntlatlamanjliaia, in intevoan.

And of the old men and the old women it was the exclusive privilege that they drink pulque. Absolutely no one of the youths, the offering priests, the maidens drank pulque.

And if anyone was noted, perforce he was seized, he was put in jail, in the granary.[26] Council was held concerning what would be done about it; whether perchance they would punish him. There was weighing [of evidence]; there were opinions given. They determined if it was his privilege, and if it was not his privilege he was condemned to die. No more did he go forth; there was no protection for him; no longer was it his half-entanglement;[27] there was no hope for him.

When whoever it was had been condemned, in the evening there was announcing to the people that there would be assembling, there would be gathering wherever [the judge's] words were to be published.

It was said: "On the morrow there will be dying. All of the commoners will be troubled. Some of those who drank we shall leave alone. Fear will fall upon them."

[The condemned] came with wrists bound together. [The constables] placed them in the middle [of the market place]. Thereupon the high judges spoke. They admonished the people. They spoke about pulque, which no youth was to drink. Only later, when they matured, when they had become old [might they drink it]. And those who had youths, who already had maidens, verily their privilege it was that they might drink pulque.

And when this was done, when the judgment ended, when Moctezuma's slayers, his executioners, struck the backs of each [of the criminals'] heads. They were the Quauhnochtli, the Ezuauacatl, the Ticociauacatl, the Tezcacoacatl, the Maçatecatl, the Atempanecatl.[28] These were not lords; they were only constables under command, appointed, approved, courageous, able, who spoke well.

And when [the criminals] had been killed, there was terror because of it; the intelligent, the clear thinkers were terrified. But the perverse, those badly brought up, those who could not think, the effeminate, the rebellious only laughed at it, only jested at the admonitions. They only listened mockingly; they

Auh in ueuetque, yoan in jlamatque, çan inneixcaujl catca in tlaoanaia: çan njmã aiac tlaoanaia in telpuchtli, in tlamacazquj, yn ichpuchtli.

Auh intla aca, oittoc, vel iujuj ic oanoc, quauhcalco tlalilo, petlacalco: ipan nenonotzalo in tlein ipan muchioaz, yn aço qujtzacutiaz neetitilo, neixpãtitilo: qujpantia intla ie ynemac: auh intlacamo ie ynemac, tlatzontequjlilo, mjquiz, aocmo qujçaz, aoctle itzacujl, aocmo ichicomatl, aoctle ynetemachil.

In aq'n oixnaoatiloc, teutlacpa in tetlalujlo, in necenqujxtiloz, necentecoz, in çaço cãpa ie moteneoaz, in jtlatollo:

mjtoaia, muztla micoaz, ixqujch tlacatl oliniz in maçeoalli cequjntin tiqujncaoa in tlaoãque, inca mauiztli uetziz.

Mamailpitiuitze, tlanepantla qujntlalia: njman ie ic tlatoa, in tecutlatoque, tenonotza, itechpa tlatoa in vctli, in aiac qujz in telpuchtli: ça qujnjquac in otlachicalujque, yn oueuetique: yoan in telpuche, in ie ichpuche, vel innemac catca in tlaoanazque.

Auh in ie iuhquj yn ontzonquiz, in tecutlatolli: njman ic qujncuexcochujujtequj, yn itemicticaoan, in itequacaoan in moteçumatzin: in quauhnochtli, iezoaoacatl, ticociaoacatl, tezcacoacatl, maçatecatl, atenpanecatl: in iehoantin yn, amo tetecuti, çan achcacauhti, tlanaoatilti, tlaixquetzalti, tlaqualitalti, iollotlapaltique, iollochicaoaque, yoan iolloque, in vellatoa.

Auh yn iquac ie mictilo, ic necujtiuecho, ic mocujtiuetzi in tlacaqujni, in uel monotzanj: auh in iollotlaueliloque, yn atlanonotzalti, yn auel monotza, in tlacioaizcaltilti, in tzonteme, çan qujuetzca, çan qujcamanaloa in tenonotzaliztli, çan qujcamanalcaquj,

26. See Plate 27.

27. *ichicomatl*: cf. Dibble and Anderson, *Book VI*, p. 220.

28. For these officials, cf. Clark's *Mendoza Codex* (ed. and trans. James Cooper Clark, 3 vols. [London: Waterlow and Sons, 1938]), Vol. III, fol. 65.

only listened in vain; they took the discourse ill. Not thus were they terrified of death.

And when this was done, when there had been slaying, then there was dispersing, there was disorder. They raised dust. There was repeated shaking out [of capes], there was scattering of each one, there was breaking up, there was repeated breaking up, there was spreading out,[29] there was going on the part of each; they went to their various homes. Then the place where they had been quieted.

Here finishes, here ends the way in which was celebrated the feast called Uey tecuilhuitl.

çan caujlcaquj, avampa qujtta in tlatolli, amo ic mauhcaçonequj, in temjctiliztli.

Auh in ie iuhquj, yn onmjcoac: njman ic tlatzomonj neacomanalo, teuhtli qujquetza, netzetzelolo, cecenmanoa, xitinoa, xixitonoa, moiaooa, viujloa, viuj yn jnchachã: njman cactiuetzi yn vncan onooaia.

Nican tlamj, njcan tzonqujça, inic ilhujtl muchioaia: yn jtoca Vey tecujlhujtl.

29. The *Real Palacio MS* has *momoyaoua*.

Twenty-eighth Chapter, which telleth of the feast and of the offerings which they made during all the days of the ninth month, which was named Tlaxochimaco.[1]

The ninth month was known as Tlaxochimaco. It also was of twenty days.

Two days [before the feast] there was the seeking of flowers. There was scattering over the mountains when there was looking for every flower — various flowers, mountain flowers, dahlias,[2] hummingbird flowers,[3] mountain tagetes,[4] ranunculus,[5] bocconias,[6] tiger lilies,[7] plumerias,[8] didymeas,[9] forest magnolias,[10] talaumas,[11] earth plumerias,[12] tagetes,[13] lobelias,[14] white water lilies, red water lilies,[15] castalias.[16]

And when they had been gathered, when they had come bringing the flowers, when there had been coming bringing [them], when it was dawn, then they were strung together. There was stringing; they strung them. And when the flowers had been strung together, then they were twisted, they were wound [in garlands] — each indeed long, each very long, each thick, indeed thick.

And when there had been the arranging, then carefully they were each set down; they were indeed handled with esteem, they were cared for with reverence.

Jnic cẽpoalli on chicuei capitulo, itechpa tlatoa in ilhuitl, yoan in tlamanaliztli: in quichioaia in ipan ic cemilhujtl, ic chicunauhtetl metztli, in moteneoaia Tlasuchimaco.

Inic chicunauhtetl ilhujtl: moteneoa tlasuchimaco, no cempoalilhujtl:

viptlatica in suchitemoloa, necenmanalo in tepepan in tlatemolo in ixqujch suchitl, in nepapan suchitl, in tepepan suchitl, yn acocosuchitl, vitzitzillacusuchitl, tepecempoalsuchitl, nextamalsuchitl, tlacosuchitl, ocelusuchitl, cacalosuchitl, ocusuchitl, anoço aocusuchitl, quavelosuchitl, iollosuchitl, tlalcacalosuchitl, cempoalsuchitl, acasuchitl, atlacueçona, tlapalatlacueçona, atzatzamolsuchitl.

Auh yn omonechico yn ocaaxitico suchitl, yn oaxioaco, yn otlatujc, njmã ic moçoço tlaçolo, tlaçoa: auh yn omoçoçoc, suchitl, mec momamalina, mjlacatzoa, vel viujac viujtlatztic, totomaoac, vel tomactic.

Auh yn otlacencaoaloc, mec tlamatzin motlatlalia, vel momalhuja, momauizpia:

1. Cf. Orozco y Berra, *Historia antigua*, Vol. II, p. 38: "Miccailhuitzintli, Tlaxochimaco. *El primero era nombre usado por los de Tlaxcalla. . . . El nombre mexicana es Tlaxochimaco, palabra que Torquemada interpreta, cuando son dadas y repartidas las flores; mientras Veytia dice, estera de flores. En la fiesta principal del mes, consagrada á Huitzilopochtli, la estatua de éste y de los demas dioses eran adornadas profusamente con flores. . . ."* Clavijero, *Historia antigua*, Vol. III, pp. 162–63, further writes: "*. . . adornaban de flores a todos los ídolos, no solamente a los que se veneraban en los templos, sino también a los que tenían por devoción en sus casas; que por esto daban al mes el nombre de* Tlaxochimaco."

2. *acocosuchitl:* Dahlia coccinea Cav. in Dibble and Anderson, *Book XI*, p. 199.

3. *vitzitzillacusuchitl:* "*Prob.* Gallium *sp.,* Didymea mexicana," in Sahagún, Garibay ed., Vol. IV, p. 337.

4. *tepecempoalsuchitl:* cf. Chap. 26, n. 16.

5. *nextamalsuchitl:* Ranunculus petiolaris H. B. K. in Dibble and Anderson, *Book XI*, p. 200.

6. *tlacosuchitl:* Bouvardia termifolia Schl. in *ibid.*, p. 208.

7. *ocelosuchitl:* Tigridia pavonia in *ibid.*, p. 212.

8. *cacalosuchitl:* Plumeria rubra in *ibid.*, p. 205.

9. *ocusuchitl:* Didymea mexicana Benth. in Sahagún, Garibay ed., Vol. IV, p. 347.

10. *quavelosuchitl:* eloxochitl is identified as *Magnolia dealbata* Succ. in Dibble and Anderson, *Book XI*, p. 201.

11. *yollosuchitl:* Talauma mexicana Don in *ibid.*, p. 201.

12. *tlalcacalosuchitl:* prob. *Plumeria acutifolia* in *ibid.*, p. 198.

13. *cempoalsuchitl:* cf. Chap. 26, n. 16.

14. *acasuchitl:* Lobelia fulgens, L. laxiflora in Dibble and Anderson, *Book XI*, p. 211.

15. *atlacueçona:* cf. Chap. 26, n. 5.

16. *atzatzamolsuchitl:* Castalia gracilis in Dibble and Anderson, *Book XI*, p. 126.

And when this was done, all the common folk together fell to making tamales for themselves. In the evening they plucked turkey hens and [killed] dogs; also in the evening they singed them. Those were singed which would be required early in the morning.

There was confusion. There was indulging in sleeplessness; there was wakefulness. There was living for the feast day. It was as if each one was active; there was preoccupation on the part of each one so that there would be preparation.

And when the day broke, the guardians of the god thereupon each made offerings to Uitzilopochtli; they adorned him with garlands of flowers; they placed flowers upon his head. And before him they kept spreading, they kept lining up, they kept placing in rows, they kept hanging in rows all the various flowers, the precious flowers, the gifts made as offerings.

Thereupon flowers were offered all at the same time to all of the gods, the images of the gods, the demons. They were adorned with flowers, they were girt with [garlands of] flowers; flowers were placed upon their heads there in the temples.

Thereupon all at the same time in all the houses, in the homes of the stewards, in the homes of the great noblemen, and [in] each of the young men's houses, they all laid them out [before the idols]; they all spread them out in people's homes.

And when this was done, when they had been ornamented, then there was eating, there was drinking. Everywhere there was eating, there was celebration of the feast day.

And when midday came, then[17] there were singing and dancing. Verily they ornamented all the youths, the masters of the youths, the leaders of the youths, the seasoned warriors, the shorn ones, the Otomí. There in the god's courtyard, in the courtyard of [the Temple of] Uitzilopochtli, there was dancing.

And those who led were the shorn ones, the great, brave warriors, each of whom was considered [equal to] a battle squadron, who did not hide themselves behind something in war; they who turned [the enemy] back, they who wheeled them around.

Also the women danced — not one's daughters [but] the courtesans, the pleasure girls. They went, each one, between [pairs of the men]; they each went grasped in their hands; they were grasped

auh yn iquac muchioaia yn, yn ixqujch maceoalli, cenuetzi in motamalhuja, teutlacpa in qujujujtla totolti, yoã in chichime, no teutlacpa in qujnchichinoa, techichinolo, in monequizque ioatzico:

neixpololo, acuchiztli nechioaltilo, necuchiçololo, yilhujnemoa, iuhqujn tlatlaciuj, netetequjpacholo, injc tlacencaoalo.

Auh yn otlatujc in iehoantin teupixque, njman ie ic qujtlamamaca in Vitzilopuchtli, qujsuchicuzcatia, conicpasuchitia: yoan ixpan qujtetequjlia, qujtetecpanjlia, qujujujpana, qujtetecpiloa, in ixqujch nepapan suchitl, in tlaçosuchitl, in manquj, in tlamantli:

njman ie ic tesuchimaco, cenvetzi in ixqujchtin teteu, yn imixiptlaoan teteu, tlatlacateculo, tesuchitilo, tesuchiapano, teicpacsuchitilo, in vncan in teteupan:

njman ie ic cenvetzi in noujan calpan, in calpixque inchan, in veuei pipilti inchan: yoan in tetelpuchcali, qujcentzacutimanj, qujcentzacutimomana in techachan.

Auh in ie iuhquj yn otecencaoaloc mec tlatlaqualo, haatlioa: noujan tlatlaqualo, yilhujtlamacho.

Auh yn oacic nepantla tonatiuh mec cujcoianolo, vel ixqujch qujcencaoa, in telpuchtli, in teachcaoan, in telpuchiaque, in tequjoaque, in quaquachictin, in otomj: vncan in netotilo in teuitoalco, yn itoalco Vitzilopuchtli.

Auh in teiacana, iehoantin in quaquachicti, in veuei tiacaoã yn iuhquj cecentecuti momatia, yn amo mitzacujlia iaoc, in tecuepanj, in temalacachoanj.

No iehoantin in cioa mjtotiaia, amo iehoan in teichpuchoan, iehoantin in mahaujltianj, yn avianjme intzatzalan mantiuj, inmatitech maantiuj, mo-

17. For *mec* the *Real Palacio MS* has *nimã ye yc*.

about the waist. They were all in line; they went all in line; they went winding to and fro. Nowhere did the line break; nowhere were hands loosed. They went in order.

And the singers, those who sang for them, those who beat the drums for them, who beat the ground drums for them, were quite apart, quite to one side. They were against a building, against a round altar [or pyramid]. And the altar was completely round, circular, like a spindle whorl. Against it, by it, stood [the musicians].

And as they danced, they did not keep leaping nor did they make great movements; they did not go making dance gestures; they did not go throwing themselves continually[18] about, they did not go dancing with arm movements, they did not continually bend their bodies, they did not continually go whirling themselves, they did not keep going from side to side, they did not keep turning their backs.

It was quite quietly, quite calmly, quite evenly that they went going, that they went dancing. Very much as a serpent goeth, as a serpent lieth,[19] was the dance. None disturbed, none intruded, none encircled,[20] none broke in.

And those who embraced the women were only the great, brave warriors. But those who were only masters of the youths did not embrace them.

And when there was an end to the dancing, there was only a little sun; already the sun was about to set. There was dispersing, there was going on the part of each one.

And everywhere in the houses, there was singing; there was singing in each one. They sang for their gods: perhaps Omacatl, or Chicome coatl, or Ehecatl, or Coatl xoxouhqui. Over here, over there, there was singing; song was widespread. Cries were widespread; cries were widespread as there was singing. The singing kept reechoing in a great din.

And only the revered old men and the revered old women drank pulque. And he who became really drunk cried out at people or boasted of his manly deeds.

cujtlanaoa, çan cenpanti, çan cenpantitiuj, mococolotiuj, acan cotonj, acan momacaoa vipantiuj.

Auh in cujcanjme, in qujncujcatia, in qujntlatzotzonjlia, qujnueuetzotzonjlia, çan nonqua, çan chico, caltech in manj, emomoztitech: auh in momoztli, çan iaoaltic, teujlacachtic, malacachtic, yn jtech, yn itlan manj.

Auh ynic mjtotia, amo chocholoa, amono ontlayiaoa, amo ontlayiauhtiuj, amo motlatlaztiuj, amo momaitotitiuj, amo mopapachoa, amo momamalacachotiuj. amo aujc onviuj, amo tzitzinqujça:

çan yujian çan matca, çan tlamach yn iatiuj, yn mjtotitiuj: cēca çan coamantiuh, coanotiuh in netotiliztli, aiac tlaolinja, aiac tlaamana, aiac tlepeionja, aiac tlaixneloa.

Auh in cioa in q'nnaoa, çan iehoantin in veuey tiacaoan: auh in çan tiachcaoan, amono iehõatin, amo qujnnaoaia.

Auh in necaoalo in netotilo, ça achi tonatiuh, ie oncalaquiz tonatiuh, cecenmanoa viujloa.

Auh in noujan calpan, cujcujco, qujncujcujcatia yn inteteuoan: yn aço omacatl, anoço chicome coatl, anoço hecatl, anoço coatl xoxouhquj, nanachca in cujco, quitzacutimanj, in cujco, tlacaoacatimanj, tlacaoacatinemj in cujco, xaxamacatimanj in cujcatl.

Auh çanyioque, in ueuentzitzin, yoã yn ilamatzitzin, in tlaoana: auh yn aqujn vel oiujntic, tetzatzilia, anoçe moqujchitoa.

---

18. *momatlatlaztiui* in *ibid.*
19. *coaonotiuh* in *ibid.*
20. *tlapeyonia* in *ibid.*

Twenty-ninth Chapter, in which are named the feast and the debt-paying which they celebrated during all the days of the tenth month, which was called Xocotl uetzi.[1]

The tenth feast, Xocotl uetzi, likewise was of twenty days.[2] They concluded it in twenty days.

And when they set up the *xocotl*, it was on the day after Tlaxochimaco[3] that at dawn they began it. Thus during one day was their strength used. Shouting was widespread. The overseer,[4] as he hastened it, shouted; he shouted at one.

He said: "[Use] all your strength! Pull upon [the ropes]! Pull with strength!"

And when he shouted at them he was hoarse. It was as if his voice broke.

There was piled up for themselves, there was provided a mound of earth by means of which [the *xocotl*] was erected.[5] Strength was indeed exerted; they each took hold of it with all their force.

And the *xocotl* was twenty-five fathoms long. They removed its branches; only its main stalk was left. Thus, in the manner in which they set it up, it was for twenty days. When they had brought it, it had no adornment.

And when twenty [days] had gone by, then verily it was the time of the feast day, Xocotl uetzi. And when the feast was to be observed two days hence, once again they laid it out; quite gradually, quite carefully they laid out [the *xocotl*]. They took pains lest it break, lest it crack, lest it snap. They went resting it upon wooden supports;[6] they went laying it down upon wooden supports with much caution.

Jnic cempoalli on chicunauj capitulo, vncan mote- neoa in ilhujtl, yoan in nextlaoaliztli: in qujchioaia, in ipan ic cemilhujtl, ic matlactetl metztli: in mitoaia Xocotl vetzi.

Inic matlactetl ilhujtl, iehoatl in xocotl vetzi: no cempoalilhujtl vel qujtlamja, in cempoalilhujtl.

Auh in qujquetza xocotl, oiuh ialoa tlasuchimacotl, ioatzinco in qujpeoaltia, ic cemilhujtica vel ontlamj, yn jntlapaliuiz, tlacaoacatimanj in tepan manj, in tlaciujtia, tzatzi, tetzatzilia:

qujtoa. Ixqujch amotlapal, xitlatilinjcan, ximotilinjcan, ximotlapaltilican:

auh in tetzatziliaia içaoacaia, iuhquj yn jntozquj tzatzaianja.

Mololhujaia, mocentlatilulcaujaia, ynic meoatiquetzaia, vel motlapaltiliaia, ixqujch caanaia yn intlapaliuiz.

Auh in xócotl, injc viac catca, cempoalmatl ommacujlli: muchi qujtepeviliaia in jmatzocol: ça yio in jzcallo mocaoaia: inic iuhquj in oqujquetzque, cempoaltica in çan oqujvicaca, aiatle itlatquj.

Auh in oacic cempoalli: vel iquac ilhujtl in xócotl vetzi: auh in oqujuh viptla ilhujtl iez, oc ceppa qujteca, can jvian, çan tlamach in qujteca, qujmalhuja in ma cuetla, in ma natzin, in ma poztec: quauhtonmaçatl, quioalquechilitivi, quauhtonmaçapã in motecatiuh, cenca çan tlamach.

---

1. Garibay ("Relación breve," p. 303) translates *Xucutl valuetzi* as "*El Xócotl viene a caer.*" Seler, *Einige Kapitel*, pp. 160, 161, has "*der Xocotl fällt herab*" for both *xocotl valuetzi* and *xocotl uetzi*.

In *Gesammelte Abhandlungen*, Vol. II, pp. 449, 1039, and Vol. III, pp. 289–92, however, Seler argues that Xocotl uetzi should have been celebrated as the feast of Otontecutli, god and ancestor of the Otomí, rather than for Xiuhtecutli; because the *xocotl*, which was set up at the feast on the top of the tree, was the likeness of Otontecutli. As evidence, Seler mentions the adornment of the *xocotl* and a passage from the *Real Palacio MS: iquac in itech motlaliaia yn inacaio Otontecutli.* Sometimes, Seler adds, the figure was a mummy bundle.

Cf. also Jiménez Moreno, "*Primeros memoriales,*" pp. 41–45.

2. *cẽpoualilhuitica* in the *Real Palacio MS*.

3. The *Real Palacio MS* reads: *O yuh yalhua tlaxochimacoc.* The sentence could be translated: "And when they set up the *xocotl* the previous month of Tlaxochimaco had been celebrated." The cutting and bringing in of the *xocotl* occurred during the previous month of Tlaxochimaco. Sahagún's corresponding Spanish reads: "*en passando la fiesta de tlasuchimaco, cortauan vn gran arbol.*" For more discussion see Seler, *Einige Kapitel*, p. 161, n. 1, and Jiménez Moreno, "*Primeros memoriales,*" pp. 38–40.

4. In the Garibay ed., Vol. I, p. 202, Sahagún defines the duties of the *tepan mani* as "*los que tenían cuidado de recoger la gente.*" The corresponding Spanish text for Xocotl uetzi appears to use the term *tlayacanques* as a synonym, here rendered into Spanish as *cuadrilleros*.

5. See *Codex Borbonicus, Codex Féjérváry-Mayer*, and Jiménez Moreno, "*Primeros memoriales,*" for illustrations of this scene and others for the month Xocotl uetzi.

6. Cf. *quauhtomacatl* (Siméon, *Dictionnaire*, p. 370); the term is *quauhtonmaçatl* in the Nahuatl and *quauhtomaçatl* in the corresponding Spanish text.

And when they had laid out the *xocotl* in some fashion, then there was entering of the houses on the part of each one, there was resting on the part of each one. And they piled up all the heavy ropes on the *xocotl*; they placed them scattered over it.

And when it dawned, then the carpenters came forth; they assembled. They brought their equipment; they had with them adzes, hatchets. Well did they make even, did they smooth [the *xocotl*] where it had knots, where it was broken off, where it was uneven.

They smoothed another pole of five fathoms. They joined it to strengthen the main stalk of the *xocotl*. They made its main stalk very even. They girded, they held its tip with ropes; they placed [main stalk and pole] within the ropes.[7]

And when this was done, thereupon the fire priest took charge. The old priests helped; also those who cast [victims] into the fire helped. There were three of them. They were very powerful; they were each tall; they were very tall; they were exceedingly tall. They were lords.

The first was named Coyoua; the second was named Çacancatl;[8] the third was named Ueicamecatl. As such were disguised those who knew the task of adorning [the *xocotl*].

And the *xocotl* image they fashioned as of flesh. They formed it of a dough of fish amaranth and maize. They arranged pure white papers for it, each of which they placed on it. They had no design.

On it they set its shoulder sash of paper, its paper breechclout, its papers designed with falcons, its paper wig, its *xocotl* shifts. There were two *xocotl* shifts. They were not put on; they were only on the tree in two of its incisions. Then also they placed in another of its incisions large papers, wide — a yard wide;[9] they were ten fathoms long. They were reaching one-half the length of the *xocotl*.

And also they made three tamales of amaranth seed. They pierced them with sticks. In three places they set them up [over the image]. And thereupon on the *xocotl* they bound ropes there, half way up the *xocotl* — ten [of them].

And when it was made ready, thereupon they set it up. Then there was an outcry, there was shouting.

Auh in oquentel qujtecaque xócotl: njman ic cacalacoa, nececevilo: auh in ixqujch vepanmecatl ipan cõtepeuhtitlalia in xocotl, ipan contoxauhtitlalia.

Auh in otlatvic: njman oalhuj, oalnechicavi in quauhxinque, qujoalitquj, intlatquj oalietiuh in matepoztli, tlaximaltepoztli, vel qujpetlaoa, qujxipetzoa, in vncan yixe, in vncã titicujtztic, in vncã xixipochtic.

Oc ce qujxima quaoacatl macujlmatl: qujtlaçalhuja, qujtoctia in jzcalo xocotl, vel cõnevivilia in jzcalo, in jquapitzaoacan, qujmecatecuja, qujmecacuja, qujmecatitlantlalia.

Auh in ie iuhquj: njmã ie ic qujtlamamaca, in tlenamacac, tlapalevia in quaquacujlti, no iehoantin tlapalevia, in tetlepãtlazque. Eintin, cenca chicaoaque, quaquauhtique, quauhticapopol, quauhcholpopol, tetecutin catca.

In ce itoca: coiooa. Injc vme, itoca: çacancatl. Injc ei, itoca: veicamecatl: iuhqujn mjxpolotinemj,, motequjmati in tlachichioa.

Auh in jxiptla xócotl, in qujnacaiotiaia: mjchioauhtzoalli qujtlaliaia, çan cemjztac in amatl in qujmamaca, in jtech qujtlatlalia: amo ma tlacujlollo.

In jtech qujtlaliaia: yiamaneapanal, yiamamaxtli, itlotloma, yiamatzõ, ixoxocovipil, ixocovipil, vme: amo onacticac, çan quauhtitech caca: vme itzitziqujlpan: njman no contlalia oc ce itzitziqujlpan, vevei amatl, patlaoac: injc patlaoac, ceniollotli: matlacmatl injc viac, itlacapan acitica in xocotl injc viac.

Auh no etetl tzocoiotl in qujchioa, qujquaquauhço: excan in qujquequetza: auh njman ie ic qujilpia in xócomecatl, in vncan inepantla in xócotl, matlactli.

Auh in omocencauh: njmã ie ic qujquetza, njman ie ic tlacaoaca, tzatzioa:

7. Corresponding Spanish text: *"labraban otro madero, de cinco braças delgado: hazianle concabo, y ponjanle en la punta desde donde començaua el gujon: y recoxian las ramas del gujon: dentro del concabo del otro madero, y atauanle con vna soga, ciñjendole desde donde començaua las ramas, hasta la punta del gujon."*

8. Probably *çacamecatl* is meant. Cf. the Jourdanet–Siméon edition of Sahagún, p. 129.

9. Cf. Chap. 24, n. 17.

They said: "Go on there,[10] brave warriors! Pull with all your strength!"

Thereupon they went to setting it upright; they went about raising it [by using] the wooden supports, and they pried it up with levers. And likewise when already it went, when already it went rising, there was a great outcry, there was much shouting, there was much din.

And when this was done, it was quickly erected. Much did the earth stir; much did it move and swirl. When this was done, thereupon they filled [the hole] with stones, all these round rocks. They threw large stones in;[11] they cast them in. And when it was filled with stones, thereupon it was covered above with earth. Thereupon there was going on the part of each one; there was entering the houses on the part of each one. It was quiet; silence prevailed.

And thereupon came out the captors [with] their captives who were to be cast into the fire. [The captors] were well arrayed; they were adorned. They were painted with yellow ocher;[12] their faces were stained red. They bore upon their backs butterfly devices purely of flaming red feather composition. And their shields were [decorated with] shanks; either eagle legs or ocelot shanks were designed there on their shields in feathers. Hence were the shields called "shanks."

Thus did they go dancing. They went dancing with the captives; they went winding back and forth. Thus they proceeded by twos. The captives, they who were to be cast into the fire, also went dancing. They covered their bodies with chalk; they had their paper breechclouts, their paper shoulder sashes, then their paper wigs. They decked their heads with feathers. They had their feather lip pendants; they were strained chili-red about the mouth; they were stained black in the hollows of their eyes.

And when the sun had set, thereupon it ceased. They shut the captives in, and the captors departed. Likewise in the same place reposed those who owned the captives. They guarded their captives.

And then they started holding a vigil for them. It was already far into the night when the old men of the *calpulli*, the elders of the *calpulli*, there where they belonged, departed. And when they ended the

qujtoa. Maecuel tiacahoane, ximotilinjcan, ixqujch amotlapal:

njmã ie ic queoatiquetztivi, conquechilitivi, in quauhtonmaçatl, yoan qujquãmjvia: auh in iequene ie iauh, in ie meoatiquetztiuh: cenca tlacaoaca, cenca tzatzioa, cenca chachalacoa:

auh in ie iuhquj ommoquetztivetzi, vel tecujnj in tlalli, vel olinj, yoã comonj: in ie ihuquj, njmã ie ic qujtetema: muchi iehoatl in teololli, in vevei tetl conmaia, contepeoa: auh in omoteten, njman ie ic motlalpachoa in panj, njman ie ic viviloa, cacalacoa, cactivetzi, cactimomana.

Auh njman ie ic valqujça in tlamanjme: in immalhoan, in motlepantlazque, vel mocencaoa, mochichioa, motecocauhaltia, mjxtlapalhuja, in qujmama tlaviztli, papalotl: çan cuecalin in tlachiuhtli: yoã in jchimal tetepontli, aço quauhicxitl, anoço ocelomatetepontli, in vncã chimalpan icujliuhtica, hivitica: ic moteneoa in chimalli, tetepontli:

ic mjtotitivi, momalitotitivi, momamãtivi: ic vmpatitivi in mamalti in motlepantlaçazque, no mjtotitivi, qujntiçavia, imaamamaxtli, imamaneapanal, njmã ie imamatzon, qujnquapotonja; imjvitençac, motenchichiloa, mjxtentlilcomoloa.

Auh in oncalac tonatiuh: njmã ie ic mocacaoa, qujncalcaquja in mamalti: auh in tlamanjme vivi: çan no vncan ommotlalia in maleque, qujnpia in immalhoan.

Auh in peoa in qujntoçavia, ie tlaquauhiova in qujça: iehoantin in calpolvevetque, in calpoleque, in vncan povi: auh in mocacaoa in tetoçavia, iovalnepantla, iovalli itic, ioalli xelivi:

---

10. *ma ye cuel* in the *Real Palacio MS*.

11. *cõmayaui* in *ibid*.

12. *motecoçaualtia* in *ibid*.

vigil, it was midnight, in the midst of the night, [when] night divided in half.

When this was done, thereupon there was the taking of hair [from some of the captives]; the captors took hair from the crowns of the captives' heads, a little of the captives' hair; they cut it from the crowns of their heads; they bound it at the middle with chili-red thread, on which were two forked heron feathers. And the obsidian knife with which they cut their hair they named "obsidian falcon."

When this was done, when they had taken [the hair], then they put it into a small, woven reed coffer, called "hair coffer." This hair coffer the captor carried to his home. He hung it high. Thus it was shown that he was indeed a taker of captives; thus his manly exploits were boasted. Always it hung from the roofing of his house, from the roof beams. It never came down until the time that he died.

And when [the captives'] hair had been cut, the owners of the captives yet slept but little. They guarded [the captives] well; they watched them well; they were indeed careful lest those who were to be cast into the fire should flee.

And when it dawned, when the earth showed clearly,[13] thereupon they arranged [the captives] in order before the skull rack. And when they were arranged in order, a man [a priest] set upon them; he set upon them there; he pulled off of [these] others their banners and their paper adornments,[14] and perchance their wretched little capes. He placed them in the eagle vessel. There they burned.

Thereupon all who were going, the captives who were following, continued to place their banners and their little capes [in the fire]; there they all burned up. Indeed already they were to leave the earth forever. Futilely they were in order there. They were awaiting their death; indeed in truth it was already the time.

And there they were awaiting Paynal, the envoy of Uitzilopochtli. And when Paynal came to arrive, thereupon he ascended to the place where men were sacrificed, where the unhappy captives were to perform their service. And when this was done, no sooner had Paynal arrived than he thereupon descended [from the pyramid]; it was only that

in ie iuhquj, njman ie ic tetzoncujva, in tlamanjme: qujntzoncuj in mamalti, inquanepantla, aqujton intzõ in mamalti, qujntequjlia in inquanepantla, chichilicpatica qujcujtlalpia, aztatl itech ca, vme, maxaltic: auh in jtztli injc qujtequja intzon: qujtocaiotiaia, itztlotli:

in ie juhquj in oconcujque, njmã ic cõtema petlacaltonco, itoca: tzonpetlacalli: inin tzonpetlacalli, qujvica in jchan tlamanj, aco qujpiloa, ic monextia in ca tlamanj, ic moqujchitoa, muchipa pilcac calquac, itech in calquavitl, aic oaltemo ixqujch cavitl in mjqujz:

auh in otetzoncujoac oc achi concochi, in maleque: vel qujmpia, vel qujmjxpia, vel imjx intequjuh, in ma choloti in motlepantlaçazque.

Auh in otlatvic, in otlatlalchipaoac, njmã ie ic qujntecpana, tzompãtli ixpan: auh in ie tecpantimani, njman çe tlacatl compeoaltia, qujmonpeoaltia, qujmontzintilinja in oc cequjnti: in jpan yoan in jamatlatquj, yoan in aço itilmaçoltzin contlalia quauhxicalco, vncan tlatla.

njman ie ic mochintin õiatimanj, ommotocatimanj in mamalti, contlalitimanj in impan, yoan in intilmatzitzi, vncan centlatla, ca ie iccen cõcaoazque in tlalticpactli, çaçan ie vncã tecpantimanj, qujchixtimanj in immjqujz, ca nel ie otlaimmãtic:

auh vncã qujchixtimanj in Painal, in jxiptla vitzilobuchtli. Auh in jquac oacico Painal: njman ie ic tleco in tlacacouhcan, in vncan tlacotizque, mamaltzitzinti: auh in ie iuhquj: çan tequjtl onaci in Painal, njmã ie ic oaltemo: çan ce tlacatl in qujoaltemovia, qujciacavitivitz: inin qujoaltemovia, moteneoa

---

13. *ontlachipauac* in *ibid.*
14. *quimõtzintilia* in *ibid.*

114

a man [a priest] brought him down; he came carrying him under one arm. He who brought him down was called his father, or his elder brother. And when he had descended, he came forth before the captives; he came forth in their presence.

Once again Paynal quickly went up. And a captor stood for the purpose; he awaited him. Then the captor seized [the captive] by the head; he grasped in his hand[15] [the hair of] the crown of his head. Thereupon he went off leading him. When he had gone taking him to the landing at the foot of the pyramid, there he left the captive.

Then those who cast men into the fire came down; they seized him. First they threw *yauhtli* in his face. Then they bound his wrists; they brought each hand behind his back, and they bound his ankles.

Thereupon they placed him upon their backs to carry him up. And when they had gone taking him up, then they cast him into the fire.[16] High[17] did the ashes shoot up; they indeed billowed.

And the brave warrior's flesh thereupon sputtered; blisters quickly formed; burning spots quickly arose.

Then the old priests quickly seized him; they quickly drew him forth. They stretched him out on the offering stone. They cut open his breast; they split open his chest. Then they cut out, they tore out, his heart; they cast it before Xiuhtecutli, the representation of fire. And in just the same manner died all the captives whom Paynal delivered up here.

And when this was done, when the brave warriors had come to an end, thereupon there was dispersing, there was departing. There was going to people's various homes. There was eating; the feast day was observed.

And [as for] Paynal, his old men carried him. They went encircling him, they went crowding about him. They left him, they placed him in his place, the place where he was guarded. And when they had gone to leave him, thereupon they descended; they went in single file. And when they had come reaching the base, thereupon they dispersed, each one; they went, each one, to their various homes. They each ate.

And when this was done, when there had been eating, then there was coming forth, there was the assembling here of all the men, the youths, and the

jta, anoço iach. Auh in ooaltemoc: imjxpan oalqujça, imjxtlan oalqujça in mamalti:

ie no ceppa tlecotivetzi in Painal. Auh in tlamanj, ça iqujcac, qujchixticac: njmã ie icpac conana in tlamanj, amatica in cõtzitzquja, in jquateiolloco: njmã ie ic qujvicatiuh; in ocaxitito in apetlac, vncã qujcaoa in malli:

njmã ie ic oaltemo, in tetlepantlazque, qujoalana: achtopa, qujxiiauhtemja, çatepan qujmailpia, icampa qujviviqujlia in jma, yoan qujcxilpia:

njman ie ic iquechpan conteca, injc qujtlecavia: auh in oqujpantlacato, njmã ic contlaça in tleco, cẽcalli moquetztivetzi in nextli, vel molonj.

Auh in tiacauh njmã ie ic cuecuepoca in jnacaio, aquaqualacativetzi, yoan tletlecaleoativetzi:

njman ic conantivetzi, convilantivetzi, in quaquacujlti, qujoalteca techcac, coneltequj qujoalixtlapana in jielchiqujuh: njmã ic concotona, contlatzcotona in jiollo; ixpan cõmaiavi, in xiuhtecutli: in jxiptla tletl: auh çan ie moch ivi in momjqujlia in mamalti, qujnoalçaçaca in Painal.

Auh in ie iuhquj, in otlanque tiacaoan njmã ie ic tlaxitinj, viviloa viloa in techachan, tlatlaqualo, ilhujtlamacho.

Auh in Painal, njmã qujvica, cololhujtivi, qujtepevitivi, in jveveioan, concaoa, contlalia in jieian, in jpieloian: auh in ocõcaoato, njmã ie ic oaltemo, oalcenpantitivi. Auh in oacico tlalchi: njmã ic momoiaoa, vivi in inchachan ontlatlaqua.

Auh in ie iuhquj in otlatlaqualoc, njmã ic oalhujloa, oalnenechicolo, ixqujch tlacatl in telpochtli, yoan

15. *amatica*: read *imatica*.

16. *oquipãtlaçoto* in the *Real Palacio MS*.

17. *cẽcalli* may be in error for *cenca*. The *Real Palacio MS* reads: *cenca, lli moquetztiuetzi*.

boys, the small boys, those with a small tuft of hair at the back of the head,[18] those with a little tuft of hair at the back of the head. They put all in order.

At this time was begun the singing and dancing,[19] at midday. In this manner was it danced: the serpent dance was performed. Between [the men] the women were going, as hath been told. The courtyard was well filled, it was well crowded, it was well packed. No longer was there coming forth among the people. There was much jostling.

And when they grew tired, thereupon there was leaving on the part of each one. Then there was shouting. Then they passed over there where the *xocotl* stood. Indeed there was continual trampling; indeed there was hurrying; indeed there was a press of people.

And the masters of the youths kept people away [from the *xocotl*]. Their pine staves lay in the hands of each one. They did not hold back as they struck one, they did not spare their staves as they struck one. And those who in some way, somehow, quickly broke through [as the others] held them back, thereupon put their strength to the ropes, the heavy ropes.

Thereupon there was climbing on the ropes. On one rope maybe twenty climbed as if each were hanging. Not all reached the top; only some reached the top. The one who went leading, he indeed could reach the *xocotl* image. It was only of amaranth seed dough. He took all — its shield, its tipless arrow, and its dart thrower.

And the amaranth seed dough pieces he cast down there; he scattered them on the people. All the people who stood below looked up. When the amaranth seed dough fell, everyone stretched forth his hands. As if there were brawling, so was there shouting. Also some grasped the head ornaments of the amaranth seed dough [figure]; they also scattered them on the people. They were carried off down below.

And when this was done, then, thereupon he who had captured the *xocotl* [image] came down. When he had descended, when he had come to reach the ground, thereupon the old men seized him; they took him up to the place of sacrifice. There they gave him gifts. And everyone thereupon pulled the ropes; there indeed was pulling; strength was indeed

in telpopochtotonti, in telpopochpipil, in cuexpaltotoneque, in cuexpaltzitzineque: ixqujch qujcencaoa:

in jquac peoalo cujcoanolo nepantla tonatiuh, inic netotilo, necocololo, intzatzalan mamantivi in cioa in juh omjto, in jtvalli vel temj, vel cacatzca, vel tzitzica, aoc vel tetlan qujxoa, cenca nepapatzolo.

Auh in otlatziuhque nimã ie ic necacaoalo, njman ic tlacaoaca: njman vmpa onxoqujvi, in vmpa icac xocotl: vel nequequeçalo, vel netotocholo, vel nepitzmamalioa.

Auh in teachcaoan, tetzaqua, imoocoquauh in immac oonoc, amo motlamachvia injc tevitequj, amo iloti in inquauh injc tevitequj: auh in oqueztel, in oquezteltzin in oqujnpetlatiqujzque tetzaqua: njmã ie ic muchi motilinja in mecatl, in vepãmecatl:

njman ie ic tlecoa in mecatitech: in ce mecatl, aço cen tecpantli in jtech tleco, iuhqujn tlapipilcac: amo mochintin in vmpanvetzi, çan quezqujntin in vmpanvetzi, in aqujn iacatiuh, vel iehoatl caci in xócotl ixiptla, çan tzoalli: muchi qujcujlia in jchimal, in jmjuh tlaoaçomalli, yoan yiatlauh.

Auh in tzoalli, vmpa qujoaltetepeoa, tepan qujoalcecẽmana, muchi tlacatl, onacopatlachia in tlatzintlan manj, in jquac oalhuetzi tzoalli muchi tlacatl maçoa, iuhqujn ipan nemjmjctilo, iuhquj tlatlacaoaca: no cequjntin conaci, in jtzõcoiol in tzoalli, no tepã qujoalcecẽmana, namoielo in tlatzintlan.

Auh in ie iuhquj njmã: njman ie ic oaltemo, in xócomanj: in ooaltemoc, in otlaltitechacico: njmã ie ic conana: in tlacacouhcan, vmpa qujtlecavia in vevetque, vmpa qujtlauhtia: auh in jxqujch, tlacatl, nimã ie ic qujtilinja in mecatl, vel netilinjlo, vel ontlamj in tlapaliviztli: auh in xocotl, njmã ic vetzi

---

18. Corresponding Spanish text: "*todos aquellos, que tenjã vedixas de cabellos en el cogote, que llamauan cuexpaleque.*"

19. *cuicoyanolo* in the *Real Palacio MS*.

expended. And the *xocotl* then fell to the ground. There was a sudden billowing of dust; it suddenly broke to pieces. Into three parts or into four parts it quickly flew.

When this was done, thereupon there was going on the part of each one. All was quiet; all was clear. And afterwards they took the captor of the *xocotl* [image] to his home. They arrayed him in a brown cape with an edge striped with feathers.[20]

And if one were a captor [of the *xocotl* image], he could [thus] array himself, he could [thus] go wrapping himself; no one might dispute him over it. But if one were not [such] a captor, he only kept it; it would be only in his care. And mayhap he would sell it when he was already poor or during a sickness.[21]

And thus they left him at his home; two old priests went grasping him; they went holding him by the arm. Behind came the offering priests. They blew wind instruments for him; they went sounding shell trumpets for him. And he went carrying his shield on his back. And when they had gone to leave him, then they turned back [to the temple].

Thus in truth here ended, [here] concluded the feast day.

tlalpã, tlalipototztivetzi, popoztectivetzi, aço excan, anoço nauhcan qujztivetzi.

In ie iuhquj, njmã ie ic viviloa, cactivetzi, cactimomana: auh çatepã, concaoa in jchan in xocomanj, ic caapana camopalli in tilmatli, tenjvivavanquj.

Auh intla tlamanj, vel qujmoquentiz, vel qujmolpilitinemjz, aiac ic qujtlatzoviliz: auh intlacamo tlamanj, çan qujmotlatiliz, çan ipiel iez: auh anoço qujmonamaqujliz, in jquac ie motolinja in jcocoian.

Auh injc cõcaoa ichan: caantivi, qujtzitzitzqujtivi yiacolpã; in quaquacujlti: vmentin, icãpa mantivi tlamacazque, qujtlapichilitivi: iehoatl in tecciztli qujpichilitivi: yoã qujmamatiuh in jchimal. Auh in ocõcaoato, mec oalmocuepa:

ic vel oncan ontzonqujça, õtlamj in jlhujtl.

---

20. Corresponding Spanish text: *"lleuaua esta manta, vna franja en la orilla de tochomjtl, y pluma."*
21. Corresponding Spanish text: *"podianlas tener en su casa, y vender todos los que querian, pero no traerlas."*

Thirtieth Chapter: here are related the feasts and the honors observed during all the days of the eleventh month, which was called, which was known as Ochpaniztli.[1]

The eleventh feast day was the one known as Ochpaniztli. Before the very time, the very day, had come, for five days nothing more was done; only silence still prevailed. But when the five days had passed, then began the hand-waving dance. At that time it was fifteen [days] to Ochpaniztli. This was done for eight days.[2]

And thus was the hand-waving dance danced: there was the arranging of various rows;[3] four rows were formed; there was the forming of four rows. Thus they danced: they only went walking; they kept circling about. Their hands each went filled with flowering tagetes branches. They went grasping them in their hands on both sides.

They did not sing; none called out; they went in complete silence.

Yet if some of the perverse youths became drunk, they imitated the ground drums. As the ground drums sounded, just so they went about doing. On both sides they went circling their arms. They only went in rows; they only went as one. None broke ranks; none turned another aside; none went astray.

And when the hand-waving dance began, it was already late afternoon. And when there had been ceasing on the part of each one,[4] the sun had already set. And when eight days had passed, then began the mock battle [of the women physicians]. For four days this was done there before the house of song and dance.

In this manner was it done; in this way this was done: there were all the women physicians — the old women as well as the maidens as well as some of the pleasure girls.

Injc cempoalli on matlactli capitulo: vnca motene- oa in ilhujtl, yoã in tlamaviztililiztli: in muchioaia in jpã ic cemjlhujtl, ic matlactetl oce metztli: in mjtoaia, in moteneoaia: Ochpanjztli.

Injc matlactetl oce ilhujtl: iehoatl in moteneoa, Ochpanjztli: in aiamo onaci, in vel iquac vel ilhujtl: oc macujlilhujtl, in aiatle muchioaia, in çan oc cactimanj: auh in õqujz macujlilhujtl njmã ic vmpeoa in nematlaxo, iquac in tlacaxtolti ochpanjztli: chicueilhujtl in muchioaia.

Auh injc nematlaxo, netetecpanaloia, nappantioa, nenappantililo: injc mitotiaia, çan nenentivi, tlatlaiaoaloa, cempoalsuchitla mapoztectli in immac tetẽtiuh, nenecoc in immac qujtzitzitzqujtivi:

amo cujcaia, aiac naoatia, çan nõtitivi:

tel intla cequjntin in telpuchtlaveliloque, in mjivintia contlaeecalhuja in vevetl: in juh caqujzti vevetl, çan no iuh qujchiuhtivi, necoccampa in conjauhtivi imma, çan tecpantivi, çan cemonotivi, aiac chicopetonj, aiac tepatilia, aiac onchicoqujça.

Auh in peoaia in nematlaxo, ie teutlac: auh in necacaoaloia ie õcalaquj tonatiuh. Auh in otzonqujz chicueilhujtl: njmã ic vmpeoa in çonecali, navilhujtl in muchioaia: vncan in cujcacalli ixpan.

Ivin in muchioaia, iuhquj in, in muchioaia: in jxqujchtin cioatitici, in jlamatque, yoan in jchpupuchti, yoan cequjntin avienjme:

---

1. *Barrimiento de caminos* in Garibay's rendering ("Relación breve," p. 306); *das "Wegfegen,"* according to Seler, *Einige Kapitel*, p. 171; *fiesta barredera* in Durán, *Historia*, Vol. II, p. 190.

2. The corresponding Spanish reads: *"los cinco dias primeros deste mes no hazian nada, tocante a la fiesta. Acabados los cinco dias; quinze dias antes de la fiesta començauan a baylar, vn bayle: que ellos llamauan, nematlaxo: este bayle, duraua ocho dias."* Seler, in *Einige Kapitel*, p. 172, translates the Nahuatl as follows: *"Als der eigentliche Festtag noch nicht erricht war, noch fünf Tage (fehlten), geschah nichts, alles bleibt noch still und leer. Und nachdem die fünf Tage zu Ende sind, beginnt der Handbewegungstanz. Wenn noch fünfzehn Tage bis zum Ochpanizli sind, wurde er acht Tage lang vollführt."* Cf. also Sahagún's summary of Ochpanizli in Chapter 11.

3. *nappanti* is added in the *Real Palacio MS*.

4. *necaualoya* in *ibid*.

They divided themselves; they divided themselves into two equal parts. [The likeness of] Teteo innan went with a certain number; likewise as many went opposing her, keeping a skirmish against her. Thus they banished her sorrow, they kept gaining her attention, they kept making her laugh that she might not be sad. But if there were weeping, it was said, it would be an omen of evil. It was said that many eagle-ocelot warriors would die in war or that many women would become *mociuaquetzque* when from their wombs [children] would go.

And in this manner was the mock fighting done: first the Teteo innan [party] began to pursue the others. With her were going the great women physicians. These were Aua; second, Tlauitequi; third, Xoquauhtli. These three were her old women.

Thus did they pursue [the others]: they went pelting them. Thus did they pelt them: it was with [matted] tree parasites[5] gathered into balls, gathered into many balls, and reeds [pressed into] balls, and cactus leaves, and tagetes flowers. And all tied their tobacco gourds to their waists. Again [the others] turned [Teteo innan] back; they went pelting them. It was not for long; it was only sometimes that they were pursued.

And when this was done they took [the likeness of] Toci[6] where she was guarded. This was for four days that they did the skirmishing.

And when the four days of skirmishing had ended, then, upon the morrow, toward sundown, she tramped over her market place.[7] As she came forth, the [women] physicians came encircling her. And as she came along, then the Chicome coatl [priests][8] received her here. And when they had received her here, then they made a circle [about her]. And when a procession had been made [about her], then she stopped in the middle of it. Then she kept scattering cornmeal there. Then she tramped over her market place for the last time before she took leave of the market place.

And when she had gone tramping over it, then they took her where she was guarded in her temple. Much did the [women] physicians console her. They said unto her: "My dear daughter, now at last the ruler Moctezuma will sleep with thee. Be happy."

moxeloaia, monepātlaxeloaia, izquj intlan mātivi, in teteu innan, no izquj in qujnamjctivi, in qujtiia-iavtla, ic qujpopololtiaia in jtlaocul, qujtlatlacaavi-loaia, qujvevetzqujtiaia, injc amo tlaocuiaz; auh in tlachocaz, qujlmach tlatetzaviz: qujl mjec iaumj-qujz, in quauhtli ocelutl: anoço mjequjntin mocioa-quetzazque in cioa in jmiti ic iazque.

Auh ivi in, in muchioaia injc çonecalia: achto peoa in teteu innan in tetoca, itlan mantivi in vevei titici. Iehoatl in Aoa: Jnjc vme Tlavitecquj. Injc ei xo-quauhtli. In iehoantin im eixtin y, ilamaiooa:

injc qujntoca, qujntepachotivi: injc qujntepachoa, papachtli ica, tlaolollalilli, tlaoolollalili, yoan toltapa-iolli, yoan nupalli, yoā cempoalsuchitl: yoā muchin-tin imjiietecō ic mocujcujtlalpia: enocuele qujnte-putztia, qujntepachotivi: amo vecaoa çan quezqujpa, in ommototoca.

Auh in ie iuhquj, njmā ic qujvica in toci, in vmpa pielo: inin navilhujtl in qujchioaia in mjicali:

auh in otzonqujz in çonecali, navilhujtl: njmā imuztlaioc in qujoalicça itianqujz, ie teutlac: injc oalqujça cololhujtivitze in titici: auh in ie iativitz, njmā ic qujoalnamjquj in chichicomecoa: auh in oqujoalnamjcque njmā ic oallaiaoaloa: auh in ontla-iaoalo, vncā vmmoquetza, in tlanepantla: njmā vncā contetepeoa, tlaoltextli: njmā ic conjcça in jtianqujz, ça iiopa, ça ie cōnaoatia in tianqujztli.

Auh in oconjcçato, njman ic qujvica, in vmpa pielo, in jteupan, cenca qujiollalia in titici:

qujlhuja. Nochputzin, ca iequene axcā mote-tzinco aciz in tlatoanj Motecuçoma, ma ximopapac-tzino:

5. Spanish beard; *Tillandsia usneoides* L. in Clark, *Codex Mendoza*, Vol. II, p. 106.
6. Toci: identical with Teteo innan and with Tlaçolteotl. Cf. Seler, *Gesammelte Abhandlungen*, Vol. II, p. 1064.
7. Corresponding Spanish text: *"A este passeo llamauan acozeamjento del tianquez porque nunca mas auja de boluer a el."*
8. Corresponding Spanish text: *"rescebianla luego los satrapas, de la diosa llamada chicome coatl."*

They did not tell her of her death; it was as if she died unaware. Then they adorned her, they arrayed her.

And when midnight came, then they took her [to the temple]. No one at all spoke, none talked, nor did anyone cough; it was as if the earth lay dead. And everyone gathered round in the darkness.

And when they had taken her to where she was to die, then they seized her. They stretched her out on the back of one [of them]. Then they quickly cut off her head. And when they had cut off her head, then also they quickly flayed her; they swiftly flayed her. And when they had flayed her, then a man [a priest] quickly put on her skin. He was called Teccizquacuilli — a very strong [man], very powerful, and very tall.[9]

And her thigh they had then also quickly flayed; they hastened it there to Pochtlan. [The likeness of Toci's] son put it on. His name was Cinteotl. There he went to take it.[10]

And when this was done, when the Teccizquacuilli had [donned] her skin, then she quickly placed herself here on the edge [of the pyramid].[11] As she quickly placed herself here, it was with great speed. Then she quickly came down. There followed her swiftly, on each side, two of her Huaxtecs coming [with her]. And the offering priests went helping her. They went behind her; they went crowded about her; they went guarding her.

And a number of noblemen and great brave warriors were awaiting her. And when already she went, then they set forth; they went spreading out before her; they went gathering before her. Much did they run; much did they hasten; as if they flew, so did they run. They kept going to turn back toward her; they went striking their shields, they went striking their shields against each other. Also they swiftly turned to her; they kept crowding, they kept pressing as they ran. There was much fear; fear spread over the people; indeed fear entered into the people.

And when they thus ran, it was called "They fight with grass"; because it was indeed grass, it was indeed straw [brooms] that each of them went carrying in their hands; they were bloody; they were

amo qujmachitiaia in jmjqujz, çan iuhquj in ichtaca mjquja: mec qujchichioa, qujcencaoa.

Auh in jquac ie onaci iooalnepantla njmã ic qujvica, çan njmã aiac naoati, aiac tlatoa, anoac tlatlaci, ça iuhqujn tlalli mjctoc: auh ixqujch tlacatl, cenquiçaia in iooaltica.

Auh in oconaxitique vncã mjqujz: njmã ic qujoalana, çan tecujtlapan in cõteca, njmã ic qujoalquechcotontivetzi: auh in ocõquechcotonque, njmã no iciuhca qujxipeuhtivetzi, qujxipeuhtiquiça. Auh in oqujxipeuhque: njmã ic cõmaqujtivetzi ce tlacatl in jeoaio: itoca Tecizquacujli, cenca chicaoac, chichicactic, yoan cenca quauhtic.

Auh in jmetz njmã no iciuhca qujxipeuhtivetzi, qujmotlalochtia, in vmpa puchtlan: conaquja in jconeuh: itoca, Cinteutl, in vmpa canatiuh.

Auh in ie iuhquj, in ocõmaquj Tecizquacujlli: mec oalmoquetztivetzi tlatempan: in ooalmoquetztivetz, cencan iciuhca: mec oaltemotivetzi, qujtzatzacutivitze, nenecoc, oomemãtivitze in jcuexoan. Auh in tlamacazque qujpalevitivi, icãpa onotivi, qujtepevitivi, qujpixtivi:

auh in cequjntin qujchixtoque in pipilti, yoan in veve in tiacaoã. Auh in jquac ie iauh: njman ic oneoa, ixpã mãtivi, ixpã onotivi: cenca motlaloa, cenca paina: iuhqujn patlanj, ic motlaloa; oalmocuecueptivi, in jvicpa, qujoalhujtectivi in inchimal, oalmochimalhujtectivi: no ceppa ic mocueptivetzi, ontetemj, ompipilcatoque in motlaloa: cenca nemauhtilo, maviztli tepan moteca, vel tetechaquj in maviztli.

Auh injc iuh iauh in: moteneoa, çacacali: iehica ca çacatl, ca popotl in immac tetentiuh, ehezço, tlaezvilli: auh injc qujntoca, çan momoiaoa, cecenmanj, cenca momauhtia.

9. We use "the likeness of" to refer to the representative of the goddess Toci (Teteo innan) until her ritual death. The priest who subsequently put on her skin is referred to as "the impersonator."

10. For the purpose of distinguishing the acts of the impersonator of Toci from those of the impersonator of Cinteotl, the former is referred to in subsequent passages as a woman (*she*) and the latter as a man (*he*).

11. Corresponding Spanish text: "*luego se leuantaua al canto del cu.*"

covered with blood. And when [the impersonator and her companions] set upon [the warriors], they just were scattered; they dispersed. Greatly were they terrified.

And when [the impersonator] had gone arriving at the base, at the foot of [the Temple of] Uitzilopochtli, then she raised her arms, she spread her arms at the foot of [the Temple of] Uitzilopochtli. She placed herself facing [the god]; then she turned about; she placed herself by her son, Cinteotl.

Here this one had been waiting. He had with him his thigh[-skin] mask,[12] and he had put on his peaked cap, curved back and serrated. And this [cap] was given the name Itztlacoliuhqui, "curved obsidian knife."[13] This [Itztlacoliuhqui is god of] frost. [Cinteotl] went accompanying [the impersonator]; they went along together. They did not run; it was only at their leisure that they went along. There they went facing, there they slowly approached [Toci's] temple, where [the likeness of Toci] had died. Again they took their places there.

And upon the morrow, when there was the breaking of day, the rising of daylight, then [the wearer of the skin of Toci's likeness] placed herself here upon the edge [of the pyramid]. And every one of the noblemen already stood awaiting her. There was hastening upward. Then they each ministered unto her.[14] One of them applied feathers to her head and her legs, with soft eagle down; one of them painted her face; one of them offered her her shift with the eagle design, and her skirt, which was only painted; one of them beheaded quail for her; one of them set incense before her. It was all very swift. Then it was quiet; then there was departing on the part of each.

And when there had been departing, then came forth her great vestments, called her paper crown and her market place banners. And her paper crown was wide; in the middle a market place banner went upright. There were five: in the middle a market place banner went erect, and four were on the sides, two each. They each went in order. [This headdress] was called *meyotli*.[15]

Auh in oacito tlacxitlan, in jicxitlan vitzilobuchtli: njmã ic maana, moteteoana, mamaçoa in jicxitlã Vitzilobuchtli: conjxnamjctimoquetza, mec oalmocuepa, itlan oalmoquetza in jconeuh in Cinteutl:

in vncan oqujchixticaca, imexaiac ietivitz: yoan cõmaquja, icopil, quacoltic, yoan tzitziqujltic: auh inin motocaiotiaia, itztlacoliuhquj: iehoatl in çetl: qujvicativitz, neoã mantivitze, amo motlaloa, ça yiolic yiativitze, vmpa itztivi, vmpa tlamattivi in jteupan, in vmpa omjc: oc ceppa vmpa ommotlalia.

Auh in otlatvic, in otlatlavilotleoac, tlatlavillotl eoa, mec oalmoquetza tlatenpan: auh in jxqujch tlacatl pipilti, ie qujchixtoque ipan õnetepeoalo: njman ic qujtlatlamaca: in aca qujpotonja icpac, yoan icxic, quauhtlachcaiotica: in aca qujxaoa: in aca cõmaca iquavipil, yoan icue, çan tlacujlolli: in aca çolin in qujcotonjlia: in aca copalli in contemjlia cenca çan iciuhca: njmã ic cactivetzi, njman ic viviloa.

Auh in oviviloac: njmã ic oalqujça in jveitlatquj moteneoa: yiamacal, yoan itianquizpan: auh in jamacal, çan patlachtic, inepantla icatiuh in tianqujzpanjtl, macujlli manj: in tlanepantla icatiuh, iehoatl in tianqujzpanjtl: auh navi necoccampa oome qujtzatzacutiuh: moteneoa meotli.

<hr>

12. Corresponding Spanish text: "*Este cinteutl era vn mancebo: el qual lleuaua puesto, por caratula, el pellejo del muslo de la muger que aujan muerto.*" Garibay ("Relación breve," p. 307) translates *imexaiac* as "*máscara de muslo.*"

13. This headdress is illustrated in the Tonalamatl of the *Codex Borbonicus* and of the Aubin Collection.

14. *quitlamamaca* in the *Real Palacio MS.*

15. According to Seler (*Gesammelte Abhandlungen,* Vol. II, p. 501), *meiotli* is to be read as *miotli,* derives from *mitl (pfeil),* and means "*Ausstrahlung.*" He sees it as the headdress of Teteo innan pictured in the *Codex Borbonicus* for the month of Ochpaniztli. In Sahagún, Garibay ed., Vol. IV, p. 342, Garibay derives the word from *metl* (maguey), and translates it as "*Hilera de magueyes.*" It is *meyotli* in the *Real Palacio MS.*

And when they had attired her, then four captives were given first place before [the other captives]. Then they stretched one of them out on the offering stone; she herself slew him. She opened the breasts of each of the four; in like manner did she do.

When she had slain the four, then she left [the others] in the hands of the fire priests, that they might slay the rest of the captives. Then she went where [earlier] she had gone to get her son; she went to bring her son, Cinteotl or Itztlacoliuhqui. Her Huaxtecs led her; they went at a distance from her. They were adorned with their rope breech-clouts and their mirrors for the small of the back, their cotton blossoms, with the precious feather spindles [with unspun cotton].

And the [women] physicians and the lime vendors went ranged on both sides. They went singing. The old priests went intoning a song for them. They were beating a small horizontal drum to which was fastened a small water gourd. Hence it was called "the hanging gourd." [16]

When they had gone reaching the place of the skull rack, then [the wearer of Toci's likeness's skin] tramped upon her drum.[17] And the seasoned warriors already stood awaiting [Cinteotl]. From there he departed with his thigh[-skin] mask in order to leave it in enemy land. From there the brave warriors departed. They went surrounding him — the strong, the agile ones. Swiftly did they run.

And when they who there placed [the mask] had gone to reach the land of the foe, upon the mountain top, one of the side peaks of Iztac tepetl, a place called Popotl temi, not without struggle did they put it in its place. [The foe] set upon them, or else they pursued [the foe]. On both sides there were deaths.

And when they had gone setting her thigh[-skin] mask upon a wooden frame,[18] then there was quick departing. Then also the foe went.

And when this was done, when [the wearer of the skin of the impersonator of] Toci had gone leaving her son, thereupon she went to her home there at Atempan. Then there was an assembling of the brave warriors, all the shorn ones, the leading

Auh in ocõcencauhque, njmã ic ommoiacatia, in mamalti injxpan, navintin: mec ce conteca, in techcac: inoma yioma in qujmjctia, qujmeltetequj: navixtin, iuhquin chioa:

in oqujmõmjcti in navixtin, mec immac qujnoalcaoa in tletlenamacaque, injc qujnmjctizque, in oc cequjntin mamalti: mec iauh in vmpa ocanato iconeuh: qujvicatiuh in jconeuh, in cinteutl ano itztlacoliuhquj: qujiacana in jcuexoan vecapa qujtztivi, omocencauhque, inmemecamaxtli, yoan incujtlatezcauh, imjichcasuchiuh, mamalacaquetzallo.

Auh in titici, yoan in tenexnamacaque, necoc onotivi, cujcativi: qujncujcatlaxilitivi in quaquacujlti, qujtzotzontivi in teponaztontli, itech tlaçalolli, atecontontli: ie injc moteneoa, tecomapiloa.

In oacito tzompantitlan: njmã ic conjçça in jveveuh: auh in tequjoaque, ie qujchixtoque: vncan oneoa in jmexxaiac injc qujcaoazque iauc: vncã oneoa cololhujtivi in tiacaoan, in chicaoaque, in tlaçanj: cenca motlaloa.

Auh in oacito, in vmpa contlalianj in iaupan, in vmpa tepeticpac: inacaztlan in iztac tepetl: itocaiocan, popotl temj: aivian in contlalia, qujnoaltoca: anoce qujntoca, necoc mjcoa.

Auh in ocõtlalito quauhticpac, in jmexxaiac: mec viloatz, mec no vi in teiauoan.

Auh in ie iuhquj, in iehoatl Toci: in ocõcaoato, iconeuh: njman ie ic iauh in jchan, in vmpa atempã, njmã ic cenqujxoa in tiacaoã, in jxqujchtin quaquachictin, in quaquauhiaca, in tlatlacochcalca, in tlatlacatecca: yoan in ie ixqujchtin tequjoaque, in

16. Cf. Chap. 27.

17. Garibay ("Relación breve," p. 306) translates *ic motenevaya iveveuh quicza* as *"con que se decía: 'golpea su tamboril.'"* Jiménez Moreno, *"Primeros memoriales,"* p. 46, translates *iueuéuh — quicza* as *"su tambor lo pisa."*

18. Corresponding Spanish text: *"el pellejo ponjanlo colgado, en vna garita."* Durán, *Historia*, Vol. II, pp. 186, 191, refers to *"vna ermita a manera de umilladero."*

warriors, the generals, the commanding generals,[19] and all the seasoned warriors, the chosen ones, the respected brave warriors, those valiant of their own will, who set no value upon their heads, their breasts, the fearless of death who in truth hurled themselves upon our foes.

And when this was done, when there had been the assembling, then there was their arranging in order, their placing in rows, before Moctezuma. He was seated upon the eagle mat; this was verily the flayed skin [with feathers] of an eagle upon which he was seated. And he was reclining upon an ocelot [skin] seat with back rest. It was in truth the hide of an ocelot with which the seat was covered.

Each one stood saluting him. Before him lay all the various devices, shields, and clubs set with obsidian blades, and the capes, and the breechclouts.

They stood saluting him. Then each one stood taking his gifts. They went there where was the adorning, the putting on of devices. To the great brave warriors was given this costly array. But to all of those who were only commoners were given the Huaxtec devices.[20]

And when this was done, when it was concluded, when there had been the arraying, then once more there was their arranging in order before Mocte-zuma. Each one stood saluting him. Then they came forward; they went up there.

And when the dancing took place, the hand-waving dance was danced. Those to whom insignia had been given, who went there, displayed their devices there. And the devices which thus had been given them became their reward, which became like what was their covering. And in this manner was the hand-waving: they went in various rows as hath been said; they moved like flowers. They indeed went in glory.[21] They kept circling the temple.

And all the onlookers, the beloved old women, all the beloved women, raised a tearful cry; their hearts were compassionate.

They said: "These are our beloved sons whom we see here. If in five days, in ten days, the sea, the conflagration are announced,[22] that is, war, will they

tlatzonanti, in ovelittoque in tiacaoan, in jiolloco chi-caoaque, in amo qujtlaçotla in intzontecon, in jmel-chiqujuh, in amo mjqujzmauhq̄, in vel in ca momo-tla in toiauoan.

Auh in ie iuhquj, in ocenqujxoac: njmã ic ixpan onnevipanalo, onnecenpātililo, in jxpā Motecuçoma, iehoatica quauhpetlapan, vel iehoatl in quauhtli, tlaxipeoalli in jpan eoatica, yoan ocelotepotzoicpalli in jpan motlaztica, vel ie in ocelotl yieoaio, injc tla-qujmjlolli icpalli:

ceceiaca contlapalotimanj, ixpan onoc, in jxqujch nepapan tlaviztli, in chimalli, yoan in macquavitl yoã tilmatli, yoan maxtlatl:

contlapalotimanj, njman ic concujtimanj, ceceiaca in innetlauhtil: vmpa oniatimanj in vmpa nechichi-oalo, onneaqujlo tlaviztli: in vevei tiacaoan, in quj-momaca iehoatl in tlaçotlanquj: auh in ie ixqujch, ça tlacujtlapiloa, iehoatl in qujmomaca cuextecatl tlaviztli.

Auh in ie iuhquj in ontlamoac, in õnechichioaloc: njmã ic oc ceppa õnevipanolo, in jxpan Motecu-çoma: ceceiaca contlapalotimanj, njmã ic oalqujzti-manj, njman ic vmpa oniatimanj.

Auh in jquac in ie netotilo, nematlaxo: vmpa onia-timanj in omotlavizmacaque, vncan tlaviznextia. Auh in tlaviztli, ic qujmomaca, iuhqujn impatiuh muchioa, in qujmjliuhca muchioa: auh injc moma-tlaça tetecpātivi in juh omjto iuhqujn suchitl man-tiuh, vel maviçotivi, qujiaiaoalo in teucalli.

Auh in jxqujchtin tlatlatta, in jlamatzitzin, yie ix-qujch tlacatl cioatzitzinti, tlachoqujztleoa, icnoioa in iniollo:

qujtoaia. Inin topilhoantzitzin nican tiqujmitta, intla macujl, matlac oalmjto, tehoatl tlachinolli, id

19. Cf. Arthur J. O. Anderson and Charles E. Dibble: *Florentine Codex, Book III, The Origin of the Gods* (Santa Fe: School of American Research and University of Utah, 1952), p. 53, and Dibble and Anderson, *Book VI*, p. 76.

20. See Seler, *Gesammelte Abhandlungen*, Vol. II, pp. 604–606. Seler mentions a pointed, cone-shaped hat; a disc or rosette fastened to the hat; a crescent-shaped nose plate; a golden ear pendant; and spindles. Either these relate to the wars of Axayacatl among the Huax-teca or else "the Mexicans wore [them to proclaim] themselves to be the servants, followers, likenesses of the old mother of the gods, Teteo innan, the Huaxtec earth goddess, . . . mother and inventor of war, . . . who was supposed to be at home among the Huaxteca, and perhaps was actually received by the Mexicans from there."

21. *mauizçotiui* in the *Real Palacio MS*.

22. Cf. Dibble and Anderson, *Book VI*, p. 244.

perhaps come returning? Will they perhaps come making their way back? Verily, they will be gone forever!"

And [the wearer of the skin of the likeness of] Toci, and her Huaxtecs, and the [women] physicians went apart [from the others]; they went dispersed behind [the dancers]. They alone went singing. Thus did they sing: it was a high falsetto; like a mockingbird they raised their song. When the hand-waving dance began, it was midday, and when it stopped, with it the sun set.

And when dawn broke, when it was the next day, again there was an assembling; still there was also dancing the hand-waving dance. None ceased, indeed even once. Then, later, insignia were offered to the noblemen, no longer to many but to some. And those which they were given were very costly insignia, with much gold, covered with gold, with many quetzal feathers, full of quetzal feathers.

And when they had been given them, thereupon they went to perform the hand-waving dance. Moctezuma led it; in great glory did he go. Before the people they displayed the insignia; for a great distance did they scintillate; much did the devices gleam.

And when this was done, when it had ceased,[23] then it was already late afternoon. Then came forth the Chicome coatl [priests], who were also the impersonators of the *tototecti*, who had also died when Toci['s likeness] died.

Then they came forth from their temples. They strewed seeds [of maize] there at [what was called] the banquet table of the devil [Uitzilopochtli,[24] a small pyramid which was] not very high. And when they had climbed up, then they each flung forth, they each dispersed here, they each scattered here on the people the seeds — white maize grains, yellow maize grains, black, red; and squash seeds. As if there were stealing, as if there were scratching up, gathering up, there was indeed continued brawling over it.[25]

And the maidens who belonged with the Chicome coatl [priests] were known as offering priestesses. They bore upon their backs the ears of dried maize, seven ears each, each ear of dried maize painted with liquid rubber. And they wrapped them each in paper. And they were with precious capes. The

est, iaoiutl, cujx oc mocuepaqujuj, cuix oc ymiloch qujchioaqujuj, ca ic ceniazque.

Auh in toci, yoan ycuexoan, yoan titici, çan nonqua mantiuj, iteputzco tepeuhtiuj: çanjioque in cujcatiuj, ynic cujca cenca tlapitzaoa, iuhqujn tzõtli cana incujc: in peoa nematlaxo nepantla tonatiuh, auh in necaoalo, ic oncalaquj in tonatiuh.

Auh yn otlatujc, in ie ymuztlaioc, oc cepa cenqujxoa, oc no nematlaxo, aiac mocaoa ca ça yiopa: qujniquac motlauizmacaia in pipilti, aocmo mjequjnti, ca quezqujntin: auh in qujmomacaia, cenca tlaçotlanquj in tlauiztli, cenca teucujtlaio, moca teucujtla cenca quetzallo, moca quetzalli.

Auh yn oconmomacaque, njman ie ic uj momatlaçazque, qujiacana in Motecuçoma, cenca mauizçotiuj: teixpan qujnextia in tlauiztli, cenca veca in motonameiotia, cenca mihiiotia in tlauiztli.

Auh in ie iuhquj, yn onecacaoaloc in jquac ie teutlac, mec oalquiça in chichicomecoa, in jmjxiptlaoan no tototecti: in jquac mjquj toci, no iquac mjqui.

Mec oalquiça in inteteupan, oalxinachpixoa: vncan in jtlaquaian diablo, amo cenca vecapan. Auh in otlecoque: njman ic qujoalchachaiaoa, qujoaltetepeoa, qujoalcecenmana tepan, in xinachtli: iztac tlaolli, coztic tlaolli, iavitl, xiuhtoctli, yoã aiovachtli, iuhqujn namoialo, iuhqujn momotzolo, netlapepenjlo, vel ipan nemjmjctilo.

Auh in jchpopochti in intech povi chichicomecoa: moteneoa, cioatlamacazque: qujmomamaltiaia in cintli, chichicoomolotl, oltica qujxaxaoaoaia in cintli, yoan amatica in qujnqujqujmjloaia, yoã tlaçotilmatica in qujnmama in cioatlamacazque, moxaoaia,

---

23. *onecaualoc* in the *Real Palacio MS.*

24. Corresponding Spanish text: "*Estos se subian, encima vn cu pequeño, que se llamauan* [sic] *la mesa de uitzilobuchtli.*"

25. *ipampa* in the *Real Palacio MS.*

ILLUSTRATIONS

Al tercero mes, llamavan tocoztontli: enel primer dia deste mes, hazian fies
ta al dios llamado Tlaloc: que es dios de las pluuias. E nesta fiesta, mativa
muchos niños, sobre los montes: offecian los en sacrificio aeste dios, y asus com
pañeros. paraque los diessen agua.

Cap. 3.

		K L tocoztontli.		
1	c		c	14
2	d	E nesta fiesta: offecian las primicias de	d	15
3	c	las flores, que aquel año primero nacian enel cu, llamado iopico: y antes que las o freciessen, nadie osaua oler flor.	e	16
			f	17
4	f	Los officiales de las flores, que se llaman	g	18
5	g	sochimanque: hazian fiesta, a su diosa lla mada coatl ycue, y por otro nombre coatl tona.		
6	A	Tambien eneste mes: se desnudauan, los q̃	A	19
7	b	trayan vestidos, los pellejos, de los muertos, q̃ aujan desollado el mes pasado: y van los aechar en vna cueua, enel cu, que llama uan iopico: y van ahazer esto, con procesi	b	20
8	c	on: y co muchas cerimonjas, y van hedien do, como perros muertos: y despues que	c	21
9	d	los aujan dexado: se lauauan, con muchas cerjmonjas: Algunos enfermos hazian voto,	d	22
10	e	de hallarse presentes, aesta procesion, por sanar de sus enfermedades: y dizen, que	e	23
11	f	algunos sanauan.	f	24
12	g	Los dueños de los catiuos, con todos los de su casa, hazian penjtencia, veynte dias: que nj	g	25
13	A	sebañauan, nj se lauauan las cabeças: has ta que se ponjan los pellejos, de los captiuos	A	26
14	b	muertos, en la cueua arriba dicha: dezian que hazian penjtencia, por sus captiuos.	b	27
15	c	Despues que aujan acabado la penjtencia: bañauanse, y lauauanse, y conbidauan a	c	28
16	d	todos, sus parientes, y amigos, y duanles conjla: y hazian muchas cerjmonjas, con	d	29
17	e	los huesos, de los catiuos muertos.	e	30
18	f	Todos estos veynte dias, hasta llegar al mes que viene: se exercitauan en cantar en las casas, que llamauan cujcacali, no baylaua sino estando sentados: cantauan cantares	f	31
19	g	aloor de sus dioses. Otras muchas cerjmo njas, se hazian enesta fiesta: las quales,	g	1. Aprilis habet dies xxx.
20	A	estan escriptas, ala larga en su historia. fol. 45.27.	A	2 Mariæ egiptiace.

Page from *Florentine Codex* (Chater 3)

Cochina, cochina, cocochi ie njemia
ololonjcanj, ie cihoatl njcochinay
teo, oaies yho, yia, yia.

q Xippe icuje, totec iovalla
vana.

Ioalli Havana, iʒtleican, timone
nequja xjiaquj mjtlatia teucuj
tlaquemjtl, xjcmoquenti quetlovjia.

Notzuhoa chalchimmana tlacoa
pana itzmoia, oiquetzallaveuetl,
ayquetzal xiujcoatl nech taiquj no
cauhquetl ovjia.

Manjiaryia, njia, njia poliviʒ
njyoatzin, achalchiuhtla noiollo,
afeucujtlatl nocoiaittas nciolce
visqujtlacatl achto quetl tlaqua
vaia otlacatquj iautlatoa quetl
ovjia.

Notzuhoa centlaco xaiailiviʒ ço
noa yioatzin motepeiocpa mjtʒ
valitta motzuhoa, visqujntla
catl achtoquetl tlaquavaia etla
catquj iautlatoa quetl ovjia.

q Chicomecoatl icuje.

Chicomolotzin, xaia mehoa,

—*After Paso y Troncoso*

1-7. Tlacaxipeualiztli (Chapter 21)

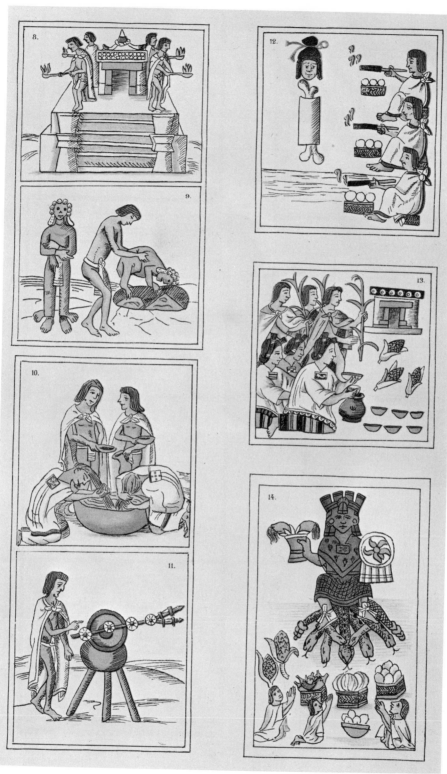

—*After Paso y Troncoso*

8-12. Tlacaxipeualiztli (Chapter 22)
13-14. Uei toçoztli (Chapter 23)

15-21. Toxcatl (Chapter 24)

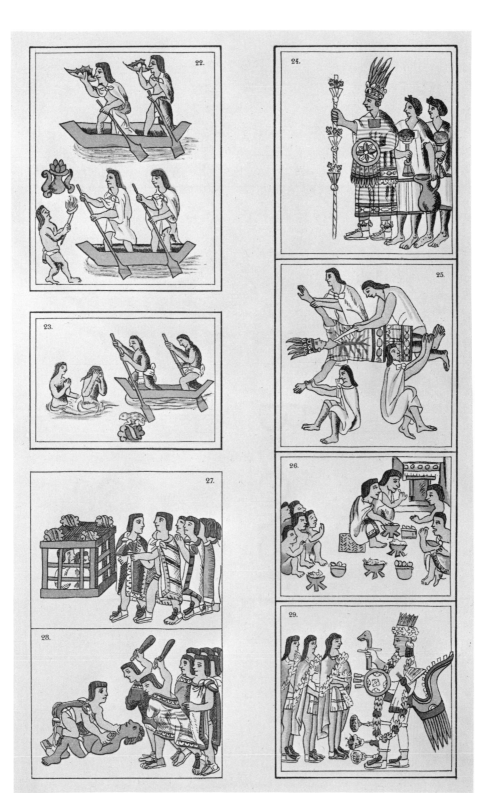

—After Paso y Troncoso

22-23. Etzalqualiztli (Chapter 25)
24-25. Tecuilhuitontli (Chapter 26)
26-28. Uei tecuilhuitl (Chapter 27)
29. Tlaxochimaco (Chapter 28)

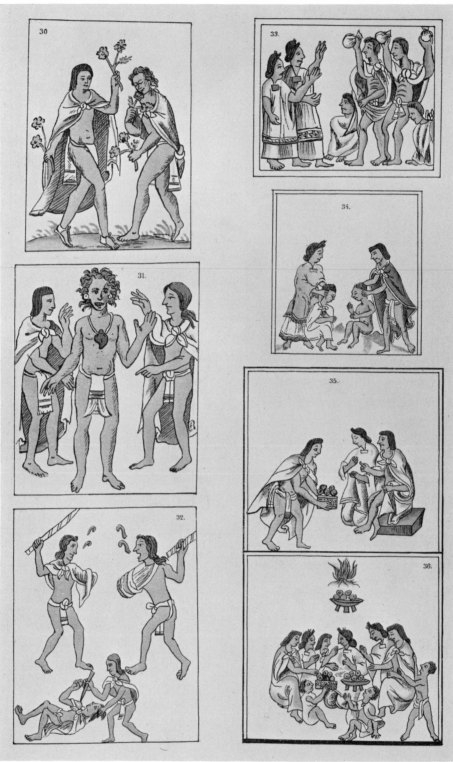

30. Ochpaniztli (Chapter 30)
31-32. Panquetzaliztli (Chapter 34)
33. Tititl (Chpter 36)
34. Izcalli (Chapter 37)
35-36. Ixcoçauhqui (Chapter 38)

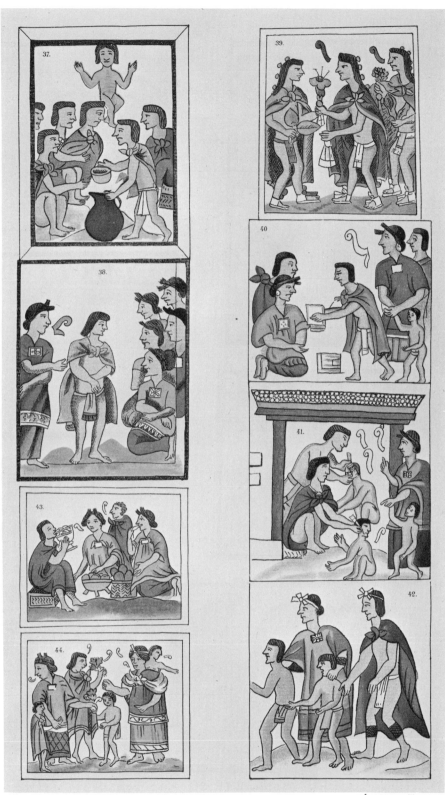

37-44. Ixcoçauhqui (Chapter 38)

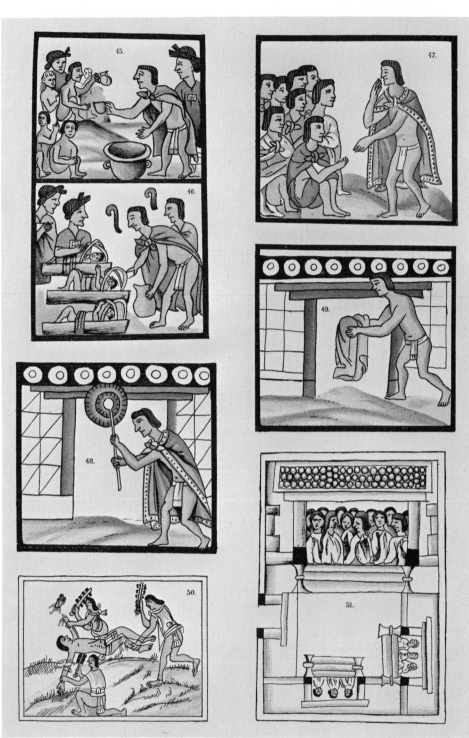

—*After Paso y Troncoso*

45-49. Ixcoçauhqui (Chapter 38)
50. Macuilcalli (Appendix)
51. Calpulli (Appendix)

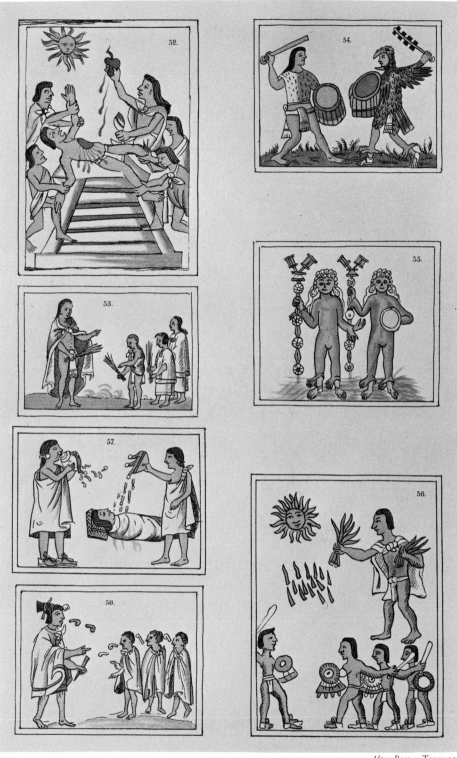

—*After Paso y Troncoso*

52. Tlamictiliztli (Appendix)
53. Tlachpanaliztli (Appendix)
54. Tlauauanaliztli (Appendix)
55. Çacapan nemanaliztli (Appendix)
56. Neçacapechtemaliztli (Appendix)
57. Tlatica tlauiliztli (Appendix)
58. Mexicatl teuhoatzin (Appendix)

59. Tepan teuhoatzin (Appendix)
60. Tlenamacaliztli (Appendix)
61. Iouallapializtli (Appendix)
62-63. Song of Xipe (Appendix)
64. Song of Chicome coatl (Appendix)
65. Song of the Totochtin (Appendix)
66. Song of Atlaua (Appendix)

offering priestesses who carried them on their backs had their faces painted; [their arms and legs] were pasted with feathers. Also they went singing. The Chicome coatl [priests] intoned the chant for them.

And when this was done, when they had scattered the seed,[26] thereupon they went to hide themselves away. Thereupon came down the [white] chalk and [white] feathers; they lay in a wooden vessel above [in the Temple of] Uitzilopochtli. And he who brought down the chalk was the fire priest. When he had come reaching the bottom, then he placed it there on the landing.[27]

And when he had placed it, then set forth the brave warriors. They ran hard; they ran fast. In truth those who ran swiftly, those who were agile, appeared there. He who went leading quickly took up feathers.[28] Then they billowed up. Thereupon there was falling upon [the feathers] as [the others] went off with them. Then they left; indeed they ran off.

And Toci['s impersonator] there stood awaiting them; she stood facing them. Then she sent them forth; she set after them; she pursued them; she went crying war cries. And when Toci['s impersonator] went, everyone spat at her; anyone whose flowers lay in his hands spat at her; he cast [the flowers] at her.

And Moctezuma also ran with the others. He followed them only a little way; sometimes he quickly entered the Bird House;[29] sometimes he quickly entered [the Temple of] Tecanman.[30] And everyone [else] went stopping when they left her; there were only few who indeed brought her, who indeed left her there at Tocititlan. However, the offering priests did not leave her; rather, they went guarding her.

And when they had arrived, then they took her up to the top of a wooden [structure]. Well did they set in place [the skin so that] its head looked forth. Similarly they made an end of all her adornments.

mopotonjaia, no cujcativi, qujncujcatitivi in chichicomecoa.

Auh in ie iuhquj, in oxxinachpixooa njman ie ic vi in motlatizque: njmã ie ic oaltemo in tiçatl yoã hivitl, quauhxicaltica manj, in jcpac vitzilobuchtli: auh in qujoaltemovia tiçatl, tlenamacac: in ocaxitico tlatzintlan, mec qujmana in vncã Coaxalpan.

Auh in oqujman: njman ic eoa in tiacaoan, cẽca motlaloa, cenca totocoa, vel vncan neci in painanj in tlaccani: in aqujn iacattiuh, qujmotzolotiqujça in jvitl: njman ic molonj, njmã ie ic ipan onnetepeoalo in qujnamoia in hivitl, njman ic qujztimanj, vel motlaloa.

Auh in toci vncan qujnchixticac, vncã qujmjtzticac, njmã ic qujmevitia, intech ietiqujça, qujntoca, tlacaoacatiuh. Auh in jquac ie iauh toci, muchi tlacatl conchicha: in aca isuchiuh oinmac onoca, conchichicha ic cõmotla.

Auh in Motecuçoma, no teoan, motlaloa, çan achiton in contoca: in quenman, totocalco in calactivetzi: in quẽman tecãman, in calactivetzi. Auh in jxqujch tlacatl, çan iuh ontlantivi in qujtlalcavia, çan quezqujnti in vel qujmonaxitia, in vel ompa qujmoncaoa Tocititlan: tel in tlamazque amo qujcaoa, çan qujpixtivi.

Auh in oacic, njman ic contlecavia in quauhticpac, vel qujtlatlalia, oalitztica in jtzontecon, çan iuh tlã-

---

26. *oxxinachpixoco* in *ibid*.

27. Corresponding Spanish text: *"ponjalo abaxo, en vn lugar que se llamaua coaxalpä, que era vn espacio, que auja entre las gradas del cu, y el patio abaxo, al qual espacio subia por cinco, o seys gradas."*

28. *quimatzolotiquiça* in the *Real Palacio MS.*

29. *totocalli*: *"la recámara de Mocthecuzoma . . . que se llamaba* Totocalco, *que quiere decir, la casa de aves"* (Sahagún, Garibay ed., Vol. IV, p. 46); and *"Alli se guardaba lo que era propio de Motecuhzoma, en el sitio de nombre Totocalco"* (*ibid.*, p. 112).

30. Tecanman is mentioned as a place or district in Chapter 24. Seler, *Gesammelte Abhandlungen*, Vol. IV, p. 154, says Tecanman was *"dem im Norden gelegenen Quartier und Tempel der Feuergöttin* Chantico."

And when they had gone setting it in place, then there was a turning about; there was a quick departure.

This is all. Here ended, here concluded the feast day which was known as Ochpaniztli.

tica in jxqujch inechichioal: in ocontlalito, mec oalnecuepalo, viloatz:

Ie ixqujch njcan tlamj, njcan tzonqujça, in ilhujtl, in moteneoa, Ochpanjztli.

Thirty-first Chapter, which telleth of the feast and the debt-paying which were observed during all the days of the twelfth month, which was named Teotl eco.[1]

The twelfth feast day was the one named Teotl eco.

After five days,[2] right there began the placing of the fir [branches].[3] The fir [branches] were [really] reeds, which they bound together in threes. Only the youths placed them everywhere on the small pyramids in the temples of the Ciuateteo,[4] and everywhere in people's homes where were kept the images of the devils.

And when they were placing fir [branches] everywhere in people's homes, [the householders] gave [the youths] perhaps a small basket of dried grains of maize, or else four ears of maize; in some places, three ears of maize; if [the householder] were very poor, it was two ears of maize[5] that he gave them. It was stated: "They are tongs,"[6] for the youths ate the maize toasted on the embers. And no one just idly ate the maize toasted on the embers; only those who were diligent, acceptable, careful, wakeful, who trusted not [too much] their [own] diligence.

And on the third day of placing fir [branches], at that time arrived Telpochtli, named Tlamatzincatl.[7] He came here ahead; this one arrived first. For this reason did he come here ahead: he indeed still was a youth; he was still strong; he had calves [to his legs]. For this reason he arrived here first.

And they laid out an offering for him; that which they offered him was fish amaranth seed dough. First they roasted [the seeds]; they broke them up on an earthen griddle. Then they ground them up. And when they had ground them up, then they

Inic cempoalli on matlactli oce capitulo: itechpa tlatoa in ilhujtl, yoan in nextlaoaliztli; in muchioaia, in jpã vel ic cemjlhujtl, injc matlactetl omume metztli: in motocaiotiaia, Teutl eco.

Injc matlactetl om ume ilhujtl: iehoatl in motocaiotia, Tetl eco:

in ie iuh tlamacujlti, njmã vncan vmpeoa in acxoiatemalo: in acxoiatl, iehoatl in acatl, êei in qujlpiaia; çan iehoantin in telpopochtin qujtemaia, novian in momozco, in cioateucalco, yoan in novian techachan, in vncan pipielo in jmjxiptlaoan diablome:

auh in techachã novian onacxoiatemaia, qujnoalmaca, aço cen chiqujuhtzintli in tlaolli, anoço cintli, naolotl: in cana ieolotl: in cenca motolinja, omolotl in cintli qujoaltemaca: moteneoa, cacalotl ca qujmocalhuiaia in telpopochtli: auh aiac çan nê mocalhuiaia, can iehoantin in jmel, in tlacelianj, in tlamocujtlavianj, in cochiçanj, in amo tlatlacanequjnj in jmel.

Auh in ie ic ieilhujtl acxoiatemalo: iquac heco in telpochtli, itoca Tlamatzincatl, oaliacattivia, iehoatl achto heco: ipampa in oaliacattivia, ca oc telpochtli, oc chicaoac, tlaçcanj, cotze: ipampa in achto oalaci,

yoan qujtlamanjliaia: in qujmanjliaia, mjchioauhtli, in tlapololli: achtopa qujcequj, qujtzomotza comalco, çatepan qujteci: auh in oqujtezque, çatepã qujpoloaia, atica: cequj necutica, in qujpoloaia: aço macujltetl, aço nauhtetl in coololoa, quauhcaxic in

1. *Teteu heco* — *Los dioses llegan*, in Garibay ("Relación breve," p. 307). Clavijero, *Historia Antigua*, Vol. III, p. 165, refers to *teotleco* as *la fiesta de la venida de los dioses*. The spelling *"Tetl eco"* is in the *Florentine Codex*.

2. The Nahuatl text should read "fifteen days." The rituals described took place during the last five days of the month. Sahagún's corresponding Spanish text reads: "*A qujnze dias andados, deste mes, enrramauan vnos altares, que ellos llamauan momoztli.*" See also Sahagún's summary of the month in Chap. 12.

3. See Chap. 23, n. 4. In the Spanish text of Chap. 34 (Panquetzaliztli), fol. 83, Sahagún explains that "*por ramos lleuauã cañas verdes, y espinas de maguey,*" and in Chap. 25 (Etzalqualiztli), fol. 41, "*luego yuan a cortar ramos que llaman acxoiatl: y donde no auja estos ramos, cortauan cañas verdes, en lugar de acxoiatl.*"

4. See the Eighth Movable Feast in this volume.

5. *olotl*: maize cob in Sahagún, Garibay ed., Vol. II, p. 34; however, Sahagún usually renders it maize ear.

6. "*cueruo, o tenazuela . . . para comer granos de mayz tostado en el rescoldo*" (Molina, *Vocabulario*). In the corresponding text, Sahagún states: "*llamauan a esto cacalotl, como qujen dize agujnaldo.*"

7. These names are synonyms for Tezcatlipoca. Cf. Chap. 12 and Sahagún, Garibay ed., Vol. I, p. 152.

moistened them with water. Some they moistened with honey. Perhaps four pieces, perhaps five pieces it was that they made into balls. They went filling a wooden vessel. Then they went off carrying it. When they arrived in his presence, then they put it in place; they put it in place for him.

And when it was already night, then there was pulque drinking; there was the drinking of pulque. It was the esteemed old men, the esteemed old women [who did so]. Thus they said: "It is said they bathe [the god's] feet."

And when the fourth day came, then ended the placing of the fir [branches]. At that time they threw away the fir [branches]. And when the fifth day came, it was in truth the time of Teotl eco, with which ended the twenty days.[8]

It was midnight when [the priests] made cornmeal. They pressed it together hard; they pressed it together. They made it circular. It was on a reed mat that they placed it.

When it was time that the gods were reaching here, were arriving, they made preparations. They all set themselves in action, since the gods were arriving.

And the old priest, [the god's] old man, named Teohua [the god's keeper], kept going back to look upon [the cornmeal on the mat]. Often he looked upon it. He never sat down; his only office was to look on it. Never did he get off his feet when he was looking on the cornmeal. It was called "his foot."

And when [the god] arrived, [the priest] saw there a little foot[print], which was there on the cornmeal or at its edge. When [the god] stood upon the cornmeal, he crumbled the cornmeal.[9] It then appeared that the gods had indeed arrived.

Then he who kept the god said to them: "Indeed the lord hath deigned to come."

When this was heard, then [the priests] came together to go in procession, while shell trumpets were blown. It became generally known; then it was known that indeed the gods had arrived.

And all the common folk then went; there was going on the part of each one to lay offerings, each one, in their temples, the temples of the devils. All offered them balls of dough.

tetentiuh, mec qujtqujtiuh: in oacic ixpã mec contema, contemjlia.

Auh in jquac ie ioa, mec tlatlaoano, tlatlaoanalo, in veventzitzin, in jlamatzitzin: in juh qujtoaia, qujlmach qujcxipaca.

Auh in oacic ic navilhujtl, vncan ontlamj, in acxoiatemaliztli: iquac qujtepeoa in acxoiatl. Auh in oacic ic macujlilhujtl, in ie vel iquac Teutl eco, in ie ic ontlamj cempoalilhujtl:

ioalnepantla, in qujchioaia, iotextli, qujtepitztlaliaia, qujpachoaia, iaoaltic injc qujtlaliaia, petlapã in contlaliaia:

in jquac muchintin oalacia, hecoia in teteu, qujcencaoaia, cemolinja, injc iecoia teteu:

auh in quacujlli, in jveveio, itoca: Teuoa, mocujtlacueptinemj, in conjtta, achca in conjtta, aquẽmã motlalia, çan jc nemj in conjtta, aquẽman conjcxicaoa, in conjtta iotextli, moteneoa: icxi.

Auh in ohecoc, vncan conjtta, iexitontli, in vncan icac, iotexpan: anoço itenco, in moquetza iotextli, texxitinj: njmã ic neci, ca ohecoque in teteu:

njman ic qujoalitoa, in teuoa. Ca omecavi in tlacatl:

in ocacoc: njmã ic maantimoquetza in tlapitzalo, qujtzacutimomana: njmã ic macho, ca ohecoque in teteu.

Auh in jxqujch maceoalli, njman ic vivi, viviloa, in tlatlamanazque inteupã, in inteteupan diablome: çã moche in tlapololli, in qujnmanjlia.

---

8. Cf. note 2. Corresponding Spanish text: *"al qujnto dia, era la fiesta de teutl eco, es la llegada de los dioses, que era el vltimo dia deste mes."*

9. The word *xitinia* is explained by Garibay ("Relación breve," p. 307): *"Auh quil mach in icuac vallacia teteu xitinia in iuhqui xamitl tlaultextli"* — *"y dizque cuando venian los dioses, se partia el como adobe de harina de maíz."*

And when each had made the offerings, then all was still.

And when already night fell, in the same manner as they had done [previously], the old men, the esteemed old women each drank pulque. It was said: "They bathe the feet of the gods who have arrived."

And when it was the next day, it was the time that Yacapitzauac arrived; this one was Yiacatecutli; he was the merchants' god. And Ixcoçauhqui: this one was Xiuhtecutli; he likewise was the merchants' god. These came here only at the last, they came here only following, they came here only last of all because indeed they were already old.

And at this time then there began the casting [of victims] into the fire there on the large altar.[10] Indeed many were the poor captives whom they cast into the fire.

And when they were being cast into the fire, [one arrayed as a] squirrel went dancing there. He was ornamented only with a small crest of feathers on his head; he had a crest of feathers. He had bi-colored face painting. He went carrying his carrying frame on his back; in there went lying a small dried rabbit. When they cast one into the fire, [the dancer] whistled repeatedly through his fingers.

And one [in the likeness of a] bat was there. He went dancing. Indeed like a bat was he arrayed.[11] He had two gourd rattles. They were in each hand as he went rattling the rattles.

And when the captives had been cast into the fire, then the offering priests formed themselves into rows in order to descend here. They had their paper stoles, which were painted with designs.

They grasped one another; with their hands they grasped one another; very firmly they grasped one another. When [in the line of procession] they were cut off, when they were in a gap, it was as if each one was thrown off. Some thus struck the ground; they quickly bit the earth. This was called *mama-tlauitzoa*.[12]

And next day there was the assembling of each one, at the same time; there was a serpent dance. There was the decking of each one with feathers — yellow, chili-red, dark brown, blue-green. Thus were they decked with feathers — [even] all the small

auh in ontlatlamanaloc, njman ic cactivetzi.

Auh in ie iooa: çan ie no ivi in qujchioa, tlatlaoana in vevetque, in jlamatzitzin, qujlmach, qujmjcxipaca in ohecoque teteu.

Auh in jmuztlaioc, iquac heco in Jacapitzaoac, inj Jacatecutli: pochteca inteouh catca, yoa in Ixcoçauh-quj, iehoatl in Xiuhtecutli, çan no pochteca inteouh catca, ça oallatzacujtivia, ça oallatoqujlitivia, ça qujoalcentzacujtivia: iehica ca ie vevetque.

Auh in jquac in, njman ic peoa in tetlepantlaxo, vncan in teccalco: vel mjequjntin, in qujntlepantla-çaia, mamaltzitzinti:

auh in vncan tetlepãtlaxo, vncan mjtotitinemj techalotl, çan mochichioaia quachichiqujltone, qua-chichiqujle, mjxtecujcujlo: ioacalton qujmamati-nemj, vncan onotinemj, tochtlaoatzaltontli: in jquac ce contlaça tleco, mapipitzoa:

yoan ce tzinacan vncan nenca, mjtotitinemj, vel iuhqujn tzinacan: ic no mochichioaia vntetl in jaia-cach, vccampa in aiacachotinemj.

Auh in ontetlepantlaxoc, mec oalmotecpana in tlamacazque: injc oaltemo, imaamaneapanal, tlacuj-lolli:

maana, in matitech maana, cenca moteteuhtzitz-quja: inon omocotonque, in omotlacavilique, iuh-qujn mochichiccanauhtivi, in aca tlalli ic movitequj, tlalli qujjquativetzi. Inin moteneoa mamatlavitzoa.

Auh in jmuztlaioc, onnenechicolo, cenvetzi, in necocololo, hivitica necujcujlolo, in coztic, in chichil-tic, in vitztecolli, in xoxoctic, injc mjvicujcujloa, muchintin in pipiltotõti, in manel coçolco onoc, cenca ixqujch tlacatl, çan iehoantin in oqujchtin:

---

10. See a description of the *teccalco* in the appendix of this volume.

11. *yc momochichiuaya* in the *Real Palacio MS*.

12. *momatlauitzoa* in the *Real Palacio MS*; *mamalauitzoa* in the corresponding Spanish text; the appendix on the temple square build-ings, below (see Teccalco), uses the term *amatlauitzoa*. See also *tlauitzoa* in Siméon, *Dictionnaire*, p. 630.

children, although they [still] lay in the cradle; indeed everyone, [but] only the males.[13]

Thereupon was begun the serpent dance, at midday. There was grasping of one another; there was singing. It was no matter what they intoned; just pleasure songs. And when there was stopping on the part of each, it was already dark. And he who was taking much pleasure indeed remained there until night fell.

And these two festive days they had already taken from Tepeilhuitl, [the next month].

Enough. Here ended, here concluded the feast [of the month] Teotl eco.

njman ie ic peoalo in necocololo, nepātla tonatiuh, neaano, cujco, çaço ac tle queoa, çan avilcujcatl: auh in necacaoalo, ie iooa: auh in aca cenca compaquj, vel vncan iovilia:

auh in jiomjlhujixti y, ie cuel cōcujlia in tepeilhujtl.

Je ixqujch njcan tlamj, njcan tzonqujça in ilhujtl Teutl eco.

---

13. This ceremony is further described in the appendix of this volume.

Thirty-second Chapter, in which are related the feast day and debt-paying which were observed during all the days of the thirteenth month, which was known as, which was called Tepeilhuitl.[1]

The thirteenth feast day was known as Tepeilhuitl.[2]

All the [wooden] serpent [representations] which were kept in people's houses, and the small wind [figures][3] they covered with a dough of [ground] amaranth seeds.

And their bones were likewise fashioned of amaranth seed dough. They were cylindrical. Either fish amaranth[4] or ash amaranth [was used].[5]

And also they fashioned [images in the form of] mountains [for] perchance one who had died in the water, who had been drowned, or else had been struck by lightning.

And [for] whoever had died who had not been burned, who had only been buried,[6] they also at this time made representations of mountains. They made them all of amaranth seed dough.

And upon the eve of the feast, toward sundown, there was the bathing or the washing of the surfaces [of the figures' frames].[7] When they bathed them there, they went blowing wind instruments for them; they went blowing pottery whistles and little seashells.

And they bathed them there at the Mist House; with fresh cane shoots they washed their surfaces. And some bathed them only at their own shores.[8]

And when they had been bathed, then they were returned here; in the same manner they came blowing wind instruments for them; it was as if they

Inic cempoalli on matlactli omome capitulo: vncan moteneoa in jlhujtl, yoan in nextlaoalli, in muchioaia in jpã ic cemjlhujtl, ic matlactetl omei metztli in moteneoaia, in mjtoaia Tepilhujtl.

Injc matlactetl omei ilhujtl iehoatl in moteneoa tepeilhujtl:

in jxqujchtin cocoa im pipialo techachan, yoan in ecatotonti, qujtetepetlaliaia, tzoalli injc qujnpepechoaia:

auh in jmomjo muchioaia, çan no tzoalli, mjmjmjltic, aço mjchioauhtli, anoço cócotl:

auh no qujtepetlaliaia, in açaca atlan mjc, in jlaqujlo, in anoçe viteco:

yoã in aqujn omomjqujli, in amo tlatilo, in çan qujtoca, no tepetl ipan qujqujxtiaia, çan moch tzoalli in qujnchichioaia:

Auh in oqujuh muztla ilhujtl teutlacpa in teaaltilo, anoço teixamjlo: injc qujmonaltia qujntlapichilitivi, in qujnpichilitivi, cocovilotl, yoan tecciztotonti.

Auh in qujmonaltiaia, vmpan aiauhcalco, acatzontli iehoatl in celtic ic qujmjxamja: auh in cequjntin çan imatenco in qujmonaltia.

Auh in ontealtiloc, mec oaltecuepalo, çã no ivi, qujntlapichilitivitze, iuhqujn tlacaoacativitz, njmã ie ic tetlacatililo, techichioalo qujmpepechoa:

---

1. "*Fiesta del cerro,*" according to Garibay ("Relación breve," p. 308); "*Fest der Berge,*" in Seler, *Einige Kapitel,* p. 189.

2. After *tepeilhujtl* the *Real Palacio MS* adds: "*no cempoalilhujtl ynic moteneua tepeylhuitl*" — "also twenty days. For this reason was it known as Tepeilhuitl."

3. See the explanation of *cocoa* and *ecatotonti* in Chap. 13. Juan de Torquemada, in *Segunda parte de los veinte i un libros rituales i monarchia indiana* (Madrid: Nicolas Rodrigo Franco, 1723), p. 279, writes: "*Para cuia solemnidad, lo primero era, hacer unas Culebras de palo, ò de raìces de Arboles, labrandoles las cabeças, lo mas pulidamente que sabian. Hacian tambien de troçuelos pequeños vnas figurillas, à manera de las Muñecas, que acostumbran las Niñas, en nuestra Nacion Española, las quales llamaban Ecatotonti. . . .*"

4. According to Garibay, in Sahagún, Garibay ed., Vol. IV, p. 343: "*Michyauhtli.* — 'Bledos de pez.' . . . Prob. la misma que la Argemone mexicana (*Chicalote*)." Cf. also Dibble and Anderson, *Book XI,* p. 287.

5. Cf. *ibid.,* p. 286.

6. Torquemada, *Segunda parte,* p. 279, further explains: ". . . *en memoria de algunos difuntos, en especial de los que se avian ahogado en Agua, ò avian muerto de muerte, que no pudieron ser quemados sus cuerpos, ò fueron enterrados por alguna causa.*"

7. Both Sahagún (corresponding Spanish text) and Seler, *Einige Kapitel,* pp. 190–91, differ from this version. In Sahagún, the people wash the mats upon which the images rested; in Seler, the people are washed.

8. Corresponding Spanish text: "*el agua, que passaua junto a su casa.*"

came shouting. Thereupon they were given human form; they were adorned. They gave them their foundation.

And some gave them their foundation well on into the night. Thus did they give them human form: they applied liquid rubber to the faces [of the figures][9] and they placed [a spot of] fish amaranth upon [each] of their cheeks; they dressed them in paper banners and they fitted them with their paper headdresses, their forked heron feather ornaments.

And for those who had died in the water, they placed their images only on circular jar rests of grass.[10] They made [the images] of amaranth seed dough.

And when it dawned, then they were set up in each one's house upon reed foundations made perhaps of thin, fine reeds; perhaps of wide reeds; of large white reeds; perhaps of hollow reeds.[11] On these they placed them.

And when this was done, when they had arranged them, thereupon they laid offerings before them. They offered them fruit tamales, and stews, or dog meat, or turkey hen. And they offered them incense.

And at this time it was stated: "They are laid in the houses." And where there was riches,[12] there was singing, and there was drinking pulque for them. But elsewhere all they did was make offerings to them.

And upon the feast day there died some women who were representations of the mountains.

The first was named Tepexoch; the second, Matlalcueye; the third, Xochtecatl; the fourth, Mayauel, representation of the maguey. The fifth was named Milnauatl; this one was a man who represented a serpent.

Their array, their paper headdresses, their paper vestments were painted with liquid rubber; they had much rubber; they were full of rubber. And the adornment of Milnauatl was in the same manner.

Early in the morning they started them off. They went carrying them in their arms on litters. It was stated: "They provide them with litters." There they each went; there they each sat up in the litters. They took them in a roundabout procession. Only

auh in cequjnti oc vecaioan, in qujnpepechoa, injc qujntlacatilia, qujmixolhuja, yoan mjchioauhtli in quimõtlalilia incamapan, qujmõquentia in tetevitl, yoan qujmõaquja imamacal, yiaztatzon.

Auh in atlan mjquja, çan iaoalco in qujntlaliaia, in jmjxiptla, tzoalli in qujnchichioaia.

Auh in otlatvic: mec tetlatlalilo in techachan, tolpepechpan, aço tolpitzaoac, aço tolpatlactli, aztapili, aço axali in impã qujtlaliaia:

Auh in ie iuhquj, in otecencaoaloc: njman ie ic qujntlamanjlia: in qujnmaniliaia xocotamalli, yoan tlatonilli, anoço itzcuinnacatl, anoço totolin: yoan qujntlenamaqujlia.

In jquac in moteneoa cali onoac: auh in netlacamachoia, cujcatilo, yoan tlatlaoanjlilo: auh in cana çan ixqujch in qujntlamanjliaia.

Auh in jpan in ilhujtl, mjquja cequjntin cioa, imjxiptlaoan Tetepe.

Injc ce itoca Tepoxoch. Injc vme: Matlalquae. Injc ei: Xochtecatl. Injc navi, Maiavel: ixiptla metl. Jnjc macujlli: itoca Milnaoatl: inin oqujchtli, ixiptlan coatl:

in jnechichioal, in jmamamacal, in jmamatlatquj: tlaolhujlli, cenca ollo, moca olli: auh in Milnaoatl, çan no iuhquj in jnechichioal, in jtlatquj:

ioatzinco in qujmpeoaltiaia in qujnnapalotinemj, tlapechtica: moteneoa, qujntlatlapechvia, vncan mamantivi, vncan yicativi in tlapechco, qujntlatlaiaoalochtia: çan no cioa in tlanapaloa, qujncujcatitivi.

---

9. The corresponding Spanish text reads, besides: "*La cabeça de cada vn monte tenja dos caras, vna de persona, y otra de culebra. . . .*"

10. Spanish text: "*rodeos, o roscas, hechos de heno, atados con sogas.*"

11. Cf. Chap. 25, n. 3. See also Dibble and Anderson, *Book XI*, pp. 136, 195.

12. *netlacamachoa* in the *Real Palacio MS.*

the women carried [the litters] in their arms.[13] They went singing for [the victims].

And [the women] who carried [the litters] were well arrayed; they were properly set up. All new were their shifts, their skirts, which they had put on them. And their faces were painted; they were pasted with feathers.

And when it was the time for it, when it was time for them to die, thereupon they set down the litters. Then they were each brought up [to the top of the pyramid]; they went leaving each one there at [the Temple of] Tlaloc. And when they had brought them there, then they stretched them on the offering stone. Then the officiating [priests], the slayer stood forth. Thereupon they cut open their breasts.

And when [the victims] had given their service, when they had died, then they brought [their bodies] down here. And thus did they bring them down here: they only went rolling them here; it was slowly that they went turning them over and over.

And when they had come bringing them down, then they took them to the skull rack. And when they had taken them [there], then they cut off their heads; they decapitated them. There they inserted into their heads [the crosspieces of the rack].

And when they had cut their heads off, their bodies they then took to the various *calpulcos* [whence the victims had been sent]. And next day, at dawn, when it was said, "They are dismembered," they were each dismembered.

Thereupon they dismembered the amaranth seed dough [figures]. And when they had dismembered each one, then they took them up to the roof tops. There they dried hard, they dried stiff. Little by little they went taking some of it when they ate it; gradually they finished it.

And with the paper array which had been [theirs] they covered the circular grass jar rest which they had [used]. And when they had covered them, they hung them from the roof of the *calpulco*. For one year they went caring for them; [then] they went to throw them away, they went to scatter them there at the Mist House. Only the paper vestments did they scatter; but the circular grass jar rests they brought back.

Here ended the feast day which was called Tepeilhuitl.

auh in tlanapaloa, vel moçencaoa, ieccan moquetza, mochi iancujc, in intech qujtlaliaia in incue, in invipil, yoã moxaoa, mopotonja.

Auh in otlaimmãtic in ie iquac mjqujzque: njmã ie ic qujteca in tlapechtli: mec tetlecavilo, qujmooncavitivi in vmpa tlalocan. Auh in oqujmonaxitique, mec qujmõteca in techcac: mec oalmoquetza in tequjpaneque, in temjctianj: njmã ie ic qujmelтetequj.

Auh in ontlacotique, in ommjcque, njmã ic qujnoaltemovia: auh injc qujnoaltemovia, çan qujnoalmjmjlotivi, cenca çan quẽmach, in qujncuecueptivitze.

Auh in oqujntemovico, njmã vmpa qujnvica, in tzompantitlan: auh in oqujmonaxitique, njmã ic qujnquechtequj, qujnquechcotona: vncã qujmõçoço in intzonteço.

Auh in oqujmõquechcotonque, in intlac: njmã ie qujvica in incacalpolco: auh in jmuztlaioc, in ooallatvic: in mjtoaia, Texinjlo, texixitinjlo:

njmã ie ic qujxitinja in tzoalli: auh in oqujxixitinjque, njmã ic tlapanco qujtlecavia, vmpa oaquj, quauhvaquj, tepioaquj: achchi concujtivi in qujqua, can juh qujtlamja.

Auh in jmamatlatquj ocatca, qujqequentia in jiaoallo ocatca: auh in oqujqequẽtique calquac compiloa, calpulco, çe xivitl qujmattiuh, in qujtlaçativi, in qujtepeoativi, in vmpa aiauhcalco: çanjo in jmamatlatquj, contepeoa: auh in iaoalli qujoalitquj.

Nican tlamj in jlhujtl, in moteneoa Tepeilhujtl.

13. *tenapaloa* is added in *ibid*.

Thirty-third Chapter, in which are related the feast day and the debt-paying with which they gave service, which they observed during all the days of the fourteenth month, which was called Quecholli.[1]

The fourteenth feast was the one called Quecholli.

When Tepeilhuitl ended, nothing was done for another five days.[2] All still remained quite quiet.

And when the five days had passed, upon the next day there was an offering of reeds there; each seasoned warrior took a load upon his back in Tenochtitlan, in Tlatelolco, when reeds were offered there at the foot of [the Temple of] Uitzilopochtli. And when they had been offered, then [others] came carrying them; they each bore them upon their shoulders [to their homes].

And, upon the morrow, once again there was going to the courtyard of [the Temple of] Uitzilopochtli. They were to straighten them over a fire; the reeds were to be straightened over a fire. Only this was still all that was done. And when they had been straightened in the fire, once again they were borne away; once again their burdens went away with them.

And on the third day, once again there was going. The reeds were carried. Indeed all moved together — seasoned warriors, youths, young men of marriageable age. And the small boys they took, each one, up [the pyramid] to the temple. There they each sat blowing shell trumpets, and they sat bleeding themselves. They cut their ears; they pressed out their blood; they anointed their temples [with it]. It was said: "They anoint themselves with blood because of the deer." They fasted for the deer, so that [the deer] would be hunted.

And when there had been assembling in the temple courtyard, those of Tenochtitlan were spread on one side, those of Tlatelolco were spread on the other side. Thereupon spears were made. It was said: "Spears are born, or their [points] of oak."

Injc cempoalli õmatlactli omei capitulo: vncan mo-teneoa in ilhujtl, yoã in nextlaoalli, injc tlacotia: in qujchioaia, in jpã ic cemjlhujtl, ic matlactetl on navi metztli, in moteneoaia, Quecholli.

Injc matlactetl on navi ilhujtl: iehoatl in moteneoa Quecholli:

in õquiz tepeilhujtl, oc macujlilhujtl in aiatle muchioaia, çan oc cactimanj:

auh in õqujz macujlilhujtl: in jmuztlaioc, vncã in neacamaco, cecen tlamamalli in conanaia tequj-oaque, in Tenuchtitlan, in Tlatilulco: in neacama-coia, vncã in icxitlan Vitzilobuchtli: auh in õnema-coc, njmã ic qujitqujtze qujquequechpanoa.

Auh in jmuztlaioc, ie no ceppa ic viloa in jitoalco Vitzilobuchtli, tlatlemelaoaloz, motlemelaoaz in acatl: çan oc ixqujch, in muchioaia y: auh in vmmo-tlemelauh, oc ceppa çan no oalmotquji, oc ceppa intlatquj oalietiuh.

Auh injc eilhujtl, no ceppa viloa, mootqují in acatl, vel ixqujch cemolinj, in tequjoaque in telpuchtli, in tlapalivi: auh in oqujchpipiltotonti, qujtletlecavia in teucalli, vncã tlatlapitztoque, yoan mjçotoque: quj-tequj in innacaz, in jmezço compatzca, incanaoacã conalaoa: mjtoaia, momaçaíço, qujnneçaviliaia in mamaça, injc amjoaz.

Auh in ocẽqujxoato teuitoalco: cecnj moteca in tenuchca, cecnj moteca in Tlatilulca: njmã ie ic mu-chioa in mjtl: mjtoaia tlacati in tlacochtli, anoço yiaoaio.

---

1. *Quecholli:* "Pájaro 'flamenco' (Platalea ajaja)" in Jiménez Moreno, "*Primeros memoriales,*" p. 52. The *teoquechol* or *tlauhquechol* is identified as *Ajaia ajaja,* "roseate spoonbill," in Dibble and Anderson, *Book XI,* p. 20. Torquemada, in *Segunda parte,* p. 280, writes: ". . . *nombre de vn Paxaro de pluma azul, y colorada, que ai en esta Tierra, en especial en vnos manantiales, y ojos de Agua, que ai junto del Pueblo de Quecholac.*"

Tovar, while mentioning the bird of rich plumage, adds that captains raised their banners and performed warlike exercises. He describes it as a month of unrest and dissensions (Kubler and Gibson, *The Tovar Calendar,* p. 32).

2. Corresponding Spanish text: "*salido el mes passado, cinco dias, no se hazia cerjmonja ninguna, nj fiesta en los cues.*"

And at the time that the spears were being born, there was fasting; they fasted for them. Everyone anointed himself with his blood. And if anyone was seen who did not anoint himself with his blood, they repeatedly stripped him; nevermore did they give him his cape. The overseers took it from him for good.

And when spears were being born, no [man] lay with a woman. And the old men drank no pulque; they became not drunk. They abstained; they abstained from pulque.

And when spears were being made, their measure came forth. They were made all quite the same, and the bolts were all quite the same. None were unequal in length; on none did they make changes.

Thereupon the reeds were cut. They went to put them in the hands of those who fitted the bolts, those who put on the bolts. Well did they tie the [ends of the] reeds with maguey fiber; well did they keep binding them with maguey fiber, so that the bolt would not split back. They set [the points] in glue so that they would indeed hold fast, so that they would be well embedded.

And when they had [thus] prepared them, thereupon they applied pine pitch to the heads and the ends. This was done quite quickly.

And when they were finished, thereupon they were bound together at the middle; in twenties were they bound together at the middle. And when they were assembled, thereupon there was their arranging in rows, their ordering in line, their arranging in file to leave [the bundles] there at the foot of [the Temple of] Uitzilopochtli. There they heaped them together. And when they had come to make [this] offering, then there was departing on the part of each one [to their homes].

And the fourth day was called "They are made to live in the houses." Everyone used arrows, each one at his home, only to amuse themselves with them. Yet there were continual trials of skill with them; there was continual learning with them. They would put up a maguey [leaf] at a distance; they shot arrows at it continually. There appeared some who could knock it down, those who were dexterous, who shot arrows well.

And upon the fifth day one was concerned only with the dead. For each of them were made very small arrows, each one of a hand's length.[3] Also

Auh in jquac tlacatia, tlacochtli: neçaoaloia, qujneçaviliaia, ixqujch tlacatl, mjçoia: auh in aquj itto, in amo mjço qujpepetlaoaia, aocmo qujmaca in jtilma, iccen qujtqujlia in tepāmanj.

Auh in jquac tlacatia mjtl, aiac cioacochia: auh in vevetque, amo quja in vctli, amo tlaoanaia, motlacaoaltiaia, qujmocaoaltiaia in vctli.

Auh in muchioaia mjtl, oalqujça itamachiuhca, çan much ixqujch, in muchioaia: auh in tlaxichtli, çã much ixqujch, atle chicoviac, atle tlapatiliaia:

njmā ie ic tlateco in acatl, inmac qujoallaztivi, in tlatlaxichaquja in qujtlaxichaquja, vel qujchtecuja in acatl, vel ichtica qujtetecuja, injc amo cujtlatzaianjz in tlaxichtli: tzacupā in cōquetza, injc vel tilinjz, injc vel tzitzicaz.

Auh in ocōcencauhque: njmā ie ic cocotzovia, in jquac, yoan itzintlan, çan iciuhcā muchioa.

Auh in oiecauh, njmā ie ic tlacujtlalpilo, cecempoalli in mocujtlalpia: auh in otlacenqujz, njmā ie ic onnetecpanalo, onnevipanolo, oncempantioa in mocaoaz in vmpa icxitlan Vitzilobuchtli, vncan concentecpichoa: auh in ōmomamanato, njmā ic viviloa.

Auh injc navilhujtl, mjtoaia, calpā nemjtilo, ixqujch tlacatl momjtiaia intechachan, çan iuhquj injc neaviltilo, tel ic neieiecoloia, ic nemamachtiloia: ce veca qujoalquetzaia metl, qujmjmjna, vncan neci in aqujque vel qujmaiavi, in vel momaimati, in vellamjna.

Auh injc macujlilhujtl, çã mjxcaviaia in mjmjcque, qujnchichiviliaia, mjtotonti, çeçemjztitl, no achitoton ic conoocotzovia: auh in jtlaxichio, çan

3. Corresponding Spanish text: "eran largas, como vn xeme, o palmo."

they applied only a little resin on each one. And their bolts were only sticks. They bound four arrows [and] also four pine torches about the middle with loose cotton thread; they laid each [bundle] where the dead lay buried. And they placed on each one two sweet tamales. There they stayed all day. And at sundown, they thereupon burned them for [the dead], in the same place. There they set them on fire.

And when they had burned, they buried their charcoal and their ashes there.

And the streamers, and the costly banners, and the shields, and the capes, and the breechclouts of those slain in battle they placed on a dry maize stalk. They tied them on. From it hung loose, twisted, red cotton thread. At its end went hanging a [dead] hummingbird and four hundred [white] heron [feathers]. They pasted many cords with feathers. At the ends heron [feathers] went hanging. They left them in the eagle vessel; there they burned.

And of the sixth day it was said: "There is issuing on the grass." [4] And for this reason was it said, "There is issuing on the grass": grass was scattered [in the Temple of Mixcoatl]; it was pine-tree grass.[5] There were ranged the old women [who served in the temple]. Before them lay a mat.

Thereupon came forth women with children. Each one heaped upon the mat five sweet tamales. All together, by fives, they laid them down. They came to give their children to the old women. And the old women came to take the children; then they dandled them in their arms. Then, when they had dandled them, they gave the mothers [back] their children.

Then [the mothers] departed to their homes. It was yet early morning when this started. And it was already time to eat when it was finished. And when this was done, thereupon[6] there was the departure to hunt. They went to come upon Çacatepec, there at Ixillan tonan.

And at the end of ten days of this month, as hath been said above, they there celebrated a feast in

tlacotl: navi mjtl, no navi ocotl, concujtlalpia ica potonquj, impã contetema, in vncan toctitoque, mjmjcque: yoan ontetl tzopelic tamalli, contetema, vncan cemjlhujtia: auh in ie oncalaquj tonatiuh, njman ie ic qujntlatlatilia, in çan ie no vncan: vncan contlecavia:

auh in ontlatlac, in jtecollo, yoan inexo, vncã contoca.

Auh in oiaomjcque in inmecapan, yoan intlaço-pan, yoan inchimal, yoã intilma, yoan inmaxtli, ooaquauhtitech in qujtlaliaia, qujlpiaia, itech pilca-tiuh chichilicpatl, potonquj ic tlamalintli, yiacac pilcatiuh vitzitzilin, yoã cẽtzonaztatl, mjec in mecatl, qujpotonjaia hivitica, yiacac pilcatiuh aztatl, vmpa concaoa in quauhxicalco, vmpa tlatlaia.

Auh injc chiquacentlamantli: moteneoa, çacapã qujxoa: auh injc moteneoa, çacapan qujxoa, motze-tzeloa, çacatl: iehoatl in ocoçacatl, vncan motecpana in jlamatque, ce petlatl imjxpan onoc.

Nimã ie ic oalmoiacatia in pilhoaque çioa, conten-timanj petlapan mamacujltetl in tzopelic tamalli: ceniauh, in mamacujltetl contema: qujmõmacativi in impilhoan, in ilamatque: auh in jlamatque, qujn-oalantimanj in pipiltotonti, njmã qujmonjtotia in-mac: njmã ic qujmõmaca, in tenanoan, in oqujmon-jtotilique inpilhoan:

njmã ic iatimanj in inchachan, oc iooatzinco in peoaia. Auh in ie tlaqualizpan in necaoalo: auh in ie iuhquj, njman iec viloa in amjoaz, vmpa tlamattivi in çacatepec, vmpa in jxillã tonan:

Auh in jmatlacioc metztli y, in tlacpac omote-

4. For zacapan quixoaya Garibay ("Relación breve," p. 309) gives: "se salía a la grama"; in "Primeros memoriales," p. 53, Jiménez Moreno translates: "se salía (la gente) al zacate."

5. ocoçacatl: "tendian mucho heno, que lo trayan de las montañas," Sahagún says in the corresponding Spanish text. Molina, in his Vocabulario, gives: "paja particular para hazer bohios, o casas de paja" for ocoçacatl — perhaps Andropogon schoenanthus Linn. or A. citratum D. C. (Hernández, Historia de las plantas, Vol. II, pp. 395–96).

6. For niman iec read niman ie ic as in the Real Palacio MS.

honor of the god of the Otomí, who was named Mixcoatl, which in its time will be told.[7]

And when there had been arrival at Çacatepec, nothing was done; there was only each one's arriving; there was the making of grass shelters on the part of each one. There was sleeping there on the part of each one. There was the lighting of fires on the part of each one; there was being warmed by the fire on the part of each one.[8]

And at dawn, thereupon food [and] drink were eaten [and] drunk. Thereupon there was arraying, there was dressing on the part of each one.

Then there was departing; there was arranging in order, there was disposing in rows. Like a rope they stretched; nowhere was it cut. Everyone in this manner encircled all the deer, coyotes, rabbits, jack rabbits.[9] Cautiously they closed in upon them.

And when they were able to come upon them, then there was the seizing [of the game]; it was fallen upon on the part of each one. All that escaped their hands did not yet die.[10]

And when this was done, thereupon they dispersed. There was returning. But the captors were still left there; they yet slew [more game]. To those who yet caught a deer or a coyote, Moctezuma gave gifts of capes whose edges were striped with feathers.

If one were a captor, one would array oneself [in it]. But if one were not a captor, one would place it in a basket or one would sell it. And Moctezuma gave the captors food, and they drank.

And when the slaughtering had been done up on Çacatepec, thereupon there was a quick departure. They took with them only the heads of [the game]; they carried them each with them in their hands; they went dripping blood. When they reached their homes, they hung each [of the heads] high. And they left Moctezuma there [in his palace].

And when there was going forth on the grass, at that time they would give their paper vestments to as many as were to die. For [the god] Tlamatzincatl[11] many of his bathed sacrificial victims were arrayed. For the second [god], Izquitecatl, perhaps

neuh: vncan qujlhujqujxtiliaia, in inteouh otomj: in mjtoaia Mixcoatl in jpan jn moteneoaz.

Auh in onaxioac in vmpa çacatepec aiatle muchioaia, çan oc qujxqujch haaxioa nexaxacaltilo, in vncan cocochioa, tlatlatlatilo, neezcolo.

Auh in otlatvic, njman ie ic tlatlaqualo âatlioa: njmã ie ic nechichioalo, nehaapanalo:

mec viloa, netecpanalo, nevipanolo: iuhqujn mecatl motilinja, acan cotonj: muchi tlacatl im juh, qujniaoaloa in jxqujchtin mamaça, in coiotl, in tochtli, in citli: çan jvian impan ommonamjquj.

Auh in ovel impan ommonamjc, mec tenamoialo, tecujcujtivecho, ixqujch in tematitlampa qujça in aiamo imjquja.

Auh in ie iuhquj, njmã ie ic tlaxitinj, oalnecuepalo: auh in tlamanjme, oc ompa ommocaoa, oc tlamjctia: in aqujn maçatl oc acic, anoço coiotl, qujntlauhtia in Motecuçoma, tenjvivavanquj in tilmatli:

intla tlamanj, qujmoquentiz: auh intlacamo tlamanj, çan qujtlatiz tanaco, anoço qujmonamaqujliz: yoan in tlamanjme qujntlamaca in Motecuçoma, yoã atli.

Auh in ie iuhquj motlamjctiloc, in jcpac çacatepetl: njman ie ic viloatz, çaiio in intzontecon qujoalhujvica intlan qujmaana, chichipicativitz in eztli, in oacico inchachan, aco qujnpipiloa auh çan vmpa concaoa in Motecuçoma.

Auh in jquac çacapan qujxooaia: iquac qujnmacaia in imamatlatquj in jzqujntin mjqujzque: iehoatl in Tlamatzincatl, mjequjntin mochichioaia, itlaaltilhoan: injc ome iehoatl in Izqujtecatl, aço

---

7. This paragraph appears to be parenthetical. The corresponding Nahuatl text is missing in the *Real Palacio MS.*

8. *neezcolo*: read *neozcolo*.

9. Cf. Dibble and Anderson, *Book XI*, p. 12.

10. Reference to the corresponding Spanish text suggests that *çan quezquintin* might better be read for *ixquich*. Cf. also Seler, *Einige Kapitel*, p. 199.

11. Tlamatzincatl was a Chichimec pulque god and is to be distinguished from the same name as applied to Tezcatlipoca in the month of Teotl eco. Cf. Seler, *Gesammelte Abhandlungen*, Vol. II, p. 481.

two or three. Those who bathed [the victims] were the pulque makers and the ruler's pulque makers.

Third, there died for Mixcoatl and his consort, a woman named Yeuatl icue, only two [victims]. Only the stewards displayed them. And also there were the women [each named] Coatl icue, wives of Tlamatzincatl and Izquitecatl. These also took upon their heads their paper array.

And when [the time] had arrived, when it was verily the feast of Quecholli, with which the twenty [days] ended, there was going into the sand there;[12] those who were to die went into the sand there. After midday they then took them to the place where they were to die. They took them in procession about the offering stone; they went in line. And when they had come to encircle it, then they came down [from the pyramid]. No longer were they taken where they had been guarded; they only took them to their various *calpulcos.* There they kept them in vigil all night. They guarded them; they continually guarded them.

And when midnight arrived, thereupon there was the taking of hair [from the crowns of their heads]. And when they had taken the hair, thereupon [their belongings] were burned. [If the bathed one was] a man, he burned his streamers, and his cape, and his breechclout, and whatever his comforts had been, and his water gourd. All of them he burned.

And a woman burned all her womanly belongings: her basket, her spindle whorl, her chalk, her spinning bowl, her warping frame, her cane stalks, her batten, her large straw for weaving, her divided cord which held up [the textile], her waist band, her weaving stick, and her thorns, and her skeins, her heddle, and her measuring stick.[13] All of it she burned herself.

For this reason they thus did it: it was said that they would be required there where they were to go; when they died, [these things] would await them there.

And when it dawned, then they were adorned, they were arrayed. They put on them their paper vestments in which they were to die. When they had arrayed them, then they were taken where they were to die. Two escorts took them; they were to take them up. Lest they faint somewhere, they held them tightly. And the two were to bring them down,

vmentin, anoço eintin: iehoan qujmaltiaia in tlachicque, yoan in tecutlachique:

injquein, mjquja iehoatl in Mixcoatl, yoan inamjc cioatl, itoca: Jeoatl icue, çan omextin, çan calpixque in qujnnextiaia: auh no iehoãtin in cioa, Coatl icue: in jnamjcoan Tlamatzincatl, yoan izqujtecatl: no iquac qujcuja in jmamatlatquj.

Auh in oacic, in vel iquac ilhujtl, Quecholli injc tlamj cempoalli: vncã xalacoa, vncã xallaquj, in mjqujzque: vmmotzcalo, in tonatiuh: mec qujnvica in vmpa mjqujzque: qujmõiaoalochtia in techcatl, motecpantivi: auh in ocõiaoaloto, njmã ie ic oaltemo, aocmo vmpa vico in vmpa opieloia, ça vmpa qujnvivica in incacalpulco, ceioal in qujntoçavia, qujnpia, qujnpipia.

Auh in ie onaci, ioalnepãtla: njmã ie ic tetzoncujva: auh in oqujmõtzoncujque, njmã ie ic motlatlatlatilia: in oqujchtli, qujtlatia, in jpan yoan itilma, yoan imaxtli, yoã in quezquj itlaçevil, yoã iiatecõ muchi qujtlatia.

Auh in cioatl, muchi qujtlatia in jxqujch icioatlatquj: in jtana in jmalac, in jtiçauh, in jtzaoalcax, in jtzatzaz, in jotlauh, in jtzotzopaz, in jteçac, in jmecamaxal, ineanaia, yoã itzopaia, yoan ivitz, yoan iquatzon, ixiouh, yoan yioctacauh: muchi qujtlatia inoma.

Injc iuh qujchioa y, qujlmach vmpa intech monequjz in vmpa iazque, in jquac mjqujz vmpa qujoalchiaz.

Auh in otlatvic, mec tecẽcaoalo, techichioalo, qujmonaaquja in amatlatqujtl, in jpan mjqujzque: in oqujmõchichiuhque, mec tevico in vmpa mjqujzque, qujnvica in teanque, vmentin qujntlecavizque, in ma cana çotlaoa, qujntzitzqujzque: yoã vmẽtin tetemovjzque, in qujnoaltemovizque, in jquac ommjcque: yoan ce panoa, in qujvicatiuh panjtl: yoan

12. See Chap. 27.
13. These weaving implements were tentatively identified with the assistance of the late Dr. Gladys Reichard, Barnard College, Columbia

they were to bring them down here when they had died. And there was one flag-bearer who went carrying a flag. And there were two women who were face-washers. Thus they took each one of the ceremonially bathed [victims].

And when they had brought them [there], four captives went ahead to die. At the landing at the foot of the pyramid they bound their feet and their hands. Then they took them up; four [priests] carried each one of them; they went pulling them by their arms [and] their legs; [the captives] went bobbing their heads up and down; their heads went hanging toward the ground.

And when they had brought them, then they stretched them on the offering stone. There they slew them.

And as they took them up, it was said: "Thus they slay them as deer; they serve as the deer who thus die." And the rest of the captives climbed up purely of their own will. And when they had died, when they had given their service, then [the likeness of] Mixcoatl died. And when he had died, at the Temple of Mixcoatl, then [the likenesses of] Tlamatzincatl died; they died there at [the Temple of] Tlamatzincatl. And thus did they die: they climbed up purely of their own will; of their own accord they ascended. Then they went straight to the offering

vmentin, teixamjque cioa: çan much ivi in qujnvivica, cecenme tlaaltilti.

Auh in oqujmaxitique: iacattivi in mamalti mjquj navintin: apetlac in qujmjilpilia imjcxi yoã inma: mec qujntlecavia, qujnnanauhcavia, qujntitilinjlitivi in jnma, in jmjcxi: âaquetztivi, tlalchi oalpipilcatiuh in intzontecon.

Auh in oqumonaxitique, mec qujmõteca in techcac vncã qujmõmjctia.

Auh injc iuh qujntlecavia, y, qujlmach ic qujnmaçapoloa, qujntlaehecalhuja in mamaça, in juh mjquj: auh in oc cequjntin mamalti, çan õmonomavia in ontleco. Auh in õmjcque, in ontlacotique: çatepan in ommjquj Mixcoatl. Auh in mjquja y Mjxcoateupã: njman iehoantin in tlamatzĩca, vmpa mjquj tlamatzinco: auh injc mjquj, çan õmonomatlecavia, çan in iollotlamati in ontleco: njmã techcac ontlamelauhtimanj: auh in mjquja y, vncan in tlamatzinco.

University, N.Y., and Dr. Bertha P. Dutton, late of the School of American Research, Santa Fe. The accompanying drawings of weaving and weaving implements are from Books VIII and X, after Paso y Troncoso.

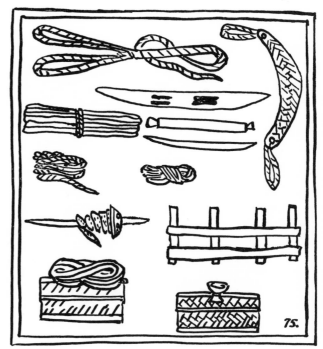

139

stone and then they died there at [the Temple of] Tlamatzincatl.

And the women died when it was indeed still dawn there at [the Temple of] Coatlan. When they ascended, they went singing lustily. Some went dancing. Some indeed wept. And the escorts went holding them by the hand.

When they had died, when they had given their service, then [they whose office it was] brought them down. As they brought each of them down, most carefully did they roll them here. And when there had been the slaying, then there was dispersing, there was departing on the part of each one.

This concluded [the feast]; already at that time one day had been counted [in the month of] Panquetzaliztli.

Here endeth [the account of the feast of] Quecholli.

Auh in cioa vel oc ioatzinco in mjquja, vmpan coatlan: in jquac tleco, cenca cujcativi, cequjntin mjtotitivi, in cequjtin vel choca: auh in teanque qujmaantivi.

In ommjcque in ontlacotique: mec qujnoaltemovia, in tetemovique, çan jvian in qujnoalmjmjloa: auh in ommjcoac, mec tlaxitinj, viviloa.

Inin tzonqujça, ie cuel ipan icemjlhujtlapoaloc in Panquetzaliztli:

njcan tzonqujça in Quecholli.

Thirty-fourth Chapter, which telleth of the feasts and the debt-paying which were observed during all the days of the fifteenth month, which was called Panquetzaliztli.[1]

The fifteenth month was the one known as Panquetzaliztli.

Before the feast of Panquetzaliztli arrived, the offering priests had been fasting for eighty days and had been laying down fir [branches]. The time that they began this was thus the day following [the month of] Ochpaniztli. At midnight they spread out the fir [branches] on all the mountain tops and upon the circular altars, [even those] which were distant.

And this they did until [the month of] Panquetzaliztli arrived. When they were laying down the fir [branches], they went quite naked; nothing went on them. They went carrying fir [branches; actually] they were green reeds and thorns. And they went blowing their shell trumpets and the pottery whistles. They went alternating them as they blew them.

And when the feast of Quecholli ended, then began the singing and dancing. The song which was intoned was called Tlaxotecayotl; it was the song of Uitzilopochtli. When it was begun, it was at the time that night fell, and when there was stopping on the part of each one it was at the time that the conch shells were repeatedly blown, when already the conch shells were blown.

And with one the women, the pleasure girls, sang and danced. They went between [pairs of men] (as hath been told). Daily they did this until twenty days [had passed].

And when the ninth day [before the feast] arrived, there the ceremonially bathed [victims] or those to die the flowery death were bathed in sacred water.[2] The old men of the *calpulli* would get the water; they got the water there at Uitzilopochco; there indeed was [the spring called] Uitzilatl, in a cave. With cypress [branches][3] they went stop-

Inic 34 capitulo: itechpa tlatoa in ilhujtl, yoan in nextlaoaliztli, in muchioaia in jpan ic cemjlhujtl, ic caxtoltetl metztli, in mjtoaia: Panquetzaliztli.

Injc caxtoltetl ilhujtl: iehoatl in moteneoa, Panquetzaliztli:

in aiamo aci ilhujtl Panquetzaliztli: in tlamacazque, nappoalilhujtl in moçaoaia, yoan acxoiatlaliaia: iquac qujpeoaltiaia, in iuh onquiz imuztlaioc, Ochpanjztli: in ioalnepantla onacxoiatema, in novian tetepeticpac, yoā in momomozco, in veca.

Auh inin qujchioaia, ixqujchica onaci in Panquetzaliztli, in onacxoiatlaliaia, çan pepetlauhtivi, atle intech vetztiuh, qujtqujtivi in acxoiatl, iehoatl in acatl xoxouhquj, yoan vitztli, yoan intecciz, yoan in cocovilutl qujpitztivi, qujpapatlativi in qujpitza.

Auh in ōqujz Quecholli ilhujtl: njmā ic peoa in cujcoianolo, in cujcatl in eoa itoca tlaxotecaiotl, icujc in Vitzilobuchtli: im peoaloia, iquac in tlatlapoiaoa: auh in necacaoaloia, iquac in tlatlapitzalizpā, in ie tlatlapitzalo:

no teoan cujcoianoa in cioa in avienjme, tetzatzalan mantivi (in juh omjto) mumuztlae in muchioa, ixqujchica cempoalilhujtl.

Auh in oacic tlachicunaviti, vncan moteualtiaia in tlatlaltilti, anoço suchimjcque: in calpulvevetque, conanaia atl: vmpa in vitzilobuchco conanaia atl, vmpan ca vitzilatl, oztoc, avevetica in qujoaltzatzacutivi, intlan qujoalaantivi:

---

1. *"Elevación de banderas"* in Garibay, "Relación breve," p. 312; *"el acto de enarbolar el pendón"* in Clavijero, *Historia antigua*, Vol. III, p. 170 — possibly a reference to the raising of the standard and the statue of Paynal up to the altar in the Temple of Uitzilopochtli. According to Tovar (Kubler and Gibson, *The Tovar Calendar*, p. 32), it was the special festival of the war captains who set up a banner in the middle of the temple courtyard.

2. Cf. Charles E. Dibble and Arthur J. O. Anderson, *Florentine Codex, Book IX, The Merchants* (Santa Fe: School of American Research and University of Utah, 1959), pp. 45–49.

3. *Taxodium mucronatum* in Dibble and Anderson, *Book XI*, p. 108.

ping each [jar mouth]; they each went holding [the jars] with them.

When they had carried [the water] here, thereupon they sprinkled it upon [the victims] there at the foot [of the Temple of] Uitzilopochtli, and there they gave them their paper vestments, their paper adornment, in which they were to die. And they painted blue stripes on them, on their legs up to their thighs and on their arms up to their shoulders. And their faces they stained in horizontal stripes;[4] they each went striped in light blue [and] in yellow. And they placed on them nose pendants [shaped like] arrows,[5] and reed headdresses surmounted by feathers.[6]

And when this was done, when they had adorned them, when they had prepared them, then [the bathers, who owned the slaves] took them each to the various *calpulcos*. They only quickly took them away. Thereupon the bathers [of victims] each went to their homes. There they took apart, they set down the array [of each victim]. They placed [their ornaments] in palm leaf baskets for them. And there, with one, [the owners] began singing and dancing; they went, each one, taking their women.[7]

And when the fifth day arrived, then the bathers of [sacrificial victims][8] began to fast there, and the old men of the *calpullis* fasted[9] and bathed themselves at midnight. They bathed themselves there at the Mist House. From these they departed to their *calpulcos*.

And a woman who was to bathe [sacrificial victims] just bathed herself there at her water's edge. She set up a thorn, stained with blood, on the bank. And when the four days of fasting ended, then at nightfall the serpent dance was danced. The bathed victims danced the serpent dance, as well as the bathers, and the escorts, and those who brought the victims down, and the flag-bearers, and the women who were face-washers. When conch shells were blown, [at midnight, the dancing] ceased.

in oqujoalhujcaque: njman ie ic qujmatzelhuja, vncan in jcxitlan Vitzilobuchtli, yoan vncan qujnmamaca in jmamatlatquj, in jmamanechichioal in jpan mjqujzque, yoan qujntexovavana in imjcxic, inmetzpan tlatlamj, yoan in inma, imacolpã tlatlamj: yoã imjxtlan tlatlaana, ic tlatlapantiuh in texotli, in coztic, yoan qujmontlalilia iacapilolli, mjtl muchioa, yoan anecuiotl.

Auh in ie iuhquj in oqujmõchichiuhque, in oqujmõcencauhque, njman ic qujnvivica in incalpulco, çan oalqujqujztiqujça njmã ie ic vivi in inchachan tealtique, vmpa qujnxixitinja, qujntlatlalilia in intlatquj, qujmõtanatemjlia. Auh vncan in teoan compeoaltia in cujcoianoa, qujnvivicativi in incioaoan.

Auh in oacic, vncã tlamacujlti: njmã vncã compeoaltia in moçaoaia tealtique, yoan in calpulvevetque: tlacatlaquaia, yoan maltiaia in ioalnepantla: vmpã aiauhcalco in ommaltiaia, vncan oneoa incalpulco.

Auh in cioatl tealtiz, çan vncã in jatenco ommaltia: ce vitztli cõquetza atenco ezço: auh in otzõqujz navilhujtl, injc moçaoa: njmã ic oaliova in coanecujlolo, coanecujloa in tlaaltilti, yoã in tealtique, yoan in teanque yoan in tetemovique, yoã im panoaque, yoan in teixamjque cioa: in mocaoa iquac in tlatlapitzalo.

4. Seler, in *Gesammelte Abhandlungen*, Vol. II, p. 425, describes this face painting (*yixtlan tlaanticac*) as *"Die Querstreifung des Gesichts, mit abwechselnd hellen und dunklen Streifen."* The stripes, although of different color, are characteristic of Tezcatlipoca.

5. Corresponding Spanish text: *"ponjanles en las narizes vna saetilla atrauesada, y vn medio circulo, que colgaua hasta abaxo."*

6. Corresponding Spanish text: *"ponjanles vnas coroças, o coronas, hechas de cañjtas atadas, y de lo alto salian vn manojo de plumas blancas."* The *anecuyotl* was a headdress worn by the Centzonuitznua in Book III of the *Florentine Codex*. It is described in Book XII of the *Florentine Codex*: *"hivitl in tlachichioalli, mjmjltic, achitzin vitztic, achi tzimpitzaoac"* — "of featherwork, cylindrical, a little pointed, a little narrow at the base." Cf. also Seler in *Gesammelte Abhandlungen*, Vol. II, p. 425.

7. *iciciuaũa* in the *Real Palacio MS*.

8. Corresponding Spanish text: *"dueños de los esclauos."*

9. *"comjan al medio dia, por el ayuno"* in corresponding Spanish text; *"Sie assen (nur einmal) am Tage (am Mittag)"* in Seler, *Einige Kapitel*, p. 206; *"comía a medias"* in Garibay, "Relación breve," p. 312.

And hence was it said that the serpent dance was danced: they took one another's hands; they were ranged in line. In their hands they grasped circular jar rests; it was perhaps reeds or cords which they arranged as jar rests. The bathed ones went trotting among [the others]. Much did they run; they continually hopped; they kept hurrying. It was as if they hastened, as if they were breathless. They kept winding about; they did not sing, they did not sing at all.

And the old men of the *calpulli* kept beating the drums for them; and only they sang. Some looked on; they marveled at [the dance]. And it was much admired; much was the fasting respected. Indeed everyone abstained, especially the bathers. No [man] lay with a woman, nor did any [woman] lie with a man.[10]

And when the serpent dance had been danced, thereupon they dispersed.

And when it dawned, on the twentieth day, when it was verily the feast day, thereupon the bathed ones went to take leave at the various [bathers'] houses. They dissolved stains for them: black; perhaps blue mineral earth; or red ocher. And as they went to take leave at the various [bathers'] houses, they went singing as if they each cracked their voices,[11] as if they were hoarse. When they reached the houses of the bathers, then they dipped their hands in the blue stain or the black stain or the red ocher. Thereupon they placed their hands on the posts and on the door lintels wherever they came out of the homes of the bathers.

And when they had proceeded to the several places where their relatives were, thereupon they again went to [the bathers'] homes. These in vain offered them food. Some still ate, but some no longer ate.

And at this time, gifts lay for them. Capes lay waiting for them, breechclouts, shifts, skirts. And when the gifts were laid out, thereupon the bathed ones arrayed themselves; they put their banners on their backs. Quite of their own will they arrayed themselves. And the women likewise of their own accord put their baskets [with] all their womanly belongings on their backs. Thereupon those who bore burdens arose; they carried the gifts in their arms. At the entrance, in the street, they placed themselves in order. And the bathed ones thereupon

Auh injc moteneoa coanecujlolo, maana, motecpana: injc maana iaoalli, aço toli, anoço mecatl in qujiaoallalia: in tlaaltilti intlan aactivi, cenca motlatlaloa, chichitonj, vivicinj, iuhqujn tlaixtotochca, iuhqujn tlacica: moiaiaoaloa, amo cujca, amo ma cujca.

Auh in calpulvevetque, qujntlatzotzonjlia: auh çanjoque in cujca: cequjntin tlatlatta, tlatlamaviçoa: auh cenca tlamaviztililoia, cenca qujmaviztiliaia in neçaoaliztli: vel ixqujch tlacatl, motzitzqujaia: oc cenca iehoantin, in tealtique: aiac cioacochia, auh in cioa, ano ac oqujchcochia.

Auh in onnecocololoc, njmã ie ic tlaxitinj.

Auh in otlatvic, in vncan tlacempoalti, in ie vel iquac ilhujtl: njman ie ic vi in tlaaltilti, mocacalnaoatizque: qujnpatilia tlilli, aço texotli, anoço tlavitl: auh in jquac ie vi mocacalnaoatizque, cujcativi, iuhqujn no intozquj tzatzaianj, omach içaoacaque: in onacique inchan tealtique, njmã conaquja in imma texotitlan, anoço tliltitlan, anoço tlauhtitlan: njman ie ic commamana tlaquetzaltitech, yoã tlaixquatl itech, izquicã qujça in inchachan tealtique.

Auh in jzqujcan onqujzque, in inoaniolcaoacan: njmã ie ic no ceppa vi in inchachã, in nen qujntlamaca; in cequjntin oc ontlaqua; auh in cequjntin aocmo tlaqua.

Auh in jquac in, ie ic onoc in tetlauhtilli, ic qujchixtoc in tilmatli, in maxtlatl, in vipilli, in cueitl: auh in omotetecac, tetlauhtilli; njmã ie ic mochichioa in tlaaltilti commomamaltia in impã, çan monomavia in muchichioa: auh in cioa çan no innoma in cõmomamaltia, intana, in jxqujch incioatlatquj: njmã ie ic moquetza in tlanapaloa, in qujnapaloa tetlauhtilli, qujiaoac, vtlica oalmotecpana: auh in tlaaltilti, njman ie ic calaquj in cioapan, qujoaliaoaloa in tlecujlli: mec oalqujça mec ommoiacatia

10. *anoyac* in the *Real Palacio MS.*

11. *yuhquin o yntozqui tzatzayā* in *ibid.*

entered the women's quarters; they went around the fireplace. Then they came out. Then those who bore burdens went leading. They went quietly to the *calpulco*. The bathed ones only went following them; they only went last.

And when they had gone to reach the *calpulco*, thereupon the bathed ones danced in the courtyard. And they put the gifts in the *calpulco*. Also they placed aside the capes, the breechclouts, the skirts, the shifts. Then came first the bidden guests. [The bathers] offered each one of them their gifts. And the women stood apart in line. They also offered them their gifts.

And this was the doing of only the merchants, the bathers, the buyers [of slaves].

And when they had been completely arrayed, when they had come together, when they had been given their gifts, thereupon they took the bathed ones to enter into the sand.[12] When they reached the [pyramid] temple of the devil, then they climbed up to the top of the temple. When they had come to the top, then they circled about the sacrificial stone. They came right down [the other] side.

And when they had come climbing down to the ground, when they had come to reach the ground, then they each ran to the various *calpulcos*. But some went going quite slowly. When they entered [the *calpulcos*], thereupon they disposed for them their paper vestments; then they sat down on reed mats. They kept food for them, or pulque, whatever they would require. All night they had them keep vigil.

And when midnight arrived, then they ranged them in a row, while they cut hair [from the crowns of their heads]. When they had cut hair [from the crowns of their heads], then they put it away for themselves (as hath been told in [the account of] Quecholli).

And when this was done, then were eaten [tamales of] amaranth seed, all at the same time, everywhere among the common folk. None failed to eat [tamales of] amaranth seed. And none broke the amaranth seed [tamales] with his hand; it was with [a length of] maguey fiber that they sliced it. And when the amaranth seed [tamales] had been eaten, thereupon were taken up the mats. They rolled them up, they set them each down at the entrance. Thereupon there was stretching out on the part of each

in tlanapaloa, vmpa tlamattivi in calpulco, ça tetocativi in tlaaltilti, ça tlatzacutivi.

Auh in oacito calpulco: njman ie ic mjtotia, in tlaaltilti, in jtoalco: auh in tetlauhtilli, qujcalaquja in calpulco: no nonqua qujtlalia in tilmatli, in maxtlatl, in cueitl, in vipilli: mec ommoiacatia in tlacoanotzalti, qujoalmacatimanj, ceceniaca in innetlauhtil: auh in cioa, nonqua mocempanoa: no qujnoalmacatimanj, in innetlauhtil:

auh inin çan mjxcavia in pochteca, in tealtianj, in tecoanj.

Auh in õtecencaoaloc, in oncenvetz, in ontetlauhtiloc: njman ie ic qujnvica in tlaaltilti, xalaqujzque: in onacique tlacateculotl iteupan, mec tleco in teucalticpac, in vmpanvetzito: mec qujoaliaoaloa in techcatl, can jc oaltemotimanj, centlapal.

Auh in otemoco tlalchi, in otlaltitech acico, mec oalmotlatlaloa in incacalpulco: auh in cequjntin, çan jvian in iativi: in ocalaqujto, njmã ie ic qujntlatlalilia in jmamatlatquj, mec motlalia in petlapã qujnchieltia in tlaqualli, anoço vctli, in catle cõnequjzque, ceioal in qujntoçavia.

Auh in oacic iooalnepantla: mec qujntecpana, in qujntzoncujzque: in oqujmontzoncujque, mec motlatlatlatilia (in juh omjto ipan quecholli).

Auh in ommochiuh y, mec tzoalqualo, cĕvetzi in novian maceoalpan, aiac in maca tzoalqua: auh in tzoalli, aiac imatica qujcotonaia: ichtli injc qujxotlaticate: auh in ontzoalqualoc, njmã ie ic meeoa in petlatl, qujilacatzoa, qujiaoac qujoalmamana; njmã ie ic neteteco, çan tlalpan, tlalitzticapan, ça tilmaçolli, anoço aiaçolli in commopepechtia, in commopepechia.

---

12. Cf. Chap. 27, n. 23.

only on the ground, on the cold ground. It was only of old capes or old maguey fiber capes that they made beds for themselves, that they made couches for themselves.

And upon the morrow, when still a little darkness lay about, thereupon [he who carried the figure of] Paynal came down from the top of [the Temple of] Uitzilopochtli.[13] When he had come down here, then he went direct to [the place] called the god's ball court.[14] There they slew four [victims], two [honoring the god] Amapan, two [honoring the god] Uapatzan.[15] When they had slain them, then they dragged them about the ball court. It was as if they painted it with [the victims'] blood.

And when this was done, then [the priest bearing the figure of Paynal] departed. Much was he made to run. He proceeded to Tlatelolco. Then he went direct to Nonoalco. To that place there quickly took him [the priest bearing the image of the god] named Quauitl icac, [Paynal's] helper, his elder brother.[16] His adornment was similar[17] [to that of] Paynal, but he was striped with chalk.

And when [the latter] had quickly taken [Paynal], then [both] departed. They circled about there to Tlaxotlan. Thereupon they went straight to Popotlan. There also they quickly slew victims — very swiftly.

Then once more they went on, straight to Chapoltepetl; they passed before it. And when they had gone arriving at the river bank, at a place named Izquitlan, there also they quickly slew a victim. He whom they slew was named Izquitecatl.

Then they went on; they quickly passed on to Tepetocan. Already they were at the outskirts of Coyoacan. They then went direct to Maçatlan. There they doubled back. Then they went direct to Acachinanco.

And when they had come to reach Acachinanco, then the rolling up of the paper stopped. Those who rolled up the paper began at the time that Paynal had begun to follow his path.

And thus was the paper rolled up. The bathed ones remained in a separate group; those of Uitz-

Auh in otlatvic ça oc achi tlatlaiovatoc, njmã ie ic oaltemo in teucalticpac in Paynal in jcpac Vitzilobuchtli: in ooaltemoc, mec tlamelaoa, in moteneoa Teutlachco: vncan qujmõmjctia navintin; vme amapan, vme vappatzan: in oqujmõmjcti, mec qujnvivilana, tlachco: iuhqujn ic tlatlacujloa imezço.

Auh in ie iuhquj, mec oaleoa, cenca qujmotlalochtia, vncan qujça in Tlatilulco, njmã ic tlamelaoa nonooalco: vncan cantiqujça itoca Quavitl icac, itepalevicauh, itiacauh: canno iuhquj in jnechichioal, tel çan ie motiçaoaoan:

auh in oconantiqujz, mec vi, vmpan ommocoloa tlaxotlan: njmã ie ic ontlamelaoa popotlan: no vncã ontlamjctitiqujça, çan iciuhca:

njmã oc ceppa ontlamelaoa, chapoltepetl ixpan qujça: auh in oacito atoiac, itocaiocan Izqujtlan: no vncan ontlamjctitiqujça in conmjctia, itoca Izqujtecatl:

mec vi, vncã qujztiqujça in tepetocan, ie coiooacã caltenco, mec oallamelaoa, maçatlan, vncã oallacoloa: njman ic qujoalmelaoa in acachinanco.

Auh in oacico acachinanco, njmã ic mocaoa in tlaamavia: in iehoãtin tlaamavia, iquac peoa, in jquac vmpeoa, vtlatoca Paynal.

Auh injc tlaamaviaia; in tlatlaaltilti, nonqua manj: in vitznaoa nonqua manj, qujmpalevia cequjntin

---

13. Corresponding Spanish text: *"descendian el dios paynal, de lo alto del cu de vitzilopuchtli."* The priest who carried the figure was dressed in the trappings of Quetzalcoatl, according to Torquemada, *Segunda parte*, p. 282.

14. See the description of *teotlachco* in the appendix of this volume.

15. Seler, in *Einige Kapitel*, p. 210, apparently does not regard Amapan and Uapatzan as gods. See, however, the corresponding Spanish text and the discussion of *teotlachco* in the appendix of this volume.

16. Corresponding Spanish text: *"alli le salia a rescebir, el satrapa de aquel cu, con la ymagen del dios Quavitl ycac."*

17. The *Real Palacio MS* reads *çã no.*

nauac remained in [another] separate group. [These latter] a number of brave warriors aided. Moctezuma gave them yellow quilted cotton jackets and shields [painted with] bears'[18] eyes. Only pine staves lay in their hands.

And [the warriors] who aided those of Uitznauac had spears with which they battled, which they cast. And the bathed ones met them only with bird arrows, which they shot. They had flint points. Verily, battle was joined. Verily, there were deaths.

And of them who aided those of Uitznauac, if one were taken, he also would die. The bathed ones themselves slew him; it was only on a horizontal drum that they cut open his breast.

And the onlooker, he who oversaw [the battle], when he noted, when he saw that [he who bore the likeness of] Paynal already was coming, then cried out: "Mexicans! Now indeed he cometh! Now already the lord cometh! Enough!"

And when they heard this, then the bathed ones took after [the others].[19] From there they each dispersed; there was dispersing. Those who aided [those of Uitznauac], who had been rolling up the paper, each went.

Thereupon came [he who bore] Paynal. First arrived the standards and two devices for seeing, made of feathers, with a hole in their midst. They who brought it here were still only small boys. Much did they make it hasten here. Then the brave warriors took [the seeing devices] from them — [warriors] who could hasten, who could run fast.

And when they had run along a certain distance, again two more [warriors] took [the devices] from them. It was as if they went sharing them.

And when they had come to reach the eagle portal [of the temple square],[20] no one could take these from them; they took [the devices] up to the top of [the Temple of] Uitzilopochtli. These who indeed came ahead, when they had reached the top, cast the devices for seeing upon the image of Uitzilopochtli, which [was made of] amaranth seed. [There] they each fell to the ground; indeed each one was faint; each one lay exhausted.

And the fire priest thereupon went [to] cut their ears with a flint knife so that they opened their eyes, so that they revived.

tiacaoan: qujnmacaia in Motecuçoma ichcavipilli, coztic, yoan chimalli, cujtlachixxo: çan ocoquavitl in immac oonoc.

Auh in vitznaoa qujmpalevia tlatzontectli injc tlaiecoa in qujtlaça: auh in tlaaltilti qujnnamjquj, çan totomjtl in qujtlaça, iacatecpaio, vel iauiotl in muchioaia, vel mjcoaia.

Auh in tlapalevia in qujmpalevia vitznaoa, intla çe axioacã, no mjqujz: vel iioma qujmjctia in tlaaltilti, çan teponaztli in jpan coneltequj.

Auh in tlachixquj, in oqujttac, in oconjttac in ie vitz Paynal: mec tzatzi, qujtva, Mexicae, ca ie vitz, ca ie movicatz in tlacatl, ma ixqujch.

Auh in oqujcacque: mec tetoca in tlaaltilti: vncan xixitinj, tlaxitinj, vivi, in otepaleviaia, in otlaamaviaia.

Niman ie ic vitz in Paynal: achtopa oaleoa in machiotl, auh in tlachielonj vntetl hivitl in tlachioalli, yiticoionquj, çã oc pipiltotonti in aujoalitquj, cenca qujoalmotlalochtia, njman qujncujlitiqujça in tiacaoan, in vel paina, in vel totoca:

auh in oquexqujch oqujoaltoctique, oc ceppa no vmẽtin, qujncujlitiqujça, çan juhqujn qujmomamacativi.

Auh in oacico quauhqujiaoac, aocac vel qujncujlia, ieeoan qujpantlaçazque, in jicpac Vitzilobuchtli: in vel iacattiuh, in opanvetzito in tlachielonj, ipan contlaça in jxiptla Vitzilobuchtli, in tzoalli ça onchachapantivetzi, vel çoçotlaoa, ça cicintoque.

Auh in tlenamacac, njman ie ic iauh, qujnnacaztecpavia, ic oallachia, injc mozcalia.

---

18. Suggested identifications in Dibble and Anderson, *Book XI*, p. 5, are *Ursus horriaeus* or *Euarctos machetes*.

19. In the *Real Palacio MS* Sahagún has crossed out *tetoca* and inserted *quintoca*.

20. Corresponding Spanish text: *"hasta llegar a la puerta del patio del cu, de Vitzilopuchtli, que se llamaua quauhqujiaoac."*

And when they revived, then they climbed down; they came bringing the amaranth seed [image] which they had captured.[21] They took it with them to their homes, for it was in truth their captive. They ate it. They offered it to each of their kin and to those of the neighborhood; they ate it all.[22]

And when this was done, then those who were to die were taken in procession around [the pyramid]; only once did they circle them about. When this was done, then they were arranged, they were placed in order. The captives were in the lead. Thereupon they brought down [from the top of the pyramid] the sacrificial papers;[23] it was a man [a priest] who brought them down. When he reached the ground, he raised them in dedication to the four directions. Then he laid them there in what is called the eagle vessel.

Thereupon likewise descended the fire serpent.[24] It was just like a blazing pine firebrand. Its tongue was made of flaming red feathers. It went [as if] burning [like] a torch. And its tail was of paper, perhaps two fathoms or three fathoms long. As it came down, it was like a real serpent; it showed its tongue; it was as if it bent back and forth.

And when [the priest] had brought it to the base [of the pyramid], he proceeded carefully there to the eagle vessel. Then he went up [to the eagle vessel]; also he raised [the fire serpent] in dedication to the four directions. When he had [so] raised it in dedication, then he cast it upon the sacrificial papers; then they burned.

And when he had come to leave it, when he went ascending to the top, then shell trumpets were blown. Thereupon [the image of] Paynal, the representative of Uitzilopochtli, came down; in great haste [the priest] brought it down.

Auh in omozcalique mec oaltemo, qujtqujtze in ocacique tzoalli, qujmotqujlia in inchan, ca nel immal, qujqua, qujnmamaca in inoaniolque, yoan in tlaxillacaleque, qujcenqua.

Auh in ie iuhquj mec tetlaiaoalochtilo, in mjqujzque, çan ceppa in qujnoallaiaoalochtia: in ie iuhquj mec temanalo, tetecpanalo, iacattimanj in mamalti: njman ie ic qujoaltemovia in teteuhpoalli: ce tlacatl in qujoaltemovia, in ocaxitico tlalchi, nauhcampa conjaoa; mec cõmana, in vncan moteneoa quauhxicalco:

njman ie ic no oaltemo in Xiuhcoatl, çan juhqujn in ocopilli; cueçalin in jnenepil muchioa, tlatlatiuh in ocopilli: auh in jcuitlapil, amatl, aço vmmatl, anoço ematl injc viac: injc oaltemo, iuhqujnma nelli coatl, nenepilotivitz, iuhqujn mocuecuelotivitz.

Auh in ocaxitico tlatzintlan, vmpa tlamattiuh in quauhxicalco: mec tleco, no nauhcampa in conjaoa: in oconjauh mec cõmaiavi in jpan teteppoalli, mec tlatla:

auh in oconcaoaco mec tleco, in opanvetzito tlacpac, mec tlapitzalo: njmã ie ic oaltemo in Paynal, in jxiptla Vitzilobuchtli, cenca qujoalmotlalochtia.

---

21. Clavijero, *Historia antigua*, Vol. III, p. 168, says such images had been made of both Uitzilopochtli and Paynal: ". . . *fabricaban . . . dos estatuas de aquellos dioses, de la pasta de varias semillas con sangre de niños sacrificados, y le ponian por huesos algunos leños de acacia.*"

22. In *ibid.*, pp. 169–70, Clavijero writes: "*aquella noche que era la última del mes, velaban también los sacerdotes y a la mañana siguiente llevaban a la estatua de masa de Huitzilopochtli a una sala que había en el recinto del templo, y en presencia solamente del rey, de cuatro dignidades del templo y de cuatro superiores de los seminarios, el sacerdote de Quetzalcoatl, que era jefe de los tlamacazques o penitentes arrojaba un dardo a la estatua con que la atravesaba de parte a parte. Con esto decían que ya había muerto su dios; uno de los sacerdotes le sacaba el corazón y lo presentaba al rey para que lo comiese; el cuerpo se dividía por medio y la una mitad se daba a los tlatelolcas y la otra quedaba para los mexicanos; de esta se hacían cuatro partes para los cuatro cuarteles de la ciudad, y cada parte se dividía en menudas partículas que se distribuían entre todos los individuos del sexo masculino. Esta ceremonia explicaban con la palabra* teocualo, *comer a Dios. Las mujeres no probaban de esta sagrada masa por razón, como se puede creer, de no pertenecer a su sexo el empleo de la guerra.*"

23. Corresponding Spanish text: "*vn volumen grande, de papeles blancos, que llaman* teteppoalli, *o por otro nombre* teteujtl." The Nahuatl text here has *teteuhpoalli*; subsequently it is spelled *teteppoalli*.

24. Corresponding Spanish text: "*Luego descendia otro satrapa, que traya vn hachon de teas muy largo, que llamã* xiuhcoatl: *tenja la cabeça y la cola como culebra.*" In Chap. 14 of *Book IX* (Sahagún, Garibay ed., Vol. III, p. 54), which describes the same ceremony, the priest wears the fire serpent as a disguise: "*luego descendía un sátrapa que venía metido dentro de una culebra de papel, el cual la traía como si ella viniera por sí, y traía en la boca unas plumas coloradas que parecían llamas de fuego que le salían por la boca.*"

147

And when he had brought it to the ground, he passed before the eagle vessel. Quickly he passed before the captives and the bathed ones, as if he guided them. Then they ascended the pyramid steps.

When they had gone reaching the summit, first the captives died; it was as if they became the fundament of the bathed ones.[25] And when, first, the captives had died, the bathed ones just followed them.

And when one died, then shell trumpets were blown. Then they brought them down here; they came rolling them down. So did they with all the bathed ones.

And also there was dying in Uitznauac. They who died were only those of Uitznauac. Only they [died]; none were their fundament.[26]

And when there had been dying, then there was departing on the part of each one. And upon the next day there was the drinking of pulque; the leftovers were distributed.[27] The pulque which was drunk was called blue pulque. Everyone of the old men, the old women, and the seasoned warriors of noble lineage who already had wives, the men of marriageable age, and the lords, and the leaders of the marriageable ones were those who drank pulque.

And the rulers of the youths, those who were already mature, drank pulque, but they drank only in secret. They did not disclose themselves. They hid themselves well in the dark; they indeed crouched behind bushes in order not to be seen.

And if anyone discovered them, if they made it known that indeed they drank pulque, that indeed there had been gathering together, that indeed there had been arranging among themselves, they beat them repeatedly with pine staves; they bruised their bodies sorely, and they shaved their heads like servants — they cut [the hair from] the heads of each one. They dragged them each; they went kicking them; on the ground they struck them repeatedly; they cast stones at them. Verily, they afflicted them. From time to time death came from this.

And after they had taken their pleasure [with them], then they cast them hence, they threw them out of the portals. Thus fear fell [over the people].

And in the homes of the bathers there was sing-

Auh in otlaltitech caxitico, ixpan qujqujxtia in quauhxicalli, imjxpan qujztiqujça in mamalti, yoan in tlaaltilti, iuhqujn, qujnoaliacana, mec tleco:

in oacito tlacpac, achto mjquj in mamalti: iuhqujn impepechoan muchioa, tlaaltilti: auh in oachto om-mjcque, mamalti; ça qujmõtoqujlia in tlaaltilti.

Auh in jquac çe õmjquj; njman tlapitzalo: njman ic qujnoaltemovitimanj, qujnmjmjlotivitze; much iuh qujnchioa in tlaaltilti.

Auh no mjcoa in vitznaoac: çanjoque in mjquj vitznaoaca, çan mjxcavia, aiaque inpepechõ.

Auh in õmjcoac, mec viviloa: auh in jmuztlaio, tlatlaoano, haapeoalo: in vctli mja itoca matlalvctli, ixqujch tlacatl in vevetque, in jlamatque: yoã in tla-paltequjoaque, in ie cioaoaque, in otlapaliuhcatque, yoã in tetecutin, yoan in tlapaliuhcaiaca, in quja vctli.

Auh in telpuchtlatoque, in ie chicaoaque, quja in vctli: iece çan qujchtacayia, amo mjxmanaia, vellaio-valli qujmotoctiaia, vel moxiuhtlapachoaia, injc amo ittozque.

Auh intla aca qujnnexxotlaz, intla machililozque, in ca otlaoanque: in ca necentlaliloia, in ca nenono-tzaloia: qujnvivitequj, ocoquauhtica vel qujnnacate-poçaoa, yoã qujnquatexoloxima, qujnquatetequj, qujnvivilana, qujntilicçatinemj, tlaltitech qujntzo-tzona, qujntetentimaiavi, vel qujmellelaxitia: nema-maco injc mjctiloia.

Auh in oimellel onqujz, njmã in ca oalmaiavi, qujnnoalchiccanaoa qujiaoac, ic maviztli vetzia.

Auh in inchan tealtique, cujco, vevetzotzonalo,

25. Corresponding Spanish text: "assi hazian a todos los esclauos, que matauan a honrra de vitznaoa, solos ellos morian, ningun captiuo moria, con ellos matauanlos en su cu de vitznaoatl."

26. After inpepechõ the *Real Palacio MS* adds *mochiua*.

27. *haapeoalo (apeualo)* was the ritual distribution of the leftovers after the ceremony. Cf. Sahagún, Garibay ed., Vol. I, pp. 74, 363.

ing; ground drums were beaten, gourd rattles were rattled, turtle shells were beaten. Only as they were [seated] on the ground was there singing; only as they were [seated] on the ground were the ground drums beaten. Gifts were given one. They gave gifts to all who worked, who served [the guests] — those who cared for the tobacco, who were with the tobacco; and those who cared for the chocolate, who were with the chocolate, or who were with the water; and those who watched over one, who served [the guests]; and the honored women, those who were among the [cooking] vessels, who were with the tamales, who were with the meat, who set forth the meat, who stood over the meat; and those who stood over the pulque, the pulque-makers; and all those of the neighborhood. Everyone was given gifts.

And the third day [of Atemoztli] was known as "the mock-fight of the Chonchayotl." One [man] was set up as Chonchayotl; one [man] was his likeness. His hair was wild, his hair was disorderly; it was bloody; he was frightful.[28] And when they arrayed the Chonchayotl, then they separated [into bands]. Apart were the offering priests; with them went, with them stood the Chonchayotl. And [also] apart were the youths.

Then at midday they began fighting each other; they skirmished. They struck one another with fir branches, with fir staves, and long reeds, long stout reeds. They bound them each in the middle; they bound them firmly, they bound them tightly; they wrapped them in cords; they placed cords about them. As they were repeatedly struck, it was as if waves were breaking on the shore. Verily they harmed one another; verily they were hurt.

And if [the youths] caught an offering priest, if one were taken, they rubbed him with [ground up] maguey thorns; much did he burn; he itched. It was as if his body were deadened. And if one of the youths were taken, the offering priests bled his ears with a [maguey] thorn, [and] his shoulders, his breast, his thighs. Indeed they made him cry out.[29]

And if [the priests] chased the youths into the palace, they looted it; they stole all the [reed] mats, the mat cords, the seats with backs, the couches, the backless seats. And if they found horizontal drums, ground drums, they took away all; they took all.

aiacacholo, aiochioalo: çan tlalpan cujco, çan tlalpan veuetl in motzotzona: tetlauhtilo, qujntlauhtia yn ixqujchtin otlatequjpanoque in techixquj, in qujmocujtlauja yietl, yn iiepã ca, yoan in qujmocujtlauja cacaoatl, in cacaoapan ca, anoço apan ca, yoan in techia, in techixquj: yoan in cioatzitzinti, in contitlan nemj, in tamalpan ca, in nacapan ca, in nacatlatlali, in nacatl ipã icac: yoan in vctli ipan icac, yn vctlali: yoan in ixqujch tlaxilacaleque, ixqujch tlacatl motlauhtia.

Auh injc eilhujtl moteneoa chonchaiocacalioa, ce moquetzaia, ce qujxiptlaiotiaia in chonchaiotl: quatatapatic, quapaçoltic, ieço temamauhti: auh yn oqujcencauhque chõchaiotl, mec moxeloa, nonqua manj, in tlamacazque inoan eoa inoan icac in chonchaiotl: auh nonqua momana in telpupuchti:

mec peoa nepantla tonatiuh, in moiaiaotla, micali, ynjc moujujtequj, acxoiamaitl, iehoatl yn oiametl, yoan acapitzactli, yoan otlapitzactli, qujcujcujtlalpiaia, qujcacatzilpiaia, qujtetevilpiaia, qujmecatetecujaiaia, qujmecatitlan tlaliaia ynic moujujtequj: iuhqujn tlatlatzcatimanj, vel mococoltia, vel mococoaia.

Auh intla oce cacique tlamacazquj, intla oce axioac, qujmealtia, cenca cuecuetzoca, quequexquja: yuhqujn iolmiquj ynacaio. Auh intla ce axioa, telpuchtli, in tlamacazque qujçoçoia vitztica yn jnacazco, yn jacolpan, yn ielpan, yn jmetzpan, vel qujtzatzatia.

Auh in telpupuchti, intla qujntocaticalaquizque, in vmpa tecpan, tlanamoia, muchi qujnamoia in petlatl in petlamecatl, in tepotzoicpalli, in netlaxonj, in tzinicpalli: auh intla qujpãtilia teponaztli, in veuetl muchi qujqujxtia, muchi qujcuj.

---

28. See Pl. 31.
29. *quitzatzatzitia* in the *Real Palacio MS*.

And if [the youths] chased the offering priests into the *calmecac*, they also robbed them;[30] they removed things from them. They took away all the mats, the shell trumpets, the seats with backs.

And they just dispersed from there, each one; there was stopping toward evening when there was still a little sun.

And the fourth day [of Atemoztli] was called "Ashes are scattered." The old people said: "Indeed the bathed ones who died, it is said, still walk [on the earth] for four days. Not yet do they depart to the place of the dead. But when ashes are scattered, then they go down to the place of the dead."

And at that time were burned their paper vestments in which they had died, which had been laid in reed coffers. And at that time there was head-washing with *amolli* soap; there was bathing. Then there was departing on the part of each one; thus there was dispersing, [each to his own house].

Here ended the feast of Panquetzaliztli; already it had taken four days from [the month of] Atemoztli.

Auh intla qujntocaticalaqujzque tlamacazque in calmecac, no qujntlanamoielia, qujntlaçaçaqujlia, muchi qujnqujxtilia, in petlatl, in tecciztli, in jcpalli:

auh çan vncã xixitinj, necacaoalo, oc achi tonatiuh ie teutlac.

Auh injc navilhujtl moteneoa, nexpixolo: qujtoaia in vevetque. Ca in tlaaltilti in omjcque: qujl oc nemj navilhujtl, aiamo vi in mjctlan: auh in jquac nexpixolo, qujnjquac temo in mjctlan;

yoã iquac motlatia, mopetlacaltema, in jmamatlatquj in jpã omjcque, yoan iquac neamovilo, neaaltilo, mec viviloa, ic cecẽmanoa.

Nicã tzõqujça in jlhujtl Panquetzaliztli, ie cuel ic naujlhujtl cõcujlia in Atemuztli.

---

30. *quintlanamoyalia* in *ibid*.

Thirty-fifth Chapter, which telleth of the feast day and the honors which they observed during all the days of the sixteenth month, which was called Atemoztli.[1]

The sixteenth feast was the one known as Atemoztli.

For this reason was it called Atemoztli: it was indeed the time that the rains newly broke out, growled, thundered. All the common folk said: "Water cometh down" or "The Tlalocs descend."

And at this time the fire priest of the Temple of Tlaloc was very solemn, was very devout; he was trusting, he was expecting that in its time the rain would break out.

And when the rain broke out, then he forthwith arose; he seized his incense ladle. Its handle was indeed very long, quite thin. The incense ladle rattled. It was in the form of a serpent. And the serpent's head also rattled; it also [had a stone in] its hollow center.

Then he quickly scooped up the burning embers, the fire; he then quickly put on *yauhtli*. Only this did he do. Then he offered incense; to the four directions he raised [the incense ladle]. Much did it rattle; [the incense] spilled out; it fell out. Then he departed. He walked everywhere; he issued everywhere into the temple courtyards; everywhere he offered incense; everywhere he spread warmth. Thus he attended to the matter; thus he called upon the Tlalocs; thus he prayed for rain.

And a number of the common folk made vows that they would make figures of the mountain [gods]. And five days [before the feast] they arranged paper, they bought paper, and liquid rubber, and obsidian knives, and maguey fiber. They bought them.

They paid great honors to [the mountain gods], and they did penances so that they might make the figures and cover them [with paper]. They did not soap themselves when they bathed themselves; only their necks did they wash. Neither did [a man] lie

Inic cempoalli on caxtolli capitulo: itechpa tlatoa in jlhujtl, yoan in tlamaviztililiztli, in qujchioaia in jpan ic cemjlhujtl ic caxtoltetl occe metztli in moteneoa Atemuztli.

Injc caxtoltetl, oce ilhujtl iehoatl in moteneoa Atemuztli:

injc moteneoa Atemuztli, ca iquac iancujcan oalanj, oaoalaca, titicujca in qujavitl: qujtoaia in jxqujch maceoalli, atemo, anoço temo in tlaloque.

Auh in jquac y, in tlalocan tlenamacac, cenca tlaocuxtica, tlateumattica, muchixcaca, motemachitica: in quenmã oalanjz qujavitl:

auh in ooalan qujavitl, njmã ic moquetztiqujça, qujcujtivetzi in jtlema, vel hujtlatztic, çan pitzaton in jquauhio, cacalaca in tlemaitl, coatl ipan qujça: auh in jtzontecon coatl no cacalaca, no iollo:

njmã qujxopilotivetzi in tlexochtli, in tletl: njman contentivetzi in jiauhtli, ça mjxcavia: mec tlenamaca, nauhcampa in conjaoa, cenca cacalaca, ixaoaca, ichaiaca: mec iauh novian nemj, novian qujça in teujtoalco, novian tlenamaca, novian tlatotonja, ic tlatemachia, ic qujnotza in tlaloque, ic qujauhtlatlanj.

Auh in cequjntin maceoalti, monetoltiaia injc tepiqujzque: auh macujltica in amatemaia, in amacoaia, yoan olli, yoa itztli, yoan ichtli in qujcoaia:

cenca qujmaviztiliaia, yoan qujneçaviliaia injc tepiqujzque, yoã tequentizque: amo mamoviaia injc maltiaia, çan moquechaltiaia, amono cioacochia: auh in cioatl amono oqujchcochia.

---

1. "*Bajada de el agua*," according to Torquemada, *Segunda parte*, p. 299, "*porque este Mes suele llover, y nevar algunos Años.*" Garibay ("Relación breve," p. 313) has the same.

Concerning the term Atemoztli, Tovar refers to frequent, extraordinary drizzles in the region, attributed to Tlaloc. Kubler and Gibson, *The Tovar Calendar*, p. 33.

with a woman, and neither did a woman lie with a man.

And [until] the feast day dawned, when the twenty days of Atemoztli were completed, thus was all night lived, thus indeed was there spending of the night as paper was cut, that the spotted paper banners might be completed, might be finished. And when they were completed, when they were finished, they were each attached to poles. On the ground they began; they reached the top [of the poles]. They set them each up in the middle of the courtyard. There indeed they spent the feast day.

And the producers of figures of the mountain [gods] first entertained the offering priests, so that they would make for them the paper adornment of the small mountain gods. But only there in the *calmecac* did they array them.

And when all [the adornment] had been finished, then they quickly took them to the homes of those who had undertaken to provide the figures. And their belongings went with them: their two-toned wooden drums, and their gourd rattles, and their turtle shells. Then they adorned the figures of the mountain gods; they offered them food; they dressed them.

And one who produced the figures [provided] perhaps five; [another] perhaps ten; [another] perhaps fifteen. And [the figures] which they adorned were all [made] purely of amaranth seed dough.

And they fashioned figures of these mountains: Popocatepetl, Iztac tepetl or Iztac ciuatl, Tlaloc, Yoaltecatl, Quauhtepetl, Cocotl, Yiauhqueme, Tepetzintli, Tepepolli, Uixachtecatl; also [the god of] fire, Chicome coatl, Chalchiuhtli icue, Ecatl.[2]

And when they had adorned them, then they set food before them; they did it for each one alone. And their tamales were exceedingly small, exceedingly tiny, each one long and small, each one long and tiny. And they put them into each one's small wooden vessel and their small sauce bowls; and their small earthen vessels contained a very little chocolate.

And four times during the night they made offerings of food. And before them lay two "green stone" jars; pulque was [in them]. And the "green stone" jars were made of green gourds.[3] They split them; they took out their seeds; they removed the

Auh in ie iuh oallatvi ilhujtl, in jquac tlacempoalti Atemuztli, iuh ceioal in nemoa, vel neixpololo, in amaxotlalo: in tlamj, in iecavi tetevitl: auh in otlan, in oiecauh, matlaquauhtitech movivipana, tlaltitech peuhticac, onaciticac in jtzonco; itoalnepantla in qujquequetza, vel oncã cemjlhujtia:

auh in tepicque achtopa qujnmolcaoaltiaia in tlamacazque, injc qujnchivilizque imamatlatquj, tepictotõ: auh çan vmpa in calmecac in qujchichioaia.

Auh in omuchi iecauh, mec qujtqujtze in inchã tepiqujnj, yoan intlatquj, oalietiuh in inteponaz, yoã imaiacach yoan in jmaiouh, mec qujnchichioa in tepicme qujntlamamaca, qujntlaquẽtia:

auh in aca qujpiquja, aço macujltetl, in aca aço matlactetl, in aca aço caxtoltetl: auh in qujchichioaia çan muche in tzoalli.

Auh in qujnpiquja iehoantin in tetepe: in popocatepetl, in jztactepetl, anoço iztac cioatl, in tlaloc, in iooaltecatl, in quauhtepetl, in cocotl, yiauhqueme, in tepetzintli, in tepepolli, in vixachtecatl, no ie in tletl, in chicome coatl, chalchiuhtli icue, ecatl.

Auh in oqujncencauhque, mec qujntlamaca, cececnj mjxcavia: auh in intamal cenca çan tepitoton, cenca çã achitoton, papatlachtotonti papatlachpipil: quauhcaxtotonco in qujntetemjlia, yoã inmolcaxtoton, yoan inçoqujtecõtoton, çan no tepitoton cẽcã achi in onaquj cacaoatl:

auh nappa in qujntlamaca ceioal, yoan imjxpan manj vntetl chalchiuhtecomatl vctli oncaca: auh in chalchiuhtecomatl muchioa, iehoatl in tzilacaiotli, xoxoctic, qujxtlapanaia, qujoalqujxtilia in jaiovachio, qujoalaiooachqujxtia: yoan qujoalqujxtilia in jcuj-

2. These are in the chapter on Atl caualo. Tepetzintli and Tepepolli are probably the Tepetzinco and Tepepulco named in that chapter.

3. *Cucurbita ficifolia* Bouché in Seler, *Einige Kapitel*, p. 221. Cf. Dibble and Anderson, *Book XI*, p. 288.

seeds. And they removed their pith as if it were a cord. There they put in the pulque with fermentation plants added.[4] Thus all night they sang for [the images]; they held vigil for them, and they blew trumpets for them, they played flutes for them.

And they who sounded the trumpets were not those whose office it was [to blow trumpets] but youths. They were much honored; they were given food, they were given drink.

And when this was done, when it dawned, [the priests] then sought weaving sticks. Thereupon they planted them in the hearts [of the images].[5]

And when they had set in the weaving sticks, then they bent back the necks of the amaranth seed [figures]. Then they took from them what had served as their hearts. They gave them to those who had produced the figures; [the priests] placed them in the green gourd bowl.

And when this was done, when [the priests] had slain the amaranth seed [figures], then they gathered, they heaped up all the mountain images' paper vestments. They burned in the middle of the courtyard; they burned them, they set fire to them. And their little vessels, the little wooden vessels, all burned together.

And all the reed mats on which they had stood, and the reed staves, and all the little vessels from which they had eaten, and the "green stone" jars, all [these] they left in the Mist House.

When they had gone to leave these, thereupon first arrived the bidden guests to feast in honor of the images. Then food was offered them, each severally. Nothing else was done. When they had eaten, thereupon they gave them pulque.

And the women also entered. It was said: "They leave the tamales." None came emptyhanded; everybody went bringing their dried grains of maize; the women carried them in their skirts. But those who brought their ears of corn [brought] perhaps fifteen or twenty.

And when they had assembled, when they had sat down, then they gave them food; food was given them. Then also they gave them pulque; they made them drunk. They set before them pulque

tlaxcol, in juhquj mecatl, vncan conteca in aioctli, iuh ceioal in qujncujcatia, qujntoçavia, yoan qujntlapichilia, qujnvilacapitzalhuja.

Auh in tlapitzaia amo iehoan in tequjppaneque, çan telpopochtin, cenca no mavizmachoia, tlamacoia, tlaitiloia.

Auh in ie iuhquj in otlatvic, mec conjtlanj in tzotzopaztli, njmã ie ic qujmonaqujlia in iollopan.

Auh in oconaqujli, njmã ic qujoalquechcollalia in tzoalli, mec conanjlia in jiollo muchioa, qujoalmaca in tepiqujnj, xoxovic xicalco, in qujoallalilia:

auh in ie iuhquj in oqujmõmjctique tzoalti: njmã ie ic qujncenqujxtia, qujtecpichoa, in jxqujch imamatlatquj tepictoton, itoalnepantla in tlatla, in contlatia, in cõtlecavia, yoan in incacaxxototon, in quauhcaxtotonti, muchi centlatla.

Auh in jxqujxh aztapilpetlatl in jpan onoca, yoan oztopilquavitl, yoan in jxqujch in tlaquaia in caxtotonti yoan in chalchiuhtecomatl much vmpa concaoa in aiauhcalco.

In ie vi qujcaoazque, njmã ie ic ommoiacatia, in tlacoanotzalti, in tepictlaquazque: mec tetlamaco, cececnj, neixcavilo: in ontlaquaque, njmã ie ic qujnmaca in vctli.

auh in cioa no calaquj, moteneoa ontamalcaoa, aiac çan juh iauh, muchi tlacatl itlaol qujtqujtiuh in cioa qujcuecuexanotivi: auh in aca icintzin in qujtquj, aço caxtolololotl, anoço tlamjc.

Auh in omotecaque, in omotlalique, mec qujntlamaca tetlamaco: njmã no qujmaca in vctli, qujntlaoãtia, qujnoalmanjlia tlilapaztica in vctli, yoã

4. Sahagún, Garibay ed., Vol. I, p. 363: *"otras veces daban* pulcre *hechizo de agua y miel, cocido con la raíz, al cual llaman* ayoctli, *que quiere decir* pulcre *de agua."* In Vol. IV, p. 324, Garibay defines *ayoctli* as *"Ingrediente vegetal, raíz, planta, o madera usado para hacer fermentar el pulque. . . . Conjeturalmente . . .* Mimosa *sp.,* Acacia *sp."*

5. Torquemada, *Segunda parte*, p. 284, thus describes it: *"abrianlos por los pechos, con vn Tzotzopaztli, que es vn palo ancho, con que texen las Mugeres, à manera de espada, ò machete, sacabanles el coraçon, que tambien les avian puesto, en lo interior de la masa, y cortavanles las cabeças, como acostumbraban hacer à los Sacrificados, y guardavanlas."*

in black vessels. And they set before them, when they made them drunk, cups, drinking vessels, also black.

And when they left the paper banners, when they set down the debt-payment, they bound them upon the poles.

Enough. Here ended this feast, which was named Atemoztli.

qujoalmana in tetlaoan, in tlaoanonj, in tlaoãcaxitl, çan no tliltic.

Auh in jquac concaoa tetevitl, in nextlaoalli cõmamana, conjilpia cuenmantitech.

Iie ixqujch, njcan tzonqujça inj ilhujtl in moteneoa Atemuztli.

Thirty-sixth Chapter, where are related the feast day and the debt-paying which were observed during all the days of the seventeenth month, which was called Tititl.[1]

The seventeenth feast was the one known as Tititl.

At the time of this feast there died a person named Ilama tecutli — [one in] her likeness, a ceremonially bathed one. The stewards displayed her.

And her adornment was that of Ilama tecutli. She had her white skirt, her white shift — completely white. And over this she was dressed in what was named her star skirt. This was made with small shells on cured skin cut into long, thin strips, the shells set in at the end of each [strip]. She wore it about her hips over [the other skirt]. When she walked, loudly did it jingle; it was audible for a distance. And her sandals had white toes, each toe woven with cotton thread.

And her shield was only a chalky shield pasted with eagle feathers. Its center was made of eagle feathers sewn to the middle of the shield, and it had pendants of heron feathers at the edges [and tassels shaped like] grasshopper heads, of eagle feathers; they hung by their points. And on the [other] side she held her weaving stick.[2]

And her face was painted. It was in diverse colors; it was painted in various colors. About her lips they spread black; it was said: "She is painted black [about] the lips."[3] And upon her nose and her forehead they spread yellow ocher.

And her eagle feather headpiece was a headdress on which stood arrayed eagle feathers; only they were the hair. They were twisted, arrayed, disposed,

Injc cempoalli on caxtolli oce, capitulo vncan mo- teneoa in ilhujtl, yoã in nextlaoalli, in muchioaia in jpan vel ic cemjlhujtl ic caxtoltetl omume metztli in mjtoaia Tititl.

Injc caxtoltetl omume ilhujtl iehoatl in moteneoa, itoca Tititl:

in jpan in ilhujtl, ce tlacatl mjquja, itoca: Ilama tecutli, ixiptla, tlaaltilli: calpixque in qujnextia.

Auh in jnechichioal catca in Ilama tecutli, iztac in jcue, iztac in jvipil, çan cemjztac: auh in panj qujmocuetia, itoca citlalli icue: inin cuechtli in tlachioalli, cuetlaxtli in tlapipitzaoacaxotlalli, tlapipi-tzaoacatectli, yiacac in tlatlatlalilli cuechtli; panj ic ommotzincuetia: in jquac nenemj cenca xaxamaca, veca caqujzti: yoan icacac, iztac in jquetzil, in jquequetzil: icpatl injc tlaqujttli,

yoan ichimal, çã tiçachimalli, quauhpachiuhquj: in jnepantla quauhivitl in tlachioalli, inepantla in tlatzõtli, chimalli, yoan tentlapilollo, aztatl in tlapi-lolli quauhivitl in jiacachapollo, in jiacac pipilcac: yoan centlapal qujtzitzquja, itzotzopaz:

yoã moxauh mochictlapana, mjchictlapana: in jtenco qujteca tlilli: mjtoa, motentlilhuja: auh in jiac ipan, yoan ixquac tecoçavitl in qujteca,

yoan iquauhtzon, tzoncalli in jtech tlavipantli in quauhivitl, çan mjxcavia in tzõtli, tlamalintli, tlavi-

1. "*Estiramiento*," Garibay suggests in "Relación breve," p. 314. Orozco y Berra, in *Historia antigua*, Vol. II, p. 39, writes: "Tititl. *Torquemada traduce, tiempo apretado; Boturini, vientre ó nuestro vientre. Gama rechaza como falsa la interpretacion de Boturini, y saca la suya del verbo* titixia, *rebuscar despues de la cosecha.*" Torquemada, in *Segunda parte*, p. 300, amplifies his version thus: "*porque lo era de frios, y heladas, las quales sentian mucho por la poca ropa de que vsaban, y porque por este mismo tiempo, andaban apretados, con Guerras, y Asaltos, que tenian las vnas Provincias contra las otras, y se mataban, y destruian vnos à otros.*"

Durán (*Historia*, Vol. II, pp. 301–302) writes: "*quiere decir estirar . . . imaginaban en el cielo dos niños estirándose el uno al otro. . . . había bailes de mugeres y hombres asidos unos con otros de las manos.*"

2. The shield and the entire costume of the goddess are clearly illustrated several times in the *Codex Borbonicus*. Paso y Troncoso, in *Descripción, historia y exposición del códice pictórico de los antiguos nauas* (Florence: 1898, p. 273), thus describes the shield: "*la rodela, que se acomoda muy bien á la descripción que han dejado los indios, es blanca; tiene un corro de plumas de águila pegadas en el centro; y lleva como rapacejos otras 2 clases de plumas: unas pequeñas de garzotas, redondas (que algunos han tomado por conchas, porque lo parecen; pero que no son sino plumas), é ingeridas en estas primeras, y de ellas pendientes, otras plumas grandes de águila.*"

3. *motentetlilhuia* in the *Real Palacio MS*.

sewn to it, sewn to each other. The headdress was called *tzompilinalli*.

And before she died, she danced. The old men beat the drums for her; the singers sang for her; they intoned her song. And as she danced she could weep for herself, and she sighed; she felt anguish.[4] For indeed it was only a short time, only so much time, only a brief time until she was to give her service when she would bring an end to earthly things.

And when the sun was past its zenith, thereupon they took her up to the top of the temple. All the impersonators of the devils went laying hold of her, went accompanying her; they went in file. Yet another impersonator of [Ilama tecutli] went leading them, one whom verily they thought a god[dess] on earth; it was only a man whom they [so] adorned.

And when they had taken her [to the summit], then they cut open her breast. And when she died, then they severed her head. And her head they gave to him who went leading. He took it with him; in his right hand he went grasping it; he went dancing; with the severed head he went making dance gestures. He went before them; he went leading all the impersonators, the representatives of the devils. They circled the temple; then they descended in the same way [as they had ascended]. They came ranged in a row; they came in line. And when they had come to descend to the ground, thereupon they each went, they dispersed; they went, each, to their homes, to their several *calpulcos*, where [the gods' raiment] was guarded.

And the impersonator, the likeness of Ilama tecutli, thus danced: he kept stepping back; he raised his legs up behind him; and he kept supporting himself upon his staff, a cane.

At its end, at its head, it was divided into three [points], like a three-pronged harpoon. It was called his thorny staff. And when he thus danced, it was said: "Ilama tecutli backeth away." And they put on him a mask; it looked in two directions. It had large lips, it had huge lips; and it had big, round, protruding eyes. And upon his head stood a row of small banners; they stood in line. They seemed like a wreath of flowers upon his head.

And when this [took place], it also was said: "Her grain bin burneth." Her grain bin was

pantli, tlavipanalli, itech tlatzontli, tlanetech itzontli: in tzõcalli, mjtoaia, tzompilinalli.

Auh in aiamo mjquj mjtotiaia, qujtlatzotzonjliaia in vevetque, in cujcanjme, qujcujcatia, quevilia in jcujc. Auh in jquac mjtotiaia, vel mochoqujliaia, yoan elcicivia, mociappoa: iehica ca ça achitonca, ça ixqujch cavitl y, ça ixqujch cavitontli y, in ie ontlacotiz, in ie compoloz tlalticpactli.

Auh in jquac õmotzcalo tonatiuh: njmã ie ic qujtlecavia in teucalticpac, qujtzitzqujtivi, qujtocativi in jxqujchtin im jxiptlaoã diablome cempantitivi, teiacãtiuh in oc ceppa ixiptla, in vel qujmoteutia tlalticpac, çan tlacatl in qujchichioaia.

Auh in oconaxitique, njmã ic coneltequj: auh in õmomjqujli, njmã ic qujoalquechcotona: auh in jtzontecõ, qujoalmaca in teiacantiuh, itlan conana imaiauhcampa in qujtzitzqujtiuh, mjtotitiuh ic ontlaiiauhtiuh in tzõtecomatl, imjxpan icatiuh, qujniacantiuh in jxqujchtin imjxiptlaoan, in impatillooan Diablome, qujoaliaoaloa in teucalli, njman ic oaltemo, çã no ivi, motecpantivitze, cenpantitivitze: auh in otemoco tlalchi, njmã ie ic vivi, momoiaoa, vmpa vivi in inchachan, in incacalpulco, in vmpa pipielo.

auh in teixiptla, in jxjptla Ilama tecutli: injc mjtotiaia tzitzintlacça, itzintlampa in conjaoa icxi: yoan ic motlatlaquechitiuh itopil, v̂tlatl:

in jiacac, in jquac, excan in maxaltic, iuhqujn mjnacachalli: motocaiotia, yiotlavitzil, auh in juh mjtotiaia y, mjtoa, motzineoa in Jlama tecutli: yoã xaiacatl cõmaquja, occampa tlachia, texxaxacaltic, tenxaxacalpul, yoan ixtotolonpol, auh in jcpac pantotonti tecpantoc, vipantoc: iuhqujn icpacsuchiuh muchioa:

yoan in jquac y, no moteneoa icuezcõ tlatla: in jcuezcon qujchichioaia ocoquavitl in qujnenepa-

4. Torquemada (*Segunda parte*, p. 284) writes, however, that "*a esta Muger le era permitido llorar, y entristecerse mucho (caso negado en otras, que morian otros Dias) y asi se entristecia, suspiraba, y lloraba, con la memoria de la muerta, que de proximo, y cerca esperaba.*"

fashioned[5] of pine branches which they joined together; like a framework did they arrange it.[6] They wrapped paper about it; they caulked it with paper. They placed it there upon the eagle vessel.

And a fire priest arrayed himself; he was bedight as a young [warrior]; he imitated a youth [with] his netting cape, his forked heron feather device, his deer hoof [rattles], his lip pendant. He departed from the summit of the temple; he came bringing a maguey leaf; a small banner came standing on it.

When he came to arrive on the ground, he thereupon went to the eagle vessel, where stood the grain bin. There he placed the maguey leaf.

And when he had placed it there, the offering priests thereupon appeared. They ran fast; it was as if each strove to be first. It was known as, it was called "They run for flowers"; they climbed up to the temple, where the flowers were. They were called godly flowers.

And when [the priests] had gone to reach the summit [of the temple], then [others] set fire to, ignited the grain bin. Once again [the priests] descended; they each quickly grasped the flowers. There they were casting the flowers there in the eagle vessel, there where the grain bin burned. Then the offering priests each ran off; they just left. This is quite enough.

And upon the morrow, then began the casting of bags at people. Everybody, each one, made bags for themselves. They carried grass nets; there they filled them with the flowers of reeds or with scraps of paper. They shredded paper; they shredded it fine; they bound it inside [of the nets]. And some carried nets [made like] gloves; they also filled them with reed flowers; they were called hand bags. And some only prepared themselves green maize leaves, which they made into bags for themselves; they pressed the leaves into balls.

And at this time it was commanded that none should put stones [in the bags]. Those who were yet small boys only began in fun when they began the mock-fighting with bags; only gradually it quickened. As the mock-fight was fought, it was as if it quickened as blows were repeatedly struck perchance at the heads [of the participants], perhaps at their backs, perhaps at their breasts as they dealt blows.

noaia, iuhqujn colotli, ic qujtlaliaia camaqujmjloaia, camapepechoa, vncan qujquetza in quauhxicalco:

auh ce tlenamacac in muchichioaia, motelpuchchichioaia, telpuchtli ipan qujça icuechin, yiaztaxel, ichochol itenpilol: vmpa oaleoa in teucalticpac, metl qujvicatz, pãtontli itech icativitz.

In oacico tlalchi: njmã ie ic vmpa iauh in quauhxicalco, in vmpa icac cuezcomatl, vmpa contlalia in metl.

Auh in ocõtlali, njmã ie ic eoa in tlamacazque, cenca motlaloa, iuhqujn mopapanavitivi: moteneoa, motocaiotia. Suchipaina, qujtlecavia in teucalli, vmpa caca suchitl: itoca Teusuchitl.

Auh in opanvechoato: njmã qujtlemjna, qujtlecavia, in cuezcomatl in tlamacazque: no ceppa oaltemo, qujoalcujcujtiqujça in suchitl: vncã qujoallaztimanj in suchitl in vncã quauhxicalco, in vncan tlatla, cuezcomatl: njmã motlatlaloa, in tlamacazque, çan ic qujztimanj, çan oc ie ixqujch.

Auh in jmuztlaioc: njmã ie peoa in nechichiquavilo, ixqujch tlacatl qujmuchichiviliaia chichiquatli: in acamatlatl in queoaia, vncã qujtentiquetza in tolcaputl, anoço amatzotzolli: in amatl qujpochina, qujpopochina, in jitic qujcacatza: auh in cequjntin iuhqujn macpalli, queoaia matlatl, no qujtentiquetza in tolcaputl: motocaiotia, macpalchichiquatli: auh in cequjnti çan izoatl in qujmuchichiviliaia, in qujmochichiquatiaia: izoatl in qujtatapaiollaliaia.

Auh in jquac nenaoatiloia, injc aiac tetl itic qujtlaliz: çan onavilpeoa, çan oc pipiltotonti in qujpeoaltiaia in muchichiquaiautlaia, çan iuh nenti veiia: injc moiaiautla iuhqujn cocomonj ic movivitequj, aço imjcpac aço incuitlapan, aço imelpan in qujmotlaxilia.

---

5. *chichiua* may be rendered in two ways. We have been guided largely by the context.

6. In the next chapter (Izcalli) Sahagún notes that "*hazian la estatua del dios, de fuego de arqujtos, y palos atados, vnos con otros, que ellos llaman colotli, que qujere dezir zimbria, o modelo.*"

And the boys cast bags at the maidens — those yet with the long hairdress; whenever these came before them, there they cast bags at them; they surrounded them; in truth some made them weep. But when some woman took forethought if she went forth somewhere, she took something with her as a staff, or else a "devil-fruit-thorn." If anyone came to cast a bag at her, she pursued him with it, she defended herself with it.

But if one carried nothing with her as her defense, they indeed formed a ring about her. And some of the boys only kept watch; so that some might not display their bags, they just went hiding them by their sides.

And when they came upon a woman, if they somewhat waylaid her, then they turned around; they struck her; they made it known to her only when they struck her with the bags, when they cast the bags at her. They said to her: "It is a little bag, O our mother!" Then they ran away.

And this was done when there was the casting of the bags. And all these days the women watched themselves well; they were very prudent when they walked abroad, when they followed the road.

Enough. Here ended Tititl.

Auh in telpopochpipil, qujnchichiquaviaia in ichpopochti, iehoantin in tzonquemeque, in jquac imjxpan qujça, vncan qujchichiquavia, coololhuja, in aca vel qujchochoctia: auh in aca cioatl monemachtia, intla canapa iaz itla quavitl qujtquj, anoço tlacatecoloxocovitztli: intla aca ie vitz, qujchichiquaviz, ic qujtoca, ic momapatla.

Auh in aca atle qujtquj, inemapatlaia, vel coololhuja: auh in cequjntin telpopochtotonti, çã motepapachivia: in aca amo qujnextitiuh in jchichiqua, çan itlan caqujtiuh.

Auh in jquac qujnamjquj cioatl, intla achi ocompatili, njmã oalmocuepa, qujoallaxilia, çan ic qujmachitia in jquac qujoallaxilia, chichiquatli, in quioalchichiquavia: qujlhuja, chichiquatzin, tonãtze, njman ic motlaloa.

Auh inin muchioaia, in nechichiquaviloa: auh in jzqujlhujtl y, çẽca mopiaia in cioa, cenca mjmati, in jquac nememj, in jquac vtli qujtoca.

Ie ixqujch njcan tlamj Tititl.

Thirty-seventh Chapter, which telleth of the feasts and the honors performed during all the days of the eighteenth month, which was called, which was known as Izcalli.[1]

The eighteenth feast was the one known as Izcalli.[2]

Upon the tenth day of Izcalli, tamales stuffed with greens were eaten. It was maintained, it was said: "Our father, the fire, roasteth [food] for himself." They set up his image; it was only a framework [of wood] which they made.[3] They gave it a mask. His mask was made of green stone horizontally striped with turquoise. It was very awesome; much did it gleam; it was as if it shone; it cast much brilliance.

And they fitted upon its head a quetzal feather crown, quite narrow at the bottom, large enough to fit around the head. The quetzal feathers were outspread. And there were two head-fire-drills; they became as his horns; they were on two sides. And the head-fire-drills both had quetzal feather vases. And to the base of the quetzal feather crown was sewn yellow hair. Very even was the head trimming; very evenly was the hair cut. His lordly hair fell to his loins. Very evenly was his head trimmed, his hair cut.

And when they put it on him, it was verily like his [own] hair.

And they dressed him in a cape of quetzal feathers, replete with quetzal feathers. Very far did it lie dragging; it was dragging a great deal on the ground. The wind penetrated it; it was as if it kept raising it up; it was as if it glittered, it was as if it gleamed.

And his mat was an ocelot skin; the ocelot skin mat lay with paws extended; in the same way its head lay face down. And this [image of] Xiuhtecutli was before a brazier. At midnight [the priest] used the fire drill [to make a fire]. And when a

---

Jnic cempoalli oncaxtolli omume, capt. ytechpa tlatoa, yn ilhuitl, yoan in tlamauiztililiztli, in motequjpanoaia, in ipan vel ic cemilhujtl, ic caxtoltetl omey metztli, in mjtoaia in moteneoaia Yzcalli.

Inic caxtoltetl omey ilhujtl: iehoatl in moteneoa Yzcalli:

in izcalli tlamatlacti in qualoia oauhqujltamalli, moteneoa, mitoaia, motlaxqujan tota, iehoatl in tletl, qujtlaliaia, yxiptla, çan colotli, in qujchioaia, qujxaiacatiaia, yn ixaiac chalchiujtl in tlachioalli, xiujtl ynic ixtlan tlatlaan, cenca mauiçoticatca, cenca pepetlaca iuhqujn cuecueioca, cenca mihiiotia:

yoan conaquja yn itzontecõ quetzalcomjtl, çan tzinpitzaoac, vey ynic quamalacachtic, iuhqujn xexeliuj quetzalli: auh vme in quammalitli, iuhqujn iquaquauh muchioa, nenecoc in mamanj. Auh in quammalitli, quetzaltzontecomaio yiomexti: auh yn jtzintlan quetzalcomjtl, itech tlatzontli tzoncoztli, cencan quenmach in tlaquatectli, cencã quenmach in moquatec: auh ycujtlacaxiuhian vetztica yn itecutzon, cencan no quenmach in tlaquatectli in tlatzontectli.

Auh yn iquac oconaqujque, iuhqujnma nelli itzon.

yoan conquentia in quetzalquemjtl, çan motqujtica quetzalli, cenca veca in vilantoc, tlalpan vivilantica: in ehecatl itlan calaquj, iuhqujnma acomana, iuhq'n cuecueioca, iuhqujn cuecueiaoa.

Auh yn jpetl muchioa, ocelueoatl, ocelupetlatl mamaçouhtoc, çan iuh ca in jtzontecon, ixtlapach onoc: auh in iehoatl xiuhtecutli ixpan ca tlecujlli, iooalnepantla in tlequauhtlaça. Auh in ovetz tletl, njman ie ic qujpitza, mec tletlalia:

---

1. In the *Real Palacio MS*, fols. 123, 124, and 125 were bound out of correct sequence in the MS (pp. 45–50 in the Paso y Troncoso edition). Seler (*Einige Kapitel*, pp. 230–48) arranges the text in accordance with the consecutive numbering of the folios (119–26).

2. "Growth," or "the growing," according to Garibay ("Relación breve," p. 316). Torquemada favors the meaning "rebirth" (*Segunda parte*, p. 300): "*quiere decir: Resucitado, ò el de la resurreccion: porque por aquel tiempo ià queria mudar el tiempo, y pasar de frio à calor, y començar la Primavera.*" In Clavijero's *Historia antigua*, Vol. III, p. 172, n. 54, it is suggested that the literal meaning of *izcalli* is "here is the house."

3. Sahagún's corresponding Spanish text says: "*hazian la estatua del dios, del fuego de arqujtos, y palos atados, vnos con otros, que ellos llaman colotli, que qujere dezir zimbria, o modelo.*"

flame fell, thereupon he blew upon it; then he made the fire.

And when the fire had been made, when it was dawn, when it grew bright on the land, then there ranged themselves, there came first the youths, the small boys; they were giving the old men the snakes which they had caught. The old men were spread about taking them from [the boys]; they were spread about casting them into the fire. And everything, whatever anyone had captured—all the birds, the reed thrushes,[4] boat-tailed grackles,[5] western grebes,[6] all the various birds, and salamanders,[7] large lizards,[8] long-tailed lizards,[9] thick dark fish,[10] thick white fish,[11] small white fish,[12] shrimps,[13] frogs,[14] dragonfly larvae[15] — all of them they were spread about casting into the fire.

Then [the boys] were spread about coming forth; [the priests] were spread about offering each one a tamal stuffed with greens. And everyone of the common folk made themselves tamales stuffed with greens. They laid them before [the image of] Xiuhtecutli. As many as laid them out before Xiuhtecutli did so purely voluntarily. But some laid them as offerings only in their *calpulcos*.

And the tamales stuffed with greens they also named precious green stone tamales. And all the common folk gave one another their tamales stuffed with greens; they were given one another. Whoever first cooked her tamales stuffed with greens then went to offer them to her kin. Thus she showed her self-esteem.

And the sauce of the tamales stuffed with greens was a shrimp sauce. And the sauce was called "red [chili] sauce." And when the good common folk ate, they sat about sweating, they sat about burning themselves. And the tamales stuffed with greens were indeed hot, gleaming hot. They ate them hot; they sat about steaming their noses. And the husks

auh in omotlali tletl, in otlatvic, in otlatlalchipaoac, mec ommotecpana, õmoiacatia in telpopochti, in pipiltotonti, qujmõmacatimanj, in vevetque, in cocoa in oqujmacique: qujnoalcujlitimanj in vevetque, tleco qujmontlaztimanj, yoan in ie ixqujch, in aqujn çaço tlein ocacic, in jxqujch tototl, in acatzanatl, in teutzanatl, in acatechichictli, in ie ixqujch nepapã tototl, yoan in axolotl, in acaltetepon, in mjlquaxochtli, xovili, in amjlotl, in xalmjchi, in acocilin, in cujatl, anenez, moch tleco qujmõtlaztimanj:

njmã ic oalqujztimanj, qujnoalmacatimanj, cecentetl in oauhqujltamalli. Auh ixqujch tlacatl in maceoalli mooauhqujltamalhuja: ixpan ontlamanaia in xiuhtecutli: çan teiollotlama, in quezquj ontlamanaia ixpan Xiuhtecutli: auh in cequjntin çan incacalpulco in tlamanaia.

Auh in oauhqujltamalli, no qujtocaiotiaia, chalchiuhtamalli: auh in jxqujch maceoalli netech qujmomacaia, in inoauhqujltamal: netech motlatlamacaia: in aqujn achto oicucic, ioauhqujltamal: mec iauh qujmacaz in joãiolquj, ic qujnextia in netlaçotlaliztli:

Auh in oauhqujltamalli in jmollo catca, acociltlatonjlli: auh in tlatonjlli, motocaiotiaia, chamolmolli: auh in jquac tlaquaia maceoaltzitzinti, mjîtonjtoque, mochichinotoque: auh in oauhqujltamalli, vel totonquj totontlapetztic qujtotoncaqua, iaiacapoçontoque: auh in jzoaio, çan nonqua qujtlaliaia, aiac tleco conaxitiaia: muchi atlan contepeoaia.

4. *"Tordo de las cañas o milpero"* in Francisco J. Santamaría, *Diccionario de Mejicanismos* (Mexico: Editorial Porrúa, S. A., 1959, hereafter referred to as Santamaría, *Diccionario*), p. 18. Cf. also Dibble and Anderson, *Book XI*, p. 50.

5. *Cassidix mexicanus* (Gmelin) in *ibid.*, p. 50.

6. *Aechmophorus occidentalis* (Lawrence) in *ibid.*, p. 31.

7. *Amblystoma tigrinum* L., *Proteus mexicanus, Sideron humboldti* in *ibid.*, p. 64.

8. *Heloderma horridum* in Santamaría, *Diccionario*, p. 15.

9. *Cnemidophorus sexlineatus gularis* in Dibble and Anderson, *Book XI*, p. 61.

10. *Cyprinus americanus* or *Algansae tincella* C. in *ibid.*, p. 62.

11. *Chirostoma humboldtianum* in *ibid.*, p. 62.

12. *Amilotl, xouilin* and *xalmichi* are said to be the same, differing only in size and color. See n. 11.

13. *Cambarellus montezumae* in *ibid.*, p. 64.

14. *Rana esculenta, R. temporaria* in *ibid.*, p. 63.

15. *Larva de libélula* (dragonfly) in *ibid.*, p. 64.

they only set apart. No one took them to the fire; they strewed them all in the water.

And when this was done, when there had been eating, thereupon pulque was drunk. It was said: "There is cooling off at the oven; the old men cool off at the oven there at the Temple of Xiuhtecutli." And thus did they cool off at the oven: they sat about drinking pulque, they sat about singing until it was dark. Here ended, thus concluded [the time when] tamales stuffed with greens were eaten, or the eating of tamales stuffed with greens.

And when Izcalli arrived, when twenty days were counted, at that time Milintoc roasted something for himself. He likewise was [god of] fire. They also set up his image; it also was only a framework which they made.[16] They put a mask upon it made of [a mosaic of bits of] seashell. The lower part of the face was blackened, made black [with] black stones called *teotetl* [jet], and the face was striped horizontally with black mirror stones.

And upon his head they fitted a ball of yellow parrot feathers. His tuft of hair at the back of his head was made of turquoise-browed motmot feathers: they were his motmot-tuft of hair at the back of his head. And they set on him his fire-flowers, made of turkey hen neck feathers.[17] It was as if this flared up, and [it had] plucked [single] flaming red feathers; and they were set in order.[18] When they put it on, it was as if in truth it lay burning. And his vestments were made only of flaming red feathers — a flaming red feather cape which also trailed far.

And they laid before him tortillas made of uncooked ground maize,[19] or bracelet tortillas. They ground the maize, and when it was already cornmeal, then they moistened it with hot water; then it was sweetened. Then they offered the tortillas. Some were with shelled beans — cooked shelled beans, not raw shelled beans.

And when they had set Milintoc in place, then offerings were laid before him. The common folk, each one, [made offerings]; they went together each [with] five [tortillas]. A great quantity of bracelet tortillas were heaped up before him.

And in the same way [as for Xiuhtecutli] the youths [and] small boys were ranged in order; they

Auh in ie iuhquj, in ontlatlaqualoc, njmã ie ic tlaoano: mjtoa, texcalcevilo, texcalcevia in vevetque in vmpa iteupan xiuhtecutli: auh injc texcalcevia vctli, tlaoantoque, cujcatoque, çan iuh iooa, njcã tlamj ic tzonqujça, in oauhqujltamalli qualo, in anoço vauhqujltamalqualiztli.

Auh in onacic Izcalli, in jquac tlacempoalti: iquac motlaxqujaia in Milintoc, çan no ie in tletl: no qujtlaliaia ixiptla, çan no colotli in qujchoaia, conaquja ixaiac, tapachtli in tlachioalli, motentlilhuj, in tlilli muchioa, iehoatl in tliltic tetl, motocaiotiaia teutetl, yoan ixtlan tlatlaan, tezcapoctli ica:

auh in conaquja itzontecon, iehoatl in tozpololli in jcuexpal muchiuhtica, tziuhtli in tlachioalli, itziuhcuexpal, yoan contecatica itlachinolsuchiuh, totolquechtapalcatl in tlachioalli: iehoatl in juhquj xoxotla, yoan cueçalin in tlaxconolli: yoan tlavipantli: in jquac conteca iuhqujnma nelli tlatlatoc: auh in jtlaquẽ çã no cueçalin in tlachioalli, cueçalquemjtl, no veca vilantoc.

Auh ixpan qujmanaia vilocpalli, anoço macuextlaxcalli: tlaolli in qujteci: auh in ie iotextli, njmã catotonjlpachoa, çatepan tzopelia: njmã ic qujmana in tlaxcalli, cequj tlaoio, epaoaxtlaoio, amo xoxouhcatlaoio.

Auh in oqujtlalique Milintoc, mec tlamanalo ixpan, ceceniaca in maceoalti, ceniauh in mamacujlli, ixachi in jxpã motepeuhtitlalia, macuextlaxcalli:

auh çan no ivi in motecpana in telpopochti, in pipiltotonti, quauhtitech qujnpipiloa in cocoa, yoan

16. Corresponding Spanish text: "*hazian otra vez, estatua del dios, del fuego, de palillos, y circulos atados, vnos con otros.*"

17. Corresponding Spanish text: "*Tenja aquella corona adornado el chapitel, de vnas plumas muy negras, que resplandecian, de negras: que crian las gallinas, y los gallos en el pescueço.*" Cf. also *tapalcatl* in Dibble and Anderson, *Book XI*, p. 54.

18. Corresponding Spanish text: "*entrepuestas vnas pestañas, de plumas peladas, que parescian como pestañas de tafetan.*"

19. *uilocpalli*: "*una manera de tortas que llaman* uilocpalli, *de maíz molido, hechas sin cocer*" (Sahagún, Garibay ed., Vol. III, p. 57).

hung on sticks the serpents and all the small animals mentioned. They spread about offering them to the old men, and the old men spread about casting them into the fire. And the quite small serpents and the other quite small animals indeed burned; they charred. But the well-grown serpents, when they had been roasted, they went taking out. They spread about casting them on the hearth. There they were placed in a pile. Later the old men of the *calpulli* ate them.

And the youths [and] small boys then were spread about coming forth; [the old men] would offer them the bracelet tortillas. Then they each went. And when this was done, the bracelet tortillas were eaten.

Thereupon there was cooling off at the oven; the old men cooled off at the oven there at the Temple, the *calpulco*, of Milintoc. And the pulque makers, the lords' pulque makers, left with each [of the old men] a bowl of pulque, or a gourd, with each one, or a small earthenware jar with each one; quite freely, quite of their own accord, they left the pulque; they would pour it into a large earthenware vessel. And the old men sat drinking the pulque; they sat cooling off at the oven. They did not become drunk.

Enough of this.

And when the twenty [days] of Izcalli had passed, thereupon were established the five days of Nemontemi or Nenontemi.[20] They belonged nowhere. And the Nemontemi were indeed feared; they were held in awe. No one disputed with others, no one wrangled. And if anyone disputed with others, then it was said that they would continue it. And he who was born then they named Nemo. They said: "It is said that nothing is his desert, nothing becomes his merit. He will live in misery, he will live in poverty there on earth."[21]

And when it was the time of Izcalli, in the first year, and in the second year, and in the third year, nothing was done. But later, in the fourth year, a great [festival] was observed. Then died those [adorned as] Ixcoçauhqui, the impersonators of Xiuhtecutli, ceremonially bathed ones. Sometimes many died; sometimes not many.

And upon the morrow, when already [the feast of] Izcalli had dawned, the ceremonially bathed

in jxqujch omjto in ioiolime: qujmonmacatimanj, in vevetque: auh in vevetque, tleco qujmõmaiauhtimanj: auh in çan tepitoton cocoa, yoan in oc cequjntin çan tepitoton in ioiolitoton, vel tlatla, tecoltia: auh in veveintin cocoa, in õmoxcaque, qujmonantivi, tlecujllan qujnoallaztimanj, vncã motepeuhtitlalia, çatepan qujnqua in calpulhuevetque.

Auh in telpopochtin, in pipiltotonti, ic oalqujztimanj, cecen qujnoalmacatimanj, in macuextlaxcalli: njmã ic vivi. Auh in ie iuhquj in onqualoc, macuextlaxcalli:

njmã ie ic texcalcevilo, texcalcevia in vevetque in vncan iteupan, in jcalpolco Milintoc. Auh in tlachicque, in tecutlachicque, qujoalcaoa cecen caxitl in vctli, anoço cecen xicalli, anoço cecem apiloltepitotõ, çan in iollocopa, çan in iollotlamati, in concaoa vctli, qujoaltecatimanj apazco: auh tlaoãtoque in vevetque, texcalcevitoque, amo ivinti:

ie ixqujch.

Auh in onqujz y, cempoalli Izcalli, njmã ie ic oalmotlalia in macujlilhujtl in nemotemj, anoço nenontemj, acampouhquj: Auh in nemontemj, vel imacaxoia, mauhcaittoia, aiac teaoaia, acac maoaia: auh in aca vncã teaoa, qujlmach cenqujcuj. Auh in aqujn vncan tlacati qujtocaiotiaia. Nemo: qujtoaia, qujlmach atle ilhujtl, atle imaceoal muchioa, qujhiiovitinemjz, vmpa onqujztinemjz in tlalticpac.

Auh in jpan jn Izcalli: injc ce xivitl, yoan ic oxivitl, yoan iquexivitl, atle muchioaia: auh qujn ic nauhxivitl in moveichioa, qujniquac mjquja in Ixcoçauhque, in jxiptlaoan Xiuhtecutli: tlaaltilti, in quemã mjequjntin in mjquja, in quemã amo mjequjnti.

Auh in ie iuh muztla, in ie oallatvi Izcalli: in tlaaltilti, onxalaqui, qujmonxalaquja in vmpa tzom-

---

20. Corresponding Spanish text: "*estos cinco dias, a njngun dios, estan dedicados: y por esso, los llaman nemontemj.*" *Nenontemi* means "not filled" and refers to an incomplete ritual month of 20 days.

21. Cf. Dibble and Anderson, *Book VI*, p. 225.

ones entered the sand; they brought them to the sand there at Tzonmolco. The women carried everything, all their womanly array, and the men carried everything, all their array (as hath been told elsewhere). And they carried for them all their paper array; these various things went upon a wooden globe.

And when they had brought [the bathed ones] there, thereupon they arrayed them; they were arrayed. They put on them all their paper array. And when they were prepared and arrayed even as Ixcoçauhqui was arrayed, and the women were arrayed in the same manner, thereupon they climbed up to [the Temple of] Tzonmolco; they went in rows. And when they reached the top, thereupon they circled about the offering stone. Then once again they came down. They also came in rows.

And when they came descending, thereupon they took them to the *calpulco*. Then they took apart the various [vestments]; there [the victims] were gathered in a house; they guarded each of them well. They fastened the men with a rope about the waist; [guards] held them tightly [with it] when they [went forth to] urinate. And when midnight arrived, then there was the cutting of hair; they cut hair from [the crowns of] their heads as hath been told, as hath been published. And when hair had been cut from them, thereupon they had feathers pasted [on their heads]. They also pasted feathers on [the heads of] the women. And, as during the night, none of the stewards might sleep by day.[22]

And when day broke, when already it grew bright on the land, thereupon was burned [the bathed ones'] various [raiment] (as hath been told). When each of these had been burned, thereupon once again they entered indoors. But some did not burn their various belongings; they only gave them as gifts to others; they gave them to others.

And when it had dawned, then once again they were adorned. Thereupon they went there where they were to die; they were in order. When they reached there where they were to die, thereupon they danced, they sang; they made an effort. It was said that [they sang until] their voices cracked; it was said that they were hoarse.

And when the sun had already passed its zenith, thereupon descended [he who was arrayed as] Paynal; he led the captives here; he came at their head.

molco: in cioa muchi qujtquj, in jxqujch incioatlatquj: yoan in oqujchtin, muchi qujtquj in jxqujch intlatlatquj (in juh omjto cecnj): auh in jmamatlatquj, muchi qujmjtqujlia: quauhtzontapaioltica ieietiuh.

Auh in oqujmonaxitiq̃, njman ie ic qujnchichioa, techichioalo, qujmonaaquja in jxqujch imamatlatquj. Auh in ontecencaoaloc: auh injc muchichioa, ivin muchichioa Ixcoçauhquj: auh in cioa, çan ie no ivin muchichioa: njmã ie ic tleco in tzommolco, tecpantivi: auh in vmpanvetzito: njmã ie ic qujoaliaoaloa in techcatl: njmã ic no ceppa, oaltemo, no motecpãtivitze.

Auh in otemoco njmã ie ic qujnvica in calpulco, mec qujnxixitinja, vncan mocencaltilia, vel q'npipia: in oqujchtin qujnxillãmecaiotia, in jquac maxixa qujntitilinjtivi. Auh in oacic iooalnepantla: njmã ie ic tetzoncujoa, qujntzoncuj: in juh omjto, in juh omoteneuh: auh in ontetzoncujoac: njmã ie ic tepotonjlo, no qujnpotonja in cioa: auh in juh ceiooal, aocac ma ontlacacochi in tlapixque.

Auh in otlavizcalli moquetz, in ie tlatlalchipaoa: njmã ie ic motlatlatlatilia (in juh omjto) in ommotlatlatlatilique: njmã ie ic no ceppa calaquj in inieian: auh in aca amo qujmotlatlatilia in jaxca, çan qujtetlauhtia, çan qujtemamaca.

Auh in otlatvic, njmã ic no ceppa techichioalo: njmã ie ic vi in vmpa mjqujzque, motecpana: in onacique vmpa mjqujzque: njmã ie ic mjtotia, mocujca ellaquaoa: omach intozquj tzatzaian, omach ihiçaoacaque:

Auh in ie ommotzcaloa tonatiuh; njmã ie ic oaltemo in Paynal, qujnoaliacana, iacattivi in mamalti,

22. "*En aquella noche nadie dormja*" seems to be the corresponding Spanish text of the *Florentine Codex*. See, however, Angel María Garibay K., "Paralipómenos de Sahagún," *Tlalocan*, Vol. II, No. 2 (1946), p. 171, for a discussion of *tlaca* in composition.

They became the fundament of [the bathed ones]. When the captives died, then [they slew] the bathed ones, [the impersonators of] Ixcoçauhqui.

And when they had completely ended the slaying, when it was so, [then] all the rulers, the lords, those much to be revered, then already were spread about; they just stood about waiting. They were arrayed. Moctezuma led them. He had put on the turquoise ruler's miter, the [symbol of] rulership.

And all put in place the turquoise nose rods and inserted the turquoise ear plugs, indeed of turquoise; but some were only made of wood painted like turquoise. And they put on the sleeveless jackets, the turquoise [blue] jackets, well ornamented, and the Xolotl jewel like a little dog which went with it. These were made of paper painted turquoise [blue]. And they had their paper breechclouts painted with stripes. And these were painted only with black.

And in their hands wooden staves went lying; they were small, shaped like weaving sticks, painted in two colors — red above and chalky below. On either side they grasped a paper incense bag. Thereupon they came down [from the temple]; they came dancing.

And when they had come descending, then they went encircling [the courtyard]. Only four times did they go encircling. And when they had danced, then there was dispersing on the part of each one; there was dispersing of each person. Thereupon there was entering the palace; there was going into the palace. And of this it was said: "There is lordly dancing; the lords dance the lordly dance." It was the privilege only of the rulers that they should dance the lordly dance. This was done every four years.

So it was.

It was still early morning when was begun the piercing of the ear [lobes], when they pierced the ear [lobes] of the small children. And they pasted them with yellow parrot feathers and with soft [white] feathers which went mingled with the yellow ones.

And for a gift they made pinole.[23] And the mothers sought out some brave warrior, perhaps a seasoned warrior or a leader of youths who might wish to be as a parent, thus to become [their children's] uncle. Also some sought out a woman who might be as an aunt.

in impepechoan muchioa: in ommjcque mamalti: njmã iehoã in tlaaltilti in ixcoçauhq̃.

Auh in oncentlanque mjquj in ie iuhquj: auh in jxqujchtin tlatoque, in tetecutin in cenca maviztililonj, ie ic manj, ça qujchixtimanj omocencauhq̃, qujniacana in Motecuçoma: ocontlali xiuhvitzolli, in tlatocaiotl:

yoan contlalia iacaxivitl in muchinti, yoã conaquja xiuhnacochtli, vel xivitl. Auh in cequjntin çan quavitl in tlachioalli, tlaxiuhicujlolli yoan cõmaquja xicolli, xiuhtlalpilli, vel tlaiecchioalli, yoã in xolocozquj iuhqujn chichiton ic ietiuh; amatl in tlachioalli, tlaxiuhicujlolli, yoan iamamaxtli, acaxilquj injc tlacujlolli: auh çan tlilli injc tlacujlolli.

Auh in immac oonotiuh quavitl, çan tepitoton tlatzotzopaztectli, chictlapãquj; in aco chichiltic, auh in tlanj tiçaio: cecectlapal qujtzitzquja amaxiqujpilli; njmã ie ic oaltemo mjtotitivitze.

Auh in otemoco: njmã ie ic tlaiaoaloa, çã nappa in tlaiaoaloa: auh in ommjtotique mec nexixitinjlo, texixitinjlo, njmã ie ic calacoa in tecpan tlatecpanoloz. Auh in iehoatl y, moteneoa: netecujtotilo, motecujtotia in tetecutin, çan inneixcavil catca in tlatoque, in motecujtotiaia: nauhxiuhtica in muchioaia;

ie iuhquj.

Oc vecaiooan in peoaloia in tenacazxapotlaloia in qujnnacazxapotla pipiltotonti: yoan qujnpotonja, tocivitica, yoan itlachcaioio neneliuhtiuh in toztli.

Auh in ventli in qujchioaia pinolli: auh in tenanoan cequj temooaia, iehoatl in tiacauh aço tequjoa, anoço telpochiaquj iuhqujn tlanenequja impilhoaque injc Tetlatizque: no cequj temoa cioatl in teavitiz,

---

23. The *Real Palacio MS* here contains the line *yeuatl yn chinampinolli*, which probably identifies the *pinolli* as ground dried maize and chía seeds.

They gave gifts to the man; they gave him perchance a tawny cape or a coyote fur cape. And also the woman was given gifts; they also gave gifts to her.

And when there had been the piercing of ear [lobes], thereupon they took each of the children to singe them. They laid a fire, they made a fire; indeed much incense did they spread on the fire.

And hence was it said: "They are singed." The old men of the *calpulli* were spread about taking the small children; they were spread about dedicating them over the fire. Then they were spread about giving them uncles and aunts. And it was as if the children kept crying out, it was as if they whimpered. Then they went each to his home.

And when they had gone to their homes, thereupon there was eating, there was drinking on the part of each one.

And when the singing and dancing were begun in the temple, it was noon. Then once again there was going to the temple. The uncles [and] the aunts carried the children. Those who carried things went with the pulque; what was poured they carried in small gourds, some in earthen jars. And when they went to arrive, there was singing there. Then was quieted the dance; they carried the children on their backs. There they were spread about giving them pulque; they went giving it to them; they gave it to one another.

And for drinking, for drinking the pulque, there were quite small drinking vessels; only exceedingly small ones. And all were giving pulque to the small children.

Hence this was named "pulque drinking for children."

And in the evening, when there had been ceasing on the part of each, there was going on the part of each to their several homes. And when there had been going on the part of each to their several homes, once again they danced in their courtyards. All the kin [of those who celebrated], each one, drank pulque — the revered old men, the revered old women.

Here ended Izcalli.

And for this reason was [the feast] named Izcalli [The Growing]: at this time they lifted by the neck all the small children. It was said that thus they

qujtlauhtiaia: in oqujchtli in qujmaca, aço quappachtilmatli, anoço coioichcatilmatli: auh no motlauhtiaia, no qujtlauhtiaia in Cioatl.

Auh in ontenacazxapotlaloc; njmã ie ic qujnvivica, in qujnchichinozque pipiltotõti: qujtlalia tletl, tletlaliaia, vel mjec in copalli contepeoa tleco.

Auh injc moteneoa techichinolo in calpulhuevetque, qujnoalantimanj in pipiltotonti tleco qujmonjauhtimanj: njman ic qujnoalmacatimanj in tetlati, in teaviti: auh in pipiltotonti iuhqujn tlatzatzatzi, iuhqujn tlacaoacatimanj: njman ic iatimanj in inchachan:

auh in oniaque inchan, njmã ie ic tlatlaqualo, haatlioa.

Auh in opeoaloc teupan in ie cujco in ie netotilo, nepantla tonatiuh: njmã ic no ceppa viloa in teupan: in Tetlaoan, in teavioan qujnvivica in pipiltotonti, in tlatlatquj ietiuh in vctli, in tlatoiaoalli xicalhujcoltica in qujitquj, cequj apiloltica: auh in oacito vncã cujco: njmã ie ic ommomana in mitotia, qujnmamama in pipiltotonti: vncã qujmomacatimanj, qujmomacatinemj in vctli: netech qujmomamaca.

Auh injc quja injc tlaoanaia, in tlaoancaxitl, çan tepiton, çã tetepiton: auh muchintin qujntlaoantiaia in pipiltotonti:

ie injc moteneoa, pillaoano.

Auh ie teutlac in necacaoaloia, viviloa in techachan: auh in onviviloac techachan, ie no ceppa mjtotia in jmjtoalco, muchintin tlatlaoana in tehoaniolque, in veventzitzin, in jlamatzitzin.

Oncan tlamj in Jzcalli.

Auh injc moteneoa Jzcalli: vncã qujnquechanaia in jxqujchtin pipiltotonti: qujlmach, ic qujmjzcalloana: qujmjzcalana, injc iciuhca quauhtiazque.

grasped them for growth; they grasped them for growth that they might quickly grow tall.

Enough. Here ended, here concluded the feast of Izcalli.

Ie ixqujch njcan tzonqujça, njcan tlamj in jlhujtl Jzcalli.

Thirty-eighth Chapter, which telleth of the feast which was named Uauhquiltamalqualiztli [The Eating of Tamales Stuffed With Amaranth Greens], which was celebrated at the time it was the tenth [day] of the aforesaid month; and when it was [this time], they celebrated a feast for him who was their god, whose name was Ixcoçauhqui.

Izcalli and Izcalli tlami: these verily are placed in the month of January, after there have been eight days, already after eight days, after the eighth day. When it was this [time], tamales stuffed with amaranth greens were eaten.[1] Everywhere [the custom] was general; it was everywhere; nowhere was it left out. In each house, and in each city, they indeed consumed two [tamales] when there was the making of tamales stuffed with amaranth greens, when there were tamales stuffed with amaranth greens. And there was giving of them to one another, there was giving of them to one another on the part of each one. In this manner was there the giving of them: there was giving in company; there was giving among themselves; there was giving to friends; there was giving to those whom they knew. There was no giving in ill will; there was giving in gladness.

And she who first cooked her tamales stuffed with amaranth greens then went to give them to [those of] houses like hers, her neighbors, those who lived in nearby houses. And first she made offerings for her distant kin.

And when this was done, when she had given them to each of the others, then they sat down to eat their tamales stuffed with amaranth greens. They were arranged in a circle. They rounded up, gathered together, brought together, assembled their children. This formed the family.

And first they made an offering to the fire; they laid five tamales stuffed with amaranth greens before the fire. These were in a wooden vessel; they went covered up. Then they set them in place, they laid them as offerings for each of their dead, there where they each lay buried.

Injc cempoalli on caxtolli omei capitulo: itechpa tlatoa in jlhujtl, in moteneoaia: Oauhqujltamalqualiztli, in muchioaia in jpan ic tlamatlacti in metztli in tlacpac omjto: auh in jquac y, qujlhujqujxtiliaia, in inteouh catca, in jtoca Ixcoçauhquj.

Izcalli, yoan Izcalli tlamj: inin vel ipan motlalia in metztli henero, ie iuh chicueilhujtl manj, ie ichicueilhujoc, ie iuh chicueilhujtica: in jquac in, oauhqujltamalli qualoia: novian qujtzacutimãca, ipanoca, acã cavia: in cecencalpan, yoan in cecemaltepetl ipan, vel ontetlamja in neoauhqujltamalhujlo, in neoauhqujltamaltilo: auh nepanotl nemacoia, nepanotl nemamacoia, ic netlatlamacoia, necepãmacoia, nenetech macoia, necnjuhmacoia, neiximatcamacoia, amo netlavelmacoia, nepaccamacoia:

in aqujn achto oicucic ioauhqujltamal njman ic iauh qujmacaz in jcalpo, in jcalecapo, in jcalnaoac tlacatl: yoan in vecapa ivaniolquj, achto contonaltiaia.

Auh in ie iuhquj, in onoviampa qujtemamacac njmã motlalia in qujquazque, in inoauhqujltamal, moiaoaloa, qujncemololoa qujnnechicoa, qujncentlalia qujntecpichoa in impilhoã inin cencaltia.

Auh achtopa contlamanjlia in tletl, tlecujlixquac cõmana in oauhqujltamalli macujltetl, quauhcaxtica mantiuh, mollotiuh, çatepan cecentetl q'ntlatlaliliaia, qujnmamanjlia in immjccaoan, in vncã totoctoque:

---

1. *Uauhquiltamalqualiztli*: cf. Arthur J. O. Anderson and Charles E. Dibble: *Florentine Codex, Book I, The Gods* (Santa Fe: School of American Research and University of Utah, 2nd ed. rev., 1970), p. 29, n. 84. Much of the material in this chapter is discussed also in the previous one (Izcalli).

Thereupon they ate. They sat burning themselves, each one; they each sat sweating; indeed they were gleaming with the heat. What they ate went smoking; what they gladly ate they each gulped down, they went gulping it down; they ate panting; they sat burning their mouths.

And the [corn] husks of the tamales stuffed with amaranth greens [in which they were wrapped] they just laid apart, elsewhere. They strewed them in the water. And no one could taste the husks. Because of this they took care that none be scorched, burned, fall in the fire.

And they were eaten in no more than one day. By night they were each done; all were finished. They left nothing for the next day.

And when it grew dark, the old men [and] the old women drank pulque; only they. It was said: "They cool off at the oven."

And when this [was done], they set up the image of the fire [god] Ixcoçauhqui, Xiuhtecutli, Tlalxictentica, Cueçaltzin, Nauhyoueue. They gave it human form, they gave it a body of amaranth seed [dough]. They who did it, whose office it was, were the men of the *calpulli* temple known as Tzonmolco,[2] especially those who worshipped [fire] as a god.[3]

And when twenty days had passed, it was said to be Izcalli tlami. The bather of slaves at this time displayed to the people, made known to the people, set up before the people the one who would be his bathed one, the slave whom he had bought, who would become the impersonator of Ixcoçauhqui. At this time he adorned him; he placed on him all of Ixcoçauhqui's array. Hence it was said, "The bather gathereth [his wealth]."

And for this reason he was called the bather of a slave: he continually bathed [the slave] with warm water all the time he was going to die, all the time that [the bathed one] went knowing that there was his tribute of death at its appointed time when he would die at the time of Tlacaxipeualiztli.

And before he died, much did the bather of slaves esteem him; he paid much attention to him. He

njmã ie ic tlaqua, muchichinotoque, in jitonjtoque, vel totontlapetztic ipotoqujztiuh in qujqua, in qujpaccaqua tlatlaltequj, ontlaltectivi, neneciuhtoque, cocociuhtoque:

auh in jzoaio, oauhqujltamalli, çan nõqua, cecnj qujtlaliaia, atlan cõtepeoaia: auh aiac vel qujpalooaia in izoatl: ipampa ic momalhujaia inic amo aca mochichinoz, motlatiz, tleco onvetziz.

Auh çan vel cemjlhujtl in qualoia: in ie iooa otlatlatlan, moch tlamja, aoctle qujmocavia in jmuztlaioc.

Auh in oiooac tlatlaoana in vevetque in jlamatque, çanjoque: mjtoaia, Texcalcevia.

Auh in jquac y, qujtlaliaia in jxiptla tletl Ixcoçauhquj, Xiuhtecutli, Tlalxictentica, Cueçaltzin, Nauhioveve, tzooalli in qujtlacatlaliaia, in qujnacaiotiaia: iehoan qujchioaia in jtech povia calpoleque, moteneoa: Tzommulca, oc cenca iehoan in qujmoteutiaia.

Auh injc onaci cempoalilhujtl: mjtoa, Izcalli tlamj: in tealtianj, iquac qujteittitia, qujteiximachtia, teixpan qujquetza in jtlaaltil iez, in oqujcouh tlacotli: in jxiptla muchioa Ixcoçauhquj, iquac ic qujchichioa itech qujtlalilia in jxqujch in jnechichioal Ixcoçauhquj ic mjtoaia, tlaixnextia in tealtianj:

auh injc mjtoa, tealtianj: in jtlaaltil muchipa caltia, atotonjltica in jxqujch cavitl mjqujtiuh, in jxqujch cavitl qujmatitiuh in vncã imjqujztequjpã in jtlapoalpan: in mjqujz ipan tlacaxipeoaliztli.

Auh in aiamo mjquj, cenca qujmavizmatia, quj-

2. Tzonmolco: temple of the fire god; also one of the districts of Tenochtitlan. The temple is enumerated in the appendix on the buildings of the temple square as the sixty-fourth building. Cf. Sahagún, Garibay ed., Vol. I, p. 240.

3. The preceding Nahuatl text is not in the *Real Palacio MS*. The Nahuatl text for the remainder of this chapter appears on fols. 123, 124, 125 of the *Real Palacio MS*. These three folios have been removed from their correct sequence and placed at the beginning of Book II. The Nahuatl text is the same in the *Florentine* and *Real Palacio* manuscripts. However, the sequence of folios in the *Real Palacio MS* is fol. 125, fol. 123, fol. 124. This sequence is evidently correct as the notation, at the bottom of the folios, labels them C.ii; C.iii; C.iiii.

regaled him; he gave him things; all good was the food which he gave him.

And a pleasure girl became his guardian. She constantly amused him; she caressed him; she joked with him; she made him laugh; she gratified him; she took pleasure on his neck; she embraced him. She deloused him, she combed his hair, she smoothed his hair. She banished his sorrows. And when already it was the bathed one's time to die, the pleasure girl took all. She rolled up, she bundled up all the bathed one's belongings, each of what [the bather] had clothed him in, had placed on him when he had sent him as a messenger; [the things] with which he had lived in pretense, had gone with head high, had lived at ease, had gone about drunk, had indeed lived in pride.

And for this reason was [the time] named Izcalli tlami [The Growing is Achieved]: they took by the neck, they hung high all the small children. Thus was it said: "They take them for growth; they grasp them to grow, so that they will each quickly grow tall; they will develop; they will grow up."

And as for the magueys, they divided their cores, they split their cores, they broke up their cores, they exposed their cores. And as for the cacti, they cleaned them, they pruned their branches, because thus they would develop quickly; they would revive, they would grow.

And at this time of Izcalli, then it also came to pass, every fourth year, that there was the bringing out of the children, that there was pulque drinking by the children. And then the rulers danced the lordly dance along with their noblemen. And they put on their wigs of long locks of hair; they were head pieces made of long hair; they covered them with many green stones. [The hair] fell, verily, to the rulers' waists.

And for this reason was it said that there was bringing out of the children: the children's fathers [and] mothers first sought out a woman [and] a man whom they summoned to bring [the children] to the *calmecac* at a place called Tezcacoac. It was said that they would be their uncle [and] their aunt; they became uncle [and] aunt.

And not their kin did they take; only their friends. To those whom they took, those whom they chose, they gave gifts. They laid out capes, breechclouts for us men; in the same way for a woman they laid out her skirt, her shift.

çeçēmatia in tealtianj, qujtlanenectia qujtlacuecue-pilia: muchi qualli tlaqualli in qujmacaia:

auh ce avienj, in jtepixcauh muchioaia: muchipa caviltia, caavilia, qujcamanalhuja, qujvetzqujtia, quj-quequeloa, iquechtlan âaquj, qujquechnaoa, caate-mja, qujtzitziquaoazvia, qujpepepetla, qujtlaoculpo-poloa: auh in jquac ie imjqujzpan tlaaltilli: in avienj moch concuj, ontlacemololoa, concemololoa in jx-quich in jtlatquj tlaaltilli: in oqujquequemja, in jtech oqujtlatlaliaia in oqujtitlanja, in jpã oiztlacattinenca, oaquetztinēca otlamattinenca, omjvintitinēca omovel-itztinenca.

Auh injc mjtoa Jzcalli, tlami yn ixquichtin pipilto-tonti, muchintin qujnquechaana, qujmacopiloa: ic mjtoa qujmizcalloana, qujmizcalaana, ynic iciuhca quaquauhtiezque, manazque, mooapaoazque:

yoã in metl qujiolloxeloa, qujiollotzaiana, qujiol-lotlapana, qujiollotoma: auh yn nopalli qujtlaiecti-lia, qujmatepeoa, ipampa ynic iciuhca manaz, moz-caltiz, mooapaoaz.

Auh yn ipan y, Izcalli, no vncan muchioaia, ynic nauhxiuhtica nepilquixtiloia, pillaoanoia: yoan vn-can motecujtotiaia in tlatoque, yoan yn inpillooan: yoan contlaliaia yntzonpilinal, centlamantli, tzon-calli catca, viiac in tzontli ic tlachioalli, qujchachal-chiuhiotiaia, vel incujtlacaxiuhiã vetzia in tlatoque.

Auh ynic mjtoa nepilqujxtilo, yn jxqujchtin pipil-totonti, yn jntahoan, yn jnnahoan, achtopa qujnte-moliaia, in qujnvicazque calmecac, itocaiocan tezca-coac ce cioatl, ce oqujchtli in qujnotzaia, mjtoa: qujntlatia qujnmavitia, tetlati, teaviti:

auh amo inoaniolque in qujmanaia, çan incoapan in tlaanaia, in tlapepenaia, qujntlauhtiaia: tilmatli, maxtlatl, contlaliliaia in toqujchtin: no ivi in cioatl, icue, ivipil contlalilia

At midnight they took [the children] to the *calmecac*. There they perforated [the lobes of] their ears; they pierced [the lobes of] their ears. [The children] yelled [as] the pointed bone thus pierced [the lobes of] their ears. They there drew through a thread of unspun cotton; they bound it to them there. It was as if the small children raised a yell, kept crying out, raised a cry of weeping. And they pasted their heads with yellow parrot feathers, with soft downy feathers.

And the women who became aunts were pasted with red feathers, but only on their legs and their arms. And they went covering themselves with their paper flowers; they were called their lordly flowers.

When they had perforated their ear [lobes], then they took them each to their several homes. There they sat watching over them; they sat in vigil, they kept vigil, they sat awake; they sat awaiting the time dawn would break, the time that the light would arise, the time that the barn swallow would sing.

And when dawn broke, thereupon there was activity, there was eating, there was drinking on the part of each one. Thereupon the old men, the men of the *calpulli*, the singers sat in the courtyard while they sang for [the children]. Then they went carrying the small children on their backs. And [a child] who was already a little large his uncle and his aunt went holding by his hand. There they made him dance; they went making dance motions. And when there was still a little daylight, when the sun hung low, there was gathering together at Tezcacoac. There the dancing, the singing continued — the songs, in all, spreading the sound, crashing like waves.

And there began the giving, the giving of pulque to the people. Everyone took his pulque there; it was taken with one in earthen jars. There was giving there to each other; there was continual giving to one another; there was continual returning, there was continual reciprocating. There they gave pulque to all the small children — those who were already a little large and those who still lay in the cradle. They only made them taste it. Indeed everyone already mature was drunk; it was indeed evident that pulque was drunk.

There was no awe [of the pulque]. It was as if it bubbled up. It was not precious. It was as if it gleamed. It reached the ground. The pulque ran like water.

ioalnepantla in qujnvicaia calmecac, vmpa qujnnacazxapotla, qujnnacazcoionja pipitzcatiuh in omjtl injc qujcoionja innacaz, potonquj icpatl in vmpa conqujxtia, vncã qujmonjlpilia iuhqujn tlatzatziztleoa, tlatzatzatzi, tlachoqujztleoa in pipiltzitzinti, yoan tocivitica tlachcaiotica qujnpotonjaia in jmjcpac:

auh in teaviti cioa, çanjo imjcxic, yoã inmac in mopotonjaia tlapalivitica, yoan imamaxochiuh contecativia: mjtoa, intecuxochiuh.

In jquac oqujmõnacaxxapotlaque, njmã ic qujnoalhujujca in inchachan, vncan qujchieltitoque ixtoçotoque, toçotoque tlatlatviltitoque, qujchixtoque in quenman tlatviz, in quenman tlatlavilotleoaz, in quenmã tlatoz cujcujtzcatl.

Auh in otlatvic, njmã ie ic tlatlacivi, tlatlaqualo, aatlioa: njmã ie ic motlalia in vevetque calpoleque, cujcanjme, in jtoalco in qujncujcatiaia, vncã qujnmamatinemj in pipiltotonti: auh in ie achi qualton imatitech cantinemj in jtla, yoan iavi, vncan qujtotia, tlaiiauhtinemj: auh in ie achi tlaca in vmmopilo tonatiuh, vncan oalcenqujxoa in tezcacoac: vncã mocenmana in netotiliztli, in cujqujztli, cepã caoantimomana, xaxamacatimanj in cujcatl:

Auh vncã peoa in nemaco, in temaco vctli, muchi tlacatl yioc vmpa qujtquj, vmpa qujvica, tetlan tlaano, apiloltica, vncan netech nemaco nepanotl nemamaco, necuecuepililo, necuecuepcaiotililo, vncan qujntlaoãtia in jxqujchtin pipiltotonti in ie achi qualtoton, yoan in oc coçolco onoque, çan qujntlapaloltiaia, vel muchi tlacatl ivinti in ie veveitlaca, vel neixmanalo in tlaoano:

amo nemauhtilo, iuhqujn tlapopoçoca, amo tlaçotli iuhqujn tlapepetlaca, tlalpã aci, iuhqujn atl nemja vctli,

And they carried their drinking vessels called *tzitzicuiltecomatl*. They had three feet; they had corners on four sides.

It was as if there were reddening of faces, as if there were a din, as if there were panting, as if there were glazing of the eyes, going in disorder, quarreling, going from one side to the other, disturbances; it was as if there were repulsing, crowding together, trampling, elbowing. There was taking of one another by the hand, there was continual taking of one; there was continual persisting, there was continual pride. There was going with arm about the neck as there was entering of their several homes on the part of each one.

Thus was it said: "Indeed it is verily the feast day of pulque; indeed there was the drinking of pulque by the children."

And thus concluded, thus ended Izcalli. Then were established, were set in the Nemontemi, five days for which there were no day-names, which no longer belonged, which were no longer counted. Greatly were they feared; greatly were they held in awe.

For they were only unfortunate; there was no purpose there; nothing came forth; there was misfortune. For indeed there was no desert there, no merit; there was only misery there, poverty, purposelessness, misfortune, a life of woe.

And if one were then born, there was great fear of it, there was ignoring of it. And if it were a man, they named him Nemon, Nentlacatl, Nenquizqui. Nowhere was he counted, nowhere did he belong. He was a profitless man. And if it were a woman, she was a profitless woman.

And when it was this time, nothing was done. The palaces, the courts of justice were empty; no suits were judged. There was only staying indoors. No one swept with a broom; they only fanned [the dust] with a fan or the flight feather of a turkey hen, the primary feather of a turkey hen; or they repeatedly beat, they swept with a cape.

And none could then wrangle; there were strong deterrents to the people; there were very strict commands given one; there were stringent commands given one; people were charged not to wrangle. Nor did anyone sleep during the day. Then it was said to them: "Thou wilt do [so] always."

Nor should anyone fall stumbling, or trip, or stumble. Carefully was there walking. And to one

yoan intlaoancax qujtquja, itoca tzicujltecomatl: ei icxi, nauhcampa nacace,

iuhqujn tlaichichiliui, iuhqujn tlaçomoca, iuhqujn tlacica, iuhqujn tlaixmetzivi, tlaixnelivi, neixnanamjco, tlaixmalacachivi, tlaixmoiaoa, iuhqujn nexoxocolo, nepopotzolo nequequeçalo, netotopeoalo nematitech neaano, neaanalo, nececenquetzalo, nececenmacho, nequechnaoalotiuh in cacalacoa techachan:

ic mjtoa ca nel ilhujo in vctli, ca pillaoano.

Auh injc ontzonqujça, injc ontlamj Izcalli: njmã oalmotlalia, oalmotema in Nemontemj: macujlilhujtl in aoctle itoca tonalli, in aocmo vmpovi, in aocmo vmpouhquj cenca imacaxoia, cenca mauhcaittoia:

iehica ca çan nêqujzquj, vncã nenenqujxtilo, atle vnqujxoa, nenencolo, nenenencolo: iehica ca atle vncan ca ilhujlli, mâceoalli, can vncan icnoiotl, netolinjliztli, nenqujzcaiotl, nenqujçaliztli, âoneoatinemjliztli.

Auh in aqujn vncan tlacatia, cenca tlamauhcaittililoia, tlatêmachililoia: auh intla oqujchtli qujtocaiotiaia Nemõ, nentlacatl, nenqujzquj, acan ompouhquj acã, ompovi nenoqujch. Auh intla cioatl: Nencioatl.

Auh in jquac y, atle aioaia, çan cactimãca in tecpan in teccali, amo tecutlatoloia, çan calonooaia; aiac tlachpanaia, ochpaoaztica: çan tlaiecapeviloia, ecaceoaztica, anoço totolmamaztica, totolaavitztica, anoço tlavivitequja, tlapopovaia tilmatica:

yoan aiac vel vncan maoaia, cenca tetlacaoaltiloia, cêca tetlaquauhnaoatiloia, tetepitznaoatiloia, tecocoltiloia injc aiac maoaz: ano ac cemjlhujcochia: vncan teilhujloia. Centicujz:

ano ac vel motlavitequja, moticujnjaia, motepotlamjaia; nematca, nenemoaia: auh in aqujn motepotla-

171

who stumbled they said: "Thou hast been affected by the Nemontemi; thou hast gotten it all. Be careful."

And if at this time anyone took sick, was ill, everyone said: "He hath taken sick. Nevermore will he go forth; no more may he hope that perhaps he will recover." No longer was there doubt; no longer was there hope of it.

And if anyone yet escaped [death], no longer was it of someone's notice, no longer was it of someone's conversation. It was said: "Indeed he through whom there is life was compassionate; he only acted of his own accord; he did it on his own account."

No longer was it customary that indeed there should be courage, that there should be an effort made. His kin forgot him; indeed they laid him on the ground. No longer was there leaving such a place. Somehow he got up, caught his breath. For the time when the days of Nemontemi began terrified one.

Indeed nothing was his day sign; indeed nothing was his name. Therefore no one could then practice medicine, heal one, read [the day signs] for one. For in truth [the days] were not counted; nothing was their number in all of these four [*sic*] days.

mjaia: qujlhujaia. Otimonemovi, ocenticcujc, ma ximjmati.

Auh in aqujn ipan y, cocoliztli qujcuja mococooaia: muchi tlacatl qujtoaia, Cencocolizcuj, aocmo qujçaz, aocmo motemachiz, in aço patiz, aocmo teumeiolloti, aocmo itech ca netemachilli:

auh intla aca oc maqujça, aoc ac itlamatian aoc ac itlatoaian: mjtoa. Ca ça oicnotlama, in jpalnemoanj, ça oqujmonomavili, oqujmoioculili:

aocmo iuh catca teiollo, ca oica netlapaloloc, neellaquaoaloc, oqujxcauhque injoaiolque, ca oiqujtecaque: aocmo iuhcan qujxooaiã inon oquĕteltzin, meoatiquetz, inon oihiio qujcujc, ca temauhti in jpan opeuh ilhujtl Nemõtemj:

ca atle itonal, ca atle itoca: ipampa aiac vel vncã ticitoca, tepatia, tetlapovia: ca nel amo vmpouhquj, atle ipooallo in jzqujlhujtl navilhujtl.

APPENDIX

Apendiz del segundo libro

TEMPLE OF UITZILOPOCHTLI

COATEPETL. 1.

Uitzilopochtli's feast came three times a year, when they used to celebrate his feast day.

The first time was [in the month] named Panquetzaliztli. And this was when there ascended [to the top of the pyramid], together, this Uitzilopochtli [and another] named Tlacauepan Cuexcotzin.[1] And when they took the image of this Uitzilopochtli up, indeed all the offering priests, the youths carried it in their arms. And the image of Uitzilopochtli was [made] only of amaranth seed [dough]. It was very large; it was as tall as a man.

And the name of the second one was Tlacauepan Cuexcotzin. His image also was [made] only of amaranth seed [dough].

And when the image of Uitzilopochtli was made, when it took human form, it was there at a place called Itepeyoc. And the second one, Tlacauepan Cuexcotzin, was made, took human form, there at a place called Uitznauac *calpulco*. And during one night they gave them form, they gave them human form.

And when it dawned, they were already shapen. Thereupon offerings were laid before them. And when it was already afternoon, thereupon there was dancing, there was going round [in procession]. And when the sun had entered his house [at sunset], they took [the figures] up [to the top of the pyramid]. And after they had gone to set them in place, thereupon they descended. [The images] were there all night. And the offering priests who guarded them were called Yiopoch.

And when it dawned, thereupon Paynaltzin came forth, who was himself the representative of Uitzilopochtli. [A priest] carried him in his arms. And the image of Paynal was only of wood [formed] to go as a man. And he who bore it in his arms was titled Topiltzin Quetzalcoatl; he was richly bedight with his feather device from shoulder to flank. And the image of Paynal was thus adorned: it had its hummingbird disguise, its *anecuyotl* device, its

VITZILOBUCHTLI ITEUCAL

COATEPETL. 1.

In vitzilobuchtli, expa in qujçaia ilhujuh, in qujlhujqujxtiliaia, yn ipan ce xivitl.

Injc cepa ipan in mjtoaia panquetzaliztli: auh ynin vncan acoqujçaia, in iehoatl vitzilobuchtli, ym omextin yn jtoca Tlacauepan cuexcochtzin. Auh ynic qujtlecaujaja in iehoatl vitzilobuchtli ixiptla, vel ixqujch in tlamacazquj, in telpuchtli in qujnapaloaia: auh yn ixiptla catca vitzilobuchtli, çan tzoalli, cenca vey, cennequetzalli.

Auh ynjc vme in jtoca Tlacauepan, cuexcotzin, çan no tzoalli in jxiptla catca.

Auh in muchioaia, in tlacatia Vitzilobuchtli ixiptla: vmpa yn itocaiocan Itepeioc: auh ynic vme, in tlacauepan cuexcotzin, vmpa in muchioaia, in tlacatia, itocaiocan Vitznaoac calpulco: auh ceniooal in qujmicuxitiaia, in qujntlacatiliaia.

Auh in otlatujc, ie otlacatque: njman ie ic ymixpan tlamanalo: auh in ie teutlac, njman ie ic netotilo, necocololo: auh çan ic oncalaquj, in tonatiuh, in qujntlecaujaia: auh yn oqujmontlalito, njman ie ic oaltemoa, vmpa ceioal cate: yoan qujnpiaia tlamacazque, yn jntoca Iiopuch:

Auh yn otlatujc, niman ie ic oalqujça, in paynaltzin, in çan no ie yxiptla Vitzilobuchtli, qujnapaloa: auh yn ixiptla paynal, çan quaujtl tlacaietiuh: auh in qujnapaloa, itoca topiltzin Quetzalcoatl: cenca mochichioaia, yiapanecaiouh: auh yn ixiptla paynal ynjc muchichioaia, yvitzitzilnaoal, yianecuiouh, yteucujtlapã, ychalchiuhcozquj: auh yn icujtlapan pilcatiuh, iehoatl in cujtlatezcatl, çan muche in teuxivitl:

---

1. Cuexcotzin: the name is so spelt in the corresponding Spanish text.

golden banner, its green stone necklace. And over the small of its back went hanging the mirror device for the back, all fine turquoise. And he who led [the god] went carrying his serpent staff covered with turquoise.

And when [the priest with] Paynal came to Teotlachco, then there was the slaying [of sacrificial victims] before him. Those who died were [both] named Amapantzin; both were only impersonators. And many more captives [also] died.

And when there had been the slaying, thereupon Paynal was taken in procession. He arrived in Tlatelolco, and when he had arrived, thereupon the common folk met him; they offered him incense and beheaded many quail for him. And thereupon they started, they reached Popotlan; similarly the common folk met him; they offered him incense and beheaded many quail. And then again they started, they reached Chapultepec; similarly the common folk met them; they offered [the god] incense and beheaded many quail for him. Thereupon they started, they reached Tepetocan; the common folk also met them, offered him incense, and also beheaded many quail. Thereupon they started forth, they reached here at Acachinanco; the common folk also met them; they offered him incense; they also beheaded many quail.

Thereupon the insignia started forth. And when the insignia came to arrive, thereupon they mounted to the top of Coatepetl, where was [the image of] Uitzilopochtli. And when they had gone up, thereupon they laid out the blood banner. When there had been circling about, thereupon they descended.

auh in qujiacana qujtqujtiuh ycoatopil, xivitl ic tlaqujmjlolli.

Auh yn onacic, in teutlachco in paynal, njman ie ixpã mjcoa: iehoantin in miquja yn jntoca Amapantzitzin, çan vmẽtin teixiptlaoan: auh ieh cenca mjequjntin in mamalti miquja.

Auh yn onmjcoac, njman ie ic vnpeoa, yn tlaiaoaloz Paynal: vmpa onaci in tlatilulco, auh yno onacic, njman ie ic qujnamjquj in maceoalli, qujtlenamaqujlia yoan miec çolin qujcotonjliaia. Auh njman ie ic vmpeoa, onaci in popotlan, çan no iuh qujnamjq'a in maçeoalli, qujtlenamaqujlia: yoan miec çolin qujcotonaia. Auh njman ie no cuel vmpeoa, vmpa onaci in chapultepec, çan no iuh qujnamjquj- in maceoalti, qujtlenamaqujlia: yoan miec çolin qujcotonjlia. Niman ie ic vmpeoa onaci in tepetocan: no qujnamjquj in maceoalli, qujtlenamaqujlia, yoan no mjec çolin qujcotona. Niman ie ic oalpeoa, valaci in vncan acachinãco: no qujnamjquj in maceoalti, qujtlenamaqujlia, no mjec çolin qujcotona.

Niman ie ic oalpeoa in machiotl, auh yn oacico im machiotl, njman ie ic tleco, yn jcpac coatepetl: in vmpa ca vitzilobuchtli: auh yn otlecoc, njmã ie ic conteca, in ezpanjtl, yn otlaiaoalo: njman ie ic oaltemo.

HERE IS DESCRIBED THE FEAST WHICH WAS OBSERVED EVERY EIGHT YEARS

And this was Atamalqualiztli [The Eating of Water Tamales], which went being observed every eight years. Sometimes it was observed in [the month of] Quecholli, but perhaps sometimes it was observed in [the month of] Tepeilhuitl.

For seven days there was fasting. Only water tamales, soaked in water, were eaten, with no chili, with no salt, nor with saltpeter, nor with lime. And they were eaten [only] at noon.

And he who fasted not at this time, if he were noted, was then punished. And much was this, the eating of water tamales, held in awe. And he who did not this, if he were not seen nor noted, it was said, would be visited with skin sores.

And when the feast arrived, it was said: "Good fortune is sought," and "Gastropod shells are applied."[1] And at this time indeed all the gods danced; hence it was said: "There is godly dancing."

And all came forth there as hummingbirds, butterflies, honey bees, flies, birds, black beetles, dung beetles; in the guise of these the people appeared when they danced.

And still others appeared in the guise of sleep. [Some had] fruit tamales as their necklaces; [others had] turkey hen tamales as their necklaces. And before them was the maize bin filled with fruit tamales.

And also all of [these] came forth: those who appeared in the guise of the poor, of those who sold various kinds of vegetables, of those who sold pieces of wood.[2] And also appeared there one in the guise of one afflicted by the divine sickness. And still others imitated birds, owls, barn owls;[3] and they appeared in the guise of still other birds.

And [an image of] Tlaloc was set in place. Before it was [a pool of] water. It was full of serpents there, and of frogs. And those called Maçateca there

NICAN MITOA, YN ILHUJTL: IN CHICHICUEXIUH-TICA MUCHIOAIA.

Auh yn atamalqualiztli, chicuexiuhtica in muchiuhtiuja: in quenmanjan ipan in muchioaia quecholli: auh anoço quenmanjan ipan in tepeilhujtl muchioaia.

Chicomjlhujtl, in neçaoaloia: çan tlapactli atamalli, in moquaia, amo chillo, amo iztaio, amono tequjxqujo, amono tenexio: auh tlacatlaqualoia.

Auh yn aqujn amo moçaoaia yn ipan jn, intla machoia, njman tzacujltiloia: auh cenca ymacaxoia y, in atamalqualiztli: auh yn aqujn amo qujchioaia, intlacamo ittoa, anoço machoia, qujlmach xixiiotia.

Auh yn jquac ilhujtl qujçaia, moteneoa ixnextioa, yoan atecuculetioaia: yoan yn jquac cenca muchintin mjttotiaia in teteu: ic mjtoaia, teuittotiloia:

yoan ixq'ch vncan oalnecia in vitzitzilin papalotl, in xicotli, in çaiolin in tototl, in temoli, tecujtlaololo: yn jpan moqujxtiaia tlaca, yn ipan oalmjtotiaia.

Auh yn oc cequjntin ipan moqujxtiaia in cochiztli, inxocotamalcozquj, yoan totolnacatl yn jncozquj: yoan ymjxpan ycaca, in tonacacuezcomatl, tenticac in xocotamalli.

Auh no muchi vncan oalnecia, yn ipan moq'xtiaia in motolinja, yn motequjqujlnamaqujlia, yn motequaquauhnamaqujlilia: no yoan vncan oalnecia, in teucocoxquj ypan moqujxtiaia: yoan yn oc cequjntin totome, in teculutl, in chichtli ipan qujçaia: yoan oc cequj ipan moqujxtiaia.

Auh motlaliaia in tlaloc, ixpan mãca yn atl, vncan temja in cocoa, yoan in cueiame, yoan in iehoantin moteneoa, maçateca, vncan qujntoloaia in cocoa, çan

---

1. Garibay ("Relación breve," p. 318) translates *ixnextioaya* as *"se enceniza la cara"*; *atecocoltioaya* appears in the same text, translated as *"se baila como víbora del agua."* However, see Seler, *Einige Kapitel*, p. 249: *"man verwandelt sich in Meerschneckengehäuse."* *Atecuculli* is *"caracol de agua"* in the Molina *Vocabulario*, fol. 7*v*; as *ategogolo* it is defined as a *"gasterópodo o variedad de caracol,"* *Ampullaria monachus* or *A. yucatanensis* in Santamaría's *Diccionario*, p. 92.

2. *motequaquamaquilia* in the *Real Palacio MS.*

3. *teculutl*: generic term for owl; *chichtli: Tyto alba pratincola* (Bonaparte) in Dibble and Anderson, *Book XI*, pp. 42, 46–47.

swallowed the serpents. They were still quite alive, each one, [as well as the frogs]. The Maçateca [just]⁴ took these with their mouths, not with their hands. They just fastened their teeth in them as they took hold of them in the water there before the image of Tlaloc. And the Maçateca just went eating the serpents as they danced before it.

And he who first finished a serpent, who swallowed it, then shouted — yelled; he circled the temple. And they gave gifts to those who swallowed serpents. And there was dancing for two days.⁵ Toward evening [of the second day] there was a procession; four times was the temple circled.

And when fruit tamales were eaten, the maize bin was filled [with fruit tamales]. Everyone took [some] when the feast ended.

And the old women and the old men wept exceedingly; they bethought themselves that perhaps they would not attain [another] eight years.

They said: "Before whom [among us] will [this again] be observed?"

[And as to its being done thus, they said that]⁶ thus the maize went being rested every eight years. For it was said that we brought much torment to it — that we ate [it], we put chili on it, we salted it, we added saltpeter to it, we added lime. As we tired it to death, so we revived it. Thus, it was said, the maize was given [new] youth when this was done.

And when the feast was ended on the morrow, it was said: "[Tortillas] are dipped in the sauce"; because indeed there had been fasting for the maize.

ioioltiuja, ceceiaca, incamatica in qujmonanaia, amo inmatica: çan qujmontlanquechiaia, ynjc qujmonanaia in atlan, in vncan ixpan tlaloc: auh çan q'nquatiuja in cocoa, ynjc impã mjtotiaia maçateca.

Auh yn aqujn achtopa qujtlamjaia in coatl in qujtoloaia, njman ic tzatzi tlapapauja, qujiaoaloa in teucalli: auh qujntlauhtiaia in qujntoloaia cocoa: auh omjhujtl in netotiloia, ie teutlac in tlaiaoaloloia, nappa in moiaoaloa teucalli.

Auh in xocotamalli yquac qualoia, in tonacacuezcomac temja: muchi tlacatl concuja, yn jquac tlamj ilhujtl.

Auh in iehoanti cioa ylamatque, yoan veuetque, cenca chocaia, qujlnamjquja, yn acaçocmo acizque, chicuexiujtl:

qujtoaia. Acoc ixpan in muchioaz:

ic moceujtiuja in tonacaiutl, in chicuexiuhtica: ipampa qujlmach cẽca tictlaihijoujltia, injc tiqua, in ticchilhuja, in tiquiztauja, in tictequjxqujuja, in motenexuja: yn juhqujma ticatzonmjctia ynic ticnemjtia: qujlmach ic mopilqujxtitiuja, in tonacajutl, ynjc iuhqujn muchioaia.

Auh yn iquac otzonquiz ilhujtl, yn jmuztlaioc moteneoaia, molpalolo: iehica ca onecaujliloc, in tonacaiutl.

---

4. Following *ceceiaca*, the *Real Palacio MS* has *ioã in cueyame çã*. The omission is supplied in brackets in our translation.

5. The *Real Palacio MS* reads *auh inic omilhuitl* — "and on the second day."

6. Following *muchioaz*, the *Real Palacio MS* has *y. Auh inic muchivaya. y. quilmach*. The omission is supplied in brackets in our translation.

178

BEHOLD HERE A TRUE [RELATION] OF ALL THE [BUILDINGS] WHICH WERE THE MEXICANS' TEMPLES

All which was [in] the courtyard of [the Temple of] Uitzilopochtli was like this:

As it appeared, it was perhaps two hundred fathoms [square]. And there in the center of [the square] were very large temples; they were the temples of the devils. The one which was taller, which was higher, was the house of Uitzilopochtli or Tlacauepan Cuexcotzin. This one was very large, very tall.

And this one was in the middle [of the square]. And with it was the house of Tlaloc. They were indeed together; they were indeed joined to each other. And at the very top, [one] stood a little higher perhaps by a fathom.

Of both of these, [one] was the taller, the higher. Only they were quite similar. And at the top of each was a temple; at the top was a house.

There was the image of Uitzilopochtli, also named Ilhuicatl xoxouhqui. And in the other [temple], there was the image of Tlaloc.

And also at the top [of the pyramid] were circular stones, very large, called *techcatl* [sacrificial stones], upon which they slew victims in order to pay honor to their gods. And the blood, the blood of those who died, indeed reached the base; so did it flow off. All were like this in each of the temples which were of the devils.

And this Temple of Uitzilopochtli and Tlaloc faced there toward the setting of the sun. And its stairway was very wide; it was reaching there to the top. There was ascending there. And of all the temples that there were, all were like this. Very straight were their stairways.

TLALOCAN, THE TEMPLE OF EPCOATL

At Tlalocan there was fasting in honor of the Tlalocs when their feast day came. And when there was fasting, thereupon evil was done, bad things were done. There was dancing with dried maize stalks. And they danced in all the houses; it was

IZCATQUJ IN JMELAOACA, IN IXQUJCH CATCA INTEUCAL MEXICA.

In jtoal catca vitzilopuchtli, in jxqujch ic catca:

in juh motta, aço matlacpovalmatl: auh in vncan yitic, cenca vevei in teucalli mamanca, in jnteucal catca diablome: in oc cenca tlapanaviticatca, in veixticatca, iehoatl in jcal catca Vitzilopuchtli, anoço tlacavepan cuexcochtzin: iehoatl in cenca vei catca, cenca vecapan.

Auh injn, nepantla in jcaca: auh nevan manca in jcal catca tlaloc, vel nehoan manca, vel netech çaliuhtimanca: auh in ie vel icpac, achi veca motzticatca: aço cemmatica.

Inj vnteixti y, oc cenca tlapanaviticatca, oc cenca veveixticatca, çan vel nenevixticatca: auh in jcpac cecentetl teucalli, in jcpac manca calli:

vncan catca in jxiptla vitzilopuchtli, no yoan itoca ilhujcatl xoxouhquj: auh in oc cecnj, vmpa catca in jxiptla tlaloc:

auh no ioan in jcpac, vncan mamanca tetl iaoaltic, cenca vevey, qujtocaiotiaia techcatl, in jpan tlamjctiaia: injc qujnmaviztiliaia inteuhoan: auh in eztli, in jmezço in mjquja, vel valacia in tlatzintlan, injc valtotocaia: muchi iuhquj catca, in jxqujch inteucal catca diablome.

Auh in iehoatl in jteucal vitzilopuchtli, ioan tlaloc: vmpa itztimanca in jcalaqujian tonatiuh: auh in jtlamamatlaio, cenca patlavac: vmpa aciticatca in jcpac, in vncan tlecovaia: ioan in ie ixqujch in teucalli catca, muchiuhquj catca: cenca vel melavaticaca in jtlamamatlaio

TLALOCAN, ITEUPAN EPCOATL.

In tlalocan: vncan netlalocaçaualoia, in jquac ilhujhqujçaia: auh in onneçaualoc, njman ie ic aiectilo, ioan neaviltilo, netotilo, yca cintopilli: auh novian in calpan mjtotiaia: mjtoaia, etzalmaceoaloia. Auh in jquac oonqujz imjlhujuh, in tlatlaloque,

said that the dance of maize and beans was danced. And when the feast day of the Tlalocs ended, thereupon died those who were destined there, those called Tlalocs. And this went being done yearly.

MACUILCALLI AND MACUILQUIAUITL

There in that place there died the informers, those who imparted secret information to those who were not dwellers here — the Tlaxcalteca, or the Uexotzinca, or the Cholulteca who entered here in Mexico during war time; who took forth information.

And if they could escape, if they came to take the information, these Tlaxcalteca, or Uexotzinca, or Cholulteca, and all who entered here in war time then would emplace [themselves] to await the Mexicans. And when the Mexicans went there, very many died there.

But if they were seen here in Mexico, then [the Mexicans] seized them and they slew them; they cut them to pieces there at Macuilcalli or Macuilquiauitl.

TECCIZCALLI

Teccizcalli: there Moctezuma did penances; there he offered incense. And there the debt was paid [to the gods]. And he only fasted there when the great feasts came. And there was dying there; captives died there.

POYAUHTLAN

Poyauhtlan: there fasted Mexico's fire priest and the fire priest of [the Temple of] Tlaloc, once yearly, at [the feast of] Etzalqualiztli. Both offered incense there at Poyauhtlan. And there was dying there; captives died there.

MIXCOAPAN SKULL RACK

Mixcoapan Skull Rack: there they strung up the severed heads of those who died in the Temple of Mixcoatl.

TLALXICCO

Tlalxicco: there died he who was named [and impersonated] Mictlan tecutli. Once a year he died

njman ie ic miquj in vncan pouhque in mjtoaia tlatlaloque. Auh injn cexiuhtica in muchiuhtivia ipan

MACUJLCALLI, IOAN MACUJLQUJAVITL.

In vncan yn, vncan mjquja in tetlanenque: in qujmjlhujaia tetzauhtlatoque, in amo njcan chaneque, in tlaxcalteca, anoço vexotzinca, anoço chololteca, in valiaucalaquja njcan mexico: in qujvalcuja tlatolli.

Auh intla ovelqujzque, intla oconcujco tlatolli, in iehoantin tlaxcalteca, anoço vexotzinca, anoço chololteca, yoan in ye ixqujch valiaucalaquja: njman ic tlateca, injc qujnchia mexica: auh in jquac onvi mexica, cenca mjiec in vmpa ommjquja.

Auh intla oittoque njcan mexico: njman qujntzitzqujaia, ioan qujnmjctiaia, qujntetequja: in vncan macujlcali, anoço macujlqujavitl.

TECCIZCALLI.

In teccizcalli: vncan tlamaceoaia in iehoatl motecuçoma, vncan tlenamacaia: ioan vncan moxtlavaia. Auh çan iquac in vncan moçauaia, in vevey ilhujtl qujçaia: yoan vncan mjcovaia, vncan mjquja in mamaltin.

POIAUHTLAN.

In poiauhtlan: vncan moçauaya in mexico tlenamacac, ioan in tlalocan tlenamacac: cexiuhtica, ipan in etzalqualiztli: nehoan vncan tletemaia in poiauhtlan: ioan vncan mjcovaia vncan mjquja in mamaltin.

MIXCOAPAN TZUMPANTLI.

In mjxcoapan tzumpantli: vncan qujçoia in jntzontecon, in mjquja mjxcoatempan.

TLALXICCO.

In tlalxicco: vncan mjquja, in jtoca catca Mjctlan tecutli: cexiuhtica in mjquja, ipan in tititl qujçaia.

when the feast of Tititl came. And when the impersonator of Mictlan tecutli died, then the fire priest of Tlillan offered incense there; he deposited incense. And this was done only at night, not by day.

Uey Quauhxicalco

Uey Quauhxicalco was Moctezuma's place of doing penance. When he fasted there, it was said: "There is fasting for the sun." And every two hundred and sixty days[1] it so came to pass that there was fasting for the sun. And also they who were called Chachanme died there — only four of them. And the impersonator of the sun [god] and of the moon [goddess] died there. And likewise many captives died there. But this was after the others.

Tochinco

Tochinco: there died the impersonator of [Ome tochtli], once yearly, at the time of [the feast of] Tepeilhuitl.

Teotlalpan

Teotlalpan: there was a procession there each year when the feast of Quecholli arrived. And when there was a procession, thereupon they departed for Çacatepec. And when it was reached, thereupon there was hunting [of game]. And Moctezuma then paid the debt there. And when he had paid the debt, thereupon he departed. No longer was anyone left there. Likewise when there was going, no longer did anyone go to be left here in Mexico. And no longer did anyone follow the road. Verily, many men went there to Çacatepec.

Tlilapan

Tlilapan: there the fire priests bathed themselves, only at night, and often. And when they had bathed, thereupon they deposited incense; they offered incense there at the Temple of Mixcoatl. And when they had offered incense, thereupon they went to the *calmecac*.

Auh in ommjc in jxiptla mjctlan tecutli: njman vncan vallenamacaia, valletemaia, in tlillan tlenamacac. Auh injn muchioaia: çan iooan, amo cemjlhujtl.

Vey quauhxicalco.

In quauhxicalco, itlamaceoaian catca in Motecuçuma: iquac in vncan moçauaia, mjtoaia: netonatiuhçaualoa: auh mamatlacpovaltica vmeitica in juh muchiuaia, in netonatiuhçaualoia. Auh ioan vncan mjquja: in mjtoaia, chachanme: çan navintin: yoan vncan mjquja in jxiptla tonatiuh, ioan metztli: auh ioan cenca mjiequjn in mamalti, vncan mjquja. Auh ynjn, çan tepan ietiuh.

Tochinco.

In tochinco: vncan mjquja in jxiptla tochinco, cecexiuhtica: ipan tepeilhujtl.

Teutlalpan.

In teutlalpan, vncan tlaiaualovaia, cecexiuhtica: iquac in quecholli qujçaia ilhujtl. Auh in ontlaiaualoloc: njman ie ic vmpeoa in çacatepec: auh in onaxivac, njman ie ic amjoa: auh in motecuçuma, njman vmpa ommoxtlavaia: auh in ommoxtlauh, njman ye ic valpeoa: ayocac vmpa ommocaoa. Çan no yvi injc vilooaia, aioc noiac njcan mocauhtivia in mexico: yoan oiocac vtli qujtocaia: vel muchi tlacatl vmpa via in çacatepec.

Tlilapan.

In tlilapan: vncan maltiaia in tlenamacaque, çan iooaltica: ioan muchipa. Auh in jquac ommaltique: njman ie ic tletema, tlenamaca, in vmpa mjxcoapan teupan: auh in ontlenamacaque, njman ie ic huj in calmecac.

---

1. *mamatlacpovaltica vmeitica*: although the corresponding Spanish text (cf. Sahagún, Garibay ed., Vol. I, p. 233) translates the term as "*cada doscientos y tres días*," it should be read *mamatlacpoaltica omeipoaltica*, "every two hundred and sixty days."

TLILLAN CALMECAC

Tlillan Calmecac: there dwelt the guardians of Ciuacoatl.

MEXICO CALMECAC

Mexico Calmecac: there dwelt the penitents who offered incense at the summit of the [pyramid] Temple of Tlaloc. [This they did] quite daily.

COACALCO

Coacalco: there dwelt the gods of [foreign] cities. Wherever the Mexicans conquered, they took [the gods] captive. Then they carried them here; they put them in there. And there they were guarded at Coacalco.

QUAUHXICALCO

Quauhxicalco: there the one named Yiopoch deposited incense. And there the [impersonator of the] devil called Titlacauan blew his flute. And when he had sounded his flute, thereupon he deposited incense. And when he had deposited incense, then he went in [to his dwelling]. Quite daily he did thus, perchance by night or [perchance] by day.

A SEPARATE QUAUHXICALCO

Quauhxicalco: there danced the impersonator [who was arrayed as a] squirrel. And there was erected that which was called the *xocotl*. It was only a tree. And they distributed its shoulder sash of paper, its paper banners. And this was done at the time of [the feast of] Teotl eco, also yearly.

TECCALCO

Teccalco: there was casting [of men] into the fire there; they cast captives into the fire there. This also was done at the time of Teotl eco, also yearly. And when there had been the casting into the fire, thereupon the offering priests came down here. Thereupon [the ceremony called] *amatlauitzoa* was performed.

TLILLAN CALMECAC.

In tlillan calmecac: vncan onoca, in jtepixcauh cihoacoatl.

MEXICO CALMECAC.

In mexico calmecac: vncan onoca in tlamaceuhque, in ontlenamacaia tlalocan ijcpac: çan mumuztlae.

COOACALCO.

In cooacalco: vncan onoca in altepeteteu, in canjn ontepeoaia mexica, in qujmonacia: njman qujnvalvicaia, vncan qujncalaqujaia: ioan vncan pialoia in cooacalco.

QUAUHXICALCO.

In quauhxicalco: vncan tletemaia yn jtoca catca yiopuch, yoan vncan vallapitzaia in diablo: in qujtoaia titlacaoan: auh in ontlapitz, njman ye ic tletema: auh in ontleten, njman ic calaquj: çan mumuztlae iuh qujchioaia, aço iooan, anoço cemjlhujtl.

OC CECNJ QUAUHXICALCO.

In quauhxicalco: vncan mjtotiaia in techalotl yxiptla: yoan vncan moquetzaia, in mjtoaia: xocotl, çan quavitl, yoan qujtlamamacaia, yamaneapan, yamapan. Auh ipan in teutl eco muchioaia: no cexiuhtica.

TECCALCO.

In teccalco, vncan netlepantlaxoia: vncan qujntlepantlaçaia in mamaltin: çan no ipan in teutl eco muchioaia, no cexiuhtica. Auh yn onnetlepantlaxoc: njman ye ic oaltemo in tlamacazque, njman ye ic amatlavitzoa.

THE SKULL RACK

The Skull Rack: there they strung up the severed heads of captives whom they had cast into the fire, who had died there at the Teccalco. Likewise this was done yearly.

THE TEMPLE OF UITZNAUAC

The Temple of Uitznauac: there died those named the Centzonuitznaua, and many captives died there. And upon [the feast of] Panquetzaliztli was this done, and [it was done] yearly.

TEZCACALCO

Tezcacalco: there was slaying there; captives died there, after the others [and] not every year.

TLACOCHCALCO ACATL YIACAPAN

Tlacochcalco Acatl Yiacapan: there were guarded the spears, the arrows. Also there was slaying there; captives died there. And only at night was there slaying. And it was only at a time which was determined.

TECCIZCALCO

Teccizcalco: there also there was slaying; there captives died, also by night, also after the others, only when it was [so] determined.

UITZTEPEUALCO

Uitztepeualco: there the offering priests, at the time of their penances, scattered the thorns, or else the fir branches, when they did penance somewhere.

UITZNAUAC CALMECAC

Uitznauac Calmecac: there dwelt the penitent, the fire priest, who offered incense, who deposited incense there at the top of the [pyramid] temple which was named Uitznauac. Quite every day was it so done.

TZUMPANTLI

In tzumpantli: vncan qujçoia in mamaltin intzontecon, in qujntlepantlaçaia, in vmpa mjquja teccalco: çan no cexiuhtica yn muchioaia.

VITZNAOAC TEUCALLI.

In vitznaoac teucalli: vncan mjquja, in jntoca centzonvitznaoa, yoan mjiec malli vncan mjquja: auh ipan in panquetzaliztli muchioaia, yoan cexiuhtica.

TEZCACALCO

In tezcacalco: vncan mjcoaia, vncan mjquja in mamalti: çan tepan yetiuh, amo cexiuhtica.

TLACOCHCALCO ACATL YIACAPAN.

In tlacochcalco acatl yiacapan: vncan mopiaia in tlacochtli, in mjtl: no vncan mjcoaia, vncan mjquja in mamalti: auh çan iooan in mjcooaia, yoan çan molnamjquja yn jqujn.

TECCIZCALCO.

In teccizcalco: no vncan mjcoaia, vncan mjquja in mamalti: çan no iooaltica, çan no tepan yetiuh, çan molnamjquja.

VITZTEPEOALCO

In vitztepeoalco: vncan qujtepeoaia in tlamacazque in jntlamaceoaia, in vitztli: anoço acxoiatl, yn jquac canjn ontlamaceoaia.

VITZNAOAC CALMECAC.

In vitznaoac calmecac: vncan onoca in tlamaceuhquj, in tlenamacac: in ontlenamacaia, in ontletemaia in teucalli icpac: in jtoca catca vitznaoac: çan mumuztlae in juh muchioaia.

A Separate Quauhxicalco

Quauhxicalco: there they placed, there they nourished the skull rack within [the pyramid compound of the god] whose name was Omacatl. In carved wood Omacatl was in human form. And it came to pass that he was nourished [with the blood of victims] every two hundred and sixty days upon the day sign Two Reed.

The Temple of Macuilcipactli

Temple of Macuilcipactli: there was slaying there; captives died there, at night only. Also the day sign [Five Crocodile] was chosen.

Tetlanman Calmecac

Tetlanman Calmecac: there dwelt the fire priest, the one devoted [to the service of Chantico].

The Temple of the White Cinteotl

The Temple of the White Cinteotl: there captives died, only those with skin sores.[2] And when they died, then [the priests] buried them; they were not eaten. They died when there was fasting for the sun.

Tetlanman

Tetlanman: there died the impersonator of Quaxolotl Chantico. The rulers just determined the time that she was to died. It was after the others, and upon the day count One Flower.

The Temple of Chicomecatl

The Temple of Chicomecatl: only at certain times was there slaying there, and it was at night. Also it was after the others, only when it was determined, at the time that the day count One Flower set in.

Oc cecnj quauhxicalco.

In quauhxicalco: vncan qujtlaliaia, vncan qujzcaltiaia in tzumpantli yiollo: in jtoca catca vmacatl, quavitl tlaxixintli, tlacaietiuh in vmacatl: auh in muchioaia in qujzcaltiaia matlacpovaltica vmeitica: ipan in cemjlhujtonalli vmacatl.

Macujlcipactli yteupan.

In macujlcipactli iteupan: vncan mjcoaia: vncan mjquja mamalti: çan iooaltica, çan no tonalpepenaloia.

Tetlanman calmecac

In tetlanman calmecac: vncan onoca in tlenamacac, in tlamaceuhquj.

Iztac cinteutl yteupan.

In jztac cinteoutl yteupan: vncan mjquja in mamalti, çan iehoantin in xixijoti: auh in jquac ommjcque, njman qujntocaia, amo qualoia: ipan in netonatiuhçavaloia mjquja.

Tetlanman.

In tetlanman: vncan mjquja, yn jxiptla quaxolotl chanticon: çan qujlnamjquja in tlatoque, in jqujn mjqujz: çan tepan yetiuh: auh ipan in cemjlhujtlapoalli, ce xuchitl.

Chicomecatl yteupan.

In chicomecatl yteupan: çan quenman in vncan mjcoaia, yoan iooaltica: çan no tepan ietiuh, çan molnamjquja: yquac in cemjlhujtlapoalli ce suchitl moquetza.

---

2. *xixijoti*: *"leprosos"* in the corresponding Spanish text. However, cf. Charles E. Dibble and Arthur J. O. Anderson: *Florentine Codex, Book X, The People* (Santa Fe: School of American Research and University of Utah, 1961), p. 157.

TEZCAAPAN

Tezcaapan: there the penitents just bathed themselves; it was their bathing place.

TEZCATLACHCO

Tezcatlachco: there also there was slaying; there died the impersonator of Uitznauatl — only at times, not often. Perchance it was at the time of [the day count] Two Reed.

SKULL RACK

Skull Rack: there were sacrificed those named the Omacame [impersonators of Omacatl]. And also very many captives died there. And there was slaying every two hundred and sixty days.

TLAMATZINCO

Tlamatzinco: there died those called, those whose name was the Tlamatzinca [impersonators of Tlamatzincatl], ceremonially bathed victims, at the time of [the month] Quecholli, at its close, yearly.

TLAMATZINCO CALMECAC

Tlamatzinco Calmecac: there dwelt the fire priests of the Tlamatzinca, those who offered incense at the top of [the pyramid of] Tlamatzinco.

QUAUHXICALCO

Quauhxicalco: there the sacrificial paper descended, but only last of all did the fire serpent descend. And there the debt-payments burned at the time that, each year, the Tlamatzinca died.

THE TEMPLE OF MIXCOATL

The Temple of Mixcoatl: there [victims] were killed like deer. And thus did they take them up when they died like deer: they only went bobbing

TEZCAAPAN.

In tezcaapan: çan vncan maltiaia, innealtiaian catca in tlamaceuhque.

TEZCATLACHCO.

In tezcatlachco: no vncan mjcoaia, vncan mjquja in jxiptla vitznaoatl: çan quenman, amo muchipa: aço ipan in vmacatl.

TZOMPANTLI.

In tzompantli: vncan motonaltiaia, in jntoca catca vmacâ: auh yoan, cenca mjec in malli vncan mjquja: auh matlacpoaltica vmeitica in ommjcoaia.

TLAMATZINCO.

In tlamatzinco: vncan mjquja in mjtoaia, in jntoca catca tlamatzinca, in tlaaltiti: iquac in quechulli, itlamjan cexiuhtica.

TLAMATZINCO CALMECAC.

In tlamatzinco calmecac: vncan onoca, in tlamatzinca intlenamacacahoan: in ontlenamacaia ijcpac tlamatzinco.

QUAUHXICALCO.

In quauhxicalco: vncan oaltemoia in teteuhpoalli, auh ça oallatzacujaia in xiuhcoatl oaltemoia: ioan vncan tlatlaia in nextlaoalli, in jquac mjquja tlamatzinca cexiuhtica.

MIXCOATEUPAN.

In mjxcoateupan: vncan maçapolioaia: auh ynjc qujntlecaviaia in maçapolivia, çan aaquetztivia, qujnnauhcaviaia: yoan vncan mjquja in mjxcoatl y

their heads up and down; four [priests] carried them. And there died the impersonator of Mixcoatl and [the impersonator of] Cuetlaciuatl. And this was done at the time of the close of Quecholli, and [it was done] each year.

NETLATILOYAN

Netlatiloyan:[3] there was laid away that which was named the likeness of Nanauatl, and Xochquaye.

TEOTLACHCO

Teotlachco: there died those named Amapantzin [impersonating the god Amapan]. They died only at dawn. And [this was done] yearly at the time of [the feast of] Panquetzaliztli.

ILHUICATITLAN

Ilhuicatitlan: there died the impersonator of the [morning] star, at night only. And very many captives died there by day. Yearly was this done, at the time that the star came forth.

THE GREAT SKULL RACK

The Great Skull Rack: there also there used to be slaying; very many captives died there, by day, not by night. [This was done] likewise at the time of [the feast of] Panquetzaliztli, also yearly.

MECATLAN

Mecatlan: there was teaching there. The sounders of trumpets were taught there—the people of Mecatlan. Quite frequently each day [they sounded trumpets].

THE TEMPLE OF CINTEOTL

The Temple of Cinteotl: there the impersonator of Chicome coatl died, at night only. And when she died, then they flayed her. And when dawn broke,

ixiptla, yoan cuetlacihoatl: auh ipan in quechulli tlamj muchioaia, yoan cexiuhtica.

NETLATILOIAN.

In netlatiloian: vncan motlatiaia, in jtoca catca nanaoatl y ixiptla, ioan xochquaie.

TEUTLACHCO.

In teutlachco: vncan mjquja in intoca catca amapantzitzin, çan tlahujzpan in ommjquja: auh cexiuhtica, ipan yn panquetzaliztli.

ILHUJCATITLAN.

In jlhujcatitlan: vncan mjquja in jxiptla citlalin, çan iooaltica: auh cencan mjec in vncan mjquja mamalti cemjlhujtl: cexiuhtica in muchioaia, ipan in citlalin qujçaia.

VEY TZOMPANTLI.

In vey tzompantli: no vncan mjcovaia, cenca mjequjn in vncan mjquja mamalti, cemjlhujtl, amo iooan: çan no ipan in panquetzaliztli, no cexiuhtica.

MECATLAN.

In mecatlan: vncan nemachtiloia, vncan momachtiaia in tlapitzque, in mecateca: çan muchipa mumuztlae.

CINTEUPAN.

In cinteupan: vncan mjquja in jxiptla chicome coatl, cioatl, çan iooaltica: auh in jquac oommjc, njman qujxipeoaia: auh in otlathujc, in tlenamacac

---

3. The corresponding Spanish text identifies this place as the cave in which were deposited the skins of victims flayed in the feast of Tlacaxipeualiztli.

then the fire priest put on the skin of [the likeness of] Chicome coatl. Thereupon there was a procession; they circled the eagle vessel; they went dancing. And this was done yearly, at the time of [the feast of] Ochpaniztli.

The Temple of the Centzontotochtin

The Temple of the Centzontotochtin: there died [the impersonators of] Tepoztecatl and Totoltecatl and Papaztac. And when they died, it was not by night; it was by day, at the time of [the feast of] Tepeilhuitl. And [this was done] yearly.

The Temple of Cinteotl

The Temple of Cinteotl: there stood, there was guarded the image of Cinteotl. There the impersonator of Cinteotl died, by day.

Netotiloyan

Netotiloyan: there danced the bathed ones [for the day sign] Nine Wind, when already they were to die. And when they died, it was at midnight, not by day. [This took place] at the time of [the feast of] Xilomanaliztli or Atl caualo, also each year.

Chililico

Chililico: there died the bathed ones [on the day sign] Nine Wind, at midnight. And each year did the bathed ones die there. And only the rulers ceremonially bathed them there. Likewise at the time of [the feast of] Atl caualo [was this done].

Coaapan

Coaapan: there the fire priest of Coatlan bathed himself. Only he did so; no one else bathed himself there.

Pochtlan

Pochtlan: there dwelt the fire priests, those who

njman conmaqujaia, in eoaio chicome coatl: njman ye ic tlaiaoaloa, qujiaoaloa in quauhxicalli, mjtotitiuh: auh cexiuhtica in muchioaia, ipan ochpaniztli.

Centzontotochti inteupan.

In centzontotochti inteupan: vncan mjquja in tepuztecatl, yoan totoltecatl, yoan papaztac: auh in mjquja amo iooan, cemjlhujtl, ypan in tepeilhujtl: auh cexiuhtica.

Cinteupan.

In cinteupan: vncan ycaca, vncan pialoia in jxiptla cinteoutl: vncan mjquja in jxiptla cinteoutl, cemjlhujtl.

Netotiloian.

In netotiloian: vncan mjtotiaia in tlatlaaltilti, in chicunauhecatl, in jquac ie mjqujz: auh iquac in mjquja iooalnepantla, amo cemjlhujtl: jpan xilomanjztli, anoço atl caoalo: no cexiuhtica.

Chililico.

In chililico: vncan mjquja in tlatlaltilti in chicunauhecatl, iooalnepantla: auh cexiuhtica in vncan mjquja tlatlaltilti: auh çan tlatoque in vncan tealtiaia, çan no ipan in atl caoalo.

Cooaapan.

In cooaapan: vncan maltiaia in cooatlan tlenamacac, çan qujmjxcaviaia, aiac oc ce vncan maltiaia.

Puchtlan.

In puchtlan: vncan onoca in tlenamacaque, in

deposited incense, those who offered incense there above [on the pyramid] Temple of Yiacatecutli. [This they did] quite daily.

ontletemaia, in ontlenamacaia, vmpa jicpac yiacatecutli iteupan: çan mumuztlae.

Atlauhco

Atlauhco: there dwelt, there lived the fire priests who deposited incense, who offered incense there above [on the pyramid of] Uitzilinquatec. Likewise [this was done] daily.

Atlauhco.

In atlauhco: vncan onoca, vncan nenca in tlenamacaque, in vmpa ontletemaia, ontlenamacaia, in ijcpac vitzilinquatec yteupan: çan no mumuztlae.

Yopico

Yopico: there was slaying there; very many captives died there. And there died the ones whose names were Tequitzin[4] and Mayauel. And when they died it was by day, not by night. And they died at the time of [the feast of] Tlacaxipeualiztli; and [this was done] each year.

Iopico.

In iopico: vncan mjcovaloia: in vncan, cenca mjiequjntin mjquja in mamalti: yoan vncan mjquja in jtoca catca tequjtzin, yoan maiavel: auh in mjquja cemjlhujtl, amo iooan: auh ipan in tlacaxipeoaliztli mjquja, yoan cexiuhtica.

The Temple of Yiacatecutli

The Temple of Yiacatecutli: there the impersonator of Yiacatecutli died, by day, not by night. [This was done] at the time of [the feast of] Tititl, also each year.

Iyacatecutli iteupan.

In yiacatecutli iteupan: vncan mjquja in jiacatecutli ixiptla: cemjlhujtl, amo iooan: ipan in tititl, no cexiuhtica.

The Temple of Uitzilinquatec

The Temple of Uitzilinquatec: likewise the impersonator of Uitzilinquatec died, likewise by day, likewise at the time of [the feast of] Tititl. Also this was done yearly. It was a woman who died.

Vitzilinquatec iteupan.

In vitzilinquatec iteupan: çan no vncan mjquja, in ijxiptla vitzilinquatec: çan no cemjlhujtl, çan no ipan in tititl, no cexiuhtica in muchioaia: cioatl in mjquja.

Yopico Calmecac

Yopico Calmecac: there was slaying there; very many captives died there, also at night at the time of [the feast of] Tlacaxipeualiztli, also every year, there at the *calmecac* of Youallauan.

Iopico calmecac.

In iopico calmecac: vncan mjcooaia, vncan mjquja cenca mjec in malli: çan no iooaltica, ipan in tlacaxipeoaliztli: no cexiuhtica, vncan icalmecac in iooallaoan.

---

4. Tequitzin: the name should probably be Izquitecatl as in Chap. 19, above (fourth movable feast). See also Charles E. Dibble and Arthur J. O. Anderson, *Florentine Codex, Book IV, The Soothsayers* (Santa Fe: School of American Research and University of Utah, 1957), p. 17. Cf. also below, in the appendix on "Those Who Served in All the Houses of the Gods": Izquitlan teuhoatzin.

YOPICO SKULL RACK

Yopico Skull Rack: there they strung up the severed heads of captives and those whom they striped [slew in gladiatorial sacrifice] at the time of [the feast of] Tlacaxipeualiztli. [This] also [they did] yearly.

SKULL RACK

[This] Skull Rack was the skull rack of [the Temple of] Yiacatecutli. And there they strung up the severed heads of captives who died above on the [pyramid] Temple of Yiacatecutli at the time of the first day of [the month of] Xocotl uetzi.

THE TEMPLE OF MACUILMALINALLI

The Temple of Macuilmalinalli and of Topantlacaqui: there [priests] sang for and offered sacrifices to these [gods], Macuilmalinalli and Topantlacaqui. And they offered sacrifices to them every two hundred and sixty days. Also they came after the others. It was at the time of the day count Flower.

ATICPAC

Aticpac: there [priests] offered sacrifices to the Ciuateteo when they observed the feast of the day sign Seven Serpent.

NETLATILOYAN

Netlatiloyan: there they laid away the skins [flayed from the women impersonating] the Ciuateteo, who died there at Xochicalco each year, at the time of [the feast of] Ochpaniztli.

ATLAUHCO

Atlauhco: there they offered sacrifices to [the goddess] Ciuateotl of Atlauhco. And when [the impersonator of] Ciuateotl of Atlauhco died, it was there at Coatlan, at the base [of Atlauhco. This was done] yearly, also at the time of [the feast of] Ochpaniztli.

IOPICO TZOMPANTLI.

In yopico tzompantli: vnca quiçoia in intzontecon mamalti: auh yehoantin in qujnoaoanaia ypan tlacaxipeoaliztli: no cexiuhtica.

TZOMPANTLI.

In tzompantli, ytzompan in jiacatecutli: auh vncan qujçoia yn jntzontecon mamalti, yn jcpac mjquja yiacatecutli yteupan: ipan yn cemjlhujtlapoalli xocotl vetzi.

MACUJLMALINAL YTEUPAN.

In macujlmalinal yteupan, yoan in topantlacaquj yteupan: vncan qujncujcatiaia, yoan vncan qujntonaltiaia in yehoantin macujlmalinal, yoan topantlacaquj: auh in qujntonaltiaia matlacpoaltica, omeytica: çan no tepan ietiuh: in cemjlhujtlapoalli, ipan in suchilhujtl.

ATICPAC.

In aticpac: vncan qujntonaltiaia in cioateteu: yquac in qujlhuja chicomecooatonalli.

NETLATILOIAN.

In netlatiloian: vncan qujntlatiaia in cioateteu imeoaio, in vmpa mjquja suchicalco: cexiuhtica, ipan ochpaniztli.

ATLAUHCO.

In atlauhco: vncan qujntonaltiaia, in atlauhco, cioateoutl: auh in ommjquja atlauhco cioateoutl, vmpa in cooatlan tlatzintlan: cexiuhtica, çan no ipan in ochpaniztli.

Tzonmolco Calmecac

Tzonmolco Calmecac: from there came the fire, which they named Xiuhtecutli. There Moctezuma took the fire when he offered incense, and there the fire drill fell [to make the new fire] yearly, at the time of [the feast of] Uauhquiltamalqualiztli.

Temalacatl

Temalacatl: at that place there was the striping [gladiatorial sacrifices]; there they striped very many captives. And thus were striped indeed all men who came here from all the lands about us, whom they slew as sacrifices there upon the stone of gladiatorial sacrifice. And there, their functionary was the Bear Man; he set them up on the stone of gladiatorial sacrifice. And when he set a captive up there, thereupon he gave him a pine club, and he gave him a feathered staff. And then went an impersonator to strike him repeatedly — perhaps an eagle or an ocelot [warrior]. Then [the warrior] repeatedly struck the captive, as if a battle were fought. And there his functionary was the one named Chalchiuhtepeua. And when the captive fell, thereupon the Bear Man dragged him off. Thereupon [a priest] slashed open the captive's breast. And the one who slew him was one whose name was Youallauan; he opened [the captive's] breast. And when they had slashed open the breast of the captive, thereupon they cast him down below. And this was done each year at the time of [the feast of] Tlacaxipeualiztli.

The Temple of Nappatecutli

Nappateco: there died [the impersonator] whose name was Nappatecutli, only at night, not by day. [This was done] yearly, at the time of [the feast of] Tepeilhuitl.

Tzonmolco

Tzonmolco: there died the four [impersonators] named Xiuhtecutli. The first was named Blue Xiuhtecutli; the second, Yellow; the third, White Xiuhtecutli; the fourth, Red Xiuhtecutli. And there were still others named Iuipapaneca temilolca. And also [the woman] whose name was Ciuatontli [and] also

Tzonmolco calmecac.

In tzonmolco calmecac: vncan qujçaia in tletl, in qujtocaiotiaia xiuhtecutli: vmpa concuja in tletl, in jquac tlenamacaia motecuçoma, yoan vncan vetzia in tlequavitl: cexiuhtica, ipan oauhqujltamalqualiztli.

Temalacatl.

In temalacatl: vncan tlaoaoanoia, in vncan qujnoaoanaia, cenca mjequjntin in mamalti: auh injc tlaoaoanoia, vel ixqujch tlacatl oalhuja in cematonaoac in oallamjctiaia, in vncan temalacac: auh vncan intequjppan catca in cuetlachtli, ontequetzaia in temalacac. Auh in jquac oconquetz malli: njman ye ic conmaca in ocotzontetl, yoan conmaca quavitl tlapotonjlli. Auh njman ye iauh in teixiptla, in tevivitequjz: aço quauhtli, anoço, ocelutl: njman ie qujvivitequj in malli, iuhqujn moiauchioa: yoan, vncan itequjppan catca, yn jtoca chalchiuhtepeoa. Auh in jquac ovetz malli: njman ye ic tevilana in cuetlachtli: njman ye ic queltetequj in malli: auh in iehoatl tlamjctiaia in jtoca catca Iooallaoan, teeltetequja. Auh in jquac oconeltetecque malli: njman ye ic tlatzintlan qujoallaça: auh in muchioaia, yn, cexiuhtica ypan in tlacaxipeoaliztli.

Nappatecutli iteupan.

In nappatecco, vncan mjquja yn itoca catca, nappatecutli çan iohoan, amo cemjlhujtl: cexiuhtica ipan tepeilhujtl.

Tzommolco.

In tzonmolco. vncan miq'a yn jtoca catca xiuhtecutli naujntin. Jnjc ce ytoca, xoxouhquj xiuhtecutli. Jnic vme coçauhquj. Jnjc ey iztac xiuhtecutli. Jnjc nauj tlatlauhquj xiuhtecutli: yoã oc cequjntin intoca, ihujpapaneca, temjlolca: auh tlaelpanmjquja, yn

[the woman] named Nancotlaceuhqui died, their breasts slashed open.

And when they had died, thereupon Moctezuma came forth there to the Coacalco. Thereupon was danced the lordly dance, and all the men danced. Moctezuma led them; he led [priests impersonating] the various gods. And when there had been dancing, when there had been the serpent dance, thereupon Moctezuma offered incense [to the god].

And this was done at the time of [the feast of] Izcalli, once yearly.

COATLAN

Coatlan: there died [the impersonators] named the Centzonuitznaua, perchance when there was drilling [of new fire] or, yearly, when it was [the feast of] Quecholli tlami.

XOCHICALCO

Xochicalco: there died [the impersonators of] White Cinteotl and Red Cinteotl, and also that one [impersonating the goddess] Atlatonan.

And when Atlatonan died, thereupon they flayed her. And when they had flayed her, then the fire priest put on her skin.

And when day broke, thereupon the fire priest danced; he stood wearing the skin of [the impersonator of] Atlatonan. And this was done yearly, at the time of [the feast of] Ochpaniztli.

YOPICALCO AND EUACALCO

Yopicalco and Euacalco: there stayed the rulers of Anauac who came from distant cities.

And greatly did Moctezuma honor them. There he gave them gifts. He gave them precious capes, precious necklaces, or precious arm bands. Whatever was precious he gave to all of them.

TOZPALATL

The Yellow Waters were very precious. They flowed [as a spring]. There the offering priests took water. And when it was the feast of Uitzilopochtli, and when all the feasts were celebrated, there water was drunk. There the common folk drank water.

jtoca catca cioatontli, no iehoatl ytoca nancotlaceuhquj.

Auh yn onmjcoac, njman ie ic oalqujça, in Motecuçoma, in vmpa coacalco: njman ie ic motecujtotia, yoan ixqujch tlacatl mjtotia, teiacanaia in motecuçoma, qujniacanaia, in nepapã teteu. Auh yn onnetotiloc yn onnecocololoc, njmã ie ic tlenamaca yn motecuçoma:

auh in muchioa yn, ipan izcalli cexiuhtica.

COOATLAN.

In cooatlan, vncan mjquja in jntoca catca centzonvitznaoa: aço yquac in tlamamalioaia, anoço yquac in quecholli tlamj cexiuhtica.

SUCHICALCO.

In suchicalco, vncan mjquja in jztac cinteoutl, yoan tlatlauhquj cinteoutl, yoan no iehoatl in atla tonan.

Auh in jquac oommjc atla tonan: njman ye ic qujxipeoa: auh in jquac oconxipeuhque, njman in tlenamacac conmaqujaia yn jieoaio.

Auh in jquac otlathujc: njman ye ic mitotia in tlenamacac, conmaqujticac in jieoaio atla tonan: auh in muchioaia y, cexiuhtica, ipan in ochpanjztli.

IOPICALCO, YOAN EOACALCO.

In iopicalco, yoan eoacalco, vncan onoca in anaoac tlatoque, in veca altepetl ipan oalvia:

auh cenca qujnmaviztiliaia in Motecuçoma, vncan qujntlauhtiaia: qujnmacaia in tlaçotilmatli, anoço tlaçocozcatl, anoço tlaçomacuextli: in ie ixqujch tlaçotli, muchi qujnmacaia.

TOSPALATL.

In tospalatl, cenca tlaçotli catca, meiaia: vncan atlacuja in tlamacazque. Auh in jquac ylhujuh qujçaia vitzilopuchtli: yoan yn ixqujch ilhujtl muchioaia, vncan atlioaloia: vncan atlia in maceoalti.

Tlacochcalco Quauhquiauac

Tlacochcalco Quauhquiauac: there was [the god] named Macuiltotec. There his feast day was observed. And when the feast day of Macuiltotec came, there was slaying there; captives died there at Tlacochcalco Quauhquiauac.

Perchance it was when the [new] fire was to be drilled; perchance also not. Also it was done yearly, at the time of [the feast of] Panquetzaliztli or [the feast of] Tlacaxipeualiztli.

Tolnauac

Tolnauac: there was slaying there. Captives died there perchance [when the day sign] One Death set in in the day count.

Tilocan

Tilocan: there cooked the [amaranth seed dough for] the image of Uitzilopochtli.

Itepeyoc

Itepeyoc: there took form [the image of] Uitzilopochtli.

Uitznauac Calpulli[5]

At Uitznauac Calpulco there was made at that place, there took man's form, the image of the devil whose name was Tlacauepan Cuexcotzin.

Atempan

Atempan: there they assembled the [child sacrifices called] "human paper streamers." And when they had assembled them, thereupon they took them in a procession; they carried them in litters.

And when they had taken them in the procession, thereupon they dispersed them. Perchance they left them in the middle of the lagoon at Tepetzinco, or at Quauhtepec, above Yiauhqueme.

Tlacochcalco Quauhqujaoac.

In tlacochcalco quauhqujaoac, vncan catca in jtoca macujltotec: vncan ilhujqujxtililoia. Auh in jquac yn jlhujuh qujçaia in macujltotec. vncan mjcoaia: vncan mjquja mamalti in tlacochcalco quauhqujiaoac:

aço yquac in tlamamalioaz, acanoçomo: no cexiuhtica in muchioaia, ipan in panquetzaliztli, anoço tlacaxipeolaiztli.

Tulnaoac.

In tulnaoac, vncan mjcooaia: vncan mjquja mamalti, aço ce mjqujztli moquetza in tonalpoalli catca.

Tilocan.

In tilocan: vncan ycucia in vitzilopuchtli ijxiptla.

Itepeioc.

In itepeioc: vncan tlacatia in vitzilopuchtli.

Vitznaoac calpulli.

In vitznaoac calpulco, vncan muchioaia, vncan tlacatia in ijxiptla diablo, in jtoca catca tlacavepan cuexcochtzin.

Atenpan

In atempan, vncan qujntecpichoaia in tlacateteuhti: auh in jquac in oqujntecpichoque: njman ye ic qujntlaiaoaalochtia, qujntlapechvia.

Auh in jquac oqujmontlaiaoaalochtique: njman ye ic qujnmoiaoa, aço atlitic tepetzinco qujmoncaoaia, anoço quauhtepec, yiauhqueme ijcpac.

---

5. Here and in instances below, where Sahagún uses the term *calpulli* instead of its locative form (*calpulco*), he specifies in the corresponding Spanish text that a building is meant.

Tezcacoac Tlacochcalco

Tezcacoac Tlacochcalco: there was slaying there, only sometimes when there were very many captives. And there spears, arrows were guarded. With them there were conquests.

Acatl Yiacapan Uey Calpulli

Acatl Yiacapan Uey Calpulli: there they gathered together [the sacrificial victims called] Tlalocs. And when they had gathered them together, then they slew them there.

And when they had slain them, then they cut them to pieces there and cooked them. They put squash blossoms with their flesh.

And when they had cooked them, then the noblemen ate them, all the high judges; but not the common folk — only the rulers.

Techielli

Techielli: there fir branches[6] were placed.

Calpulli

All the small houses which were around and which surrounded the temples were called *calpulli*. There was fasting there.

And only the noblemen, the rulers, the constables, the seasoned warriors fasted there every twenty days.

[Of this] it was said: "There is fasting for five [days]."

And when they fasted, five days hence there would be a feast. And only at the time of the feast did they fast.

And thus did they fast: they abstained from food. Some ate at noon; [they fasted] until midnight arrived. And for some the time that they ate was midnight; [they fasted] also [until] the time of midday. Just so they went alternating.

And they fasted for five nights. Not by day but by night. And when it already was night, then they entered [the *calpulli*]. And when it dawned they went forth; they performed their tasks.

Thus they did daily; thus five days passed. And not then did they lie with women.

In tezcacooac tlacochcalco: vncan mjcoaia, çan quemman, yquac in cenca mjiec malli: yoan vncan mopiaia in tlacochtli, in mjtl: ynjc tepeoaloya.

Acatl yiacapan vei calpulli.

In acatl yiacapan vey calpulli, vncan qujcenqujxtiaia in tlatlaloque: auh in jquac oqujcenqujxtique, njman vncan qujnmjctiaia:

auh in jquac in oqujmonmjctique, njman vncan qujntetequja, yoan qujnpaoacia, caiosuchqujlhujaia in jnnacaio.

Auh yn jquac oqujnpaoazque: njman qujquaia in pipilti, in jxqujch tecutlatoque: amono iehoantin in maceoalti, ça yehoantin in tlatoque.

Techielli.

In techielli: vncan acxoiatemaloia.

Calpulli.

In ie muchi caltotonti in tlaiaoalotoc, ioan qujiaoalotoc teucalli: in mjtoaia calpulli, vncan neçaoaloia:

auh çan iehoantin in pipiltin, in tlatoque, achcacauhti, tequjoaque vncan moçavaia, cempooaltica, mjtoaia: nemacujlçaoaloia.

Auh in jquac moçaoaia, oc iuh macujlilhujtl qujçaz ilhujtl: auh çan ypan in jlhujtl qujçaz moçaoaia:

auh injc mocaoaia, tlaqualizcaoaia: cequjntin tlaquaia nepantla tonatiuh, ixqujchica onaci iooalnepantla: auh in cequjntin yquac tlaquaia in iooalnepantla, no yquac onaci in nepantla tonatiuh: çan iuh mopatlatiuh.

Auh in moçaoaia macujliooal, amo cemjlhujtl, çan iooan: auh in jquac ie iooa, njman calacalquj: auh in otlathujc, valqujçaia, tlatequjpanoaia:

mumuztlae iuh qujchioaia, injc onaci macujlilhujtl: yoan ayocmo cioacochia.

---

6. Reeds (*cañas*) in the corresponding Spanish text.

HERE IS TOLD IN WHAT MANNER THE MEXICANS MADE OFFERINGS AND WHAT THEY MADE AS OFFERINGS IN THEIR TEMPLES

NICAN MOTENEOA IN QUENJN TLAMANAIA, YOAN IN TLEIN IC TLAMANAIA YN JNTEUPAN, IN MEXICA.

OFFERINGS

Thus were offerings made: with food and with capes were offerings made, and with whatever kinds of living things — perchance turkey hens or birds; or capes. Or else whatever was newly grown — perchance maize, or chía, or flowers, or whatever [was newly grown].

And thus did the young [unmarried] women make offerings: before dawn their mothers, their fathers woke them. So they went making offerings carried in the palms of their hands — little tortillas, very small ones; thus they quickly went laying gifts before the devil. In bowls they took the gifts; thus they would offer them.

Only in their homes were the tortillas made. Thus did the young women make offerings.

TLAMANALIZTLI.

Injc tlamanaloia: tlaqualtica, yoan tilmatican tlamanaloia, yoan yca in tlein ioioli: aço totolin, anoço tototl, anoço tilmatli: anoço in tlein iancujcan muchioa, aço cintli, anoço chian, anoço suchitl, anoço in tlein.

Auh injc tlamanaia cioatzitzinti: iooac in qujmjxitiaia intenanoan, intetaoan: injc qujmanativi ventlamapictli, in tlaxcaltzintli tepitoton, injc yciuhca qujmanativi ijxpan diablo: caxtica in qujtquja ventli ic conmanaia:

çan inchan muchioaia in tlaxcalli, injc tlamanaia cioatzitzinti.

THE OFFERING OF INCENSE

And thus was the offering of incense performed. It was with an incense ladle made of clay, with [stones in its hollows making] a rattle. There in the ladle they laid live coals. When they had scooped them up,[1] then they filled it with copal incense; with it they came forth before the devil or else in the middle of the courtyard, where the brazier stood. [This] was made of clay.

And when they came to stand before the devil, then they raised the incense ladle in dedication to the four directions. Thus they offered incense. And when they had raised it in dedication to the four directions, then they threw [the incense and the coals] into the brazier. Then the copal was smoking.

And thus was it done: the mothers, the fathers likewise woke the children at dawn, whether men [children] or women [children]; that they might offer incense quickly, they woke them. That they

TLENAMAQUJLIZTLI.

Auh injc muchioaia tlenamaqujliztli, in jca tlemaitl: çoqujtl tlachichioalli, cacalachio, vncan contemaia in tlexuchtli in tlemaco: in oconxopiloque, njman ic contema copalli, yc oalqujça in ijxpan diablo: anoço in itoalnepantla, in vncan ycac tlequaztli: çoqujtl tlachichioalli.

Auh in ommoquetzaco ijxpan diablo: njman nauhcampa qujiaoa in tlemajtl, ynjc tlapupuchvia: auh yn jquac onauhcampa conjiauh, ic njman contema in tlequazco, vncan popocatica in copalli.

Auh ynjc muchioaia: no yooatzinco in qujmjxitiaia in tepilhoan, in oqujchtin, in anoço cioa qujmjxitiaia in tenanoan, in tetaoan ynjc tlenamacazque iciuhca

---

1. In place of *in oconxopiloque*, the *Real Palacio MS* has *yc conxopiloaya in tlexochtli ỹ ocoxupiloque tlexochtli* — "with it they scooped up the live coals. When they had scooped up the live coals...."

might not become slothful[2] this was done in the houses.

The Casting of Incense

And the casting of incense was thus done when some statement already was to be uttered; perchance a judgment already was to be uttered: first one cast incense into the fire. For whoever already was to speak, just there lay the incense in a gourd vessel. Or else a singer, when already he was to sing, thus would begin: first he cast incense into the brazier; then the singer began [to sing].

The Eating of Earth

The eating of earth was thus done when there was coming to any place: everyone ate earth; with one finger [they touched the ground and then the mouth], perhaps before the devil, or else in front of the hearth.

And thus was attested, thus was verified the statement. When not much faith was put in a statement, thus was it said to one:

"If what thou sayest is true, eat earth."

Whosoever it was then ate earth; thus he attested to his words.

The Casting of a Food Offering

And thus was done the casting[3] of a food offering: when anything was to be eaten, before it was eaten, perchance of the food first a very small morsel was cut off; it was cast[4] before the hearth. When it had been cast, then they would begin to eat the food. No one ate first; indeed the food offering was cast first, in front of the hearth.

The Pouring of a Libation

Thus was done the pouring of a libation, when there was pulque-drinking, perchance [when] the pulque feast was celebrated: when anyone newly made pulque, when he increased it,[5] at this time he

qujmjxitiaia injc amo tlatzivizcujzque techan in muchioaia yn.

Copaltemaliztli.

Auh in copaltemaliztli ic muchioaia, yn jquac in tlein tlatolli ie mjtoz, aço tecutlatolli ie mitoz, achto contemaia in copalli, in tleco: in aqujn ie tlatoz, çan vncan manca in copalli xicaltica: anoço cujcanj in ie cujcaz, ic peoaz, achto contema in copalli in tlequazco, njman ic peoa in cujcanj.

Tlalqualiztli.

In tlalqualiztli ic muchioaia, iquac in campa oalhujlooaia, muchi tlacatl ontlalquaia, ica in ce imapil, aço ispan diablo, anoço tlecujlixquac:

yoan ic tlaneltililoia, ic neltia in tlatolli: yn jquac tlein amo cenca neltocoia tlatolli: ic teilhujloia

intla nelli in tiqujtoa, tla xontlalqua:
ic njman tlalquaia in aqujn, ic qujneltiliaia itlatol.

Tlatlaçaliztli.

Auh inic muchioaia tlatlacaliztli, iquac in tlein qualoz yn aiamo qualo, aço tlaqualli, achtopa achiton tepitõ mocotonaia, tlecujlixquac onmotlaçaia: in ontlatlaçaloc njman ic peoa inic tlaqualoz: aiac achto tlaquaia vel achto tlatlatlaçaloia, in tlecujlixquac.

Tlatoiaoaliztli.

Inic muchioaia tlatoiaoaliztli, iquac in tlauanaloia, aço vitziecoloia: iquac in aca iancujcan qujtlalia vctli, yn iquac oqujtlapiuj, iquac ic tenotzaia, qujoalmana apaztica tlecujlisquac, yoan tetlaoancaxtepiton.

2. *tlatzivilozque* in the *Real Palacio MS.*
3. *tlatlatlaçaliztli* in the *Real Palacio MS.*
4. *ontlatlatlaçaloc* in the *Real Palacio MS.*
5. *oquitlapiviyyoc* in the *Real Palacio MS.*

invited people to it; he served it in a tub, in front of the hearth, and with small drinking vessels.

And when they were to have someone drink, they dipped up the pulque with the drinking vessels. Then they poured a libation in front of the hearth; they poured the pulque in a libation to the four directions.

And when they had poured a libation of pulque, then everyone drank the pulque, then all began the drinking.

Auh yn iquac ie tetlaoantiz, coxopiloa tetlaoanoantica in vctli, njman ic contoiaoa in tlecujlisquac, nauhcãpa contoiaoaia in vctli.

Auh yn jquac ocontoiauh vctli, njman ic muchi tlacatl, quja yn vctli, njman ic muchi peoa in tetlaoantiloia.

HERE ARE TOLD THE VARIOUS MODES IN WHICH BLOOD WAS SHED [AND] OFFERED

SACRIFICIAL SLAYING, ETC.

Thus were performed the sacrificial slayings; thus died captives and slaves who were called the divine dead.

Thus they took [the victim] up [to the pyramid temple] before the devil: [the priests] just went holding him by his hands. And he who was known as the arranger [of victims], this one laid him out on the sacrificial stone.

And when he had laid him upon it, four men each pulled on his arms, his legs. And already in the hand of the fire priest lay the flint knife with which he was to slash open the breast of his ceremonially bathed one.

And then, when he had laid open his breast, he at once seized his heart from him. And he whose breast he laid open lay quite alive. And when [the fire priest] had taken his heart from him, he raised it in dedication to the sun.

THE DRAWING OF STRAWS [THROUGH PARTS OF THE BODY]

The drawing of straws was thus done, only it was at a time of a reasonable day sign that straws were drawn.

And quite everywhere [was it done], perchance on one's ear [lobe], or, whoever willed it, his tongue or his thigh. And to pierce one's flesh, a thorn-like obsidian point [was used]. And then they drew through there a twig or a straw. And in order to pull them through his flesh, the twigs [were tied] with a cord in order to draw them through there, in order to perform penance.

And when the twig had been passed through, next day the twigs and straws were swept up. They were much bloodied. And this was done in the home of the devil or along roads where there were devils.

VNCAN MJTOA IN QUEZQUICAN NEÇOLOIA YN EZTLI IC TLAMANALOIA.

TLAM JCTILIZTLI, &C.

Jnic muchivaia tlamjctiliztli, injc mjquja malli yoan tlacutli in mjtoaia teumiquj.

injc contlecaviaia ixpan diablo, çan caantivi imatitech. auh in tevelteca motocaiotiaia, iehoatl contecaia in jpan techcatl,

auh in jcoac oipan contecac navi tlacatl in qujtitilinjaia in jma in icxi, auh ie imac onoc in tlenamacac tlamacazquj in tecpatl injc queltetequiz tlaaltilli,

auh njman ic coneltequj conanjlia achto in jiollo: auh ça ioltoc in queltequja, auh in jcoac oconanjlique yiollo conjaviliaia in tonatiuh.

TLACOQU JSTILIZTLI.

Jn tlacoqujstiliztli ic muchivaia, çan no ipan in tlein tonalli in tlacoqujstiloia,

auh çan novjian aço inacazco, anoço in aqujn quinequiz inenepilco, anoço imetzpan, auh injc qujcoionjaia inacaio iehoatl in vitzauhquj in itztli, auh ic niman vncan quiqujstiaia in tlacutl, anoço çacatl, auh injc qujtilinjaia in inacaio mecatica injc vncan quiquistiaia tlacutl injc tlamacevaloia,

auh in jcoac otlacuquistiloc, in muztlaioc tlachpanoia muchpanaia in tlacutl yoan in çacatl cĕca ezço, auh in muchivaia y, ichan Diablo anoço vtli in vncan manj Diablome.

197

The Offering of Thorns

The offering of thorns was thus performed: they plucked fir branches and cut maguey spines, and they bloodied them. Thus they laid two maguey spines on the fir branches as offerings.

Everywhere one laid the maguey spines as offerings in perhaps two places, or three places, or five places. It was quite of one's own will.

The Bloodying

When they bloodied themselves, thus did they do it: with an obsidian blade one cut [the lobes of] one's ears, and then they let the blood flow from about the ears.

The Cutting of the Ear [Lobes]

Likewise the bloodying was a cutting of the ear [lobes] when one bloodied oneself, when one cut one's ear [lobes].

The Twisting Off of the Heads [of Birds]

The twisting off of the heads [of birds] was thus done: when they twisted the necks[1] of small birds before the devil, also they dedicated [the blood] to him. They cast [the body] there before the devil. There the body of the small bird lay beating its wings.[2]

The Eating [of Sacrificial Victims' Blood by the Gods]

Thus was done the eating [of sacrificial victims' blood by the gods]: when [the priests] had cut open a slave's or a captive's breast, then [the owner] took [the victim's] blood in a vessel, and, perchance, cast a paper into the vessel, which drew up the blood.

Then he took it in the vessel; he placed upon the lips of all [the images of] the devils the blood of him who had died for the gods.

NEVITZMANALIZTLI.

Jn nevitzmanaliztli ic muchivaia concuja in acxoiatl yoan contequja in mevitztli, auh quezvjaia ic qujvalmanaia in ipã acxoiatl vme in vitztli

noviian in aca aço vccan anoço excan in qujmanaia vitztli, anoço macuilcan çan teiollotlama.

NEÇOLIZTLI.

Jn mjçoia injc qujchioaia itztli ica in contequja in jnacazco, auh njmã ic qujvalpipiloiaia in eztli in innacaztitlan.

NENACAZTEQUILIZTLI.

Çan ie no iehoatl in neçoliztli in nenacaztequiliztli in mjçoia in monacaztequja.

TLAQUECHCOTONALIZTLI.

Jn tlaquechcotonaliztli ic muchivaia ca icoac in tlatototzintli ixpan qujcotonaia in Diablo no conjaviliaia, vncan contlaçaia in ixpan Diablo, vncan tlapapatlatztoc in jtlac in tototzintli.

TLATLATLAQUALILIZTLI.

Jnjc muchivaia tlatlatlaqualiliztli, in jcoac oconeltecque in tlacutli anoço malli, njman qujcuja in iezço castica yoan aço amatl contlaçaia in caxic qujchichinaltiaia in eztli,

njman ic qujtquja castica in izqujntin Diablome intenco qujntlatlaliliaia in eztli muchintin in jezço teumjcquj.

---

1. *quiquechcotonaja* in the *Real Palacio MS.*
2. *tlapapatlatoc* in the *Real Palacio MS.*

The Payment of a Debt [to the Gods]

The payment of a debt [to the gods] was thus done: when mayhap something had befallen one, perchance sickness, when he recovered, then perchance he paid his debt with incense or paper [spotted with liquid rubber]. Because he had not died, he paid his debt in this manner; because, verily, [otherwise] he would have died.

The Spreading of Fir Branches

Thus was done the spreading of fir branches: from the forest they took green fir branches in order that [bloodied] maguey spines be laid upon them as offerings. First they spread out the fir branches; upon them they laid two bloodied maguey spines as offerings.

The Piling Up of Wood for the God

The piling up of wood for the god was thus done: they took green wood from the forest; they cut it in order that it burn there in the home of the devil. They piled it up for themselves. Those did it who lived in the home of the devil when they performed penances.

The Sweeping

The sweeping was thus done: much did they constrain, much were constrained the children, whether women [children] or men [children], that there in the homes, in their courtyards, they sweep.

And when they had first swept, before dawn, then they made their offerings carried in the palms of their hands, which they laid before the devil. And when they had gone to make the offerings, then they took up their incense ladles that they might offer incense.

Vigils. 1. All–Night Vigils

Thus was a vigil kept: it was at night.

They who dwelt there in the home of the devil, who kept watch during the night, remained very wakeful, that they might not leave undone their

Nestlavaliztli.

Jn nestlavaliztli injc muchivaia in jquac aço aca in tlein ipã muchivaia, aço cocoliztli in jquac opatic, njman aço copalli yoã amatl injc moxtlavaia, injc amo omjc iuhqujnma ic tlaxtlava, iehica ca omiquizquja.

Acxoiatemaliztli.

Jnjc muchivaia acxoiatemaliztli ca concuja quauhtla in acxoiatl xoxouhquj injc ipan nevitzmanaloz achto contemaia in acxoiatl ipan conmanaia in vitztli vme ezço.

Teuquauhquetzaliztli.

Jn teuquauhquetzaliztli, ic muchivaia, ca concuja in xoxuhquj quahujtl in quauhtla contequja injc vncan tlatlaz ichan Diablo qujmaquetzaia, iehoantin quichivaia in vncan nenca ichan diablo in tlamacevaia.

Tlachpanaliztli.

Jn tlachpanaliztli ic muchivaia, cenca qujncuitlaviltiaia, cenca cujtlaviltiloia in tepilhoan in aço cihoa, anoço oqujchtin in vncã inchachan in jmjtvalco injc tlachpanazque.

auh in jcoac iovatzinco in oachto tlachpanque, njmã qujchivaia in ventlamapictli in conmanaia ixpan Diablo, auh in jcoac ontlamanato, njmã ic concuja in intlema injc tlenamacazque.

Toçovaliztli. 1. ixtoçoaliztli.

Inic muchioaia toçoliztli, iquac in iooaltica:

iehoantin in vncan nenca ichan diablo, in qujpiaia ioalli, cenca ixtoçotinenca, injc amo tlacochcaoazque, ynjc qujpiaia ioalli, in ixqujchica tlathuiz:

duties because of sleeping. Hence they kept watch during the night until dawn broke.

For this reason they kept watch: it was because of those things which should be done at midnight or very late at night or already near dawn. Because of this they faithfully kept watch all night and tended the fire.

ABSTINENCE

Thus was there abstaining: there was no fasting. Only no one washed himself with *amolli* soap, no one bathed in the steam bath, nor did anyone lie with a woman. Only at the time of [the feast of] Panquetzaliztli there was fasting for seven days.

ynjc qujpiaia, iehica, in tlein muchioaz yn iquac iooalnepantla, anoço tlaquauhiooac, anoço ie tlathuj-naoac, ipampa in, vel qujpiaia in ioalli, yoã qujpiaia in tletl.

NEÇAOALIZTLI.

Inic neçaoaloia amo tlacatlaqualoia, çan ie aiac mamoviaia, aiac motemaia, anoiac cioacochia: çanyio yquac in panquetzaliztli, tlacatlaqualoia chicomil-hujtl.

HERE ARE TOLD, IN VERY TRUTH, THE OFFER-INGS WHICH THEY MADE, WITH WHICH THEY PAID HONOR TO THE DEVIL

THE SWALLOWING OF SERPENTS

Thus was it done. Those who swallowed serpents at the time that water tamales were eaten did this. They were known as Maçateca. [The serpents] went quite alive when they swallowed them. They just seized them with their mouths; they went cutting them to pieces [with their teeth], in order to swallow them. And when they had swallowed them, then they were given gifts, as was told in [its place. This was when] water tamales were eaten every eight years.

THE SWALLOWING OF FROGS

And thus did they swallow frogs. Likewise they went alive; likewise it was done at the time [that serpents were swallowed]; likewise those Maçateca did it.

MAKING BIRDS FLY

Thus was it done. Birds were made to fly at the time of [the feast of] Etzalqualiztli. The youths tied the birds to wooden poles; with them they danced at the time that there was a procession.

PROCESSIONS

Processions were thus undertaken. For whatever feast went established, when this was done, all the people went in procession perchance at dawn or at sundown. Then there was dispersing.

SINGING IN THE MANNER OF WOMEN

And the singing in the manner of women was thus done. When, mayhap, [the image] of whatever devil took form, at that time everywhere the women

NICAN MITOA, IN VEL NELLI TLAMANALIZTLI, IN QUJCHIOAIA, INIC QUJMAVIZTILIAIA TLACATECULOTL.

COOATOLOLIZTLI.

Inic muchioaia, in coatl qujtolooaia, iquac yn atamalqualoia qujchioaia: moteneoaia maçateca, çan ioltiuja in qujntoloaia, çan incamatica in qujmon-anaia, qujnxaxamatztiuja, ynic qujntoloaia. Auh yn jquac oq'ntoloque, çatepan motlauhtiaia, yn iuhquj ipan omito, atamalqualoia chicuexiuhtica.

CUEIATOLOLIZTLI.

Auh injc cuecueia qujntoloaia çan no ioltivia, çan no iquac muchivaia, çan no iehoantin in maçateca qujchivaia.

TOTOPATLANALTILIZTLI.

Jnjc muchivaia, totopatlanaltiloia iquac in etzal-qualiztli, in telpupuchtin quauhtitech quimjlpiaia in totome ic mjtotiaia in iquac tlaiaoaloloia.

TLAIAVALOLIZTLI.

Jn tlaiavaloliztli, ic muchivaia in tlein ilhujtl motlalitivia iquac muchivaia, muchi tlacatl tlaiava-lovaia, aço iohoatzinco, anoço ie teutlac, ic tlaxiti-njaia.

CIHOAPĀCUIQUIZTLI.

Auh in jcihoapan cuiquiztli ic muchivaia iquac in aço tlacatia Diablo, in tlein, iquac muchintin

201

danced along with the men, [as] at the time of the feast day of Tlaloc.

The Moistening of Chalk

Thus was done the moistening of chalk. At that time they quickly snatched the chalk. Then he who moistened the chalk ran. As he appeared, he ran fast and a number followed him. They went stoning him, and any who did not hasten fell quickly under the stones.

Grasping [Children] for Growth

Thus was done the grasping [of children] for growth. Also upon a certain day they grasped all the children for growth on the roads, as well as all the cacti and maguey which lay on the ground. Thus, it was said, thus they would quickly mature.

mjtotiaia in cihoa novian yoan oquichtin iquac inilhuiuh tlaloc.

Tiçapaloliztli.

Jnjc muchivaia tiçapaloliztli: in iquac concuitiqujça in tiçatl njman ic motlaloa in tiçapaloa injc necia in cenca tlacça yoan cequjntin qujtocaia, qujtepachotivia auh in aqujn amo tlacçaia iciuhca tetica vetzia.

Teizcalanaliztli.

Jnjc muchivaia teizcalaanaliztli no ipan in tlein tonalli muchintin in pipiltotonti qujmizcalaanaia vtlica yoã in ixqujch tlalticpac onoc in nopalli, anoço metl, ic mjtoaia inic hiciuhca mozcaltiz.

A Declaration of Still Other Offerings with Which Similarly They Paid Honor to the Devil

Tying [an Object] Over the Breast

Thus was done the tying [of objects] over the breast.[1] In order that there be the tying [of objects] over the breast, they tied their [sickly] small children with loose cotton thread about their wrists and their necks, and placed their ration of a small tortilla made of green maize there in a small carrying frame, and they set up a small earthen jar at one corner of the carrying frame. It went full of water [as] one's hand ration. And when the time of the twenty-day period when it was known as Teotl eco came to arrive, at that time they undid the feathered cords with which the small children were bound.

The Serpent Dance

And the serpent dance was thus done at the time of the feast of [the god] Acolmiztli. The small children were painted with feathers, with colored feathers, everywhere on their bodies. But the old people applied feathers only to their stomachs, over their hearts, and to their backs. For this reason did they apply feathers to them: it was said that it was because thus Acolmiztli would not bewitch them.

The Taking Out of the Children

Thus was done the taking out of the children. They took all of them there to the temple of the devil; they had indeed all of them dance before them, and they made them drunk. Hence it was said that the children were taken out, for they had all the children come out in the home of the devil.

The Act of Striping

Thus was done what was called the act of striping. When battle was joined [with] a captive, his shield,

IMELAVACA IN OC CEQUJ TLAMANALIZTLI IN ÇAN NO IC QUJMAVIZTILIAIA DIABLO.

NEELPILIZTLI.

Injc muchivaia neelpiliztli, inic neelpiloia ica icpatl in qujmjilpiaia pipiltotonti in immaquechtlan, yoan in jnquechtlan yoan in jmjtac elotlaxcaltotonti in vncan conmanaia vacaltonco yoan tecõtontli, vacalnacazco conquetzaia tentiuh in atl in jmaitac, auh in iq̃c oacico ipan cempoalilhujtl in iquac moteneva teteu heco iquac qujntomiliaia in jcpatl potonquj injc omoolpique pipiltotõti.

NECOCOLOLIZTLI.

Auh in necocoliztli ic muchivaia ipan ilhujuh acolmiztli mjhujcujcujlovaia in pipiltotonti tlapalihujtica, novjian in jtech inacaio. Auh in veuejtlaca çãyio in jmelpan, in jniollopan yoan in jncujtlapan, qujnamjctiaia in ihujtl, injc qujnpotonjaia, quilmach ipampa inic amo teiolloquaz acolmiztli.

PILQUISTILIZTLI.

Injc muchivaia pilquistiliztli vmpa muchintin qujnvicaia in iteupan Diablo, in pipiltotonti vel muchintin impan qujmjtotyaia yoã qujntlavantiaia injc moteneva pilquistilo ca muchintin qujnvalquiztia in pipiltotonti in Diablo ichan.

TLAVAVANALIZTLI.

Injc muchivaia in motenehoa tlavavanaliztli in jquac malli moiauchivaia ichimal imaquauh imac

---

1. *neelpiliztli* is omitted in the *Real Palacio MS*.

his war club lay in his hands; his war club no longer had obsidian points. But they who striped had their shields, their war clubs with which they fought in gladiatorial sacrifice as if they fought the captive or the slave.

THE LYING ON REEDS[2]

For five days there was lying stretched out on reeds as penance was done for Tlaloc. This was when [the body of the representative of Tlaloc] was placed in a cave. Leave was taken of [Tlaloc] in one's house.[3]

THE PLACING [OF XIPES] UPON THE STRAW

The placing [of Xipes] upon the straw: of those who flayed the skins of men, some put on the skins, those who were named Xipes. And straw was shaken out; on it they set[4] [the Xipes]. Hence was it said that there was the setting [of Xipes] on the straw.

THE NOURISHING [OF THE SUN OR OF THE FIRE]

The nourishing was thus done. When the ear [lobes] were cut, they spattered the blood upward or they sprinkled it into the fire. Thus, it was said, they nourished the fire and the sun.

THE SPREADING OF FRESH SPROUTS

The spreading of fresh sprouts was thus done. When there had been going to pluck fresh sprouts,[5] then they were spread everywhere upon the altars. No one failed [to do so]; it was [done] indeed everywhere. This was known as the spreading of things which had been plucked by hand.

THE SPREADING OF A BED OF STRAW

The spreading of a bed of straw was thus done. Like eating earth, it was fitting when somewhere

onoc aoc moitztzo in imaquauh. auh in tlavavanque inchimal inmacquauh ieticac injc tlavavanaia iuhqujn qujcali mali anoço tlacutli.

TEUPAN ONOLIZTLI

Macujlilhujtl in tulpan netecoia injc neçavililoia tlaloc in iquac vztoc tlaliloia vme culnavati.

ÇACAPAN NEMANALIZTLI

In çacapan nemanaliztli, iehoantin in qujxipevaia tlaca in imevaio cequjntin conmaqujaia in ehoatl in motenevaia xixipeme, auh motzetzeloaia in çacatl ipan qujnvalmanaia ipampa in motenevaia çacapan valnemanalo.

TLAZCALTILIZTLI.

In tlazcaltiliztli ic muchivaia iquac in monacaztequja acopa contzetzeloaia in eztli anoço tleco contzitzicujnjaia injc mjtoaia quizcaltia in tletl yoan in tonatiuh.

TLATZMOLINTEMALIZTLI

In tlatzmolintemaliztli injc muchivaia, in iquac omocujto tlatzmolin, njman ic motetema in novjian momuzco, acan mocava vel novjian, iehoatl in mjtoaia tlamacujtemaliztli.

NEÇACAPECHTEMALIZTLI.

In neçacapechtemaliztli injc muchivaia çan no iuhquj in tlalqualiztli ipan povia in iquac campa

---

2. *teupan*: read *tolpan* as in the *Real Palacio MS.*
3. In the *Real Palacio MS* the word is either *omocalnavati* or *omecalnavati.*
4. Following *quinvalmanaia*, the *Real Palacio MS* has *in xixipeme.*
5. Following *omocujto*, the *Real Palacio MS* has *quauhtla.*

there was issuing where stood the image of the devil. Thus [when] there was issuing in his presence, one pulled up straw; one shook it out before the devil when one issued before him.

Still others [did so] when they followed the road and when it was during war. It was as if there were supplication because of it. When someone went where there was war, in case something might go amiss with him, he said:

"Not here shall I die; it is in war that I go to die."

And when already battle was joined, he first plucked grass, shook it out toward the sun; he said:

"He will perish, this one; may he die" or "He will take captives."

It was as if thus a vow was made to the sun.

The Blowing of Trumpets

Thus was done the blowing of trumpets. When it was already late at night, when already midnight was coming to arrive, at that time trumpets were blown, so that there be the offering of blood in the home of the devil. Therefore were [the priests] wakened.

Illumination with Fire

Thus was done the illumination with fire. When we people[6] had reached midnight, trumpets also were blown. Thus were men wakened; thus those known as drum-beaters began the keeping of the watch. And on him who could not wake up they poured water or shook [coals of] fire, or else they cast him into the water there at Tlilapan or Coaapan.

The Piercing of Ear [Lobes]

The piercing of ear [lobes] was also undertaken because of the devil. Hence were ear [lobes] pierced.

The Piercing of the [Lower] Lip

In the same manner that there was the piercing of the ear [lobes], so also, because of the devil, was undertaken the piercing of the [lower] lip.

qujxovaia in canjn ycac ixiptla Diablo injc ixpã qujxoaia compia in çacatl ixpan contzetzeloaia in Diablo, in iquac tlaixpan qujçaia

Oc cequjntin in vtli qujtocaia, ioã in iquac iavc, iuhqujnma ic nenetoltiloia, jn jquac aca iauh iavc intla itla ic motolinjtinemj qujtoaia

amo njcan in njmiquiz, iavc in njmiqujtiuh

auh in iq̃c ie muchivaz iauiotl achto qujpia in çacatl qujtzetzeloaia in jvicpa in tonatiuh qujtoaia, vnpopolihuiz y in tla miquiz, anoço tlamaz

iuhqujn ic monetoltiaia ivjc tonatiuh.

Tlatlapitzaliztli.

Injc muchivaia in tlatlapitzaliztli iquac in ie tla-quauhiovac, in ie onacitiuh iovalnepantla iquac tlapitzaloia ic neçohoaia in jchan Diablo, ic teixi-tiloia.

Tlatica tlaviliztli.

Injc muchivaia tlatica tlaviliztli, in iquac ie titlaca in iohoalnepantla oacic, no tlapitzalo, ic teixitilo, ic pevaia in tlapializtli motenehoaia tlavitequjni, auh in aqujn amo vel hiça atl ipan qujnoqujaia, anoço tletl ipã qujtzetzelovaia, anoço atlan contlaçaia vmpa tlilapan, anoço coapan.

Nenacaxapotlaliztli.

In nenacaxapotlaliztli no ic tlaieiecalhujloia in Diablo injc nenacazcoioniloia.

Netexapotlaliztli.

I Çan no iuhquj in nenacazxapotlaliztli çan no ic tlaieiecalviloia in Diablo in netexapotlaliztli.

---

6. *ticatla* (at midnight) in the *Real Palacio MS.*

A Declaration of All Those Who Served in the Homes of Each of the Gods

The Keeper of the God of the Mexicans

Thus did the Keeper of the God of the Mexicans adorn himself: he had his sleeveless jacket, his incense ladle, his pouch; with them he paid honor to the devil. And so did he keep watch that indeed it was a matter of his being like a father in the *calmecac*. He was like the ruler of the [lesser] keepers of the gods indeed everywhere.

And all the children were left with him that he might train them, that he might bring them up by his words, that they might live well. And whether men ruled, or were rich, or led others, directed things, all this was the charge of the Keeper of the God of the Mexicans.

And also this one commanded in the temples everywhere; he told the [lesser] keepers of the gods what they might do. And if perchance any should err, the Keeper of the God of the Mexicans knew all of it.

The Keeper of the God of Uitznauac, Omacatl

The Keeper of the God of Uitznauac similarly maintained usages just as the Keeper of the God of the Mexicans maintained usages. Likewise he oversaw, in the *calmecac*, that they brought up the children well.[1]

The Keeper of the God over Others

The Keeper of the God over Others: his overseeing was similar to the way the Keeper of the God of the Mexicans oversaw. For in truth he commanded all how they should oversee in the *calmecac*; how they should rear the children, how they should bring them up; indeed all that [the lesser] keepers of the gods everywhere did.

Imelavaca in izqujntin tlatequjpanoaia in jnchachan cecenme teteu.

Mexicatl teuhoatzin

Injc muchivaia mexicatl teuhoatzin ixicol, itlema, ixiqujpil injc qujmaviztiliaia Diablo, yoan ic tlapiaia ca iuhquj in teta muchiuhticatca in calmecac, iuhqujn intlatocauh catca in teteuhoatzitzin injc novjian:

yoã in ixqujch in tepilhoan itech oncavaloia injc qujmizcaltiz, injc quivapavaz tlatoltica injc vel nemizque, yoã in aço tlatocatizque, anoço mocuiltonozque, anoço teiacanazque, tlapachozque muchi iehoatl itequjuh catca in Mexicatl teuhoatzin,

yoã no iehoatl tlanavatiaia in novjian teteupan qujmilhujaia in tlein quichivazque teteuhoatzitzin, auh in anoço aca tlatlacoa muchi iehoatl qujmatia in Mexicatl teuhotzin.

Vitznava teuhoatzin Omacatl.

In vitznavac teuhoatzin, çan no iuhquj injc tlamanitiaia in juhquj ic tlamanitiaia Mexico teuhoatzin no iuhquj injc tlapiaia in calmecac in quenjn vel tlacavapavaia.

Tepan teuhoatzin.

In tepan teuhoatzin çan no iuhquj in itlapializ catca, in juhquj ic tlapiaia in Mexico teuhoatzin, iehica ca muchi iehoatl qujnnavatiaia in quenjn tlapiazque calmecac, in quenjn tlacazcaltiaia, tlacavapavaia, çan muchiuhquj in qujchivaia injc novjian teuhoatzitzin.

---

1. Following *tlacaoapaoaia*, the *Real Palacio MS* has *tenonotzaia* — "he corrected them."

Ome Tochtzin

The function of Ome tochtzin was that he gathered together the Centzontotochtin [singers], indeed all of them. None should fail.[2] And over them presided [the one named] Patecatl, who became, as it were, their leader.

Then [Patecatl] set up the rabbit [pulque] jars. There he filled them with [ceremonial] five[fold] pulque, which they called sacred pulque. Then he brought forth the sucking tubes, [made of] reeds. He laid them there[3] with the sacred pulque — two hundred and sixty of them. But only one was bored through.

And when he had set them out, thereupon there was dancing, there was a procession.[4] The Centzontotochtin danced.

Thereupon they went up to the sacred pulque. There was much jostling, that whoever it was might find [the reed which was] bored through. And whoever found [and] took up the perforated [reed], then they left him alone.[5]

Only he alone stood drinking the sacred pulque. And when the sacred pulque had been drunk, then there was departing.

Epcoaquacuiltzin

The Epcoaquacuiltzin: behold what were his duties. When feasts should be celebrated, when perchance the [fifty-two] years should be bound — verily all feasts — he directed everything, so that there would be the depositing of incense. Indeed all that was to be done, all that he commanded, he directed.

The Keeper of the God of Molonco

The Keeper of the God of Molonco also had this function: he issued directions for the paper, the incense, the [liquid] rubber, the black stain, all that this one required when [sacrificial victims] died, and the black stain with which was painted [the impersonator of the god] Chiconauhecatl. And he

Vme tochtzin.

In vme tochtzin itequjuh catca in qujnechicovaia centzontotochtin in ie muchintin, aiac mocavaia, auh vncan tepan icaca im patecatl, iuhqujn tachcauh muchivaia,

njman ie quiquetza in tochtecomatl vncã conteca in macujlvctli in qujlvjaia teuvctli, njman ie qujvalquistia in piaztli acatl vncan cõmanaia in teuvctli ipan, çan matlacpoalli vmei, auh çan ce in coionquj,

auh in ocõma, njman ie ic netotilo, tlaiavalolo, mjtotia in centzontotochtin,

njman ie ic vi in jvicpa teuvctli, cenca moquequeça in ac iehoatl qujttaz coionquj, auh in aqujn oqujttac, in oquicujc coionquj, njman ic quitlalcavia,

ça icel qujticac in teuvctli: auh in onteutlaoanoc, njman ic viujlooa.

Epcoaquacujltzin.

In epcoaquacujltzin, izca yn jtequjuh catca: yn iquac ilhujtl qujçaia, yn aço xiuhtzitzqujlo: in ie muchi ilhujtl, muchi ipã tlatoaia, injc tletemaloz in ie muchi muchivaz muchi iehoatl ic tlanavatiaia, ipan tlatoaia.

Moloncoteuhoa.

In moloncoteuhoa, çan no iehatl itequjuh catca, ipan tlatoaia, in amatl in copalli, in vlli, in tlilli, in isqujch itech monequja in iehoatl in iquac miquja, auh in tlilli ic moçaia, in chicunavecatl yoan ipan tlatoaia in tlemaitl, in çolin yoan in ihujtl tliltic ic mopotonjaia in chicunavecatl.

---

2. *mocavaia*: read *molcauaia* as in the *Real Palacio MS.*

3. Following *quivalquistia*, the *Real Palacio MS* has *in pantecatl.*

4. *tlaiaoaloa* in the *Real Palacio MS.*

5. The *Real Palacio MS* text reads *Auh in oquittaq̃ in aq̃n oquicuic coionqui nimã mochintin quitlalcavia* — "And when they saw the one who took up the perforated [reed], then they all left him alone."

207

issued directions for the incense ladles, the quail, and the black feathers with which [the impersonator of] Chiconauhecatl was feathered.

[THE PRIEST OF] CINTEOTL

The function of [the priest of] Cinteotl was that he directed indeed everything; he commanded that the paper, the incense, the [liquid] rubber, the *yiauhtli* which he needed for [the goddess] Xilonen when her feast day came, be gathered together. And he issued directions for all the [things and] incense ladles required at Ococalco[6] when [the impersonator of] Xilonen died.

CINTEUTZIN.

In itequjuh catca cinteutzin çan isqujch in ipan tlatoaia, ic tlanavatiaia, injc monechicoaia in amatl in copalli, in vlli in jiauhtli in jtech monequja xilonen in jquac ilhujuh qujçaia, yoan muchi ipan tlatovaia, in tlemaitl in jtech monequja o calli in jquac mjquja xilonen.

THE KEEPER OF THE GOD OF ATEMPAN

The Keeper of the God of Atempan: behold what was his function. This one directed, issued commands that there be gathered together the feathers, and the eagle down, the eagle beaks with which [the impersonator of] Toci was feathered when she died.

And this one summoned the Huaxtec youths to do penance there at Atempan.

ATEMPAN TEUHOATZIN.

In atempan teuhoatzin, izca in jtequjuh catca, iehoatl ipan tlatovaia, ic tlanavatiaia, injc monechicovaia ihujtl, in quauhtlachcaiutl, yoan in quauhtevitztli injc mopotonjaia toci in iquac miquja

yoan iehoatl qujtzatziliaia in cuecuexteca in telpupuchtin, injc moçavazque vncã atempan.

THE CARETAKER

The Caretaker took care of the songs of the devils, of indeed all the sacred songs, that none might do ill [with them]. He took great care that they teach the sacred songs, and he issued summons so that the singers or the lords be assembled[7] so that they would be taught the sacred songs.

TLAPISCATZIN.

In tlapiscatzin qujmocujtlavjaia in jncujc Diablome in ie muchi teucujcatl injc aiac tlatlacoz, vel qujmocujtlavjaia, injc qujtemachtiaia in teucujcatl, yoan qujtzatziliaia injc monechicozque in cujcanjme anoço tetecutin injc qujmomachtizque in teucujcatl.

THE KEEPER OF THE GODDESS OF TZAPOTLAN

The function of the Keeper of the Goddess of Tzapotlan was similar to what the function of the Keeper of the God of Atempan was like. For likewise he directed, commanded all that there be gathered together the paper, the incense, the [liquid]

TZAPUTLA TEUHOATZIN.

In tzaputla teuhoatzin, çã no iuhquj in jtequjuh catca, in juhquj itequjuh catca: Atempa teuhoatzin, iehica ça no muchi ipan tlatovaia, ic tlanavatiaia, inic monechicovaia amatl in copalli, in vlli, yoan in jiauh-

---

6. *o calli*: we accept *Ococalco*, following the interpretation given by Miguel León–Portilla in *Ritos, sacerdotes y atavíos de los dioses* (Mexico: Universidad Nacional Autónoma de México, Instituto de Historia, Seminario de Cultura Náhuatl, 1958), pp. 90–91.

7. Following *monechicozque*, the *Real Palacio MS* concludes this paragraph with *in macevalti ynic vel q'matizque yn cuicatl* — "the commoners" were assembled "so that they could know the songs."

rubber, and the *yiauhtli* which [the impersonator of] Tzapotla tenan required when she died.

THE KEEPER OF THE GOD OF TECANMAN

The Keeper of the God of Tecanman directed that there be torches, faggots. And it was the function of this one that he collect the red ocher, the black stain, and the foam sandals, the sleeveless jacket, and bells which [the impersonator of] Xiuhtecutli, the old god, required when he died.

TEZCATZONCATL OME TOCHTLI

Tezcatzoncatl Ome tochtli: this one likewise issued directions for the sleeveless jacket, the bells, the foam sandals, the paper, the heron feather headdress, the pine flowers. Hence he commanded that there be gathered together, that there should come forth all the offerings which [the impersonator of] Tezcatzoncatl needed when he died. This was done at the time of [the feast of] Tepeilhuitl.

OME TOCHTLI YIAUHQUEME

Ome tochtli Yiauhqueme likewise issued directions for the paper, the incense, the [liquid] rubber, and the foam sandals, the bells, the sleeveless jacket, the heron feather headdress, the pine flowers. Hence he commanded that all that was mentioned be gathered when they were required when [the impersonator of] Ome tochtli Yiauhqueme died. This was also at the time of [the feast of] Tepeilhuitl.

OME TOCHTLI TOMIAUH

The function of Ome tochtli Tomiauh was that he issued directions for all that was required when [the impersonator of] Ome tochtli Tomiauh died — the paper, the incense, the [liquid] rubber, the bells, the sleeveless jacket, indeed all that was mentioned. This was also at the time of [the feast of] Tepeilhuitl.

ACALUA OME TOCHTLI

Acalua Ome tochtli: likewise this one's function

tli, in jtech monequja in tzaputla tenan in iquac mjquja.

TECANMAN TEUHOA.

In tecanman teuhoa iehoatl ipan tlatovaia in ocutl in tlepilli iez yoan iehoatl itequjuh catca, in qujnechicovaia in tlavitl, in tlilli yoan in poçolcactli, in xicolli, in tzitzilli in jtech monequja xiuhtecutli, veueteutl in iquac mjquja.

TEZCATZONCATL VME TOCHTLI.

In tezcatzoncatl vme tochtli, çan no iehoatl ipan tlatovaia in xicolli, in tzitzilli, in poçolcactli in amatl, in aztatzontli, in ocoxochitl, ic tlanavatiaia injc muchi monechicoz in valcenqujcaz in ventli in jtech monequja tezcatzoncatl in iquac mjquja ipã in tepeilhujtl mochivaia.

VME TOCHTLI YIAUHQUEME.

In vme tochtli yiauhqueme çã ie no iehoatl ipan tlatovaia in amatl, in copalli, in vlli, yoan in poçolcactli, in tzitzilli, in xicolli, in aztatzontli, in ocoxochitl, ic tlanavatiaia injc monechicovaia in isqujch omjto, iquac monequja in iquac miquja vme tochtli yiauhqueme çan no ipan in tepeilhujtl.

VME TOCHTLI TOMJIAUH.

In vme tochtli tomjiauh iehoatl itequjuh catca, ipan tlatovaia in isqujch in monequja in iquac mjquja vme tochtli tomjiauh, in amatl, in copalli, in vlli, in tzitzilli, in xicolli, in e ixqujch omjto, çan no tepeilhujtl ipan.

ACALVA VME TOCHTLI.

In acalhoa vme tochtli çan no iehoatl itequjuh

was that he issued directions for all that formed the function of Tomiauh Ome tochtli.

catca, ipan tlatovaia in isqujch itequjuh catca vme tochtli tomjiauh.

QUATLAPANQUI OME TOCHTLI

The function of Quatlapanqui Ome tochtli was that he issued directions for the paper, the incense, the sleeveless jacket, the bells, and the obsidian sandals which [the impersonator of] Quatlapanqui Ome tochtli required when he died. This was at the time of [the feast of] Panquetzaliztli.

QUATLAPANQUJ VME TOCHTLI.

In quatlapanquj vme tochtli in jtequjuh catca, iehoatl ipan tlatovaia, in amatl, in copalli, in xicolli, in tzitzilli, yoan in itzcactli in jtech monequja quatla-pãquj in iquac mjquja ipan panquetzaliztli.

TLILHUA OME TOCHTLI

Tlilhua Ome tochtli: likewise this one issued directions for the paper, the incense, the bells, all that was mentioned, which likewise this one, [the impersonator of] Tlilhua Ome tochtli, required at the time of [the feast of] Tepeilhuitl.

TLILHOA OME TOCHTLI.

In tlilhoa vme tochtli, çan no iehoatl ipan tlatovaia in amatl, in copalli, in xicolli, in tzitzilli, in isqujch omjto, çan no iehoatl itech monequja in tlilhoa vme tochtli ipan tepeilhujtl.

OME TOCHTLI PÂTECATL

Ome tochtli Pâtecatl: this one gave life to the five[fold] pulque; he left it in the hands of the craftsman, the one who made the sacred pulque at the time of [the feast of] Panquetzaliztli, when the five[fold] pulque was used.

VME TOCHTLI PÂTECATL.

In vme tochtli patecatl iehoatl qujiolitiaia in ma-cujlvctli imac concavaia in tultecatl iehoatl qujchi-vaia in teuvctli ipan panquetzaliztli in popolivia in macujlvctli.

OME TOCHTLI NAPPATECUTLI

Ome tochtli Nappatecutli issued directions for the paper, the incense, the [liquid] rubber, indeed all that was required when [the impersonator of] Nappatecutli died, at the time of [the feast of] Tepeil-huitl.

VME TOCHTLI NAPPATECUTLI.

In vme tochtli nappatecutli ipã tlatovaia, in amatl, in copalli, in vlli: in ie ixqujch monequja in jquac miquja nappatecutli, ipan tepeilhujtl.

OME TOCHTLI PAPAZTAC

Ome tochtli Papaztac: this one also made the pulque which was called "chalky pulque." This one gave it to Moctezuma, and at that time indeed all the small children, or the men, or the women drank pulque, at the time of [the feast of] Uey toçoztli.

VME TOCHTLI PAPAZTAC.

In vme tochtli papaztac, çan no iehoatl qujchivaia in vctli in mjtovaia tiçavctli: iehoatl conmacaia in motecoçoma, auh iquac tlanavaia ie ixq'ch pipiltzi-tzintin, in anoço oqujchtli, anoço cihoatl ipan toçoztli.

210

The Same Ome Tochtli[8]

Similar was his function. His function was [like that of] Ome tochtli Papaztac, but it was done at the time of [the feast of] Atl caualo.

Ciuaquacuilli

The function of the Ciuaquacuilli was [to assemble] all the offerings which were required there at the Temple of Atenchicalcan [Toci] — the flowers, the tobacco, which she laid before Toci; verily, all the things which the women offered when the hand-holding dance was danced. All this was the function of the Ciuaquacuilli.

Ciuaquacuilli Iztac Ciuatl

The Ciuaquacuilli Iztac ciuatl also kept watch there, took care there at [the Temple of] Atenchicalcan and issued directions for the sweeping, the laying of fires. And any who made vows there spoke to the Ciuaquacuilli Iztac ciuatl. This one pronounced judgment on all that was done in [the Temple of] Atenchicalcan.

The Keeper of the God Ixcoçauhqui at Tzonmolco

The function of the Keeper of the God Ixcoçauhqui at Tzonmolco was [to obtain] wood for [the god] Xiuhtecutli. He made public announcement that there be going to get [it] in the forest. And those who gathered it were only the youths whose function it was. And when they had gone to gather wood for Xiuhtecutli, they piled it up at the *calmecac* in Tzonmolco.

Tlaçolquacuilli

The function of the Tlaçolquacuilli was that he kept watch there, he took care there in [the Temple of] Mecatlan. And he put on his sleeveless jacket;

Vme tochtli idem.

Çan no iuhquj catca in itequjuh, in itequjuh catca, vme tochtli papaztac, auh in muchivaia ipan in atl cavalo.

Cihoaquacujlli.

In cihoaquacujlli itequjuh catca, in isqujch ventli, in vncan monequja, atenchicalcatl, in xuchitl, in ietl injc qujtlamanjliaia toci vel ixqujch in ontlamanaia in cihoa in jquac navaloia iehoatl muchi itequjuh catca, in cihoaquacujlli.

Cihoaquacujlli iztac cihoatl.

In cihoaquacujlli iztac cihoatl çã no vmpa tlapiaia, vmpa tlamocujtlavjaia in atenchicalcan yoan ipan tlatovaia in tlachpanaliztlj in tletlaliliztli, yoan in aqujn vmpa monetoltiaia, iehoatl conilhujaia in cihoaquacujlli iztac cihoatl, muchi iehoatl qujtzontequja in tlein vncan muchivaia atenchicalcã.

Iscoçauhquj tzõmvlco teuhoa.

In jscoçauhquj tzõmulco teuhoa itequjuh catca, in xjuhtecuquavitl, qujtzatziliaia injc mocujtiuh quauhtla, auh in concuja çan iehoantin in telpupuchtin intequjuh catca, auh in oqujcujto xiuhtequavitl, vmpa conquetzaia in tzõmulco calmecac.

Tlaçolquacujlli.

In tlaçolquacujlli, itequjuh catca, vncan tlapiaia, vncan tlamocujtlavjaia in mecatlan, auh in qujmaqujaia, ixicol yietecõton ietinemj, cenca tlamavizo-

---

8. In the *Real Palacio MS* this paragraph reads: *In Ome tochtli ipan tlatoaia in tlaqualli, in ietl, in xochitl ioan in amatl, in copalli, in ie isquich omito auh itech monequia in Ome tochtli, in icoac motonaltia ipan Atl caoallo"* — "Ome Tochtli issued directions for the food, the tobacco, the flowers, and the paper, the incense, all the things mentioned, and what Ome Tochtli required when offerings were made at the time of Atl caualo."

he had his gourd for tobacco. Great was the veneration in the temple there at Mecatlan. No one urinated there; but if anyone did urinate there, they then seized him, they took him within;[9] there they punished him, they bled him.

tiaia in teupan, in vncan mecatlã, aiac vncan maxixaia, auh in aqujn vncan omaxix, njman qujtzitzqujaia, qujcalaqujaia calitic, vmpa quitlatzacujltiaia quiçoçoia.

THE KEEPER OF THE GOD AT TECPANTZINCO

TECPANTZINCO TEUHOA.

The Keeper of the God at Tecpantzinco kept guard, took care at [the Temple of] Tecpantzinco, and it was his function that he issued directions about the offerings. He made public announcement that offerings be made at [the Temple of] Tecpantzinco.

In tecpantzinco teuhoa, vncã tlapiaia, tlamocujtlavjaia in tecpãtzinco, yoan itequjuh catca ipan tlatovaia in ventli qujtzatzilitiia injc tlamanaloz vncan tecpãtzinco.

EPCOAQUACUILLI TEPICTOTON

EPCOAQUACUJLLI TEPICTOTÕ.

The Epcoaquacuilli[10] Tepictoton directed the songs. When anyone was to mold figures [of the mountain gods], this [figure-molder] spoke to [the Epcoaquacuilli Tepictoton], who chose, who summoned the singers, so that they would go to sing in the home of the one who was to mold [mountain-god] figures. Verily, this one, the Epcoaquacuilli Tepictoton, passed judgment on [the songs].

In Epcoaquacujlli tepictoton ipã tlatovaia in cujcatl, iquac in aqujn tepiquiz iehoatl iehoatl conjlhujaia in qujmisquetzaz, qujnnavatiz in cujcanjme, injc qujcativi in jchan in aqujn tepiquiz, vel iehoatl qujtzontequja in Epcoaquacujlli tepictoton.

THE KEEPER OF THE GOD AT THE TEMPLE OF IXTLILTON

IXTLILCO TEUHOA.

The Keeper of the God at the Temple of Ixtlilton presided over, issued directions, made public announcements [concerning] the gifts, when the small children, whether men [children] or women [children], began to talk. They went carrying their gifts of incense, or flowers, indeed all the gifts that were made. Each of these things they bore with them.

In jxtlilco teuhoa ipan jcaca, ipan tlatovaia, qujtzatziliaia in ventli injc motenmamalia pipiltzitzinti in in aço oqujchtin, in anoço cihoa qujitquitivi in jnven in copalli, in anoço suchitl in ie isqujch ventli muchivaia cecentlamantli in qujtquja.

THE KEEPER OF THE GOD XOCHIPILLI AT ATICPAC

ATICPAC TEUHOATZIN XOCHIPILLI.

The Keeper of the God Xochipilli at [the Temple of] Aticpac issued directions concerning [the impersonator of the goddess] Aticpaccalqui ciuatl. He assembled the paper, the incense, the [liquid] rubber which the Aticpaccalqui ciuatl [impersonator] re-

In aticpac teuhoatzin xochipilli ipã tlatovaia, in aticpac calquj cihoatl qujnechicovaia in amatl, in copalli, in vlli, in jtech monequja aticpac calquj cihoatl in iquac mjquja, auh qujxipehoaia in jiehoaio

---

9. Following *calitic*, the *Real Palacio MS* reads *ȳ mecatlã vmpa quiçoçoia* — "they bled him in Mecatlan."
10. Following Epcoaquacuilli, the *Real Palacio MS* has *itequiuh catca* crossed out.

quired when she died. And they flayed her, and the fire priest put on her skin, and he went holding a [live] quail in his teeth; it went dangling from his mouth.[11]

THE KEEPER OF THE GOD OPOCHTLI AT ATLIXELIUHQUI

The Keeper of the God Opochtli at Atlixeliuhqui issued directions concerning [and] assembled the adornment, the paper, the incense, the [liquid] rubber, and the foam sandals, the sleeveless jacket, the bells, the *yiauhtli*,[12] the chalk, the dark green stain, and the heron feather headdress, the tousled hair which [the impersonator of] Opochtli required when he died at the time of [the feast of] Tepeilhuitl.

THE KEEPER OF THE GOD XIPE AT YOPICO

The Keeper of the God Xipe at Yopico took care, at the time that that one, [the impersonator of the god] Tequitzin, died, of the paper, the incense, and the foam sandals, the red ocher; and [he arranged] that this one be arrayed in feathers, white turkey hen feathers, and the *totec* cape of fine workmanship which fell his lot.

THE KEEPER OF THE GOD YIACATECUTLI AT POCHTLAN

The Keeper of the God Yiacatecutli at Pochtlan issued directions concerning [and] assembled[13] for [the impersonator of] Yiacatecutli the various feathers, the rabbit fur, all the feathers, and the precious cape, the sleeveless jacket, the bells, and the sandals of all colors.

THE SAME, FOR CHICONQUIAUITL, AT POCHTLAN

Chiconquiauitl: likewise this one issued directions for all that it was mentioned that the Keeper of the God at Pochtlan directed.

cõmaqujaia tlenamacac, yoan qujtlanquativja çolin icamac pilcatiuh.

ATLIXELIUHQUJ TEUHOA OBUCHTLI.

In atlixeliuhquj teuhoa obuchtli, ipan tlatovaia, qujnechicovaia in jnechichival, in amatl, in copalli, in vlli, yoan in poçolcactli, in xicolli, in tzitzilli, in jiauhtli, in tiçatl, in jaiapalli, yoan aztatzõtli, papatli, in jtech monequja obuchtli in jquac miquja ipan tepeilhujtl.

XIPPE IOPICO TEUHOA.

In xippe iopico teuhoa qujmocujtlavjaia, in ipan mjquja in iehoatl tequjtzin, in amatl, in copalli, yoan in poçolcactli, in tlahujtl, auh injc mopotonjaia iehoatl in iztac totolihujtl, yoan in tolectilmatli tultecajutl in jpã vetzia.

POCHTLAN TEUHOA YIACATECUTLI.

In pochtlan teuhoa yiacatecutli ipan tlatovaia qujnechicovaia in jJacatecutli in nepapan ihujtl in tochiujtl in ie ixqujch ihujtl. yoan in tlaçotilmatli, in xicolli, in tzitzilli, yoan tlatlapalcactli.

CHICONQUJAHUJTL POCHTLÃ IDEM.

In chiconqujahujtl, çan no iehoatl, ipan tlatovaia in jxqujch omjto in ipan tlatovaia pochtlan teuhoa.

---

11. Following *pilcatiuh*, the *Real Palacio MS* has *quitlanquatiuh* — "he went grasping it in his teeth."
12. Following *yiauhtli*, the *Real Palacio MS* has *in tlilli* — "the black [stain]."
13. Following *quinechicovaia*, the *Real Palacio MS* has *inic mochichioaia* — "with which he was arrayed."

The Keeper of the God at Izquitlan

The Keeper of the God at Izquitlan issued directions for the sleeveless jacket, the bells, and the foam sandals, and the sacred pulque. He took the syrup [from a maguey plant] in the fields. This [maguey plant] was afterwards broken up, so that no one might drink of it, so that no one might take it.

The Keeper of the Chachalmeca God at Tzapotlan

The Keeper of the Chachalmeca God at Tzapotlan issued directions for [this], that [the impersonator of] the man of Tzapotlan be ornamented [and supplied with] paper, incense, and incense ladle, all the things which [the impersonator of] the man of Tzapotlan required when he died at the time of [the feast of] Tepeilhuitl.

The Old Priest of Chalchiuhtli Icue Acatonal

The Old Priest of Chalchiuhtli icue Acatonal issued directions about the offerings [and] made public announcements about all that [the impersonator of] Chalchiuhtli icue required at the time that she died: the pine nut skirt, the water skirt, and all the paper, the incense, and so forth.

Acolnauatl Acolmiztli

Acolnauatl Acolmiztli issued directions about all the adornment with which Moctezuma was adorned at the time that he fasted. Only at the time of the great feasts did he fast: at the time when there was fasting for Tlaloc, and when there was fasting for the sun, and when there was fasting for [the feast of] Quecholli. He issued directions about the cape, the sleeveless jacket, and the foam sandals.

The Keeper of the God Totoltecatl at Tollan

The Keeper of the God of Tollan issued directions for what [the impersonator of] Totoltecatl required:

Izqujtlan teuhoatzin.

In izqujtlan teuhoatzin ipan tlatovaia, in xicolli, in tzitzilli, yoã in poçolcactli: yoan teuvctli, concuicuja in necutli in mjlpã, iehoatl in qujn omotlapan in aiaiac quj, in aiaiac concuj.

Tzaputla teuhoatzin chachalmeca.

In tzaputla teuhoatzin chachalmeca, ipan tlatoaia injc muchichioaia in ipan miquja in tzaputlacatl, in amatl, in copalli, yoan in tlemaitl, in ie ixqujch itech monequja tzaputlacatl in iquac miquja ipan tepeilhujtl.

Chalchiuhtli icue acatonal cuacujlli.

In chalchiuhtli icue acatonal quacuilli, ipan tlatoaia in ventli, qujtzatziliaia in jxqujch itech monequja, in iehoatl chalchiuhtli ycue in ipan miquja, in ococalcueitl, yn acueitl: yoan in ixqujch yn amatl, in copalli, in vlli, yoan in oc cequj.

Acolnaoacatl, acolmiztli.

In acolnavacatl acolmiztli, ipan tlatoaia in ie ixqujch nechichioalli, injc muchichioaia in iehoatl motecuçoma, in jpan moçaoaia: çan ipan in veuey ilhujtl moçaoaia, ipan in netlalocaçaoaloia, yoan in netonatiuhçaoaloia, yoan in nequecholçaoaloia: ipam tlatoaia in tilmatli, in xicolli, yoan in poçolcactli.

Tullan teuhoa totoltecatl.

In tollan teuhoa, iehoatl ipã tlatoaia, in jtech monequja totoltecatl: yn amatl in copalli, in vlli,

214

the paper, the incense, the [liquid] rubber, and the obsidian sandals, the heron feather headdress, and the lordly flowers, everything which [the impersonator of] Totoltecatl required when he died, at the time of [the feast of] Quecholli tlami and sometimes at the time of [the feast of] Tepeilhuitl.

yoan yn itzcactli, yn aztatzontli, yoan in tecusuchitl: in ie ixqujch itech monequja totoltecatl, in jquac mjquja, ipan in quecholli tlamj, auh in quenman ipā in tepeilhujtl.

A DECLARATION OF HOW THE SUN WAS SERVED, AND OF HOW MANY TIMES TRUMPETS WERE BLOWN DURING THE DAY AND DURING THE NIGHT, AND OF HOW MANY TIMES INCENSE WAS OFFERED

Each day, when the sun arose, quail were slain and incense was offered. And thus were quail slain: they wrung the necks of the quail; they raised them dedicating them to the sun.

And they greeted [the sun]; they said:

"The sun hath come to emerge, Tonametl, Xiuh-piltontli, Quauhtleuanitl. But how will he go on his way? How will he spend the day? Perhaps something evil will befall his common people."

They said unto him:

"Perform thy function! Work, O our lord!"

And this each day was thus done when the sun arose, [as] hath been said.

And thus was incense offered: it was four times during the day and it was five times during the night. The first time was when the sun showed itself here. The second time was when it was time to eat. The third time was when it was midday. And the fourth time was when the sun had already set.

And at night, thus was incense offered. The first time, it was when it was dark. The second time was when it was time to go to sleep. The third time was when the shell trumpets were sounded. The fourth time was at midnight. And the fifth time was near dawn. And when it was dark, incense was offered; the night was greeted.

It was said:

"Youaltecutli, Yacauiztli hath extended here. But how will his task fall?"

And the feast day of [Youaltecutli] came at the time of the day count Four Movement, every two hundred and sixty days. And when the feast day came, there was fasting; there was fasting for four days. And when the feast day of the day count arrived, at noon shell trumpets were sounded; straws were drawn through the flesh. And they cut the ear [lobes] of small children lying in the cradles. And everyone drew blood. And there were then no greetings. There was only the drawing of blood; straws were drawn through the flesh; incense was offered. Everyone [did so]; no one was abstaining.

IMELAOACA, IN QUENJN TLAIECULTILOIA TONA-TIUH: YOAN QUEZQUJPA IN TLAPITZALOIA IN CEMJLHUJTL, YOAN IN CEIOOAL: YOAN QUEZQUJPA IN TLENAMACAIA.

In mumuztlae in jquac valqujçaia tonatiuh, tlaco-tonaloia, yoan tlenamacoia. Auh injc tlacotonaloia qujquechcotonaia in çolin, conjaviliaia in tonatiuh,

yoan qujtlapalovaia qujtoaia

Oqujçaco in tonatiuh, in tonametl, xiuhpiltontli, in quauhtlevanjtl: auh quen onotlatocaz quẽ cemil-hujtiz, cujx itla ipan mochivaz in jcujtlapil, in jiatlapal

conilvjaia.

Ma ximotequjtili, ma xjmotlacotili, totecujoe.

auh injn mumuztlae iuh muchivaia in iquac valqujçaia tonatiuh mjtoaia.

Auh injc tlenamacoia, nappa in cemjlhujtl, auh macujlpa in iovaltica. Injc ceppa iquac in valmo-mana tonatiuh. Injc vppa iquac in tlaqualizpan, auh injc Expa iquac in nepãtla tonatiuh, auh injc nappa iquac in ie oncalaquj tonatiuh.

Auh in iovaltica, injc tlenamacoia. Injc ceppa tla-poiaoa. Injc vppa netequilizpan. Injc Expa tlatla-pitzalizpan, auh injc Nappa ticatla, auh injc ma-cujlpa tlatvinavac, auh in iquac tlapoiava tlenama-coia tlapaloloia, in iovalli

mjtoaia.

Ovalçouh in iovaltecutli in iacaviztli, auh quen onvetziz in jtequjuh.

Auh in ilhujuh, qujçaia ipan cemjlhujtonalli navi ollin, matlacpoalli, vmeiica, auh in iq̃c ie onaci ilhujuh, neçavaloia, navilhujtl tlacatlaqualoia, Auh in ipã cemilhujtonalli in oacic ilhujuh, in nepantla tonatiuh, tlapitzaloia, tlacoqujstiloia: auh in pipiltzi-tzinti coçolco onoque qujnnacaztequja: auh muchi tlacatl mjçoia, auh atle ic tlapaloloia, çan jxqujch in neçocohoaia, tlacoquistiloia, tlenamacoia muchi tla-catl aiac ixcauhticatca,

And there[1] was the image of that one, [the sun, upon] the so-called Quauhxicalli. There his image was set up. His image was designed as if it had the mask of a man; his sun's rays shot forth [from it].[2] His sun costume was round, enclosed by feathers, enclosed by roseate spoonbill feathers. There in his presence the fasting was done, [and] the passing of straws through the flesh, the laying of offerings, the slaying of quail.

And at the time of his feast day, also many captives died. And also it was said that those who died in war went to the home of the sun; they dwelt with the sun.

auh inon catca ixiptla, iehoatl, in motenehoaia quauhxicalli, vncan moquetzaia in jxiptla, injc mjcujlovaia in jxiptla iuhq'n tlacaxaiaque itonameio itech quiztoia in jtonatiuhtlatquj iavaltic vej ihujtica tlatzaqualli, tlauhquechol injc tlatzaqualli, vncan ixpan muchioaia nêçoliztli, in tlacoquistiliztli, in tlamanaliztli, in tlacotonaliztli.

Auh in ilhujuh ipã no mjiequjntin miquja mamalti, auh no mjtovaia in iaumiquj tonatiuh ichan vjia itlan nemj in tonatiuh.

---

1. *in vncan* in the *Real Palacio MS.*
2. See Pl. 60.

A Declaration of the Training or the Labors Which Were Done in the Temples, in the Devils' Houses

The Education of Men

The fire priest, who educated [the young priests], left them in the hands of the offering priests, those who dealt blows, those who guarded.

Admonitions

For this reason he admonished them: that they live well, that they not spend their time in pleasures, that they not live lazily.

Sweeping

So that they would sweep the courtyard of the temple, he cried out to all the little offering priests that they should sweep.

The Laying of Fires

And he constrained them to lay the fires; so that they be watched, there was reclining by the fires.[1] And indeed everywhere in the temple courtyard fires were laid in the braziers. There perchance ten rows [of them] burned — very many [of them].

Guarding During the Night

Those who were doing penance took care of the guarding during the night. It was the function of those who were prudent.

The Carrying of Wood

The carrying of wood: with it they kept guard as it burned at the *calmecac*. The very young offering priests got it, those not yet very prudent.

---

1. *in tletitlā* in the *Real Palacio MS*.

Imelaoaca in neiehecoliztli anoço tlatequjpanoliztli in muchioaia teupan in tlacateculocalco.

Tlacazcaltiliztli.

In teizcaltiaia tlenamacac, imac concaoaia, in tlamacazque, in tlavitequjnj, in tlapianj.

Tenonotzaliztli.

Ic qujnnonotzaia, injc vel nemjzque, in amo maviltizque, in amo tlatziuhtinemizque.

Tlachpanaliztli.

Injc tlachpanazque, in teuitvalco qujntzatzilia in jxqujchtin in tlamacazcatepitzitzin injc tlachpanazque.

Tletlaliliztli.

Ioan qujncujtlaviltiaia, injc tletlalizque injc tlapialoia, vncan netetecoia in tletl itla, auh çan novjian in tletlaliloia in teuitvalco, in tlequazco in vncan in vncã tlatlaia aço matlactecpantli cẽca mjiec.

In iovallapializtli.

In iovallapializtli iehoantin qujmocujtlavjaia, in tlamaceuhque, in jxtlamatque intequjuh catca.

Quauhçaqujliztli.

In quauhçaquiliztli, injc tlapiaia in tlatlaia calmecac, iehoantin concuja, in tlamacazcatepitzitzin, in aiamo cenca ixtlamati.

218

The Cutting of Maguey Spines

The cutting of maguey spines: those who cut them were the offering priests who were not yet much experienced. They were the ones who gathered them.

The Carrying of Fir Branches

The carrying of fir branches: likewise they who were offering priests got them, and these were already experienced.

The Blowing of Shell Trumpets

The blowing of shell trumpets: this was the function of the young offering priests, and those who were already experienced went mixing with them.

The Dissolving of Black Coloring

The dissolving of black coloring was the function of the young offering priests. They dissolved the black coloring. Everyone anointed himself with it; indeed they put it on like a costume when they anointed themselves. No one failed [to do so]. And they dissolved it there in the black coloring boat, and the black coloring was dissolved at night, and there was anointing at the time that the dawn arose.

Vitztequjliztli.

In vitztequjliztli, iehoantin cõtequja in tlamacazque in aiamo cenca ixtlamati, in qujnõtlacuixque.

Acxoiaçaqujliztli.

In acxoiaçaquiliztli, çan no iehoantin concuja in tlamacazq̃ auh iehoantin in ie ixtlamati.

Tlatlapitzaliztli.

In tlatlapitzaliztli, iehoantin intequjuh catca, in tlamacazcatepitzitzin. yoan in ie ixtlamati neneliuhtivjia.

Tlilpatlaliztli.

In tlilpatlaliztli, iehoantin intequjuh catca: in tlamacazcatepitzitzin, in qujpatlaia tlilli, muchi tlacatl ic moçaia, vel mocemaqujaia injc moçaia, acan mocavaia: auh in qujpatlaia vncã in tlillacalco, auh in tlilpatlaloia, çan iovaltica, auh in neoçaloia iquac in tlavizcalli iehoa.

A DECLARATION OF HOW THE DEVILS WERE PRAYED TO, AND HOW OATHS WERE MADE

When an oath was taken, when someone promised his child to the devils, in perchance two [temples] or in three he promised what he would do for the devils. Perhaps [because] his young son had been struck or for whatever had befallen him, at that time he promised that he would perform penances to them.

And also when an oath was taken, when someone made a statement to one, in order that he verify it, he was told:

"In order that thy statement be verified, in order that thou wilt not lie, eat earth."

When, then, whoever made some statement ate earth, he thus verified his statement. In order not to be thought a liar, he said:

"Well doth the sun, the lord of the earth, know that already I have eaten earth."

Like that, thus, were oaths taken.

And if it was a supplication, it was done only with these: the offering of incense, the paying of a debt, and the eating of earth, the paying of a debt.

IMELAOACA IN QUENJN TLATLAUHTILOIA DIABLOME, YOAN IN QUENJN MUCHIOAIA JURAMENTO.

In iquac muchioaia Juramēto in jquac aca qujnetoltia iconeuh ivjcpa Diablome, aço vccan, anoço Excan qujnetoltia, in tlein qujnchiviliz Diablome, aço motlavitequj piltontli, anoço tlein ipan muchioa, iquac quinetoltiaia, injc ivicpa tlamaceoaz.

Auh no ioã iquac muchioaia in Juramento in iquac aca tlein qujteilhujaia, injc qujneltiliaia, ilhujloia.

Jnjc neltiz motlatol, injc amo tiztlacatiz tlaxontlalqua.

iquac njmã tlalquaia in aqujn tlen qujteilhujaia ic qujneltiliaia in jtlatol inic amo iztlacamachoia qujtoaia,

vel qujmati in tonatiuh, in tlaltecutli ie nontlalqua.

Iuhquj in injc muchioaia Juramento.

Auh intla tlatlauhtiliztli, ic muchivaia çan iehoatl in tlenamaquiliztli, yoan nextlavaliztli, yoã tlalqualiztli, nestlavaliztli.

HERE IS TOLD WHAT THE SONGS OF THE DEVILS WERE, WITH WHICH THEY PAID HONOR TO THEM WITHIN THEIR TEMPLES AND INDEED WITHOUT[1]	NICAN MJTOA IN JNCUIC CATCA, IN TLATLACATECULO INJC QUJNMAVISTILIAIA IN JNTEUPÃ. YOAN IN ÇAN QUJIAOAC.

SONG OF UITZILOPOCHTLI

Uitzilopochtli
Leader in war[2]
Whose work is on high[3]
Who goes on his way[4]
Not in vain[5] I take the yellow feathered cape[6]
Which through me is the sunshine[7]

Evil of omen
Dweller in cloudland

VITZILOBUCHTLI ICUJC

Vitzilobuch
iaquetl *aia,*
yiaco n ai,
in ohujhujhujia
ane njcujc tociquemjtla, *yia, ayia, yia, yio vjia,*
que *ia* noca, *oia* tonacuj *yiaia, yia, yio.*

Tetzaviztli,
ia mixtecatl,

---

1. In translating the sacred songs, we have depended heavily upon Angel María Garibay K.'s versions in *Veinte himnos sacros de los nahuas* (Mexico: Universidad Nacional Autónoma de México, Instituto de Historia, Seminario de Cultura Náhuatl, 1958; hereafter referred to as Garibay, *Viente himnos*), as well as upon those in Eduard Seler's essay, "Die religiösen Gesänge der alten Mexikaner" (*Gesammelte Abhandlungen*, Vol. II, pp. 961–1107). Both authorities should be studied by the reader who wishes as full an understanding as possible of their meaning. In the *Florentine Codex*, the songs are untranslated and lack the glosses to be found in the *Real Palacio MS*.

In the *Florentine Codex*, Sahagún comments concerning them: "*Costumbre muy antigua es, de nr̃o aduersario el diablo: buscar ascondrijos, para hazer sus negocios: conforme a lo del sancto Euangelio, que dize. Quien haze mal, aborrece la luz: conforme a esto, este nr̃o enemigo, en esta tierra planto, vn bosque, o arcabuco, lleno de muy espesas breñas, para hazer sus negocios, desde el, y para absconderse en el, para no ser hallado: como hazen las bestias fieras, y las muy ponçuñosas serpientes. Este bosque, o arcabuco breñoso, son los cantares, que en esta tierra el vrdio, que se hiziessen, y vsasen, en su serujcio: y como su culto diujno y psalmas de su loor, ansi en los templos, como fuera dellos: los quales lleuan tanto artificio, que dizen lo que quieren, y apregonan lo que el manda: y entiendenlos solamente aquellos, a qujen el los endereça. Es cosa muy aueriguada, que la cueua, bosque, y arcabuco, donde el dia de oy, este maldito aduersario, se absconde, son los cantares, y psalmas, que tiene compuestos: y se le cantan, sin poderse entender, lo que en ello se trata, mas de aquellos que son naturales, y acostumbrados, a este lenguaje. De mamera, que seguramente se canta, todo lo que el quiere, sea guerra, o paz, loor suyo, o contumelia de xp̃o, sin que de los demas se pueda entender.*"

As for our transcription of the songs for our Nahuatl column: they appear in simple paragraph form in the MS, more or less as we reproduced them in our first edition of "The Ceremonies." In the present edition, we have rearranged them in the versified form we have adopted, but have not otherwise changed them except to italicize certain sounds (*aia, yia, yio, uiya,* etc.) which, according to Garibay, in *Poesía náhuatl*, 3 vols. (Mexico: Universidad Nacional Autónoma de México, Instituto de Historia, Seminario de Cultura Náhuatl, 1964), Vol. I, p. xxviii, n. 14, have only metric value or indicate the sounds of musical instruments when not accompanying voices, or are "*palabras de exclamación que probablemente eran para dar base al canto sin palabras*" (Garibay, *Viente himnos*, p. 33). These have no other meaning, and the MS does not clearly separate them in the song texts.

Whether because of surviving archaisms; or of distortions due to their poetic expression, their presentation sung and danced, their having been constantly and unthinkingly repeated; or of mistakes in copying the text, the Nahuatl is very difficult. Our notes suggest readings in keeping with the Nahuatl of the *Florentine Codex* for the most obscure passages. These are based upon both Garibay's commentaries in *Veinte himnos* and Seler's in the *Gesammelte Abhandlungen.*. It may be noted that Seler places more confidence in the explanatory glosses to be found in the *Real Palacio MS* than Garibay does, and that he is perhaps less thorough in eliminating elements which probably have only metrical value or imitate accompanying sounds, as previously noted.

Garibay's translations into Spanish are rather free. While ours follow many of his suggestions, they are in some ways perhaps freer. We do not invariably accept his translations; sometimes we have preferred Seler's and sometimes we have accepted neither. In dividing the songs into "stanzas," we have followed the arrangement of the Nahuatl text as it is in both the *Florentine Codex* and the *Real Palacio MS.*

2. *yauhqui* or *yaqui.*

3. *in aco in ai.*

4. Garibay (*Veinte himnos*, p. 34) considers *ohuihuihuiya* as a "reiterative" form of *ouia* or *ohuia* (*otli* or *ohtli*, road, path, with the transitive verbalizing suffix *-huia*). The corresponding gloss in the *Real Palacio MS* interprets this and the preceding line as *ayac nechnenevilia*, a reading with which Seler agrees — "*Niemand ist mir gleich*" (*Gesammelte Abhandlungen*, Vol. II, pp. 964, 967).

5. *anen.*

6. *tozquemitl.*

7. *que*: read *quen; tonaqui*: read *tonac.*

221

You have but one foot	ce i mocxi
Dweller in chill land of wings[8]	pichaoazteca
You open your hand[9]	tlapo ma *ia, ova yieo ayia yie.*
Feathers are given the hot region's[10] ramparts	*Ai* tlaxotla tenamitl ihujtli macoc
Broadcast they fly	mopopoxotiuh,
Proclaimers of war	iautlato *aia ayia yio,*
My god is entitled defender of men	noteouh *aia* tepãquizqui mjtoa *ia,*
Already he rises all covered with paper[11]	O ya i eva vel mamavia
A hot region dweller[12]	in tlaxotecatl
He circles in dust	teuhtla tlamjlacatzoa *ia,*
A hot region dweller	tlaxotecatl
He circles in dust	teuhtla mjlacatzoa *ia.*
The Amanteca are our foes	Amanteca toiaohoan
About me place yourselves	xinechoncentlalizqui *via,*
In battle form[13] there's going to war	icalipan iautioa
About me place yourselves[14]	xenechoncentlalizqui.

---

8. *pichauaztecatl*: Garibay (*Viente himnos,* p. 36) derives his meaning from *pichaui,* stiffen with cold, and *aztli,* wing.

9. *moma.*

10. *tlaxotla, tlaxotecatl*: we accept Garibay's derivation from the verb *xotla* (*Viente himnos,* p. 37). Seler, however, interprets the passage as the allotting of feathers to the "gens" (*tenamitl*) of Tlaxotlan (*Gesammelte Abhandlungen,* Vol. II, pp. 969–70).

11. The corresponding gloss in the *Real Palacio MS* derives *mamauia* from *mauhtia.*

12. See note 10, above.

13. In *ibid.,* the gloss interprets *icalipan iautiooa* as *tlatlaz yn incal* — "their houses will burn."

14. *xenech* . . . : read *xinech.* . . .
In the *Real Palacio MS,* the following lines end the song: *Pipilteca toyavan xinechoncentlalizquivia icalipan yautiva xinechoncentlalizqui.*

Song of Uitznauac Yaotl

My seasoned warrior's in the spear house
Such is what I hear[1]
The man puts me to shame
I think myself ill-omened
I think I go to war
Yet it has been said[2]
My seasoned warrior's in the spear house
They laugh[3]
They talk
It is my house as lord

The Tocuiltec is panting[4]
Eagle robes lie variously
In Uitztlan

By the youths of Olopan
My captive lies emplumed
I'm afraid
I'm afraid
My captive lies emplumed

By the youths of Uitznauac
My captive lies emplumed
I'm afraid
My captive lies emplumed

By the youths of Tzicotlan
My captive lies emplumed
I'm afraid
I'm afraid
My captive lies emplumed

The priest of Uitznauac[5]
Came down to the marvel[6]
The sun shone
The sun shone
He came down to the marvel

The priest of Tocuillan
Came down to the marvel
The sun shone
The sun shone
He came down to the marvel

VITZNAVAC IAUTL ICUJC

Ahuja tlacuchcalco notequjoa *aia*
ivi nocaquja
tlacatl, *ia* nech *ia* pinavia, *aia*
ca nomati njtetzavitli, *avia, aia*
co nomati njia, iauhtla
aqu itoloc
tlacuchcalco, notequjoa
i uesca
tlatoa *ia*
ay nopilchan

Ihiaquetl tocujlechcatl
quaviquemjtl nepapanoc
vitzetla

Huja oholopa telipuchtla
yvijoc in nomalli
ie njmavia,
ie njmavia
ivjioc in nomalli

Huja vitznavac telipuchtla
yvjioc in nomalli
ie njmavja
yvjioc in nomalli.

Huja i tzicotla telibuchtla,
yvjioc in nomalli
ie njmavia,
ie njmavia
ivjioc in nomalli

vitznaoac teuhoaquj
machiotla tetemoia,
ahuja aia tonac
iahuja oia tonac
ia machiotla tetemoia.

Tocujlitla teuhoaquj
machiotla tetemoia,
ahuja, oia tonac,
iavjia oia tonac
via machiotla tetemoia.

---

1. Seler (*Gesammelte Abhandlungen*, Vol. II, pp. 971, 973) takes the particle *aia* as negative.

2. *oc itoloc.*

3. *in uetzca.*

4. *ihiaquetl*: Seler (*Gesammelte Abhandlungen*, Vol. II, p. 974) equates the term with *iyac*; cf. *iaque* or *telpochiaque*. Garibay (*Viente himnos*, p. 44) equates it with *ihiyaqui*, derived from *ihiyotl*.

5. *vitznaoac teuhoaquj*: we read *teuhoaquj* as *teohua* (god-keeper or priest); cf. also Seler, *Gesammelte Abhandlungen*, Vol. II, p. 975. Garibay (*Viente himnos*, pp. 41, 46) prefers to derive the term from *teotl* and *aqui* and translates the phrase "*Se mete el dios en Huitznahuac.*"

6. *machiotlan.*

In Mexico	*Ahujia* Mexico
God's goods are borrowed	teutlaneviloc
Among paper flags[1]	amopanitla,
And[2] in the four zones	an nauhcampa
Are men standing up[3]	ie moquetzquetl
And also[4] it's their time for tears	*ao* iequena ychocaia.
But I've been formed	*Ahuja* an nehoa *ia* njiocoloc
And for my god	ã noteuh *oa*
Of bloody flowers of corn	eztlamjiaval,
A festive few[5]	*a* ilhujcolla,
I take	nic *ia* vica *ia*,
To the god's court[6]	teutivalco *ia*
You are my warrior	*Ahuja* an notequjoa
A sorcerer prince	navalpilli
And[7] though[8] it is true	aqu itla nella
That you made our food	motonacaiouh tic *ia* chjuhquj
You the first man	tlacatl achtoquetl
They only shame you	çan mitz *ia* pinavia.
Whoever shames me	*Ahuja* can aca tell *a*, nech *ia* pinavjia
Knows me quite ill	anech *yayia* velmatia,
You are my fathers[9]	anotata
My priesthood	i noquacujllo
My jaguar serpents	ocelocoatl *aia*.
In Tlalocan	*Ahuja* tlallocan *a*
In the turquoise boat	xivacalco
Is one who comes	*aia* quizquj
And is unseen[10]	aqu amotta,
Acatonal	acatonal *aia*.
To all places go	*Ahuja* xjia novia
To all places reach	*nahuja* xi *ia* moteca *ay*
To Poyauhtlan	pojauhtla

1. *amapantitlan.*

2. *an*: equivalent to *auh.*

3. As the gloss in the *Real Palacio MS* interprets the phrase, the banners stand erect: likewise Seler (*Gesammelte Abhandlungen*, Vol. II, p. 978).

4. *yequene.*

5. Read *ilhuiçolli*. Garibay, in *Veinte himnos*, p. 56, takes the meaning he assigns the word from *ilhuitl* and *çolli*, cluster, handful, which he derives from *çoa*. Seler (*Gesammelte Abhandlungen*, Vol. II, p. 985) prefers to follow the gloss, *ỹ vmpa ilhuiçololo* — "*wo man den ganzen Tag das Fest feiert.*"

6. *teoitualco.*

7. *aqu (ac)*: equivalent to *auh.*

8. Read *intlanel.*

9. Read *annotahuan.*

10. Garibay (*Veinte himnos*, p. 59) reads *ac ua motta*, which he takes to be equivalent to *auh amotta.* Seler (*Gesammelte Abhandlungen*, Vol. II, pp. 980, 988), modifying the gloss, translates the phrase "*dein Vater.*"

With mist-bringing rattles
To Tlalocan taken

My brother Tozcuecuexi
I shall go and go[11]
It's his time for tears

Dispatch me to the place of mystery[12]
His words come down
And I have told
The omen-lord
That I shall go and go
It's his time for tears

In four years
There will be swept[13] on us[14]
Unaware
No longer[15] counted men
In the land of the unfleshed
In the house of quetzal plumes
Where together rejoice[16]
The creatures of him who forms men

To all places go
To all places reach
To Poyauhtlan
With mist-bringing rattles
To Tlalocan taken

aiauhchicavaztica, *aia*
vicalo, tlallocan *aia*.

Ao nacha tozcuecuexi
njiaializquj, *aia*
ychocaia.

Ahuja queiamjca xinechiva *ia*
temoquetl *a* itlatol
a njqu *ia* ilhujq̃tl,
tetzauhpilla
njiaializquj *aia*
ychocaia.

Ahuja nauhxiuhtica *ia*
i topa necaviloc
aioc inomatia,
aymo tlapoalli ,*aia*
ximovaia
ie quetzalcalla
nepanavia *ai*
yascan *a* teizcaltiq̃tl.

Ahuja xjia novjia
ahujia xj *ia* moteca *ia*
ai pouhtla
aiauhchicavaztica, *aia*
vicallo tlalloca.

---

11. Der. *yauh*, possibly repetitive because of reduplication.

12. *quenamican.*

13. Read *necauiloz*. The gloss in the *Real Palacio MS*, evidently preferring to read the phrase as *topan ecauiloz*, is accepted by Seler (*Gesammelte Abhandlungen*, Vol. II, pp. 981, 991) — "*man hat es über uns kommen lassen.*" Garibay (*Veinte himnos*, p. 62) translates it as "*entre nosotros habrá un levantamiento general.*"

14. *topan.*

15. *ayamo.*

16. *nepan* plus *auia* or *ahuia*. Garibay (*Veinte himnos*, p. 63) prefers to derive it from *panahuia* and translates the phrase (p. 52) "*se hace la transformación.*" Seler appears to prefer to regard it as a verbal noun, *nepanavian*, "*Ort des Reichthums*" (*Gesammelte Abhandlungen*, Vol. II, p. 992).

The yellow flower blossoms	*Ahuja* coçahujc xuchitla *oia* cueponca
She's our mother	iehoa tonana
With the godly thigh-skin mask[1]	teumechaue
Tamoanchan's where you started[2]	moqujcican tamovanchan, *avaiie, avajia, yiao, yia, yieo, aie, aie, aij, aiiaa.*
The yellow flower is your flower[3]	Coçaujc suchitla, *oia* mosocha
She's our mother	iehoa tonana
With the godly thigh-skin mask	teumechaue
Tamoanchan's where you started	moqujcican tamovanchan, *ohoayia, ahoayia, yiao, yia, yieo, aie, aie, ayia, ayiaa.*
The white flower blossoms	*Ahuja* iztac suchitla *oia* cuepõca
She's our mother	iehoa tonana
With the godly thigh-skin mask	teumechaue
Tamoanchan's where you started	moqujcican tamoanchan, *ohoayia, yiao, yia, yieo, aie, aie, ayia, ayiaa.*
The white flower is your flower	*Ahuja* iztac suchitla, *oia* mosucha
She's our mother	iehoa tonana
With the godly thigh-skin mask	teumechaue
Tamoanchans' where you started	moqujcican tamohoanchan, *ohoaya, ahoayia, yiao, yia, yieo, aie, aie, ayia, ayiaa.*
The goddess on the barrel cactus[4]	*Ahujia ohoia* teutl ca teucontlipaca
Is our mother	tona, *aia*
The obsidian butterfly	itzpapalotli, *ahoayie, ahoayia, yiao, yia, yieo, ayiaa.*
Let us find her	*Ao, ava* tic *ia* ittaca
In the ninefold steppes	chicunaviztlavatla
She'll be feeding on deer hearts	maçatl yiollo, ica mozcaltizquj
She our mother	tonan
She the goddess of the earth	tlaltecutli, *aiao, ayiao, ayiaa.*
With new chalk	*Ahoie* iancujc tiçatlan
With new feathers	ie iancujc yhujtla,
Is she covered	*oia* potoniloc
In all four quarters[5]	in avicacopa
Darts lie in fragments	acatl xamantoca.
A deer's what she's become	*Aho,* maçatl mochiuhca
There on the desert plain	teutlalipan
They come to find you	mitz *ia* no ittaco
They	iehoa
Xiuhnel and Mimich	xiuhnello iehoa mjmjcha.

---

1. *teo-metz-xaue.*

2. *moquizcan.*

3. In accordance with the *Real Palacio MS* gloss, Seler (*Gesammelte Abhandlungen*, Vol. II, pp. 994, 998) translates *oia mosocha* as "*ist aufgeblüht.*"

4. *teocontli (teocomitl) icpac.*

5. Read *nauicacopa*, as indicated in the *Real Palacio MS* gloss. See also Garibay, *Veinte himnos*, p. 66.

SONG OF CHIMALPANECATL AND OF TLALTECAUA'S MOTHERHOOD

Upon his shield
From one big with birth[1]
Was the captain born
Upon his shield
From one big with birth
Was the captain born

The seasoned warrior
On Coatepec
On the mountain
Dons shield as mask
No one in truth
Does battle like him[2]
The earth quakes in fear
Who can
[Like him]
Don shield as mask?

CHIMALPANECATL ICUJC YOAN TLALTECAOANANOTL

Ichimal ipa
chipuchica vei *a*
mjxihujloc iautlato *aia*
ichimal ipa
chipuchica vei *a*,
mjxihujloc, iautlato *aia*.

Cohoatepec tequiva

tepetitla,
moxaiavalteueuel,
aiaquj nelli
moqujchtivi vi
tlalli cuecuechivjia
aquj

moxaiavalteueuella.

---

1. *chipuchica*: Garibay (*Veinte himnos*, p. 80) relates the term to modern Mexican *chipote* (bruise, bump, swelling) a term colloquially used in reference to advanced pregnancy, and to a postulated Nahuatl *chipohtli*. Santamaría (*Diccionario*, p. 403) traces *chipote* to *xipotli* (cf. *xipocheua*). Seler (*Gesammelte Abhandlungen*, Vol. II, p. 1006) derives it "*durch Metathesis aus* ichpochca *s.* ichpochtli ica ... '*von der Jungfrau.*' "

2. Garibay (*Veinte himnos*, pp. 77, 81) reads *moquichivi ivi in*.

In Tzonmolco	*Hujia*, tzommolco
My fathers	notavane
Shall I defraud you?	ie namechmaiapinauhtiz
In Tetemocan	tetemoca
Shall I defraud you?	ie namechmaiapinauhtiz
In Mecatlan	*A* oncan mecatlan
My lords[1]	notechoan
The yucca [drum] lies croaking	icçotl mjmjlcatoc
In Chicueyocan	chicueiocan
To the sorcerer's house	navalcalli,
Did the sorcerer drop[2]	navalli temoquetl *aia*.
In Tzonmolco	*Hujia* tzonjmolco
The songs are being sung	cujco
Which we have started	tipeuhque,
In Tzonmolco	*aia*, tzomjlco
The songs are being sung[3]	cujca
Which we have started	tipeuhque,
Here's why it's time	*aia*, iz tleica
To come out disguised	naval, moquizca
Here's why it's time	*via* iz tleica
To come out disguised	navalmoquizca.
In Tzonmolco	*Hujia* tzonjmolco
Let one of the people	macehoalli
Be given [the god]	ma *ia* temaco *via*.
The day's light dawns	*oia* tonaqui,
The day's light dawns	*oia* tonaqui,
Let one of the people	macevalli
Be given [the god]	ma *ia* temaco *vjia*.
In Tzonmolco	*Hujia* tzonjmolco
The servitors'[4] song	xoxolcujcatl
Loudly resounds	cacavantoc *ia*
Through hardship[5] the lords[6]	*ai* avjia mocujltonoaci tontecujtl
Attain their contentment	
Their benefits[7]	moteicnelil
Glory	maviztli.

---

1. Read *notecuhuane.*

2. In *Gesammelte Abhandlungen*, Vol. II, pp. 1008, 1013, Seler argues that "*In . . . dem Haus der Verkleidung ist die Verkleidung (der Maskentanz) herabgekommen.*" Reference to disguises in the next stanza may support his interpretation.

3. *cuico.*

4. *xoxolo*: pl. of *xolotl.*

5. *avjia*: see Garibay, *Veinte himnos*, pp. 83, 90. The *Real Palacio MS* reads *ovica.*

6. *tontecutli*: read *tetecutin.*

7. Read *iteicnelil* or *inteicnelil*, following a suggestion in the corresponding gloss in the *Real Palacio MS.*

O little woman
Summon the people
Mist-house dweller
In the region of rain
Summon the people

Hujia cihuatontla
xatenonotza
ayiauhcalcatl
qujiavatla
xatenonotza.

From bewitchèd seven caves   Chicomoztoc qujnehoaquj
Alone I went my way[1]   ca njaueponj, çan j, can j, teiomj.

From bewitchèd cactus[2] lands   Tzivactitlan quinevaquj
Alone I went my way   ca njaaueponj, çan j, çan j, teiomj.

I came down[3]   O *ia* mjtemoc,
I was born[4]   o *ia* mjtemoc,
I came down with my cactus-shaft dart   o *ia* ica njtemoc notzivaqujmjuh,
I was born with my cactus-shaft dart   a *ia* ica njtemoc notzivaqujmjuh.

I came down   O *ia* njtemoc,
I was born   *ioa* njtemoc,
I came down with my netted back-pack   o *ia* ica njtemoc nomatlavacal.

In hand I take it   Niquimacui,
In hand I take it   njqujmacuj,
And in hand I take it   yoa *ia* njqujmacuj,
In hand I take it   njqujmacuj
And in hand he has it[5]   yoan *jaaio* macuj

---

1. A "Chichimec" phrase, according to the gloss in the *Real Palacio MS*; see Garibay, *Veinte himnos*, pp. 93–95; Seler, *Gesammelte Abhandlungen*, Vol. II, p. 1021. For *can j* read *çan in*.

2. *Tzivactlan: tziuactli* is *garambullo* in the Mexican vernacular, according to Garibay (*Veinte himnos*, p. 96), which Santamaría (*Diccionario*, p. 550) identifies as *Cereus garambullo, Pisonia capitata*, or *Rosa mejicana*. Reference is to Chicomoztoc, Garibay says.

3. *nitemoc*: metaphorically it can also mean "I was born."

4. *Ibid.*

5. In the last five lines the meaning is highly problematical. These are followed in both the *Florentine Codex* and the *Real Palacio MS* by the lines *Tlachtli icpac aia, vel in cujcaia quetzalcoxcox aia, qujnanqujlia cinteutla, oay.* Since they logically belong with the Song of Xochipilli, we have included them at its beginning. See Seler, *Gesammelte Abhandlungen*, Vol. II, p. 1024; Garibay, *Veinte himnos*, pp. 98–100.

Song of Xochipilli

Over the ball court the fine pheasant sings[1]
Making replies to the corn god[2]

Already our friendly ones sing
Already the fine pheasant sings
By night did the god of corn shine[3]

He'll hear only my song
He who still has the bells[4]
He with the thigh-skin mask
He will still[5] hear my song
He Cipactonal

I give commands
As giver of things in Tlalocan

As given of things in Tlalocan
I give commands

I have only just reached here
Where the roads are united
Only the corn god am I
Where shall I go?
Where shall I follow the road?

Givers of things in Tlalocan
Gods who give rain

Suchipilli icujc

Tlachtli icpac *aia*, vel in cujca *ia* quetzalcoxcox *aia*,
qujnanqujlia cinteutla, *oay*.

Ie cujca *ia* tocniva *ia, ohoaia, ieo*,
ie cujca *ia*, ie quetzalcoxcox *a*
ioaltica tlao cinteutla *oay*.

Çan qujcaquiz nocujc
oc oioalle
teumechaue
o qujcaquiz nocujca
in cipactonalla *atilili ohoayia*.

Aiao, aiao, aiao, njtlanavati *ai*
tlallocan tlamacazquj *ayiao, aiao, aiao*.

Aiao aiao, aiao, tlallocan tlamacazquj
nitlanavati *ay, ayiao, aiao*.

Ao ça njvallacic,
vtli nepanjvia,
ça njcinteutla
campa, ie noiaz,
campa vtli nic *ia* tocaz *aoay*.

Aiao, aiao, aiao, tlallocan tlamacazquj,
qujavi, teteu, *ayiao, aia, aiao*.

---

1. Garibay (*Veinte himnos*, p. 103) identifies *quetzalcoxcoxtli* as *Pauxis galeata* or *Crax globicera*, referring to Francisco J. Santa-maría's *Diccionario general de americanismos*, 3 vols. (Mexico: Editorial Pedro Robredo, 1942), Vol. II, p. 428, under the term *pauji*.

2. As Seler (*Gesammelte Abhandlungen*, Vol. II, p. 1025) interprets the line, Cinteotl replies to the *quetzalcoxcoxtli*.

3. *tlao*: read *tlaui*. Seler (*ibid.*, pp. 1025, 1028–29) reads *tlaoçinteutla*, which he equates with *tlatlauhqui cinteotl*, "der rothe Maisgott."

4. Translated as "*der Herr der Zeit, wo es noch Nacht ist*" in *ibid.*, p. 1029.

5. *o*: read *oc*.

From watery mistland[1]   Atlaiavica
From near there[2] came I?   njsuchiquetzalli tlacia njvitz
I Xochiquetzal?
Not as yet   aiamo
It's the house at the brink   tencali
And[3] in Tamoanchan   va tamoanchan *oay.*

You have wept until[4] now   Ie quj tichoca *ia*
Wind priest Piltzintecutli   tlamacazecatla piltzintecutlon
He seeks Xochiquetzal[5]   quj *ya* temoa *ia ieo* tochiquetzalla
To mist lands of turquoise[6]   xoiavjia *ay*
For our sake he goes   topan jaz, *oay.*

---

1. *Atl-ayaui-can.*

2. *tlacia*: read *itloc.*

3. *va*: read *iuan.*

4. *ie quin.* Seler (*Gesammelte Abhandlungen*, Vol. II, pp. 1032, 1034) accepts the explanation of *yequitichoca* in the corresponding gloss in the *Real Palacio MS* (*choca*): "*Es weint der Fromme* Piltzintecutli."

5. Read *Xochiquetzalli.*

6. Read *xiuh-ayaui-yan.*

Cotiuana, cotiuana	Cotivana, cotivana
It's the house where rabbits stay[1]	cali totochmanca, *huja, yia*
You have come to linger[2]	limanjco,
At the gate of exit[3]	oqujxa
I have come to linger	nj, manjco,
At the house of darts	tlacochcalico, *ohoayia ayia,*
Stand there	ma tinica *ia*
Come to stand there	ma tonicalico, *ohoayia ia*
I only go afar	çana, çana *io* veca njvia,
I only go afar	çana, çana *io* veca njvia, *yia, yia, yiehoaia*
I only go afar	çana, çana *io* veca njvia.
Already I am taken	Ie nocujliva *ia,*
I am sent	niva, *ia,*
I am sent	niva *ia,*
It's to his duck I'm sent[4]	niva *ia, a* icanauh
I am sent	niva *hoaia,*
It's to his duck I'm sent	njhoa *ia, a* icanauh
Let him hasten[5]	Tla ie totoca,
It's his duckling	ie canauhtzin j,
Let him hasten	tla ixtotoca,
It's his duckling	ie canauhtzin j, *aio, aia,*
It's his duckling	*yvaian,* ie canauhtzin j.
With obsidian I rejoice me	*Aueia* itzipana nomahujlia
With obsidian I rejoice me	*aveia* itzipana nomavilia,
With obsidian I rejoice me	*aveia* itzipana nomavilia.

---

1. *Cotiuana*: meaning unknown. Perhaps a place? Perhaps somehow related to *tlauana*, considering the subsequent reference to rabbits? The gloss in the *Real Palacio MS* says that the entire poem is "Chichimec" and incomprehensible.

2. Read *timanico*.

3. Read *quixoa*.

4. Seler suggests that these four lines mean *"er umschleicht die Enten"* (*Gesammelte Abhandlungen*, Vol. II, p. 1037).

5. Read *ixtotoca*.

Song of Otontecutli	Otontecutli icujc
In Nonoalco[1]	Onoalico,
In Nonoalco	onoalico
Is flowery scent[2]	poma *ia, yiaia, ayio, ayio, aia, aia, aia, ayio.*
In shielding pines	Chimalocutitlana
It clothes itself[3]	motlaquevia
This will not fall[4]	avetzi nj,
In Nonoalco	nonovalco,
The eagle cactus fruit	quanochitla
In theobroma [flowers]	cacavatla
Clothes itself	motlaquevia,
This will not fall	avetzi nj.
I am the Tepaneca man Cuecuexin	Nitepanecatl *aia* cuecuexi
I am the serpent god with plumes[5]	niquetzalcoatl y, *aia*
Cuecuexin[6]	cuecuexi.
I am just the god of wind bearing the obsidian blades[7]	Ca ne, ca *ia* itziueponj
I am just the god of wind bearing the obsidian blades	ca ne, ca *ia* itziveponj.
In the land of Otomís	Otomico,
In the Nonoalcan land[8]	noioco,
In the Nahuatlacan land	navaco
The Mexicans find joy[9]	mexicame *ia* iavilili
In the Nonoalcan land	noioco,
In the Nahuatlacan land	navaco,
The Mexicans	mexicame *ia.*
With shields they yet find joy[10]	*A* chimalica *ia xo, xa* v in oqu jia, vilili
In the Nonoalcan land	noioco,
In the Nahuatlacan land	navaco
The Mexicans	mexicame *ia.*

---

1. Read *Nonoalco.*

2. Read *poyoma*: same as *poyomatli*, unidentified aromatic-narcotic fern, root, or possibly flower (Charles E. Dibble and Arthur J. O. Anderson, *Florentine Codex, Book X, The People* [Santa Fe: School of American Research and University of Utah, 1974], p. 88, n. 39). It is further commented upon by Garibay in *Veinte himnos*, p. 121.

3. *motlaquenuia.*

4. *nj*: read *inin.* Seler reads the phrase *avetzini*, "der Herabfallende" (*Gesammelte Abhandlungen*, Vol. II, pp. 1038, 1040).

5. In the *Real Palacio MS*, the spelling may be *niquetzal ce atlj* If so, it is Quetzalcoatl in another aspect, according to Garibay, *Veinte himnos*, p. 125.

6. In *Veinte himnos*, pp. 119–20, 124, Garibay regards Cuecuexin as a Tepaneca god-name related to Quetzalcoatl. Seler relates the term to *macuextli, chalchiuhcuecuextli*, etc., draws attention to *cuecuextzin* as a term of endearment applied to those dead in war, and translates it as "das Edelsteinarmband" (*Gesammelte Abhandlungen*, Vol. II, pp. 1038, 1043).

7. *ca ne, ca ia itziueponj*: read *ça ni-ecatl itziuepani*, a practical possibility suggested in Garibay, *Veinte himnos*, pp. 119, 125–26. Seler's reading (*Gesammelte Abhandlungen*, Vol. II, pp. 1038, 1044) is as *canin cueponi*, "wo blühte er auf?"

8. Garibay (*Veinte himnos*, pp. 117, 127) reads this as *noyonco* and relates the term to Nonoalco; "podremos aventurar la versión que doy," he says, while admitting as also possible Seler's translation as "im Nachbarlande" (*Gesammelte Abhandlungen*, Vol. II, pp. 1038, 1044).

9. *ia avilili, jia vilili*: Garibay (*Veinte himnos*, pp. 117, 127) reads these as *ya avilili*; the verb is applicative of *auia*. He reads *xo, xa v in oqu* as *Xaxa! Auh in oc.* For Seler, these phrases are *iyauililli*, "wurde er dargebracht" and *xaxauhyoc*, "mit Bemalung versehen" (*Gesammelte Abhandlungen*, Vol. II, pp. 1039, 1044).

10. *Ibid.*

SONG OF AYOPECHTLI	AIOPECHTLI ICUJC
Somewhere[1]	Cane
Somewhere in Ayopechtli's home	cana ichan, aiopechcatl
She lies with necklace jewels bedight[2]	cozcapantica mjxjuhtoc.
Giving birth	
Somewhere	Cane
Somewhere in Ayopechtli's home	cana ichan aiopechcatl
She lies with necklace jewels bedight	cozcapantica mjxiuhtoc
Giving birth	
Somewhere in her home	cane ichan
The little mite[3]	chacaioliva *ia.*
Is given life	
Bestir yourself[4]	Aiavalmeva *ia,*
Be sent	*via,* xiva
Bestir yourself	xivalmeva *ia avia ia*
New child	iancujpilla
Bestir yourself	xjvalmeva *ia.*
Bestir yourself	*Ahujia* xivalmeva *ia*
Be sent	*via* xiva
Bestir yourself	xihoalmeoa *ia*
Jewel child	cozcapilla,
Bestir yourself[5]	viualmeoa *ia.*

---

1. Read *cana.*

2. *cozcapantica*: cf. *apanalli.*

3. *chacaioliva: chacalli* (lit. shrimp) and *yoliua.* Garibay (*Veinte himnos,* p. 132) also accepts as a possible meaning for *chacalli* (*chacayolli?*) a thickening of the skin; the term being applicable to pregnancy, he suggests as an alternative "wombs take life."

4. Read *xiualmeua.*

5. See note 4, above.

The eagle[1]	Quavi
The eagle Quilaztli	quavi, qujlaztla
With blood of serpents	cohoaeztica
Is her face circled[2]	xaiaoaloc
With feathers adorned[3]	vivia
Eagle-plumèd she comes	quavivitl vitz
To sweep up the path[4]	alochpan
Chalmecan cypress	chalima, avevetl
Colhuacanian	ie colhoa.
Fir tree of our sustenance[5]	*Huja* tonacaacxoima
Corncob of the godly field	centlateumilco
On rattle stick upraised	chicavaztica, motlaquechizca.
The spines	Vitztla,
The thorns fill up my hand	vitztla nomac temj
The spines fill up my hand	vitztla nvmac temj,
Like corn of godly field[6]	*a* çanteumjlco
Like rattle stick upraised	chicavaztli motlaquechizca.
The broom fills up my hand	Malinalla, nomac temj,
Like corn of godly field	*a* çãteumjlco
On rattle stick upraised	chicavaztica motlaquechizca.
Thirteen Eagle[7] is our mother	*A* vmei quauhtli ie tonan *aia*
Chalmecan lady	chalmeca tecutli
His shaft of cactus is his glory	*a* tzioac imaviz
May he sate me[8]	tla nech *ia* tetemjli,
He	iehoa
My lord of cloud-snake land	nopiltzin *aia* mjscoatlan.
Our mother	*Ia* tonanj,
War woman[9]	iauchioatzin, *aia*
Our mother	tonan
War woman	iauchioatzin, *aia*
Deer of Colhuacan[10]	imaca colivacã
In plumage arrayed[11]	ihujtla ipotoca *ia*.

---

1. *Quavi: quauhin*, equivalent to *quauhtli.*

2. A compound of *xayacatl* and *yaualoa* is suggested by Garibay (*Veinte himnos*, p. 139). Seler follows the gloss in the *Real Academia MS, yc oxavaloc in coaeztli* — "mit Schlangenblut ist sie bemalt" (*Gesammelte Abhandlungen*, Vol. II, pp. 1048, 1054).

3. *vivia*: read *iuihuia (ihui(tl)-huia)*. Seler favors the gloss's *iuan* (*Gesammelte Abhandlungen*, Vol. II, pp. 1048, 1054).

4. *alochpan*: read *ualochpan*. Seler considers a headdress called *uitzalochtli* possible (*ibid.*, pp. 1048, 1054).

5. *tonacaacxoima* (*tonacaacxolma* in the *Real Palacio MS*): cf. *tonacatl* and *acxoyatl*. Garibay (*Veinte himnos*, pp. 136, 142–44) prefers "*Ea! Donde se tienden los abetos (país) de nuestro origen,*" which he supports with references concerning Xochitlalpan, Tlalocan, Xochicalco, etc.

6. Read *centeomilco.*

7. Read *matlactli omei.*

8. Seler (*Gesammelte Abhandlungen*, Vol. II, pp. 1049, 1057) translates the phrase as "*lege mir nieder*"; cf. *temi* in Siméon, *Dictionnaire*, p. 420.

9. Read *yaociuatzin.*

10. Read *imaça* or *in maçatl.*

11. *ipotoca*: cf. *potonia.*

The sun proclaims the war[12]
Let men be dragged away
It will forever end[13]
Deer of Colhuacan
In plumage arrayed

Eagle plumes are no mask
For he rises[14] unmasked

Ahujia ie tonaquetl iautlatoca *ia*
ma nevilano tlaca
cĕpoalihuiz
aia inmaca colihoacă
ihujtla ipotoca *ia*.

Ahujia quavivitl amo xaiavallj
on *avjia* iecoiametl amo xaiaivalli.

---

12. The phrase is repeated in the *Real Palacio MS.*
13. Read *cempoliuiz.*
14. *iecoiametl:* cf. *yeconi* or *econi.* Seler (*Gesammelte Abhandlungen*, Vol. II, p. 1050) translates the last two lines thus: "*Adlerfedern sind eure Bemalung. Der im Kriege tapfer kämpft, eure Bemalung.*"

My heart is a flower bursting open
It is lord of the night's half-way point[1]

Our mother has come[2]
The goddess has come
Carnality's goddess

Cinteotl[3] was born in Tamoanchan
Where the[4] flowers lift their heads
He is One Flower

Cinteotl was born in the rain-mist[5]
Where are made the children of men[6]
Where fishermen fish the jade fish

Now will the sun rise
Now will the day dawn
Let all the various firebirds
Sip nectar where flowers stand erect[7]

On earth
You stand yourself up
Near the market place stars[8]
[You] are the lord
[You] Quetzalcoatl[9]

Let there be rejoicing
By the flowering tree
Hear all the firebirds
The various firebirds
Our god speaks
Pay him heed
His firebird speaks

Suchitl noiollo cuepontimanja;
iehoa coioalle, *vaia, oovaia, ie.*

Iecoc ie tonan
iecoc ie teutl
tlaçulteutl *oaia oovaia ie.*

Otlacatquj cententeutl tamjioanjchan
nj xochitli icacanj
ce ixuchitli *iantala, iantatã, ayiao, ayiave,
tililiiao ayiaue, vayiaue.*

Otlacatquj centeutl, atliaiavican
j tlacavillachivaloia,
chalchimjchvacan *yiao, iantala, iantata, ayiao
aiave tililiiao, aiyaue, oayiaue.*

Oia tonazquj
tlavizcalleva *ia*
ma tlachichina *ia* nepapã quechol, suchitl aca,
*yiantalan, yiantata, ayiao, ayiaue,
tililiiao, ayiaue, oayiaue.*

Tlalpan
timoquetzca
tianquiznavaquj
a njtlacatla
njquetzalcoatla *aiantala, iantanta, ayiao, ayiave,
tililiiao ayiaue oayiaue.*

Ma *ia* avjialo
suchinquavitl itlanj
nepapan quecholli ma *ya* quecholli xjccaquj *ia*

tlatoa *ia* in toteuh
xiccaquj *ia*
tlatoa *ia* iquechol

---

1. *iehoa coioalle*: read *ie tlacoyoalle.*

2. *Iecoc: ecoc* (pret. of *eco*).

3. *cententeutl*: read *centeutl* as in the *Real Palacio MS.*

4. *nj*: read *in.*

5. *Atl-ayaui(tl)-can.*

6. Read *tlacapillachiualoyan.*

7. *aca* read *icac.*

8. *Tianquiznauac*: *tianquiztli* or marketplace was probably an unidentified constellation of stars (Garibay, *Veinte himnos*, p. 164). Seler (*Gesammelte Abhandlungen*, Vol. II, pp. 1060, 1067) translates it simply as "*am Marktplatze.*"

9. Read *titlacatl, tiquetzalcoatl.* Seler (*Gesammelte Abhandlungen*, Vol. II, pp. 1060, 1067) makes no change: "*ich der Fürst, der Quetzalcoatl.*"

Is it one of our dead who is piping —
Who'll be felled by a dart from a blow-gun?[10]

My flowers I shall fan with the breeze[11]
Flowers of our nourishment
Blossoms like popcorn
Where the blossoms all raise up their heads[12]

He plays with the ball
Old[13] Xolotl plays with the ball
In the magical ball court
Xolotl plays with the ball
Man of the land made of jade
See him
Is Piltzintecutli stretched out
In the mansion of night[14]
In the mansion of night?

My nobleman
My nobleman
In yellow plumage you're bedight
In the ball court you are set
In the mansion of night
In the mansion of night

The man from Oztoman
The man from Oztoman
Back-packs Xochiquetzal
He rules in Cholula
My heart is now in fear[15]
My heart is now in fear
Cinteotl has arrived
Let us approach [the priest]
The Oztoman man
The man of Chacallan
Has ear plugs of turquoise to trade
Has arm bands of turquoise to trade

The sleeper[16]
The sleeper
In sleepiness drowses
Here now with my hand
I turn the girl over
The sleeper am I

---

a mach ieva tomjcauh tlapitza
a mach iehoan tlacaloaz *ohoao.*

Aie oho yiayia ça niqujiecavizca nosucha
tonacasuchitli
ie izqujsuchitla
suchitlaca, *yiaa.*

Ollama,
ollama viue xolotl
navallachco
ollama *ia* xolutl
chalchiuecatl
xiqujtta
mach *oia* moteca piltzintecutli
yoanchan
yoanchan.

Piltzintle,
piltzintle,
tocivitica timopotonja
tlachco timotlalia
yoãchan
yoanchan.

Oztomecatla, *yiaue,*
oztomecatla,
suchiquetzal qujmama,
ontlatoa cholollan, *ayie, ayio, oie*
manj noiol, *oie*
manj noiol, *aoia*
iecoc, centeutl
ma tivjia obispo,
oztomecatl
chacalhoa
xjuhnacochtla, iteamjc
ximaquiztla iteamjco, *ayie, ayio.*

Cochina,
cochina,
cocochi
ie njcmaololo njcan, ie cihoatl

njcochina *yieo, oaieo yho, yia, yia.*

---

10. Cf. *tlacalhuaztli.* Taking *a* as a negative prefix and *mach* as *m(o)-ach(tli)*, Seler translates these lines as "*es soll dein Bruder . . . nicht erblasen werden, es soll dein Bruder nicht mit dem Blasrohre geschossen werden*" (*Gesammelte Abhandlungen,* Vol. II, pp. 1060, 1068).

11. *niqujiecaviz: ni-c-eheca(tl)-huiz.* Seler (*Gesammelte Abhandlungen,* Vol. II, pp. 1060, 1068) considers the term causative of *eco:* "*Ich werde bringen meine Blumen.*"

12. Read *xochitl icacan.*

13. Read *ueue.*

14. I.e., *yoalli ichan.*

15. *manj:* read *maui.*

16. Read *cochini.*

The night is here inebrious	Ioalli tlavana, iz
Why have you to be coaxed?	tleican, timonenequja
Consume yourself now[1]	xjia qujmjtlatia
In garments of gold	teucujtlaquemjtl,
Array yourself	xjcmoquentiquetl *ovjia.*
My god	Noteuho
Bears jade water on his back	achalchimmama
In middle watercourse	tlacoapana
His way of coming down	itemoia,
Precious cypress tree	*oi* quetzallavevetl,
Precious snake of fire	*ay* quetzalxiujcoatl
[Care] has abandoned me[2]	nech *ia* iqujnocauhquetl *ovjia.*
Let me take pleasure	Ma njiavjia,
Let me not perish[3]	njia, njiapoliviz
I am the tender corn[4]	niyoatzin,
Of jade is my heart made	*a* chalchiuhtla noiollo
The gold [of rain] I'll see[5]	*a* teucujtlatl noco *ia* ittaz
My heart will be refreshed	noiolcevizquj
The fledgling man grow firm	tlacatl achtoquetl tlaquava *ia*
The man of war be born	otlacatquj iautlatoaquetl *ovjia.*
My god of corn	Noteuhoa centla
With face held high[6]	coxaia
Feels groundless fear	iliviz çonoa
I am the tender corn[7]	yioatzin
From up your mountain top	motepeiocpa
Your god beholds you here[8]	mjtzvalitta moteuhoa,
[My heart] will be refreshed[9]	vizquj
The fledgling man grow firm	n tlacatl achtoquetl tlaquava *ia*
The man of war be born	etlacatquj iautlatoaquetl *ovjia.*

---

1. Read *quimotlatia.*

2. *Icnocauhqui.* The corresponding gloss in the *Real Palacio MS* explains: *ye otechcauh ỹ mayanaliztli* — "famine has already left us." Garibay interprets it similarly: "*me ha hecho mercedes*" (*Veinte himnos,* p. 175). Seler translates: "*es verliess mich (die Feuer-schlange, die Hungersnoth)*" (*Gesammelte Abhandlungen,* Vol. II, p. 1071).

3. Seler (*Gesammelte Abhandlungen,* Vol. II, pp. 1072, 1076) considers the verbs in these two lines optative and hence subjunctive in meaning — "*Es mag sein, das ich dahingehe, dahingehe, um zu Grunde zu gehen.*"

4. *Ni-ouatzin* (cf. *ouatl*).

5. *No-c-on-ittaz.*

6. Read *aco ixayac.*

7. Read *niouatzin.*

8. Seler transcribes these seven lines as *Noteua ce intlaco xayailiviz çonoa yyoatzin motepeyocpa mitzvalitta moteua,* and translates them thus: "*Mein Gott, ein Stück lass im Ueberflusse vorhanden sein die Maispflanze, es schaut nach deinem Berge, zu dir hin, dein Verehrer*" (*Gesammelte Abhandlungen,* Vol. II, pp. 1072, 1077–78).

9. Read *noyolceuiz.*

Song of Chicome coatl

Seven corncob
Now arise
Now wake up[1]
It is our mother
You are going to leave us bereft
You are going to your home[2] in Tlalocan

Now arise
Now wake up
It is our mother
You are going to leave us bereft
You are going to your home in Tlalocan

Chicome coatl icujc

Chicomolotzin,
xa *ia* mehoa,
ximjcotia
a ca tonan
titechicnocaoazquj
ti *ia* vjia muchi tlallocan *novjia.*

Xa *ia* mehoa
ximjçotia
a ca tonã
titechicnocavazquj
ti *ia* vjian mochan tlallocan, *novjia.*

1. Read *ximiçotia.*
2. *muchi*: read *mochan.*

SONG OF TOTOCHTIN TEZCATZONCATL   TOTOCHTIN INCUJC TEZCATZÕCATL

Iiaa, yia, yia, yia, ayia, ayio, ovjia, ayia,
ayia, ayia, yia, yio, vjia, ayia, yia,
ayia, vjia, yio, vjia.

In Colhuacan   Colivacan
An awesome place   mavizpan
Is the home of the monster[1]   atlacatl ichan *a, yio, ayio, yia, yio.*

In the palace[2] of the god   Tezcatzoncatl tepan
With the mirror in his hair
Gifts are made the god   teutl, macoc
Yet he weeps   ie choca *ia, avjia,*
It must not be so[3]   maca ivi
Gifts are made the god   teutl, macoc
Yet he weeps   yie choca *ia.*

Alas   Huja
In Axalco palace   axalaca tecpan
Gifts are made the god   teutl, macoc
Yet he weeps   yie choca *ia*
It must not be so   maca ivi
Gifts are made the god   teutl, macoc
Yet he weeps   yie choca *ia.*

In Tezcatzonco[4]   Tezcatzonco
Your abode   moiolcan
A warrior[5]   *a* yiaquetl
A rabbit   *yia* tochin
My god has created   qujiocus noteouh
I'll overthrow[6]   niqu *jia* tlacaz
I'll perforate   niqu *jia* mamaliz
Mixcoatl's mount in Colhuacan   mjscoatepetl colhoacan

Man with the voice   Tozquiva *ia,*
I've beaten the drum   njctzotzon *jiao*
Little mirror   in tezcatzintli
Little mirror   tezcatzintli
In Tezcatzonco drink up[7]   tezca xocoi
The white-headed [pulque] is cooked to a froth[8]   ehoa tzonistapalatiati,
Drink up[9] the pulque   tla oc xocon octli *aho, a.*

---

1. Seler reads *atlacatl* as *in tlacatl* — "der Fürst" (*Gesammelte Abhandlungen*, Vol. II, pp. 1083, 1086).

2. *tepan*: read *tecpan* as in the *Real Palacio MS*.

3. *maca ivi* is repeated in *ibid*.

4. In the *Florentine Codex* the poem from this point on appears as the latter half of the Song of Macuilxochitl, because, apparently, in the *Real Palacio MS*, from which the *Florentine Codex* was copied, a mistake in binding inserted a page the wrong way about. See Garibay, *Veinte himnos*, p. 196.

5. *yaqui.*

6. *nictlaçaz.*

7. *Tezcatzonco xoconi.*

8. Possibly to be read *yehuatl tzoniztapal tlatia*. Garibay (*Veinte himnos*, pp. 192, 199) transcribes the phrase as *yeva iztapalati* and suggests a similar meaning for it.

9. *xoconi.*

I am the man from Chalman	*Huja* njchalmecatl,
I am the man from Chalman	njchalmecatl
With penance sandals	neçavalcactla
With forehead sun-jewel	oljia quatonalla
Which trembles[1]	
It trembles	olia
Big	Veia,
Big is your fir branch	veia, macxoiauh
The broom[2] of Quilaztli	quilazteutl illamanj
Your branch of a fir tree	macxoiauh.
I call to you	Nimjtzacatecunotza *ia*
Lord of the reeds[3]	
Over your shield	chimalticpac
Blood is being shed	moneçoia
I call to you	njmjtzacatecunotza *ia*.
Lord of the reeds	
My darts are gone	Aiac nomjuh
Proud is their tale[4]	timalli *a* itollaca
Reeds are my darts	acatl nomjuh
None break in two[5]	acaxelivi
Proud [is their tale][6]	timalli.
Tetoman is where you abide	Tetoma ca moiolcan *a*
Maker of gifts in Tetoman	tlamacazqujn tetometl,
Not with ease[7]	açan axcan
Do I nourish	ie quetzaltototl njc *ia* izcaltiquetl.
the quetzal bird	
Opochtli is my god	Iiobuchtli noteouh,
The one with dart throwers	atlavaquetl
[Not with ease]	[açan axcã
Do I nourish	ye quetzaltototl] njc *ia* izcaltiquetl *a*.
[The quetzal bird][8]	

1. *oljia* or *olia*: possibly to be read *olinia*.

2. *illamanj*: read *itlapan*; cf. *tlapana*, which, according to Garibay (*Veinte himnos*, p. 214) means, *inter alia*, to sweep (*tlachpana?*). Though it appears as *yllapa*, Seler (*Gesammelte Abhandlungen*, Vol. II, pp. 1088, 1093) reads it as *ilama* — "*die alte (Göttin).*"

3. *Ni-mitz-aca(tl)-tecu(tli)-notza.*

4. *itollaca*: read *itoloca*.

5. Read *acan xeliui*.

6. *itoloca* is understood, as above.

7. Equivalent to *ayaxcan*. Seler (*Gesammelte Abhandlungen*, Vol. II, pp. 1089, 1095) translates *açan axcan* as "*und jetzt.*"

8. The phrases in brackets, missing in the *Florentine Codex*, are supplied from the *Real Palacio MS.*

Where flowers stand erect   *Ayia, iao* suchitl icaca
Thence do I come   vmpa njvitza
Wind[-god]-provider   tlamacacecatla
Owner of reddening dusk[1]   tlamocoioale *va,*

Likewise are you   *ayia, yiao a* ivi n tinocic *aia*
My mother's mother[2]
With the thigh-skin mask   teumechaue *oia, iao*
Owner of reddening dawn[3]   tlavico, *ia* calle
Wind[-god]-provider   tlamacacecatlo
Owner of reddening dusk   .   tlamocoioale *a.*

God of ill omen   Tetzauhteutl *a*
My lord Tezcatlipoca   notecujo tezcatlipuca
Answer the maize god[4]   qujnanqujlican cinteutla *oay.*

---

1. *tlamocoioale*: read *tlapcoyoale*.

2. *ivi in tinoci; noci*: cf. Toci.

3. Read *tlauizcocale*, i.e., *tlauizcale*.

4. Two paragraphs follow in the *Florentine Codex*. We have shifted them back to the Song of the Totochtin, as argued by Garibay (*Veinte himnos*, p. 196).

Without my knowledge was [the war]¹ declared
Without my knowledge was [the war] declared
In Tzocotzontlan was [the war] declared
In Tzocotzontlan
Without my knowledge was [the war] declared

In Pipitlan was [war] declared
In Pipitlan
Without my knowledge was [the war] declared
In Cholotlan was [war] declared
In Pipitlan
Without my knowledge was [the war] declared

I have merited our food
Not with easiness²
My priests have brought me
The heart of water
Whence sand is scattered

In a coffer of jade
I burn myself up³
Not with easiness
My priests have brought me
The heart of water
Whence sand is scattered

Anomatia *a* itoloc,
anomatia, *a* itoloc
tzocotzontlan *a* itoloc
tzocotzõtla
anomatia *a* itoloc.

Pipitla *a* itoloc,
pipitla
anomatia *a* itoloc
cholotla, *a* itoloc
pipitla
anomatia, *a* itoloc

Tonacajutl, njcmaceuh
açan axcan
noquacujllo atl jiollo, nechval *ia* vicatique

xalli ytepeuhia.

Chalchiuhpetlacalco
njnaxca
açã axcan
noquacujllo, atl jiollo nechval *ia* vicatique

xalli itepeuhia.

---

1. See Garibay, *Veinte himnos*, p. 205.
2. *ayaxcan.*
3. Read *ninixca.*

An Account of How the Women Served There in the Temples

Behold the life of the priestesses when [their mothers] vowed them [to service] there in the great temple.

When they took them into [the temple], it was when they were still very small, perhaps after they were already twenty [days old] or after they were forty [days old]. And in order to take them, in order to leave them, they just took them in their arms; they just went in their mothers' arms. And they went with their brooms, which went filling the children's arms. And they bore their incense ladles and incense. Not yet did fire go [in the ladles]; later the old priest decided where the incense ladles would be required.

And when she had gone to dedicate the little girl, then she took her [away]. She left there only the incense ladle and the incense. And this old priest commanded that the mother not abandon her child because of lack of regard, and that [the child] not leave off, because of lack of regard, going to leave the brooms and the incense, or wood shavings, every twenty days there at the *calpulco*.

And when it was seen to be proper, when already she was a maiden, purely of her own will she went into the *calpulco*. And purely of her own will she performed the face-veiling [ceremony]. Also she went taking the incense ladle, the incense.

And when she was a grown woman, if this priestess was asked [in marriage], and if the words were well based, if the fathers, the mothers, the men of the neighborhood, the noblemen consented, then a number of things were bought. They bought quail, and incense, flowers, tobacco, and an incense ladle. And food was bought.

Then this priestess thereupon went to perform the face-veiling. She took with her all that had been bought, as was told. And that with which she veiled the face was a cape called *tlacaquachtli*; it had many heads [worked upon it]. Thereupon they laid out a very large cape, a *quachtli*. Thereupon they set forth the offerings in a reed vessel; there they placed the gifts which they called fast foods. They were only

Imelaoaca in quenjn tlatequjpanoaia cioa in vmpa teupã.

Izcatquj, in jnnemiliz in cihoatlamacazque, injc qujnnetoltiaia in vmpa vej teupan.

Jnjc qujncalaqujaia, oc vel tepitoton, aço qujn ie cempoaltia, anoco qujn ie vmpoaltia. auh injc qujnvicaia, injc qujmoncavaia, çan qujnnapalotivia, çan inmac ietivj in jnnanvan, auh njman impopouh ietivia, in pipiltotonti inmac tentivia, yoan intlema qujtquja, yoan copalli aiatle vnietiuh tletl qujn iehoatl qujmatia in iehoatl quacujlli in campa moneq'z in tlemaitl.

Auh in ocõnetoltito in cihoapiltontli njman ic qujvica: çã ixqujch in vmpa concavaia in tlemaitl, yoan in copalli: auh in iehoatl, in quacujlli njman qujvalnaoatia, in nantli injc amo qujxiccaoaz in jconeuh, yoan injc amo tlaxiccaoaz, injc qujcaoatiuh in popotl, yoan in copalli, anoço tlaxipeoalli, in cecempoaltica in vmpa calpulco.

Auh in iquac in ie movelitta in ie ichpuchtli, ça monomaviaia in calaquja, in calpulco: yoan ça yiollotlama in teisquentiaia, no qujtqujtiuh in tlemaitl in copalli.

Auh in iquac in ovelmaçic cihoatl, intla ie itlano, in iehoatl in cihoatlamacazquj, auh intla vel omotlali in tlatolli intla ocezque, in tetahoan, in tenanhoan in tlaxillacaleque in pipilti, njman ie tlacocohoalo qujcohoa, in çolin, yoan in copalli, in suchitl, in jietl, yoan in tlamaitl, yoan mocohoaia tlaqualli,

njman in iehoatl in cihoatlamacazquj njman ie ic iauh in teisquentiz qujtquj in jsquich omococouh, in omjto, auh injc teisquentiaia in tilmatlj itoca tlacaquachtli, tzotzontecomaio, njmã ie ic contlalia in cenca vej tilmatli in quachtli, njmã ie ic tlamana acaquauhcaxtica, vncan contlalia in ventli in quil-

three tamales. Thereupon they set out a wooden vessel; it went filled there with only five tamales and a sauce, perhaps turkey hen, perhaps duck, which they had put together as food.

Here Endeth the
Part of Book II
Called the
Appendix

viaia, tlacatlaqualli çan etetl, in tamalli, njman ie ic conmana, in quauhcaxitl vncan tentiuh, çan macujltetl in tamalli, auh in mulli, aço totolin, anoço canauhtli, in qujnamjctiaia tlaqualli.

Nican tlami in icotonca
inic vme amuztli
yn jtoca apendiz.

DATE DUE

APR 1 6 1987		
MAY 1 9 1997		
MAY 2 7 1997		
261-2500		Printed in USA